ASSETS

AND THE

POOR

ASSETS
AND THE
POOR
A NEW AMERICAN
WELFARE POLICY

Michael Sherraden

M. E. Sharpe, Inc.
Armonk, New York
London, England

Library of Congress Cataloging-in-Publication Data

Sherraden, Michael W. (Michael Wayne), 1948–
    Assets and the poor : a new American welfare policy /
  by Michael Sherraden.
       p.   cm.
    Includes bibliographical references and index.
    ISBN 0-87332-618-0
    1. Economic assistance, Domestic—United States. 2. Public welfare—
United States. 3. Saving and investment—United States. I. Title.
  HC110.P63S49 1990
  362.5'8'0973—dc20   90-42236
                                               CIP

To my mother and father

Them that's got shall get,
Them that's not shall lose.
So the Bible says,
And it still is news.

Mama may have,
Papa may have,
But God bless the child
That's got his own.

—Billie Holiday

Contents

Tables and Figures   xi
Foreword   *Neil Gilbert*   xiii
Preface and Acknowledgments   xv

PART I.   MAINTENANCE: WELFARE AS INCOME

1   The Failure of Welfare Policy as a Failure
of National Vision   3
2   Income Distribution and Income Poverty   16
3   The State of Welfare Theory   35
4   Federal Welfare Policy—Who Benefits?   50
5   The Welfare Reform Debate   78

PART II.   DEVELOPMENT: WELFARE AS ASSETS

6   The Nature and Distribution of Assets   95
7   Inheritance of Asset Inequality   121
8   Toward a Theory of Welfare Based on Assets   145
9   The Design of Asset-Based Welfare Policy   189
10   Individual Development Accounts   220
11   Examples, Proposals, Costs   234
12   The Integration of Welfare Policy with
Economic Goals of the Nation   280
13   Summary and Conclusion   294

Selected References   303
Index   315

Tables and Figures

Table 2.1   Sources of Personal Income, November 1989   17

Table 2.2   Percentage Shares of National Income,
1970–1984   18

Table 2.3   Household Income Distribution, 1988   20

Table 2.4   Income Poverty Levels, 1989   23

Table 2.5   Estimated Family Budget of a Nonfarm Family
of Four Based on 1989 Poverty-Level
Income of $12,100   24

Table 2.6   Family Income and Poverty, 1949–1985   24

Table 2.7   Percentages of Income Poverty of the Total
Population and of Children, by Race,
1979 and 1988   26

Table 4.1   The Grand Welfare State: Estimated Federal Welfare
Expenditures to Individuals, Both Direct
Expenditures and Tax Expenditures,
Fiscal Year 1990   56

Table 4.2   Summary: The Grand Welfare State by
Major Category and Type of Expenditure,
Fiscal Year 1990   60

Table 4.3   The Poor Welfare State: Targeted Federal Welfare
Expenditures to Individuals, Fiscal Year 1990   61

Table 4.4   The Nonpoor Welfare State: Nontargeted Federal
Welfare Expenditures to Individuals,
Fiscal Year 1990   65

Table 4.5   The Poor (Targeted) and Nonpoor (Nontargeted)
Welfare States as a Proportion of the Grand
Welfare State, Fiscal Year 1990   65

Table 4.6   The Poor (Targeted) and Nonpoor (Nontargeted)
Welfare States as a Proportion of Total Federal
Expenditures, Fiscal Year 1990   69

Figure 6.1   The Relationship of Income and Assets:
Two Continua with an Area of Similarity   98

Table 6.1   Distribution of Household Net Worth, 1984   110

Table 6.2   Total Household Wealth Distribution, 1983   111

Table 6.3   Distribution of Capital Wealth, 1983   112

Table 6.4   Mean Wealth of Income-Poor and
Income-Nonpoor Households, 1983   113

Table 6.5   Median Net Worth by Monthly Household   114
Income Level and Race, 1984   114

Figure 8.1   Welfare Effects of Assets   148

Figure 8.2   Welfare Model for the Nonpoor:
Income Plus Assets   177

Figure 8.3   Welfare Model for the Poor: Income Only   179

Figure 8.4   Proposed Welfare Model for the Poor:
Income Plus Assets   180

Table 11.1   Example: Amanda Smith's IDA Account   262

Table 11.2   Estimated Costs to the Federal Government
for Individual Development Account
Proposals, First Year   268

Table 11.3   Estimated Annual Deposits under IDA Proposals 274

Foreword

Neil Gilbert

In recent years several major themes have animated the study of social welfare policy. These include the civic obligations of welfare beneficiaries; the emerging role of the private sector in the mixed economy of welfare; the increasing use of tax and credit mechanisms to deliver social welfare transfers; and the considerable extent to which these alternative mechanisms provide welfare transfers that benefit the middle classes. Drawing on the last two themes, Michael Sherraden's work opens an important new line of analysis that challenges conventional wisdom about the nature of welfare measures designed to reduce poverty.

This is an insightful study that illuminates the broad range of welfare transfers in modern society and their implications for different groups. Sherraden's analysis begins with the distinction between social transfers for welfare purposes that entail immediate consumption, such as rent supplements to low income households under the Section 8 program, and transfers that contribute to the accumulation of assets, such as tax deductions for interest payments on housing mortgages and publicly subsidized loans for housing and education. As these examples suggest, the two types of benefits are usually delivered through different mechanisms. Those linked to immediate consumption are conveyed in the form of cash or in-kind provisions financed under direct public expenditures that are highly visible, while benefits that contribute to the accumulation of assets are financed by indirect methods, such as tax expenditures and credit subsidies, that are more difficult to trace.

It is only over the last decade that serious attention has been given to the

Neil Gilbert is the Milton and Gertrude Chernin Professor of Social Welfare and Social Services at the University of California at Berkeley.

measurement of indirect expenditures. These expenditures are still not included in the Social Security Administration's standard audit of social welfare spending. Beyond differing in their degree of visibility, the two types of benefits accrue to different classes of recipients, with the middle and upper classes on the receiving end of indirect social transfers. Advancing this line of thought, Sherraden points out that many indirect transfers are asset-based. He argues that welfare transfers that stimulate asset accumulation are ultimately more powerful antipoverty measures than those designed for immediate consumption. He then goes on to formulate an alternative approach to welfare policy involving the establishment of Individual Development Accounts. This is a provocative proposal to create asset-based welfare measures for low-income people, which might be financed through partial reductions of tax expenditures that currently benefit those in the upper income brackets.

If society were to increase social transfers to the poor, why do it in the form of welfare measures that stimulate the future accumulation of assets rather than through direct cash grants for immediate consumption that would raise their current standard of living? This is the crux of the issue with which proposals for asset-based policies must come to grips. Addressing this issue, Sherraden develops an elaborate theory of the welfare effects of assets. This theory suggests that assets are not simply nice to have, but yield various behavioral consequences such as enabling people to focus their efforts, allowing people to take risks, creating an orientation toward the future, and encouraging the development of human capital. While the possession of assets correlates to some degree with these behavioral characteristics, correlation is not causality. The extent to which it is behavior that influences one's ability to accumulate assets or the possession of assets that influences one's behavior is unclear. Sherraden recognizes that the course of influences may run in either direction. The essential question raised by this theory is not whether assets lead to a desirable set of behaviors, but for whom and to what degree. That is what makes it interesting.

One function of social theory is to provide a conceptual framework for structuring problems, a service that Sherraden's work performs masterfully. Taking an original line of analysis, it generates intriguing questions about the possibilities of asset-based welfare policy. Whether or not one agrees with his thesis, the issues posed by this book elevate the discussion of welfare policy to a new level.

Preface and Acknowledgments

Over the past several years, I have been thinking a great deal about social policy in the United States, particularly welfare policy, and I have arrived at a different idea. The idea can be summarized very succinctly: Instead of focusing welfare policy on income and consumption, as we have done in the past, we should focus more on savings, investment, and asset accumulation. This idea might be summarized by the term *stakeholding*, which suggests that poor people, if they are to overcome their poverty—not only economically, but also socially and psychologically—must accumulate a stake in the system. A stake in the system means, in one form or another, holding assets. I refer to this new thinking as *asset-based welfare policy*. Instead of merely providing subsistence, asset-based welfare policy would seek to integrate social policy with economic development. My hope is that this simple, unvarnished idea will be useful for the United States, and perhaps other nations, in the years ahead.

In thinking about these issues, I have relied on suggestions and comments from many academic colleagues, policymakers, welfare recipients, friends, and family members. It is not possible to acknowledge all these people in this space, and no doubt I have forgotten many of the suggestions and bits of advice, but permit me to mention some of the most helpful people.

For early encouragement, I am indebted to Larry Davis of Washington University, Leon Ginsberg of the University of South Carolina, Sar Levitan of George Washington University, Henry Meyer (emeritus) of the University of Michigan, and William Wilson of the University of Chicago. When one begins work on a topic that is a departure from accepted wisdom, there is a great deal of uncertainty at the outset. The initial comments and support of these individuals were a tremendous help in my decision to proceed.

For thorough readings of early drafts, I am grateful for the very helpful comments of Neil Gilbert of the University of California at Berkeley and John Tropman of the University of Michigan. My colleagues at Washington University, David Katz, Martha Ozawa, Mark Rank, and Nancy Vosler, have been key commentators on various chapters.

For perceptive discussions about policy proposals and feasibility, I wish to acknowledge Edward Weaver, former executive director of the American Public Welfare Association; Erica Baum, a social welfare policy analyst formerly with the Progressive Policy Institute; Lawrence Mead, a political scientist at New York University; Duncan Lindsey, a sociologist at the University of Oregon; and Willard Wirtz, former U.S. Secretary of Labor.

For especially helpful comments on economic issues, I am indebted to Stephen Fazzari of Washington University in St. Louis; Daniel Meyer of the University of Wisconsin; Lars Osberg of Dalhousie University in Halifax; and Robert Plotnick of the University of Washington in Seattle.

Ralph Pumphrey, a social welfare historian (emeritus) at Washington University, provided information on historical precedents for asset accumulation policies in the United States.

Among a number of other people who have provided ideas, suggestions, comments, and information, I would like to thank Margaret Adamek, Ann and Tony Alvarez, Nancy Amidei, Mahasweta Banerjee, Gordon Berlin, William Birdsall, William Butterfield, George Eberle, Rona Feit, Sarah Gelhert, Robert Haveman, John Henretta, Alice Johnson, Krishna Ladha, Joel Leon, Paul Leonard, Jules Lichtenstein, Julio López, Yasuo Matsubara, Nancy Morrow-Howell, Hyman Minsky, Ada Mui, Susan Murty, Douglass North, Deborah Page-Adams, Michael Parker, Kathryn Porter, Daniel Radner, Mary Rogge, Rosemary Sarri, Georgia Scarbrough, Isaac Shapiro, Suzanne Sheppard, Madeline Sherraden, Thomas Sherrard, Vered Slonim-Nevo, Robin Sithigh, Fredrick Smith, Michael Sosin, Catherine Striley, Paul Stuart, Edward Schwartz, Edward Wolff, and John Zipp.

Tremendously useful was a sabbatical leave during 1987, which I spent as a visiting professor in the Economics Department, Postgraduate Division, at the National University in Mexico City (UNAM). At that time, my ideas on asset-based social policy were unformed and churning. Being out of the United States, away from familiar patterns of thinking, facilitated greater insight and understanding of social policy in the United States. I wish to thank Clemete Ruiz Durán, Professor and Director of the Program in Political Economy at UNAM, as well as participants in a graduate economics seminar.

Many of the people who have commented on earlier drafts have raised thoughtful questions about my ideas, logic, analyses, or proposals. In spite of their best efforts, however, I have not always followed their advice, and therefore many shortcomings undoubtedly remain in the manuscript. For these I am wholly responsible.

Several publications of my preliminary ideas on asset-based welfare have helped to stimulate discussion. *Social Policy* published "Rethinking Social Welfare: Toward Assets" in 1988. In January 1990, the Progressive Policy Institute (PPI) published a report entitled "Stakeholding: A New Direction in Social Policy." Will Marshall, President of PPI, made this possible. In March 1990, the Corporation for Enterprise Development (CfED) devoted an issue of *The Entrepreneurial Economy Review* to "Individual Development Accounts." Robert Friedman, chairperson of the board, and Doug Ross, president of CfED, made this possible; I would also like to thank Janet Topolsky for her excellent editorial work. Initial theoretical formulations were published by *Social Service Review* in December 1990 in an article entitled "Stakeholding: Notes on a Theory of Welfare Based on Assets." These publications have helped considerably to get the idea off the ground and into the academic and policy debates. In some parts, this book draws on these previous publications.

I wish to thank Dean Shanti Khinduka of the George Warren Brown School of Social Work, Washington University, for his encouragement from the very beginning and throughout the writing of this book, and for providing the support to carry it out.

Cynthia Jones and Angela Turner provided outstanding secretarial support in preparing the manuscript for the publisher. Their professional and thoughtful assistance has been greatly appreciated.

Working with my editors at M. E. Sharpe, first Barbara Leffel and later Michael Weber, has been a pleasure. The final draft of the book has been substantially improved by their sincere interest in the project and careful attention to detail.

Finally and most important, I wish to thank Margaret Sherrard Sherraden, my best critic and advisor, who has read all of the drafts and provided exceptionally valuable comments and suggestions. Our children, Catherine Elizabeth and Samuel Chapman, also played an important editorial role by voicing their challenging question (one that more academics should take seriously): Why don't you ever write something that is interesting to read? I don't know if I have lived up to this lofty standard, but I do know that the book would not have been possible without the love and support these three wonderful people, my family, my greatest asset by far.

M.S.
St. Louis
May 1990

PART I

MAINTENANCE:
WELFARE AS INCOME

1 • The Failure of Welfare Policy as a Failure of National Vision

Welfare policy is in trouble. In important respects, the policy is not working, and a majority of the population has lost confidence in it. Especially, there is widespread discontent with the failure of income transfers to the very poor, such as Aid to Families with Dependent Children (AFDC). After decades of federal programs, it cannot be demonstrated that means-tested welfare policies permanently change people's lives for the better. For example, it has been shown that during a twenty year period, income transfers did not alter levels of pretransfer poverty. Although official poverty declined from 17.3 percent of the U.S. population in 1965 to 14.4 percent in 1984, pretransfer poverty did not decline—it was 21.3 percent in 1965 and 22.9 percent in 1984.[1] The basic conclusion is that while income transfers have helped to ease hardship, they have not reduced the underlying level of poverty. Welfare policy has sustained the weak, but it has not helped to make them strong.

Arising out of this perception of failure and the public's discontent there has been, in recent years, a good deal of thinking and rethinking about welfare policy. However, most of this thinking, both conservative and liberal, has been circumscribed within a rather limited idea. In the advanced welfare states of Western Europe and North America, social policies for the poor have been constructed primarily around the idea of income, that is, flows of goods and services. Whether in health care, housing, direct financial assistance, education, or any other area of welfare, the emphasis has been on levels of goods and services received and, presumably, consumed. The underlying assumption is that poverty and hardship result from an inadequate distribution of flows of resources, and the solution is to make the flows more adequate. However, the income-based welfare state has not fundamentally reduced poverty (although it has alleviated hardship); it has not reduced class or racial divisions; it has not stimulated economic growth; and it has not developed a broad base of public support. Yet most welfare reform proposals, conservative and liberal alike, assume that income-based policies are the only answer.

I have come to believe that income is an insufficient basis for welfare policy. Income is only one measure of poverty, a measure that ignores the long-term dynamics of household well-being. The traditional approach to poverty analysis, counting income and who has it, has not led to meaningful change, nor is it likely to lead to meaningful change in the future. Income-based policy proposals sound familiar and tepid, and inspire little confidence. They are inadequate because the underlying vision, the foundation of the proposals, is itself inadequate. In my view, the current discontent with welfare policy results from an inadequate definition of household well-being, an inadequate understanding of how well-being is achieved, and a failure to integrate social policy with the broad goals and purposes of the nation.

Despite these shortcomings, income has been so completely taken for granted as the standard in antipoverty policy in the United States and other Western welfare states that we have few policy instruments with which to pursue a different approach. Perhaps this book can serve as a beginning step in constructing an alternative perspective. The purpose is to present and establish a logical foundation for a different concept of well-being and a different approach to social policy.

This is not to take up the mossy conservative argument that income transfers decrease motivation, breed dependence, and are therefore to be rejected, a very old line of thinking that Charles Murray has resurrected.[2] There is no substantial evidence that income transfers reduce individual motivation, although it is clear that income transfers reduce work participation, much as they were intended to do. The reduction is slight. A major review of available research estimates that all welfare programs together reduce total work hours in the economy by only 4.8 percent.[3] Far more significant than lost hours of work is the remarkable persistence of work effort among recipients of public assistance and among the working poor, even though economic *dis*incentives for work, in current welfare policy, are very strong.

During 1987, 1.9 million impoverished people worked full time, year round, but remained poor. An additional 6.6 million worked less than full-time, year-round, but remained poor. Of 32.5 million people living in poverty, 18 million, more than half, lived in households where at least one household member worked during the year. About 5 million of these lived in households where at least one household member worked full-time, year-round. The vast majority of poor adults who did not work were ill, disabled, or elderly, or were single mothers of young children.[4]

As a trade-off for slightly reduced work participation, income transfer policy has maintained, but not greatly improved, a minimum level of subsistence in the United States. Because a very large portion of today's poor are children, the elderly, the ill, and the disabled, who surely cannot be blamed for not working, it would be difficult to oppose such measures. In addition, welfare policy has buffered the severity of economic cycles by providing strong countercyclical fiscal stimuli.[5] In other words, when the economy declines, welfare policy has its strongest antipoverty effects. Altogether, these effects have greatly reduced human suffering in systems of advanced capitalism, especially during economic downturns.

But this is not the point. The point is that income-based social policy, even though humane and justifiable, is not the only way—nor necessarily the best way—to structure welfare assistance. There is, perhaps, another approach that would more fundamentally promote well-being of the poor and long-term growth of the nation.

Stakeholding: Assets Rather than Income

In this book, the concept of assets rather than income is proposed as a new frame of reference. While there is a strong relationship between income and assets, they are very different concepts. *Assets* refers to the stock of wealth in a household. In contrast, *income* refers to the flow of resources in a household, a concept associated with consumption of goods and services and standard of living. These are the two most fundamental financial concepts, illustrated in accounting by two basic types of financial reports, income statements (which document financial flows) and balance sheets (which document financial stocks or accumulation). In this regard, welfare policy for the poor has been constructed almost exclusively in terms of household income statements. The proposal here is that welfare policy should be constructed more in terms of household balance sheets. This new thinking would be based on the concepts of savings, investment, and asset accumulation rather than on the concepts of income, spending, and consumption that guide current policy. Such a reconceptualization would have profound implications for the goals, structure, and programs of the welfare state.

The chapters that follow examine current welfare policy and suggest that policy should be thought of in this new way. The major reason for this proposed policy shift is that income only maintains consumption, but assets change the way people think and interact in the world. With assets, people begin to think in the long term and pursue long-term goals. In other words, while incomes feed people's stomachs, assets change their heads.

Wealth accumulation by the nonpoor occurs within a variety of institutional structures designed for these purposes, but the poor have few such structures within which to accumulate assets. For impoverished welfare recipients, asset accumulation is not encouraged. In most cases, it is not even permitted. Means-tested income transfer programs such as AFDC, Food Stamps, and Supplemental Security Income (SSI) have "asset tests," which, in effect, prohibit accumulation of more than minimal financial assets. In a sense, this is indeed asset-based social policy for the poor, but it is going in the wrong direction.

The key test of antipoverty policy, from both the recipient's and the taxpayer's perspectives, should be: Is the recipient better off than he or she was prior to implementation of the policy? Specifically, does the recipient hold more assets? If the answer to this question is no, then as an antipoverty policy, the effort has failed. If the answer is yes, then the effort has succeeded.

Fortunately, some beginning experiments in positive asset-based welfare, where asset accumulation is promoted, are underway. These beginning experiments, discussed later in the book, are scattered in different parts of the country and in different categories of social welfare. Most are not yet targeted toward the poor, and they are not yet thought of as the beginning of a movement toward a different form of welfare policy, but that is what I believe they are. For lack of previous designation, I have coined the phrase *asset-based welfare policy* so that these experiments and others might be understood as an emerging new direction.

Building on these experiments, social policy should be designed, in part, to promote and institutionalize asset accumulation among the poor. The approach is in part social reform and in part financial planning. The proposals in this book would lead to greater savings and investment for long-term goals among welfare recipients. In addition, the proposals would lead eventually to greater equality in the distribution of wealth—and greater equality in social, economic, and political affairs that would follow.

The United States, especially during the 1980s, has been a spend-and-borrow society. Across all economic sectors, we spend first, and then borrow to pay the bill. Although we generally try to convince ourselves that spending is a sign of wealth, this is a very shortsighted view. Wealth is not income, spending, and consumption, but rather savings, investment, and accumulation of assets. Very few people manage to spend their way out of poverty. The implications of this simple fact for welfare policy, as for the nation, are extremely important.

I am strongly in favor of hardheaded, long-term financial planning which is, unfortunately, not currently characteristic of any major sector of the U.S. economy—corporate, government, or household. By hardheaded, I mean the simple and time-proven formula of structured, long-term savings and investment. In this book, I attempt to apply this hardheadedness to social policy. It is, in my view, an effort to bring some common sense to a gravely misguided policy and emotionally charged issue.

Welfare policy has gone off track in becoming almost exclusively preoccupied with income protection of the poor. Policy should seek to empower as well as protect. Especially, policy should take into consideration the critical role of asset accumulation in economic and social well-being.

Also, welfare policy should avoid the "leaky bucket" syndrome of many public programs, where tax dollars are poured in at the top, but administrative costs and inefficiency drain away most of the potential benefit before it reaches its final destination. Instead, wherever possible, there should be a straightforward, direct-to-client system that relies on minimal organization and bureaucracy.

Welfare Vision

Welfare policy has many meanings. Some see welfare policy as assistance to the downtrodden, but others see it as an unfair drain on hardworking taxpayers. Some see welfare policy as the Lord's work, but others see it as waste, fraud, and abuse. Some see welfare policy as rescuing the lives of children, but others see it as fostering dependence. Some think welfare policy should be for all the needy, but others think it should be only for the most deserving. Some say the rich get most of the real welfare, leaving only crumbs for the poor, but others say welfare expenditures for the poor are ruining the nation.

There are many ways to define social problems, and distortions and errors of conceptualization are common in social policy.[6] Charles F. Kettering, in a famous line, has said that "a problem well stated is a problem half solved." The underlying vision with which we see human welfare (well-being) determines how we go about trying to solve the problem of poverty. But how should we *see* welfare? What is welfare, anyway?

Unfortunately, this question has not been asked often enough in social policy-making, and when it has been asked, the answer has almost always been that human welfare is defined by some level income, either in cash or in goods and services. By and large, assets or wealth of the poor have been ignored. Indeed, the phrase "wealth of the poor" sounds peculiar to us. We do not often apply the concept of wealth to the poor. Nor, for the most part, do the poor apply it to themselves.

The word *wealth* has changed its meaning over the years. It was once a general term for goods and services, as in Adam Smith's usage in *The Wealth of Nations*, but the word has now been altered by its derivative term *wealthy*. As a result, wealth now usually means material well-being *beyond the ordinary*.[7] The idea that poor people can have some wealth has fallen by the wayside.

Billy Tidwell of the National Urban League is one of the few people who has thought seriously about assets as a welfare issue. His focus is on black Americans, and he offers this view of wealth and welfare:

> In one sense, this inattention to wealth as a measure of black economic well-being may be understandable. Popular definitions of the concept emphasize "abundance of resources" and equate wealth with "affluence." In the public view, then, the term wealth seems reserved for "the rich and the super-rich," that elite class of Americans who are positioned well beyond the mainstream of the economic order. This group is perceived to be separate and apart from the rest of us, and the

blacks among them are distinct oddities. This subject provides titillating fodder for movies, novels, and the society pages; therefore, we tend not to regard wealth as an issue that is germane to the life experiences of the vast majority of black *or* white Americans, and thus not an issue warranting analysis along racial lines.[8]

As Tidwell mentions, the issues of wealth and well-being are not confined to one race or another. Regardless of race, assets of the poor, by and large, have not been studied. There have been no theories of welfare centered on assets of the poor. Implicitly, we seem to believe not only that the poor have no wealth, but that they *can* have no wealth. This assumption has led to the dominance of misguided income-based welfare policies. A major goal of this book is to recapture wealth (assets) as an idea that applies not only to the wealthy, but to everyone, including the poor.

The underlying vision is of an expanding economic pie, wherein all members of society can achieve greater personal wealth and contribute to greater economic productivity of the nation. The income-based welfare state assumes a finite pie, taking from one person for the consumption of another, with a resulting loss in economic growth. But the asset-based vision is that everyone saves and invests and becomes more productive. In other words, the asset-based vision seeks to integrate social policy and economic development.

Is the United States Underdeveloping?

After decades of economic prominence, the United States today may be an underdeveloping nation. We may be moving backward instead of forward. Parts of my hometown, St. Louis, are unbelievably impoverished. Thousands of homeless people are crowded into temporary shelters; thousands more are doubled up in substandard housing. New York City is shocking; there are so many hungry and homeless people on the streets and in the subway that it looks like the third world. Although more hidden, poverty in rural areas of the United States is even worse than it is in the cities. Across the nation, one-fifth of all our children live in poverty. One-fifth do not learn to read beyond the fourth-grade level. Almost one-third do not finish high school. Many young adults do not bring sufficient skills to the labor market to earn a living. Average real wages are not much more today than they were in

1973, and, for nonsupervisory workers, wages have actually declined. The gap between the highest-paid and lowest-paid workers is increasing. Today, almost nine million people are working full- or part-time but earning wages below the poverty line. Thirty-seven million Americans do not have health insurance of any kind. Even in the middle-class, the outlook for young Americans is not bright. The average 25- to 35-year-old parent now earns less (after inflation and taxes) and lives in a smaller home than his or her parents did at the same age. These are not the statistics of a prospering nation.

Most observers agree that growing hardship and inequality are the result of a poorly managed economy. We have been living beyond our means, not investing in education, research, capital expenditures, and infrastructure that would ensure future growth. The poor pay first for this lack of foresight. Poverty and hardship increase. During this process, many of the nonpoor maintain the trappings of prosperity, but if fundamental changes are not made, their comfortable life-style will not last indefinitely. Much of the underlying capital has been squandered.

The dismal economic statistics are now familiar to us all. In international trade, the United States has become a net debtor nation for the first time since 1917, and very quickly we have become the world's largest. As a result, foreigners lay claim to more and more of what is earned in the United States. Debt in all economic sectors—households, corporations, and government—grew dramatically during the 1980s. America's huge appetite for borrowed capital has kept real interest rates at historically high levels, adding to the debt burden and dampening economic growth.

Americans have long preached thriftiness; and in the early part of this century, we were a nation of savers. However, that pattern has changed during the post-World War II years. Influenced by Keynesian economics, which warned of the possibility of too much savings, we created an economy driven by consumption. Savings declined. As individuals we now save less than our counterparts in the rest of the industrialized world. The U.S. personal savings rate in 1989 was about 5 percent (up from 3 to 4 percent in prior years), compared to about 15 percent in Japan, and 7 to 10 percent in most of Europe. Domestically, a generation of younger Americans, expected by now to be peak savers, is instead spending heavily. The low personal savings rate, combined with low corporate savings and governmental deficits, has led to a dismal national savings slump. With the slump in savings, investment has declined.

The growth of debt and the lack of investment have had pronounced effects on competitiveness of the U.S. economy. During the 1970s and 1980s, the rate of productivity growth was, on the average, less than half that of the 1950s and 1960s. With low productivity growth, improvement in living standards has been stagnant. The American ideal of growing prosperity is no longer an accurate description of the U.S. economy. Indeed, in many respects, we are going backward rather than forward.

Social Policy and Economic Growth

The welfare state is not entirely responsible for the accumulated debt and economic stagnation. But it is partly responsible. As Peter Peterson and Neil Howe have cogently pointed out, issues of welfare policy are intimately connected with economic growth. This is particularly true for entitlement payments to the nonpoor, which constitute some 80 percent of all social welfare expenditures. Between 1965 and 1987, entitlement benefits grew from less than 6 percent of GNP to more than 11 percent. Because of entitlement spending, the government's function as an investor, a steward of our collective future, is small and shrinking. Its function as a switchboard for income transfers is large and growing.[9] For this reason, it is essential to consider welfare policy as an integral feature of macroeconomic policy.

As part of the economic challenge facing America, we must inevitably look at the fiscal problems of the federal government. Currently, the federal budget is serving as an engine for consumption. As the largest single part of federal expenditures, social welfare entitlements are helping to drive this consumption. Most of these entitlements go to the nonpoor. Despite antiwelfare rhetoric, the problem is *not* redistribution from the nonpoor to the poor, because in fact very little redistribution across class lines occurs—the nonpoor pay taxes and receive almost all of it back in benefits. Instead, the critical issue is *consumption*. We have welfare policies that stimulate and promote far too much consumption.

It is time to think about altering welfare policies so that they stimulate not consumption alone but also savings and investment. A new direction in welfare policy is required. This is true across the board. However, in this book I concentrate on welfare transfers to the poor.

A Proposal Suited to America

For the past half century, America has been a reluctant welfare state. We have provided income-based support to the needy, but our collective heart has been ambivalent. As a nation, we have never fully believed in welfare for the poor and even less in state planning and provision of services. We tend to value self-determination above security. As a result of this ambivalence about the poor, our welfare state is markedly different in character from those of European nations. Overall, we are less generous, less universal, and more judgmental. We provide some assistance, but we are not very comfortable with it. As a nation, it is as if we are trying to wear policy clothing that does not fit, a suit that hangs baggy at the waist and falls short at the sleeve. America needs a different welfare idea, an idea more suited to capitalism, more oriented toward accumulation and economic independence. In this book, asset-based welfare is suggested as an American proposal.

This proposal fits America's history and values. More than in European nations, the agrarian roots of America are defined by widespread landholding. Even prior to the American Revolution, British North America had become the most egalitarian nation in the Western world. Land was plentiful and Americans came to believe that landholding should be available to all.[10] In his *Letters from an American Farmer*, St. John de Crèvecoeur wrote:

> The instant I enter on my own land, the bright idea of property, of exclusive right, of independence, exalt my mind. Precious soil, I say to myself, by what singular custom of law is it that thou wast made to constitute the riches of the freeholder? What should we American farmers be without the distinct possession of that soil? No wonder we should thus cherish its possession; no wonder that so many Europeans who have never been able to say that such portion of land was theirs cross the Atlantic to realize that happiness. This formerly rude soil has established all our rights; on it is founded our rank, our freedom, our power as citizens, our importance as inhabitants of such a district.[11]

Like de Crèvecoeur, Thomas Jefferson viewed America's widespread land ownership as a wellspring of political and economic strength. America's independent agrarian tradition provided the social and economic foundation upon which capitalism thrived. Somewhat

later, Alexis de Tocqueville observed of the United States: "I know of
no country, indeed, where the love of money has such a grip on men's
hearts. . . ."[12] Tocqueville recognized that money was not worshipped
in America for itself, but because, in a capitalist democracy with little
centralized control, wealth is the basis of social organization and participation.

At the turn of the twentieth century, Max Weber identified a "spirit
of capitalism" that emerged from the rise of Calvinistic Protestantism
in Western Europe and the United States. For the first time in the
history of the world, Weber said, increase in capital was widely em-
braced as an ethical duty. Weber emphasized, "It is not mere business
astuteness, that sort of thing is common enough, it is an *ethos*."[13]
Nowhere has this ethos taken hold more strongly than in the United
States. Accumulation of independent capital is the American dream; it
has deep roots in our history. It is the fabric from which we should cut
an American welfare policy.

Poverty is more than simply a humanitarian or social justice issue.
Poverty is a drain on the nation, a loss of human resources. To take but
one example, in the field of mental retardation, it is well established
that 75–90 percent of all mentally retarded individuals have acquired
their mental disabilities not through defective genes or traumatic brain
damage but from socioeconomic causes. The causes are mainly depri-
vation in infant nurture during the prenatal and postnatal periods, including inadequate nutrition, harmful substances, and inadequate stimulation. Care of these millions of mentally retarded individuals costs
billions of dollars annually, not to mention the immense loss in the
value of their labor productivity. And this is only one area of costly
social problems related to poverty. One can similarly discuss the huge
costs of violent crime, child abuse, drugs, and so forth. From the larger
perspective of the nation, poverty simply does not pay. To put this very
succinctly, poverty is an expensive way to run a country.

Therefore, we should think about welfare policy not solely as support but also as investment. We should look not solely at deficiency
but also at capacity. Welfare policy should recognize the vast unused
potential in the American people. It is a mistake to think about welfare
policy as a separate, residual function. Instead, welfare policy should
be connected to the social, economic, and political goals of the nation.
Above all, for America, welfare policy should be about investment.

An asset-based welfare policy would be consistent with a stronger and more democratic capitalism. Social policy should seek to enhance the advantages of a free enterprise society by stimulating widespread economic participation. The more people who participate, the stronger the nation.

Billie Holiday penned the lines, "Them that's got shall get, / Them that's not shall lose. / So the Bible says, / And it still is news. / Mama may have. / Papa may have. / But God bless the child / That's got his own." These words are powerful and enduring not only because of the songwriter's eloquence, but also because she has captured an important truth. People with assets tend to do well in this world, and are even seen as virtuous, while people without assets do not do well. Although Billie Holiday undoubtedly was not thinking about welfare policy when she wrote the song, the welfare implications are far-reaching. Yet the idea of asset accumulation has hardly been considered in welfare policy for the poor. As Billie Holiday sings, "It still is news." The purpose of this book is to explore this news—to discuss the concept of asset accumulation in the context of social policy in the United States.

On my bookshelf is a good-luck charm from Ecuador, given to me by my sister-in-law, who was in a rural Ecuadorian village with the Peace Corps for two years. The charm is a gleeful little man, about four inches high, loaded down with goods of all kinds. He has a minia-ture bus, a house, several bags of grain, baskets, a bundle of money, and much more. He is so loaded down that only his head and his feet stick out, and he is very happy, smiling in openmouthed glee. It is a charm for prosperity, a wish for success in obtaining the material goods of this world, a charm for assets. Perhaps welfare policy in the United States would better serve the poor, and better serve the nation as a whole, if this little charm were the vision, rather than our current vision, which is of a ragged beggar receiving a crust of bread.

This book contains new thinking about welfare, a new way of look-ing at poverty and social policy. It is a first attempt to lay out the issues, cut the theoretical cloth, and recommend solutions. As a first step, it is far from perfect, and many issues remain to be worked out, but it is perhaps a useful beginning.

Notes

1. Sheldon Danziger and Robert Plotnick, "Poverty and Policy: Lessons of the Last Two Decades," *Social Service Review* 60, 1986, 34–51.

2. Charles Murray, *Losing Ground: American Social Policy 1950–1980*. New York: Basic Books, 1984.

3. Sheldon Danziger, Robert Haveman, and Robert Plotnick, "How Income Transfer Programs Affect Work, Savings, and the Income Distribution: A Critical Review," *Journal of Economic Literature* 19, 1981, 975–1028.

4. U.S. Bureau of the Census, *Money Income of Households, Families, and Persons in the United States: 1987*, Current Population Reports, Series P–60, No. 162, 1988; Isaac Shapiro and Robert Greenstein, *Making Work Pay: A New Agenda for Poverty Policies*. Washington: Center on Budget and Policy Priorities, 1989.

5. Hyman Minsky, *Stabilizing an Unstable Economy*. New Haven: Yale University Press, 1986.

6. Edward Seidman, "Justice, Values and Social Science: Unexamined Premises," in Edward Seidman and Julian Rappaport, eds., *Redefining Social Problems*. New York: Plenum Press, 1986, 235–58.

7. Charles Carter, *Wealth*. New York: Basic Books, Inc., 1968.

8. Billy J. Tidwell, "Black Wealth: Facts and Fiction," in National Urban League, ed. *The State of Black America, 1988*. Washington: National Urban League, 1988, 193–238.

9. Peter G. Peterson and Neil Howe, *On Borrowed Time: How the Growth of Entitlement Spending Threatens America's Future*. San Francisco: Institute for Contemporary Studies, 1988.

10. William Scott, *In Pursuit of Happiness: American Conceptions of Property from the Seventeenth to the Twentieth Centuries*. Bloomington: Indiana University Press, 1977.

11. St. John de Crèvecoeur, *Letters from an American Farmer*. New York: New American Library, 1963, 48.

12. Alexis de Tocqueville, *Democracy in America*. Garden City, New York: Anchor Books, 1969 (originally published in 1835), 54.

13. Max Weber, *The Rise of the Protestant Ethic and the Spirit of Capitalism*. New York: Charles Scribner's Sons, 1958 (originally published in 1904–1905), 51, italics added.

2 • Income Distribution and Income Poverty

Before turning to ideas and policy proposals for asset accumulation, it may be helpful to "get the lay of the land" in welfare theory and policy as it currently exists. In this chapter we briefly review the distribution of income and income poverty. In following chapters, we examine theories of welfare, federal welfare policy as it stands today, and the welfare reform debate. Most of this thinking and policy can be described as income-based. The purposes of these chapters are to illuminate the current vision in welfare theory and policy and to provide a point of departure for the asset-based information and ideas that are presented in the second part of the book. In this chapter, we very briefly review the distribution of income and characteristics of income poverty.[1]

Well-Being as Income

In the United States, we assess the prominence and power of our major corporations and wealthiest individuals by their asset holdings, but for the majority of the population, we think of well-being in terms of income. This is especially—almost exclusively—true when we think about the well-being of the poor. Income is the standard assumption in most inequality research, in poverty analysis, and in most social policy. Income-based social policy was the heart of the New Deal of the 1930s and the War on Poverty of the 1960s.

Sources of Income

Income is all the money that comes into a household, or other unit, during a given period. It is the *flow* of money. Personal income comes

Table 2.1

Sources of Personal Income, November 1989
(billions of dollars and subtotal percentages)

Labor income

Wages and salaries	$2,699.5
Other labor income	255.3
Subtotal	$2,954.8
	(65.1%)

Asset income

Proprietor income, farm	40.3
Proprietor income, nonfarm	313.6
Rental income	10.2
Dividend income	115.8
Interest income	674.0
Subtotal	1,153.9
	(25.4%)

Transfer income

Transfer payments	650.4
Less contributions for social insurance	−218.2
Subtotal	432.2
	(9.5%)

| Total personal income | $4,541.0 |
| | (100.0%) |

Source: Council of Economic Advisers, 1989. *Economic Indicators, December 1989.* Washington, DC: U.S. Government Printing Office, 5.
Note: Monthly data presented as annual rate, seasonally adjusted, with adjustments for capital consumption as well.

from three major sources: labor, assets, and transfers. Of these, labor income is by far the most important, accounting for about 65 percent of personal income in the nation as a whole (Table 2.1). However, as is so often the case, the overall figures are misleading. In many families, labor income accounts for over 80 percent of personal income. In contrast, for the very rich, asset income is more important than is labor income; and for the welfare poor, transfers are the largest source of income.

Looking at national income as a whole, and dividing it into just two sources, labor income and property income, we see evidence of a

Table 2.2

Percentage Shares of National Income, 1970–1984

	Labor	Property
1970	82.2	17.8
1975	81.0	19.0
1980	80.0	20.0
1984	77.5	22.5

Source: Beach, Charles M., 1989. "Dollars and Dreams: A Reduced Middle Class? Alternative Explanations." *Journal of Human Resources* 24 (1): 162–93, citing *Statistical Abstracts* and the *Survey of Current Business*, adjusting for self-employment, stock appreciation, and capital consumption.

declining role of labor income and an ascending role of property income between 1970 and 1984 (Table 2.2). The biggest rise in property income has occurred with interest income, which increased from 1.8 percent in 1955, to 5.1 percent in 1970, to 9.6 percent in 1984.[2] These statistics suggest that labor, while still immensely important, is receding in prominence as a factor of production, whereas property (capital or assets) is becoming steadily more influential. If this trend continues, it will eventually have tremendous—but as yet largely unconsidered— implications for how we think about the income of U.S. households.

The Pursuit of Knowledge about Income

Although the distribution of income is covered in regular statistical reports and numerous academic articles, it is not always clear what these statistics mean. Sheldon Danziger and Peter Gottschalk examine the huge volume of income data and interpretation and conclude that income analysts

> often cannot agree as to what the trend has actually been, and rarely understand its underlying causes. What is common to all of these studies is the failure of analysts to do much more than describe trends and then to advocate a policy response that fits the data and their personal views. That is, the degree of inequality and its trend are a topic of intense policy interest, but of little economic understanding.[3]

This apparent frustration with income-based studies is understandable. In many cases, the studies proceed by counting income and who has it, without asking theoretically driven questions about poverty.[4] This tendency to count in the absence of theory has generated a small mountain of data, but not an equivalent advancement in knowledge. However, Danziger and Gottschalk's conclusion is perhaps an over-statement. Most income-based research is more applied than theoretical. Much of it is oriented to who, how, and when people move into and out of poverty status or "welfare" recipiency, and on these topics, we have learned a great deal. As the twentieth century winds down, we certainly know more than we previously knew about the distribution of income, demographic and societal factors associated with income distribution, characteristics of income poverty, and patterns of welfare recipiency.

The Distribution of Income

In 1988, the average standard of living was much higher than it was in 1949, but the *distribution* of income was about the same. There was a reduction of income inequality during the latter half of the 1960s, due primarily to increased welfare expenditures. However, during the 1980s, with higher unemployment, lower wages, and reduced welfare transfers, income inequality grew worse.[5]

On average, after tax family income increased by 9.6 percent between 1977 and 1988, but this overall increase masked a very skewed growth distribution. The bottom four deciles (groups of 10 percent) actually lost income, with the lowest decile losing by far the most, 10.5 percent. The next five deciles gained income, but only modestly, while the top decile gained handsomely at 27.4 percent. The top 5 percent of families did even better, gaining 37.3 percent; and the top 1 percent enjoyed a spectacular gain of 74.2 percent.[6] In short, the rich got richer and the poor got poorer. Census Bureau figures for 1988, in quintiles (groups of 20 percent), are shown in Table 2.3. The top 20 percent of the population receives 44 percent of the income, almost ten times more than the bottom 20 percent, which receives only 4.6 percent of the income.

Income Abundance

At the top end of the scale, both women's earnings and asset earnings played significant roles in increasing family income. Between 1973

Table 2.3

Household Income Distribution, 1988

Portion of population	Percentage of income	Comment
Bottom 20 percent	4.6	lowest since 1954
Fourth 20 percent	10.7	lowest ever recorded
Middle 20 percent	16.7	lowest ever recorded
Second 20 percent	24.0	
Top 20 percent	44.0	highest ever recorded
Top 5 percent	17.2	highest since 1952

Sources: U.S. Bureau of the Census, 1989. "Money Income and Poverty Status in the United States: 1988." *Current Population Reports*, Series P-60, no. 166, October. Report and comments are from the Center on Budget and Policy Priorities, 1989. "Poverty Rate and Household Income Stagnate as Rich-Poor Gap Hits Post-War High." Washington: Center on Budget and Policy Priorities, October.

and 1987, the "rich" (defined as annual income nine times the poverty level or greater) grew from 3.1 percent of all families to 6.9 percent of all families. More than half of this income growth for the rich came from working wives, and another 22 percent came from increased asset income. Among the richest 1 percent of families, asset income accounted for nearly half of the increase in income between 1973 and 1987.[7]

Income Poverty

In the early years of televised baseball, Dizzy Dean would say to Pee Wee Reese, "Give me the statics on that, Pee Wee." If Dizzy Dean were alive today, he would be amazed at the lengthy answer this query might receive. Statistics on baseball have become remarkably detailed since the 1960s. For quite similar reasons, statistics on income poverty have become nearly as detailed. Armed with computers and a steady stream of data, poverty researchers diligently and creatively present the nuances of scope, distribution, and trends in income poverty. As with baseball, detailed statistics on poverty occasionally run ahead of their usefulness in imparting information of practical value. On the other hand, with the help of these detailed statistics, poverty analysts have learned a great deal about the characteristics of income poverty.

Measuring Income Poverty

The first statistical view of poverty in the United States was by Robert Hunter, who served with the Chicago Board of Charities before working in the slums of New York. In 1904 he published *Poverty*, in which he concluded that, in a total population of about 80 million, 10 million lived "in poverty."[8] Later, the 1909 Pittsburgh Survey funded by the Russell Sage Foundation collected detailed poverty statistics and became a model for studies that followed.[9] The Great Depression of the 1930s heightened awareness of unemployment and poverty, but World War II and the prosperous postwar years removed poverty from the national consciousness. In 1962, Michael Harrington's *Other America* described 40 million to 50 million Americans living in poverty, and these startling statistics, along with the civil rights movement, returned poverty to the national agenda.[10] Another milestone was Charles Murray's *Losing Ground*, in which he argued that increased public transfers had increased the level of welfare dependency.[11] In all these studies of poverty, income statistics have been the raw material.

Despite this long history, careful measurement of income poverty on a national scale is a recent development, associated with the beginnings of the War on Poverty of the 1960s. In order to make comparisons from one place to another and from one time period to another, a standard income poverty definition was required. Mollie Orshansky, an analyst at the Social Security Administration, developed a set of income poverty thresholds between 1963 and 1965. These became official in 1969.[12] Orshansky settled on a definition of poverty as three times an emergency food budget, an idea based somewhat precariously on 1955 research indicating that families spent about three times their after-tax income on food. This "poverty level" was adjusted upward with rising food prices until 1972. At that time, with food prices rising faster than the overall price level, the inflation adjustment was switched to the Consumer Price Index.[13]

Of course, the size of income poverty depends on what is counted as income. The official poverty definition includes only money income, does not include capital gains, and does not subtract taxes. But many poor households receive noncash income such as Food Stamps, subsidized housing, and Medicaid; and many low-income households pay taxes. Therefore, alternative definitions of poverty might add noncash income and/or subtract taxes.[14]

Thus, the definition of income poverty is, at best, imprecise. Almost everyone would agree that the official poverty line is not an exact demarcation of economic distress, but the agreement stops at that point. Some believe the official poverty line is too low, and they argue for higher poverty thresholds. Others, citing noncash and other un-counted income, believe the official poverty line is too high, and they argue for lower poverty thresholds. Which of these two opposing positions one views as correct depends on politics and sentiments more than on objective analysis.

Another measurement issue is temporal. Income poverty is currently assessed on the basis of annual income. However, evidence suggests that when income poverty is assessed on the basis of monthly income, *four times* as many people enter income poverty at some time during the year, although most of the poverty spells are quite short.[15] Because most of the income poor have little or no financial assets with which to weather income shortfalls, the official poverty rate may be grossly understating the number of people who live below the poverty standard at least some time during the year.

These issues in measurement, however, do not mean that income poverty statistics are not useful. When gathered consistently from year to year, income poverty statistics do effectively show trends over time, and this ability to chart trends is their most important function.[16]

The Meaning and Pattern of Income Poverty

Some 32 million people, about 13.1 percent of the U.S. population, were officially impoverished in 1988.[17] In other words, these 32 million people did not have incomes above the minimum (roughly three times an emergency food budget) that the federal government has designated as the poverty line (Table 2.4).

Income at the poverty level does not stretch very far. Table 2.5 illustrates an estimated family budget on poverty-level income in 1989. The budget allowed only $298 per month for rent and utilities, $20 per person per week for food, and $0.75 per person per day for transportation. Most Americans would consider this standard of living extremely difficult, if not intolerable. Yet, the income poor, by definition, exist *below* this level of income.

In 1988, for example, the average amount of money needed to raise the incomes of all income-poor families to their respective poverty

Table 2.4

Income Poverty Levels, 1989

Household size	Annual	Monthly
1	$ 5,980	$ 498
2	8,020	668
3	10,060	838
4	12,100	1,008
5	14,140	1,178
6	16,180	1,348
7	18,220	1,518
8	20,260	1,688

Note: Includes income poverty levels for the District of Columbia and all states except Alaska and Hawaii, calculated by the U.S. Bureau of the Census.

thresholds was $4,851, or $1,395 per family member.[18] With 32 million people officially poor in 1988, the total U.S. "poverty gap" was about $45 billion. In other words, $45 billion of additional income, perfectly distributed, would have been enough to raise every American's income up to the poverty line—the living standard described in Table 2.5. However, because these transfers do not reduce the rate of pretransfer poverty,[19] another $45 billion or so would also be required the next year, and the next.

Although the income poverty rate remained stubbornly high at 13.1 percent in 1988, it is important to note that in the postwar period, income poverty has greatly subsided (Table 2.6). Every five years between 1949 and 1964, the income poverty rate declined in the neighborhood of 15 percent to 20 percent. These declines can be attributed almost exclusively to economic prosperity. A somewhat larger drop of about 30 percent occurred between 1964 and 1969, influenced by expanded War on Poverty transfers. Between 1969 and 1979, the income poverty rate was essentially flat. During this period, government transfers to the elderly rose rapidly, but employment earnings fell; as a consequence, income poverty decreased among the elderly, but increased among children, a trend that continued into the 1980s.[20] Following the severe recession of 1981–82 and the Reagan budgets cuts, income poverty increased. Even after several years of economic recovery, the rate stood at 14.0 percent in 1985. Although the economy continued to expand, the income poverty declined only marginally to 13.1 percent by 1988.

Table 2.5

**Estimated Family Budget of a Nonfarm Family of Four Based on 1989
Poverty-Level Income of $12,100**

Housing and utilites	$298.00 per month
Health care	126.00 per month
Clothing	22.00 per person per month
Food and household supplies	20.00 per person per week
Transportation	0.75 per person per day
Laundry and personal items	0.50 per person per day

Source: Estimates are by Nancy Vosler, George Warren Brown School of Social Work, Washington University.

Table 2.6

Family Income and Poverty, 1949–1985

Year	Median family income*	Official poverty rate
1949	$14,021	34.3%
1954	16,678	27.3
1959	19,993	22.4
1964	22,783	19.0
1969	27,680	12.1
1974	28,145	11.2
1979	29,029	11.7
1985	27,735	14.0

Source: U.S. Bureau of the Census. *Current Population Reports*, Series P-60, reported in Sheldon Danziger and Peter Gottschalk, 1988–89. "Increasing Inequality in the United States: What We Know and What We Don't." *Journal of Post Keynesian Economics* 11 (2), 174–95. The income-poverty rate for 1954 is based on unpublished tabulations by Gordon Fisher, U.S. Department of Health and Human Services.

*Median family income is reported in 1985 dollars for all years.

Dynamics of Income Poverty

In recent years, we have learned that income poverty is highly dynamic for most individuals and households. Many people become income poor at one time or another, but most do not stay poor for a long period of time. For example, data from the Panel Study of Income Dynamics (PSID) indicate that 24 percent of the population experienced income poverty at some point during the decade 1969–78. However, during this period, 68 percent were income poor for three years or less. In contrast, less than 11 percent were income poor for eight years or more. Nonetheless, at any given moment, the persistently poor account for a substantial portion, as much as 60 percent, of the income poverty population. The persistently poor are more likely to be children, to be black, to live in rural areas, to live in the South, and to reside in families headed by elderly or disabled people.[21]

In contrast to the logic of antiwelfare analyses such as Charles Murray's *Losing Ground*, the greatest increases in poverty in the 1980's have been among those who depend on earnings for income, that is, among those least likely to be welfare recipients. According to PSID data, 50 percent of people who become income poor in a year do so because of a job loss or pay cut that reduces earnings. Regardless of the causes of income poverty, a remarkable 80 percent of all moves out of poverty result from increased earnings, a figure that remains substantial at 56 percent among female-headed families.[22]

Who Is Income Poor?

In this section, we briefly review some of the major themes in income poverty.[23] Hopefully, although we miss a great deal of specificity, the key issues are illuminated. These key issues are childhood poverty, single-parent families, poverty among nonwhites, and inadequacy of employment earnings. Although two of these issues (childhood poverty and poverty among nonwhites) are usually described as "demographic" factors, and the other two (single-parent families and inadequate employment) are often discussed as "causes" of poverty, these distinctions are not particularly helpful. It is by no means clear which of these issues causes which. They are all complexly interrelated.

Income Poverty and Age: The Rise in Childhood Poverty

Until 1973, the income poverty rate for the elderly exceeded that of children, but since that time, the relationship has been reversed. One of the major social policy changes of the last two decades has been the decline in poverty among the elderly and the increase in poverty among children. By 1988, income poverty among children under the age of eighteen was 19.6 percent (about one out of every five chil-

Table 2.7

Percentages of Income Poverty of the Total Population and of Children, by Race, 1979 and 1988

	1979	1988
Overall income poverty rate		
All persons	11.7	13.1
White	9.0	10.1
Black	31.0	31.6
Hispanic	21.8	26.8
Child income poverty rate*		
All children	16.2	19.6
White	11.6	14.4
Black	40.9	44.1
Hispanic	27.8	37.8

Source: U.S. Bureau of the Census, 1989. "Money Income and Poverty Status in the United States: 1988." *Current Population Reports*, Series P-60, no. 166. Center on Budget and Policy Priorities, 1989. "Poverty Rate and Household Income Stagnate as Rich-Poor Gap Hits Post-War High." Washington: Center on Budget and Policy Priorities, October.

*Children under eighteen years of age.

dren), which was by far the highest poverty rate of any age-group.[24] By the time they reach eighteen years of age, one-third of the nation's children have lived, at one time or another, in income poverty.

Childhood poverty is strongly associated with race. As shown in Table 2.7, the income poverty rates for black and Hispanic children are considerably greater than the rate for white children. In 1988, an astounding 44.1 percent of all black children (more than two out of every five) were living in poverty, as were 37.8 percent of Hispanic children. Also, thinking about these figures over time, we must bear in mind that the population of children is changing. The numbers of nonwhite (including both black and Hispanic) children is increasing faster than the number of white children. Nonwhites will constitute the majority of children under eighteen years old during the first half of the next century. Therefore, all other things being equal, demographic trends will continue to increase the rate of childhood poverty into the foreseeable future.

Income Poverty and Families: The Problem of Single Parenthood

> To talk about the condition of children is by definition to talk about the families in which they live. That is why we are going to have to talk about two kinds of children, because—of a sudden, in a flash—we have become a society divided into two kinds of families. . . . In this dual family system, roughly half our children . . . are born without a fair chance. We know precious little about what to do about it. . . . At any given moment, about one child in four is born poor. . . . [25]

As Senator Daniel Moynihan observes above, any discussion of poor children must inevitably be accompanied by a discussion of family structure. Regarding income poverty, the United States has two very distinct types of families—two-parent families and single-parent families. The vast majority of single parent families are headed by females.

In two-parent families, poverty has dramatically diminished. Over a forty-year period, from 1940 to 1980, there was a large decline in the poverty rate of two-parent families in all demographic groups. The overall decline was from 33 percent in 1940 to 7 percent in 1980. For white families, the decline was from 30 percent to 6 percent; for black families, from 69 percent to 15 percent; and for Hispanic families, from 55 percent to 16 percent.[26] These large declines in income poverty for two-parent families, across all racial groups, are nothing short of remarkable.

But not all children live in two-parent families. Both an increased rate of divorce and a growing trend toward never-married motherhood have led to large numbers of single-parent families. Today, one child in two has lived in a single-parent household at some time before reaching the age of eighteen. Most of these single-parent households are headed by females, and these families have not, on the average, fared very well. In single-female-headed families, the poverty rate has declined much less, from 47 percent in 1940 to 36 percent in 1980. For whites, the decline was from 41 percent to 30 percent; for blacks, from 81 percent to 53 percent; and for Hispanics, from 66 percent to 52 percent.[27] Thus, the tremendous economic progress of two-parent household between 1940 and 1980 was not matched in single-parent households. Again, this was true regardless of race. Indeed, black single-parent households actually improved slightly more than the single parent households of whites or Hispanics, largely because blacks started from a worse economic position and welfare transfers helped to reduce a portion of the inequality.

Moreover, during the period between 1940 and 1980, the percentage of single-female-headed families increased. The reasons for this increase are different across racial groups. Today, black mothers are less likely to marry at all; and white mothers are more likely to divorce and not remarry. Single-female-headed families now comprise a shocking 50 percent of all black families, and about 15 percent of all white families.[28] A very large portion of single mothers are young, with limited earnings capacity, and most receive little or no child support from absent fathers. Thus, they and their children often remain mired in income poverty for extended periods of time.[29] Overall, in 1988, 53.0 percent of all poor families in the United States were headed by a single woman. By comparison, only 12.3 percent of nonpoor families were headed by a single woman.

However, the meaning of these figures is not as clear-cut as it might seem at first glance. While the increasing percentage of single-female-headed families has undoubtedly been a major factor in the rising rate of poverty among women and children, family structure alone does not cause income poverty. The erosion of employment earnings is also a major cause of increasing poverty, and these factors are very much interrelated.[30]

Income Poverty and Racial Minorities:
The Stagnation of Progress toward Racial Equality

As indicated above, income poverty is strongly associated with race. In 1988, the income-poverty rate was 10.1 percent for whites, 31.6 percent for blacks, and 26.8 percent for Hispanics (Table 2.7). However, although nonwhites have higher poverty rates, they do not comprise the majority of the income-poor population. In actual numbers, 65.1 percent of all poor persons in the United States in 1988 were white; 29.6 percent were black; and 16.9 percent were Hispanic.[31]

The proportions of impoverished whites, blacks, and Hispanics are roughly the same, regardless of age. A higher proportion of nonwhite children, relative to white children, live in single-parent households and are poor. However, single parenthood does not account for the similarly high proportion of nonwhite adults who are poor. Family structure alone does not explain high poverty rates among nonwhites.

Black income grew in relation to white income during the 1950s and 1960s due to rising wage rates, but held steady at roughly 60 percent of white income for the next twenty years. During the 1970s and 1980s, two countervailing trends occurred. The first was the continued rising wage rates among blacks, especially black females, relative to whites. By the end of the 1980s, both black males and black females, when they worked, earned roughly the same income as did white females. The second and opposing trend was an increasing proportion of non-employed blacks relative to whites—both those who were unemployed (looking for work but unable to find it) and those who were not in the labor force (not looking for work). In short, blacks are today paid somewhat better than they were before, but they are working much less. These two trends have generally canceled each other in their effects on income distribution during the 1970s and 1980s.

Income Poverty and Employment: The Increase in the Working Poor

Working is by far the best way out of income poverty. Income poverty rates are strongly related to the numbers of workers in a family. In 1988, the poverty rate for families with no workers was 29.8 percent, while the poverty rate for families with three or more workers was only 2.2 percent.[32]

Because labor earnings are such a major factor in personal income, it is almost axiomatic that unemployment and inadequate earnings are major contributors to income poverty in the United States. As individuals move into and out of adequate employment, they and their families move out of and into income poverty. Evidence indicates that

> most able-bodied heads of households demonstrate strong labor force attachment, but their employment tends to be intermittent, low-paying, or both. . . . About half of all poor able-bodied mothers whose youngest child is over age 6 work at some point during the year, as compared with about 80 percent of men who head poor households with children. Despite this work effort, poor households remain in poverty because of low annual earnings, which reflect both low weekly earnings and less than full-year work. And most of these households would remain poor even if their heads worked a full year at their current weekly earnings rate.[33]

A surprisingly large number of the income-poor are employed. Among income poor family heads, 48.3 percent worked in 1988, and 16.4 percent worked full-time, year-round. About 59 percent (almost three-fifths) of all poor families had at least one person who worked in 1986; and 17.9 percent (1.2 million) of all poor families had two or more workers.[34] Thus, work does not guarantee an escape from income poverty. Approximately one out of every ten full-time, year-round workers in the United States does not earn enough to raise a family of three above the poverty line.

The number of people who worked, yet remained poor, increased during the 1980s.[35] The labor market trends responsible for the rising number of working poor were the loss of middle-income manufacturing jobs and the huge increase in low-paying service jobs. Unfortunately there is no sign that these trends in the U.S. labor market are likely to reverse in the near future.

Conclusion

In summarizing the trends in income distribution and income poverty, I offer two main points and a thought. The first point is that labor income is a key to reducing income poverty. Many poor people are willing to work, and in fact, many *do* work. Also, a very strong case can be made that inadequate employment earnings for black males has led to the rise in single-female-headed black families.[36] Therefore, it seems logical to consider unemployment and underemployment as the most critical issues in income poverty. In recent years, a growing voice among social welfare analysts has articulated this viewpoint.[37] An effective policy of full employment, that is, a stable and adequately paying job for everyone who wants to work, accompanied by medical care and decent child care, would, without question, do more to reduce income poverty than any other approach. Given the very positive regard for work in the United States, a policy of full employment seems by far the most acceptable and most productive policy for combating income poverty. However, at this writing, the possibility of a successful full employment initiative seems remote.

The second point is that the rising income poverty among children is a national crisis.[38] We are not raising all the nation's children to be sound, productive citizens. On the contrary, we are raising millions of children to be illiterate, angry, ill, and criminal. It is abundantly clear at this point that the income-based transfer policy has been ineffective in protecting and developing the nation's children. The eventual solution to this problem, if it is to be solved at all, will be multifaceted, including more income transfers, better and more equal education, more adequate housing, less discrimination in housing, health care available to all, and expanded employment opportunities. However, the nation as a whole is skeptical about these traditional welfare state policies; the federal budget is running at a chronic deficit; and significant progress is not likely in the near future.

As a concluding thought on income poverty, the gradually rising importance of asset income should not be overlooked. The trend is accompanied by declining real wages at the bottom of the labor income scale. Thus, those who depend solely on labor income, especially at the bottom, are swimming decidedly upstream. History in not running in their favor. Although it may seem an unorthodox line of thinking, the poor would be far better off if a portion of their earnings were generated by assets.

Notes

1. In recent years there have been a number of excellent analyses of income distribution, particularly in regard to income poverty. Among these are Greg Duncan, *Years of Poverty, Years of Plenty.* Ann Arbor: Survey Research Center, Institute for Social Research, University of Michigan, 1984; Frank Levy, *Dollars and Dreams: The Changing American Income Distribution.* New York: Russell Sage Foundation, 1987; David T. Ellwood, *Poor Support: Poverty in the American Family.* New York: Basic Books, 1988; and Robert Haveman, *Starting Even: An Equal-Opportunity Program to Combat the Nation's New Poverty.* New York: Simon and Schuster, 1988.

2. Charles M. Beach, "Dollars and Dreams: A Reduced Middle Class? Alternative Explanations," *Journal of Human Resources* 24(1), 1989, 162–93.

3. Sheldon Danziger and Peter Gottschalk, "Increasing Inequality in the United States: What We Know and What We Don't," *Journal of Post Keynesian Economics* 11(2), 1988–89, 174–95.

4. Robert Haveman. "Conclusion," in Denis Kessler and André Masson, eds. *Modelling the Accumulation and Distribution of Wealth.* Oxford: Clarendon Press, 1988, 323–28.

5. Gary Burtless, "Inequality in America: Where Do We Stand?" *The Brookings Review*, Summer 1987, 9–16; Levy, 1987; and U.S. Bureau of the Census, *Money Income and Poverty Status in the United States: 1988*, Current Population Reports, Series P–60, No. 166, 1989.

6. U.S. Bureau of the Census, 1989; Thomas B. Edsall, "The Return of Inequality," *The Atlantic Monthly* 261(6), June 1988, 86–94. For the most part,

family incomes are reported in this chapter, rather than individual incomes.

7. Sheldon Danziger, Peter Gottschalk, and Eugene Smolensky, "How the Rich Have Fared," *American Economic Review* 79(2), 1989, 310–14 (Papers and Proceedings of the Annual Meeting of the American Economic Association, New York, December 1988).

8. Robert Hunter, *Poverty.* New York: Macmillan, 1904.

9. Paul Kellogg, ed., *The Pittsburgh Survey*, six volumes. New York: Russell Sage Foundation, 1909–1914.

10. Michael Harrington, *The Other America.* New York: Macmillan, 1962.

11. Charles Murray, *Losing Ground: American Social Policy 1950–1980.* New York: Basic Books, 1984.

12. Mollie Orshansky, "How Poverty Is Measured," *Monthly Labor Review* 92(2) Feb. 1969, 37–41. Orshansky's is an absolute definition of poverty rather than a relative definition, although she raises the possibility of a relative definition. For an additional comment on definitions of poverty, see chapter 9.

13. William C. Birdsall, "The Value of the Official Poverty Statistics," Working Paper 86–01. Ann Arbor: School of Social Work, University of Michigan, 1986.

14. As alternative poverty definitions, the Census Bureau has two measures of these noncash benefits, the market value measure and the recipient's perceived value measure. By the market value measure, adding noncash transfers reduces the amount of income poverty by 35–40 percent. By the recipients perceived value method, adding noncash transfers reduces the amount of income poverty by 15–20 percent.

15. Patricia Ruggles and Robertson Williams, "Longitudinal Measures of Poverty: Accounting for Income and Assets Over Time," *Review of Income and Wealth* 35(3), 1989, 225–43.

16. Birdsall, 1986.

17. At this writing, 1988 is the latest year for which systematic income data are published.

18. U.S. Bureau of the Census, 1989.

19. Sheldon Danziger and Robert Plotnick, "Poverty and Policy: Lessons of the Last Two Decades," *Social Service Review* 60, 1986, 34–51.

20. Eugene Smolensky, Sheldon Danziger, and Peter Gottschalk, "The Declining Significance of Age in the United States: Trends in the Well-Being of Children and the Elderly since 1939," in John Palmer, Timothy Smeeding, and Barbara Torrey, eds., *The Vulnerable: America's Young and Old in the Industrial World.* Washington: Urban Institute Press, 1988.

21. M.S. Hill, "Some Dynamic Aspects of Poverty," in M.S. Hill, D.H. Hill, and J.N. Morgan, eds., *Five Thousand American Families—Patterns of Economic Progress*, vol. 9. Ann Arbor: Institute for Social Research, 1981; Mary J. Bane and David Ellwood, "Slipping into and out of Poverty: The Dynamics of Spells," Working Paper No. 1199. Cambridge, MA: National Bureau of Economic Research, 1983; Duncan, 1984; and Michael Morris and John Williamson, *Poverty and Public Policy: An Analysis of Federal Intervention Efforts.* New York: Greenwood Press, 1986.

22. William O'Hare, *Poverty in America: Trends and New Patterns*, Population Bulletin 40, no. 3. Washington: Population Reference Bureau, Inc., 1985.

23. For more thorough descriptions and interpretations, see Ellwood, 1988; and Haveman, *Starting Even*, 1988.

24. More specific data on poverty by age-group are as follows: In 1988, the income poverty rate was 20.5 percent for the under-fifteen age-group; 15.7 percent for the fifteen to twenty-four age-group; 9.8 percent for the twenty-five to forty-four age-group; 7.7 percent for the forty-five to fifty-four age-group; 9.6 percent for the fifty-five to fifty-nine age-group; 10.4 percent for the sixty to sixty-four age-group; and 12.0 percent for the over-sixty-five age-group (U.S. Bureau of the Census, 1989).

25. Daniel Patrick Moynihan, "Half the Nation's Children: Born without a Fair Chance," *New York Times*, September 25, 1988, E25.

26. James P. Smith, "Poverty and the Family," in Gary Sandefur and Marta Tienda, eds., *Divided Opportunities: Minorities, Poverty, and Social Policy*. New York: Plenum Press, 1988; his computations are from public use samples of decennial census data. See also Christine Ross, Sheldon Danziger, and Eugene Smolensky, "The Level and Trend of Poverty in the United States," *Demography* 24(4), 1987, 587–600.

27. Smith, 1988. For a discussion of this and related issues, see Harrell R. Rodgers, Jr., *Poor Women, Poor Families*. Armonk, N.Y.: M. E. Sharpe, revised edition, 1990.

28. Roger Wojtkiewicz, Sara McLanahan, and Irwin Garfinkle, "The Growth of Families Headed by Women: 1950 to 1980," IRP Discussion Paper No. 822–87. Madison: Institute for Research on Poverty, 1987.

29. Additional data on family poverty are as follows: In 1988, the income-poverty rate for all families stood at 10.4 percent. For married couples, the rate was 5.6 percent; for single female heads of households, 33.5 percent; and for single male heads of households, 11.8 percent. Overall, white families had a lower income-poverty rate (7.9 percent) than did black families (28.2 percent) or Hispanic families (23.7 percent). The difference in poverty rates between blacks and Hispanics is associated with different distributions of family type between the two groups—blacks have a larger proportion of single-female-headed families. About 49 percent of both black and Hispanic families with a single female head were below the income-poverty level in 1988. Single-female-headed families constituted about 75.6 percent of all impoverished black families, and about 47.9 percent of impoverished Hispanic families (U.S. Bureau of the Census, 1989). The race of a family is defined by the Census Bureau according to the race of the householder.

30. Smolensky et al., 1988.

31. U.S. Bureau of the Census, 1989.

32. Ibid.

33. Sheldon Danziger and Peter Gottschalk, "Work, Poverty, and the Working Poor: A Multifaceted Problem," *Monthly Labor Review*, 109, 1986, 17–21.

34. U.S. Bureau of the Census, 1989. Additional data are as follows: Among income-poor married-couple households, 56.5 percent of householders worked in 1988, and 25.3 percent worked full-time, year-round. Of those who did not work, 38.5 percent were retired, 34.3 percent were gravely ill or disabled, and the remaining 27.2 percent were unable to find work, were keeping house, or were going to school. Among income-poor single-female-headed families, 41.6 percent

of householders worked in 1988, and 9.5 percent worked full-time, year-round. The comparable figures for nonpoor single-female-headed families were 76.5 percent who worked, and 56.1 percent who worked full-time, year-round. The predominant reason for not working among income-poor single-female-headed families was family responsibilities. In contrast, among non-poor single female-headed families who were not working, the primary reason was retirement (U.S. Bureau of the Census, 1989).

35. Sar Levitan and Isaac Shapiro, *Working but Poor: America's Contradiction*. Baltimore: John Hopkins University Press, 1987.

36. William J. Wilson. *The Truly Disadvantaged: The Inner City, the Underclass, and Public Policy*. Chicago: University of Chicago Press, 1987.

37. See, for example, Michael Harrington, *The New American Poverty*. New York: Holt, Reinhart, and Winston, 1984; Katharine Briar, ed., *The Unemployed: Policies and Services*, Report from Working Group 9. Helsinki: International Council on Social Welfare, 1986; Wilson, 1987; Ellwood, 1988.

38. For example, see Martha N. Ozawa, "The Nation's Children: Key to a Secure Retirement," *New England Journal of Human Services* 6(3), 1986, 12–19, who offers an analysis of childhood poverty in terms of supporting an aging population.

3 • The State of Welfare Theory

In both the political and the academic worlds, welfare is heavily trodden ground. Discussions and proposals go back and forth, month after month, year after year. Senators give speeches and professors write books. But curiously, despite all this attention, *welfare theory*, in the sense of well-being within households, remains largely unexplored territory. We talk a lot about welfare, but we do not know very well what welfare *is* or how families achieve it.

There is a pervasive assumption, seldom questioned, that level of household income and consumption constitutes an adequate definition of welfare. This assumption overlooks household welfare as a long-term, dynamic *process* rather than simply an amount of goods and services consumed.

Before we turn to the welfare of households, however, it is useful to review two related categories of welfare theory—theories of poverty and social class, and theories of welfare policy development.

Theories of Poverty and Social Class

There are many elaborate theories, and variations of theories, on poverty and social class. These can be simplistically lumped into two groups—theories that focus on individual behaviors and theories that focus on social structures.

Within the individual behavior school are theories of choice, expectancy, attitudes, motivation, and human capital. Overall, this group is best represented by neoclassical economic theory, which assumes that individuals are free to make decisions on their own in an open market of choices. This perspective is consistent with functionalist sociological theory,[1] which suggests that some functions are more important to society than others, and are rewarded accordingly. From the perspective of functionalist theory, inequality is both inevitable and desirable for society as a whole. This thinking rests on a very old assumption of the motivational benefits of inequality, described nearly two hundred years ago by Thomas Malthus:

> In society, the extreme parts could not be diminished beyond a certain degree without lessening the animated exertion throughout the middle parts. . . . If no man could hope to rise or fear to fall in society, if industry did not bring with it its reward and idleness its punishment, the middle parts would not certainly be what they are now.[2]

The opposing structuralist view, best represented by Marxist class theory, is that systemic structural barriers create unequal opportunities, conflict, and continuing oppression of the poor by the capitalist class. A large number of conflict theories have been developed, each emphasizing the illegitimate or undesirable exercise of power in one form or another. The predominant sociological orientation has been on measures of socioeconomic status as assessed by various combinations of education, occupation, and income. Variations of structural theories focus on topics such as race, gender, or geographical discontinuities in addition to, or instead of, class. Morris Janowitz, for example, follows the Weberian tradition in seeing a complex pattern of social inequality based not only on class, but also on race and ethnicity, place of residence, gender, and entitlements to welfare state benefits. Janowitz uses the term ''ordered segmentation'' to describe this growing complexity of social inequality in advanced industrial societies.[3] The large, multimethod, and multifaceted research project on poverty in Chicago directed by William J. Wilson can be seen as part of this tradition as well.[4] Wilson's interpretation is essentially structural, based on the concept of exclusion from social and economic opportunity, although his developing explanation is quite complex.

In brief, individual-level theories suggest that undesirable or unproductive behaviors cause poverty. On the other hand, structural theories suggest that circumstances of poverty cause behaviors; that is, apparently dysfunctional behaviors are adaptations to poverty. At the extreme, both types of theories are highly normative. Intertwined through the writings of individual behavior theorists is the moral judgment that people who are doing poorly are deficient in ability, training, or morality and should pick themselves up and do better. And intertwined through the writings of structural theorists is the moral judgment that the current social structure is unfair to the poor and should be changed.

In the academic world, individual-level theories held sway during the late nineteenth and early twentieth centuries, best illustrated by social Darwinist theory and research.[5] This theoretical perspective led to "scientific studies" of the infamous Jukes and Kallikaks at the turn of the century. The Jukes and the Kallikaks were two "defective" families whose defects—criminal behavior, drunkenness, feeblemindedness, weak morality, and so forth—were said to be passed along from one generation to the next, both genetically and culturally. The books published on these "defective" families were, at the time, very popular.[6] They contributed to the rise of a eugenics movement in the first half of the twentieth century. The eugenics movement resulted in large-scale sterilizations of mentally retarded people, criminals, and indigents, as well as other massive abuses of civil rights in the United States.[7]

The economic decline of the Great Depression of the 1930s led many people to believe that poverty was not solely a result of individual failure. An ideological shift occurred among sociologists and welfare analysts. This shift accompanied the New Deal and the beginning of the modern welfare state in America. From the 1930s through the 1970s, social-structural theories were dominant, perhaps best known by Michael Harrington's *The Other America*,[8] and this thinking helped to stimulate a second great wave of antipoverty federal legislation during the 1960s. Throughout this period, however, fundamental American values changed hardly at all. The general public continued to emphasize individual responsibility,[9] creating a strain between the public's values and those of more "liberal" welfare thinkers. Sensing this strain, some dissenting scholars complained of "an oversocialized conception of man" in the academic world.[10]

This ideological rift was compounded by massive budget deficits and a resurgence of conservative ideology during the 1980s. In this revenue-short and welfare-hostile environment, the academic world again shifted, reverting back to individual theories of welfare, dominated by the neoclassical economic conceptualization of human capital. This shift was so pronounced that structurally oriented scholars began to complain of an "undersocialized concept of man."[11]

These differences of opinion on welfare have generated a heated debate. In recent years, an almost monumental literature has arisen, including well-publicized books by Stuart Butler and Anna Kondratas, Greg Duncan, Marian Wright Edelman, David Ellwood, Neil Gilbert, Neil and Barbara Gilbert, Robert Haveman, Sar Levitan and Isaac Shapiro, Lawrence Mead, Ramesh Mishra, Robert Morris, Charles Murray, Michael Novak, Isabel Sawhill, and William J. Wilson.[12] Among these, Butler and Kondratas, Mead, Murray, and Novak have concentrated on individual behavior. Duncan, Edelman, Haveman, Levitan and Shapiro, Mishra, Morris, Sawhill, and Wilson have focused more on structural causes of poverty. Ellwood and the Gilberts are perhaps in the middle. Many of these books represent major contributions to our understanding of poverty and welfare policy. Altogether, the past few years have been a very productive period in welfare analysis, the most productive such period in more than two decades.

Each of the two major schools of thought, individual and structural, has generated huge bodies of research and writing, under many labels, and it is impossible and unnecessary to repeat the full discussion here. However, it is perhaps worth noting that both neoclassical economic theory and Marxist class theory, in pure form, are extreme interpretations, and that neither, in pure form, has been particularly successful in guiding social welfare policy.

Between the extreme viewpoints are a large number of middle-ground positions. Among the best known of these is the culture-of-poverty theory, as described by Oscar Lewis[13] and Edward Banfield.[14] This theory suggests that features of lower class culture, particularly present-time orientation and absence of delayed gratification, perpetuate poverty from one generation to the next. In various forms, culture-of-poverty theory has adherents on both the political left (Lewis) and the political right (Banfield). On the left, the perspective is sometimes known as the situation of poverty, indicating that apparently dysfunctional behaviors are, in fact, functional adaptations to difficult circumstances. In other words, the left tends to view culture as a result of social structure. In contrast, on the right, the view is that lower-class culture and behavior cause lower-class position in the social structure.

One would hope that middleground theories would begin to make connections between individual-level theory and structural-level theory; that is, that the two major schools of inequality theory might be integrated and made sense of as a whole. Unfortunately, only limited progress has been made in this direction. We tend to have macro (structural) theories on the one hand, and micro (behavioral) theories on the other, with few connections between them.[15]

In a sense, it can be said that individual-level theories connect with social structure on the basis of an assumption that certain behaviors lead to one's position in the social and economic structure. However, this assumption is not entirely satisfying when one asks why profligate and gratification-oriented behaviors by the very rich do not often lead to poverty, and why so many poor families work so hard yet remain poor. On the other hand, structural theorists have not explained very well why a very large number of impoverished individuals and families do indeed manage to work their way out of poverty.

However, there is perhaps reason for optimism. A recent revival of institutional analyses in both economics and sociology seeks explicitly to connect individual behaviors with social and economic relationships. Among the simplest and most well developed of these theories is the principal-and-agent theory,[16] which envisions a world of two actors, the superior principal and the subordinate agent. The theory deals with the alignment of incentives that facilitate optimal functioning of such relationships. Principal-and-agent theory is, more or less, neoclassical economic thinking applied to a pattern of incentives and behaviors among two parties, rather than to a single individual. For the most part, the problems of agency have been pursued in neoclassical analyses of risk, responsibility, and performance. But problems of agency and the ways in which social structure interacts with individual volition have been raised among analysts on the left as well, especially by Anthony Giddens and more recently by Alex Callinicos.[17]

Perhaps the most promising middle-ground work to date is a line of theoretical contributions originating with Max Weber,[18] continuing with Ralf Dahrendorf,[19] and expressed more recently in the work of William J. Wilson.[20] Weber, the great institutional sociologist, challenges the Marxist position on economic determinism. Weber sees a far more complex array of "life chances" that depend not only on economic class position, but also on political power, historical precedents, social status relationships, and so forth. These chances represent probabilities for social and economic mobility. The frequent use of the concept of chance by Weber reflects his underlying vision of human societies as systems of possibilities, or denial of possibilities, for individual action.

Building and borrowing from Weber, Dahrendorf explicitly makes connections between social structural variables and life chances for individuals:

> Life chances are opportunities for individual development provided by social structure, 'moulds,' as we have called them. As such, they provide an important bridge between an understanding of society which emphasizes the structural quality of things social . . . and a normative theory of society which emphasizes individual liberty.[21]

Life chances are defined as the set of opportunities available to a given individual. Life chances are restrictions, or lack of restrictions, on choices. In other words, choices are not the same for everyone, and beginning at a very early age, restrictions on choices are internalized and shape individual behavior.

Wilson has elaborated this conceptualization in detailing the modern history of black urban social structure in the United States. His analysis is that two major changes—the decline in availability of good jobs in cities, and the departure of the black middle class from the ghetto following the civil rights movement—have led to isolation and disintegration in the economic and social status of urban blacks, particularly males. This disintegration has affected the black family and has left young urban blacks without the same array of chances that their parents enjoyed, without adequate black role models, without knowledge and appreciation of the strengths of black culture, and without the guidance of black middle-class values. Wilson's current research in Chicago seeks, among other things, to decipher connections between structural changes and individual responses.

Thus, the concept of life chances and social and economic institutions that shape those chances can serve as an essential foundation for a theory of welfare. But a great deal of work remains to be done in explaining the processes through which life chances are integrated into individual behavior.

Welfare Policy Theory

Another major body of welfare theory is welfare *policy theory*. Development of policy theory has been primarily at the macrohistorical level, addressing the question of how welfare states have emerged. In this massive body of work, there are several distinct schools of thought. Among the major ones is the economic or modernization approach, which suggests that social welfare policies arise, first and foremost, as a function of economic development.[22] This thinking is very straightforward—welfare distributions are not possible until there is sufficient economic growth to create a surplus to distribute.

A second school is comprised of various neo-Marxian class analyses, sometimes referred to as logic-of-capitalism approaches.[23] These theorists argue that working class discontent is "cooled out" and leadership is co-opted by capitalist welfare handouts. In this view, welfare is a mechanism of social control more than humanitarian assistance.

A third school consists of democratic political approaches, which suggest that electoral or nonelectoral politics have led to the historical expansion of welfare state benefits.[24] One prominent subgroup, more active in Europe than in the United States, is social democratic theory, which envisions a democratic approach to socialism through expanded welfare state benefits.[25] Another subgroup of the political approach is reflected in interest group politics theory.[26] However, interest group politics is sometimes viewed as dysfunctional for both democracy and capitalism in the long term.[27]

A fourth perspective concentrates on state-centered analyses, which stress the independence of the state political structure, its institutional framework, executive actors, and/or bureaucratic elite.[28] Douglas Ashford, for example, suggests that historical development of welfare states has been a gradual response to pressing problems of the day, often with as much support from conservatives as from progressives.[29] According to Ashford, welfare states are not necessarily built on fear of unrest. Very frequently, he says, visionary and/or ambitious political reformers play a key role. In Ashford's perspective, welfare states result from an interaction of social needs and political leadership, all within the framework of preexisting institutional precedents.

The Welfare of Individuals and Households

Thus, we have elaborate theories of inequality and the evolution of welfare policies, but very little about welfare itself, in the sense of individual and household well-being. What constitutes "welfare" under the social and economic conditions of welfare capitalism? The underlying vision through which we interpret human welfare determines how we go about trying to solve the problem of poverty.[30] But how should we *see* welfare?

Household Income and Welfare

Governments collect systematic data on income. With an abundance of income data available, and with the aid of modern computers, poverty research has tended to count this income as a measure of welfare. Indeed, research has been guided more by counting than by conceptualization. Income has been analyzed by age, race, gender, geographical location, and other variables. Also, with longitudinal data sets now available, intergenerational income patterns have been studied. Many of these analyses are quite sophisticated, and we have learned a great deal about income distribution during the past twenty years. But very little of this massive body of scholarship is guided by theory. Robert Haveman contrasts wealth (assets) research with income research, and observes that the latter tends to be theoretically weak and is too often characterized by a "mindless dash to the computer."[31]

The major theoretical construct in welfare research has been the issue of a "work disincentive" in welfare transfers. The key question regarding work disincentive is whether money transfers discourage labor market participation. Charles Murray, for example, has repopularized the very old idea that welfare transfers contribute to dependence and poverty.[32] Hundreds, perhaps thousands, of analyses have been performed on this threadbare theoretical issue. There is no substantial evidence that income transfers reduce individual motivation, although it is clear that welfare policy in general slightly reduces work participation. However, Gary Burtless shows that labor supply effects of welfare transfers are much smaller than required to confirm Murray's hypotheses.[33] A review of research suggests that all welfare programs together reduce total work hours in the economy by less than 5 percent.[34] A fair summation is that income transfers reduce work behavior somewhat, but on the whole, it is noteworthy that work behavior among the poor remains as strong as it does, despite disincentives.

To be sure, opinions, viewpoints, and recommendations among welfare scholars vary a great deal. However, despite important insights and contributions from many quarters, nearly all welfare thinking, both conservative and liberal, has been circumscribed within a rather limited sphere. In all of this analysis, welfare is assumed to be directly related to household income and consumption. The major debate is over who provides, or does not provide, the income and how much it should be. Or alternatively, the focus is on the level of consumption, an approach that is more common in Europe than in the United States.[35] Whether in health care, housing, direct financial assistance, education, or any other area of social welfare, the emphasis has been on levels of goods and services provided and consumed. The underlying assumptions are that poverty and hardship are defined by insufficient consumption and the solution is, one way or another, to make the consumption more sufficient.[36]

Although sometimes unstated, two contrasting viewpoints guide most policy studies and proposals. The first viewpoint is that giving the poor more income makes them better off because it is better to consume at higher levels. In other words, consumption *is* welfare. This is the basic assumption of almost all welfare state programs oriented toward the poor. The second and counterassumption is that giving the poor more income makes them worse off because such assistance saps independence, motivation, and labor market participation, and perpetuates poverty.[37] Yet, even in this counterassumption, the idea of welfare is income-related. It is only the policy approach to make income available that is different. One group proposes that the government provide additional income, while the other group insists that the poor earn it themselves.

In short, welfare theory and research, from both major ideological perspectives, has taken for granted that a certain level of income is an adequate definition of welfare, at least for the poor. Indeed, this assumption is so fundamental to the modern welfare state, as well as to its critics, that it is seldom questioned. Each year, thousands of analyses of poverty assume that level of income (or some other proxy measure of consumption) is an adequate theory of household welfare. On this rather narrow idea, the entire edifice of the welfare state has been constructed.[38]

Household Wealth and Welfare

Governments tend *not* to collect systematic data on assets, and assets are much more unevenly distributed than is income (see chapter 6).[39] In part because of this absence of systematic data, welfare analysis tends not to include assets. As Robert Haveman notes, "Micro-data— and aggregate data—on saving and wealth are among the most scarce and unreliable of those on which any sub-field in economics relies.

And, given the intertemporal nature of the process of wealth accumulation, manipulation of the required data is particularly difficult.''[40] Haveman also observes that the debate among economists who study wealth is oriented toward the upper portion of the distribution.

Despite the neglect of studying assets of the poor, it seems reasonable to suppose that human welfare consists, in part, of access to assets. If this is the case, a dynamic theory of welfare that incorporates effects of asset accumulation is perhaps required. An asset-based welfare theory would have two principal features. First, it would view household financial welfare as a long-term, dynamic process rather than as cross-sectional financial position at a given time. Assets capture this long-term, dynamic quality better than income because assets reflect lifetime financial accumulation. Second, the theory would propose that more than consumption is involved in household financial welfare, possibly much more. In other words, according to this viewpoint, assets yield positive welfare effects that income alone does not provide—effects in addition to deferred consumption.

What are these effects? There are a number of theoretical advances regarding welfare effects of assets within households. One of the earliest theoretical statements on welfare effects of assets is by Franco Modigliani and Richard Brumberg, who identify two reasons for lifetime savings and wealth accumulation: (1) to smooth out the variability of current income, and to a lesser extent, (2) to leave an estate to one's heirs.[41] Taking an opposing viewpoint, Laurence Kotlikoff argues that saving for retirement does not explain wealth accumulation as much as the desire to make bequests and intergenerational transfers.[42] Anthony Shorrocks notes that wealth serves different welfare purposes, including: (1) a store of future consumption, (2) increased ability to circumvent financial constraints, (3) increased power and influence, and (4) transmission of advantages to future generations.[43] Denis Kessler and André Masson describe two types of financial assets, which they suggest are for two different purposes.[44] The first group, S-wealth, includes assets for future consumption and precautionary purposes. Lower- and middle-class families hold almost exclusively this form of wealth. The second group, K-wealth, includes assets held mainly for economic returns, social power, and transmission to future generations. K-wealth is considerably more concentrated than is S-wealth, and is controlled primarily by the upper class. These observations and conceptualizations constitute an important foundation for theoretical work on welfare effects of asset accumulation (a topic discussed in chapter 8).

Such a theory would begin to bridge the gap between the structural-level and individual-level theories of welfare discussed above. In brief, the theory would attempt to integrate the structural concept of class (as measured by asset position) with economic, social, and psychological variables at the individual and household levels. Integration between structural and individual viewpoints is often missing in poverty and welfare analysis. Income-based welfare theory, focused entirely on consumption, does not provide such integration. An asset-based theory of welfare might serve as a partial connection between structural and individual perspectives.

More Expansive Definitions of Social Welfare

Of course, a greatly expanded definition of welfare is possible. For example, an expanded definition is often alluded to, in a fuzzy manner, among left-leaning progressives. Typically, this takes the form of a list of desirables: rights, happiness, peace, shelter, health, fulfillment, comfort, and so forth. Few people are against these things, but they do not necessarily come, like a holiday fruit basket, in a cellophane-wrapped package with a red ribbon. Some progressives have an endearing, but not very effective, tendency to list them all together as absolutely essential for social policy, whatever the issue.

Recently, on the right, similarly fuzzy thinking has come from Charles Murray,[45] who has a different list for his definition of welfare. He emphasizes achievement of "happiness" through small social units, independence, and individual gumption. Of course, this vision is as ideologically biased and impractical as that of the progressives, and filled with questionable assumptions.[46]

I do not intend to repeat lists of ideal welfare characteristics in this book. No matter how eloquently or fervently presented, the lists are not very helpful. The task of including them in a definition of household welfare is too grand a conceptual challenge. Moreover, such an exercise is not of much practical consequence. Instead, my goal in this book is more modest, to maintain the conceptualization of household welfare on a financial basis, but to include the idea of assets as well as income.[47]

Notes

1. Kingsley Davis and Wilbert Moore, "Some Principles of Stratification," *American Sociological Review* 10(2), 1945; Talcott Parsons, *The Social System*. Glencoe, IL: Free Press, 1951.

2. Thomas Robert Malthus, *An Essay on the Principle of Population*. London: Penguin Books, 1970 (originally published in 1798), 207.

3. Morris Janowitz, *Social Control of the Welfare State*. Chicago: University of Chicago Press, 1976.

4. William J. Wilson et al., panel presentation at the Annual Meetings of the Midwest Sociological Society, St. Louis, April 1989.

5. See, for example, William Graham Sumner, *What the Social Classes Owe to Each Other*. New York: Harper and Brothers, 1893.

6. Richard L. Dugdale, *The Jukes*, fourth edition. New York: G.P. Putnam's Sons, 1910; Henry H. Goddard, *The Kallikak Family*. New York: Macmillan, 1912.

7. The legal legacy of the eugenics movement has only recently been put to rest. In 1956, eighteen states still had compulsory sterilization laws. As late as 1980, Missouri still had a law prohibiting marriage of persons with epilepsy (J.L. Dell, "Social Dimensions of Epilepsy: Stigma and Response," in S. Whitman and B.P. Hermann, eds., *Psychopathology in Epilepsy: Social Dimensions*. New York: Oxford University Press, 1986, 185–210).

8. Michael Harrington, *The Other America*. New York: Macmillan, 1962.

9. James Kluegel and Eliot Smith, *Beliefs about Inequality*. New York: Aldine de Gruyter, 1986.

10. Dennis Wrong, "The Oversocialized Conception of Man in Modern Sociology," *American Sociological Review* 26, 1961, 183–93.

11. Mark Granovetter, "Economic Action, Social Structure, and Embeddedness," *American Journal of Sociology* 91, 1985, 481–510.

12. Stuart Butler and Anna Kondratas, *Out of the Poverty Trap: A Conservative Strategy for Welfare Reform*. New York: Free Press, 1987; Greg Duncan, *Years of Poverty, Years of Plenty*. Ann Arbor: Survey Research Center, Institute for Social Research, University of Michigan, 1984; Marian Wright Edelman, *Families in Peril: An Agenda for Social Change*. Cambridge: Harvard University Press, 1987; David T. Ellwood, *Poor Support: Poverty in the American Family*. New York: Basic Books, 1988; Neil Gilbert, *Capitalism and the Welfare State*. New Haven: Yale University Press, 1983; Neil Gilbert and Barbara Gilbert, *The Enabling State: Modern Welfare Capitalism in America*. New York: Oxford University Press, 1989; Robert Haveman, *Starting Even: An Equal Opportunity Program to Combat the Nation's New Poverty*. New York: Simon and Schuster, 1988; Sar Levitan and Isaac Shapiro, *Working but Poor: America's Contradiction*. Baltimore: Johns Hopkins University Press, 1987; Lawrence M. Mead, *Beyond Entitlement: The Social Obligations of Citizenship*. New York: The Free Press, 1986; Ramesh Mishra, *The Welfare State in Crisis*. New York: St. Martin's Press, 1984; Robert Morris, *Rethinking Social Welfare: Why Care for the Stranger?* New York: Longman, 1986; Charles Murray, *Losing Ground: American Social Policy 1950–1980*. New York: Basic Books, 1984; Charles Murray, *In*

Pursuit of Happiness and Good Governance. New York: Simon and Schuster, 1988; Michael Novak et al., eds., *The New Consensus on Family and Welfare.* Washington: American Enterprise Institute, 1988; Isabel V. Sawhill, ed., *Challenge to Leadership: Economic and Social Issues for the Next Decade.* Washington: Urban Institute Press, 1988; and William J. Wilson, *The Truly Disadvantaged: The Inner City, the Underclass, and Public Policy.* Chicago: University of Chicago Press, 1987.

13. Oscar Lewis, *La Vida.* New York: Random House, 1966.

14. Edward Banfield, *The Unheavenly City Revisited.* Boston: Little, Brown, 1974.

15. Robert Pinker, *Theory, Ideology, and Social Policy*, SWRC reports and proceedings, no. 26. Kensington, New South Wales: Social Welfare Research Center, 1982.

16. John Pratt and Richard Zeckhauser, eds., *Principles and Agents: The Structure of Business.* Boston: Harvard Business School Press, 1985.

17. Alex Callinicos, *Making History: Agency, Structure, and Change in Social Theory.* Ithaca: Cornell University Press, 1988.

18. Max Weber, *Economy and Society*, two volumes, Guenther Roth and Claus Wittich, eds. Berkeley: University of California Press, 1968 (translated from the 4th edition, 1956).

19. Ralf Dahrendorf, *Life Chances: Approaches to Social and Political Theory.* Chicago: University of Chicago Press, 1979.

20. Wilson, 1987.

21. Dahrendorf, 1979, 61–62.

22. Thomas R. Dye, *Politics, Economics, and the Public: Policy Outcomes in the American States.* Chicago: Rand McNally, 1966; and Harold Wilensky, *The Welfare State and Equality: Structural and Ideological Roots of Public Expenditures.* Berkeley: University of California Press, 1975.

23. Frances Fox Piven and Richard A. Cloward, *Regulating the Poor: The Functions of Social Welfare.* New York: Vintage, 1971; James O'Connor, *The Fiscal Crisis of the State.* New York: St. Martin's, 1973; and Ian Gough, *The Political Economy of the Welfare State.* London: Macmillan, 1979.

24. Frances Fox Piven and Richard A. Cloward, *The New Class War: Reagan's Attack on the Welfare State and Its Consequences.* New York: Pantheon, 1982.

25. John D. Stephens, *The Transition from Capitalism to Socialism.* London: Macmillan, 1979; and Walter Korpi, *The Democratic Class Struggle.* London: Routledge and Kegan Paul, 1983.

26. Janowitz, 1976; and Morris Janowitz, *The Last Half-Century.* Chicago: University of Chicago Press, 1978.

27. Theodore Lowi, *The End of Liberalism.* New York: W.W. Norton, 1969; and Mancur Olson, *The Logic of Collective Action: Public Good and the Theory of Groups.* Cambridge: Harvard University Press, 1965.

28. James G. March and Johan P. Olson, "The New Institutionalism: Organizational Factors in Political Life," *American Political Science Review* 78, 1984, 734–49; Theda Skocpol, "Bringing the State Back In: Strategies of Analysis in Current Research," in Peter B. Evans, Dietrich Rueschmeyer, and Theda Skocpol, eds., *Bringing the State Back In.* Cambridge: Cambridge University Press, 1985, 3–37; and Edward O. Laumann and David Knoke, *Social Choice in*

National Policy Domains. Madison: University of Wisconsin Press, 1987.

29. Douglas Ashford, *The Emergence of the Welfare States.* Oxford: Basil Blackwell, 1986.

30. Edward Seidman, "Justice, Values and Social Science: Unexamined Premises," in Edward Seidman and Julian Rappaport, eds., *Redefining Social Problems.* New York: Plenum Press, 1986, 235–58.

31. Robert Haveman, "Conclusion," in Denis Kessler and André Masson, eds. *Modelling the Accumulation and Distribution of Wealth.* Oxford: Clarendon Press, 1988, 323–28.

32. Murray, 1984.

33. Gary Burtless, "The Work Response to a Guaranteed Income: A Survey of Experimental Evidence," in Alicia Munnell, ed., *Lessons from the Income Maintenance Experiments.* Boston, Federal Reserve Bank of Boston, 1986.

34. Sheldon Danziger, Robert Haveman, and Robert Plotnick, "How Income Transfer Programs Affect Work, Savings, and the Income Distribution: A Critical Review," *Journal of Economic Literature* 19, 1981, 975–1028.

35. Susan Mayer and Christopher Jencks, "Poverty and the Distribution of Material Hardship," *Journal of Human Resources*, 24(1), 1989, 88–114.

36. S.M. Miller and P. Roby, *The Future of Inequality.* New York: Basic Books, 1970, 66–67; and Mayer and Jencks, 1989, very cogently point out that despite commonly held assumptions, there is actually little relationship between income and level of material well-being.

37. Murray, 1984, among others in recent years.

38. Neil Gilbert points out that the government has begun to include the imputed return on equity in one's home in the definition of income for estimating poverty rates, although not yet in the "official" poverty rate. This is, in a sense, a step toward including assets in a theory of welfare, but the viewpoint is rather oddly contorted through the lens of income (see chapter 8, where I attempt to show that assets have distinct welfare effects *beyond consumption* that income alone does not provide).

39. Sar Levitan and others have suggested to me that the lack of regular, systematic data on household assets is not entirely accidental, but, to the best of my knowledge, there have been no published studies of the politics and funding of asset data collection in the United States.

40. Haveman, "Conclusion," 1988.

41. Franco Modigliani and Richard Brumberg, "Utility Analysis and the Consumption Function: An Interpretation of Cross-Section Data," in Kenneth K. Kurihara, ed., *Post-Keynesian Economics.* New Brunswick, NJ: Rutgers University Press, 1954.

42. Laurence J. Kotlikoff, *What Determines Savings?* Cambridge: MIT Press, 1989.

43. Anthony F. Shorrocks, "UK Wealth Distribution: Current Evidence and Future Prospects," in Edward Wolff, *Growth, Accumulation, and Unproductive Activity.* Cambridge: Cambridge University Press, 1987, 29–50.

44. Denis Kessler and André Masson, "Personal Wealth Distribution in France: Cross-Sectional Evidence and Extensions," in Edward Wolff, *Growth, Accumulation, and Unproductive Activity.* Cambridge: Cambridge University Press, 1987, 141–176.

45. Murray, 1988.

46. A thoughtful critique is offered by William J. Wilson. "The Charge of the Little Platoons," a review of Charles Murray, 1988, in *New York Times Book Review*, October 23, 1988, 12.

47. If I were to broaden the definition of social welfare still further, this broader definition would define welfare in terms of *participation*. In the social arena, participation is mutuality and shared actions with others. In the political arena, participation is democratic voice in decision making, including both formal voting and interest group representation. In the civic arena, participation is service to society. In the educational arena, participation is development of individual potential, or "human capital." And in the economic arena, participation is ownership of assets. In my view, each of these major forms of participation is a component of human welfare, but only the latter, financial assets, is articulated in this book.

4 • Federal Welfare Policy—
   Who Benefits?

The ''welfare state'' is comprised of a conglomeration of federally sponsored services, money transfers, and tax privileges, each of which is intended to benefit certain parties for certain purposes. As a whole, the welfare state is guided by no grand design, yet it may have certain systematic results.

It is impossible and unnecessary in this short space to review the whole of federal welfare policy in detail. I do not attempt to cover the development of the welfare state.[1] Nor do I attempt to review all the results and effects of welfare policy.[2] The purpose of this chapter is to provide an overview of the existing structure of benefits that may serve as a foundation for the discussion that follows. However, the overview is not entirely standard. I attempt to take a somewhat broad view of the welfare state and to be specific about its costs. Federal welfare policy is defined as both direct expenditures and tax expenditures of benefit to individuals in seven categories—education, employment, social services, health care, income security, housing, and nutrition. I also attempt to delineate which of these are ''targeted'' for the poor, and which are ''nontargeted'' for the general population.

Conflicting Goals in Welfare Policy

Eliminating poverty and protecting human resources for future productivity are perhaps the biggest challenges of public policy. The prospect of alleviating poverty, the renowned economist Alfred Marshall observed, ''gives to economic studies their chief and their highest interest.''[3] Not all economists today would agree with Marshall, but most would agree that the economic market generates inequality, and social policy seeks in various ways to mediate and reduce the harshest and most unfair forms of inequality.

However, these social policy challenges are approached in very different ways. Robert Lampman cogently identifies welfare policy-making as a contest between four competing mentalities.[4] He describes these as the minimum-provision mentality, the replacement-of-loss mentality, the horizontal- and vertical-equity mentality, and the efficiency-of-investment mentality.

The first mentality, minimum provision, has traditionally guided public assistance to the poor. The emphasis is on basic needs and adequacy of welfare benefits for individuals who are unable to provide for themselves. Little attention is given to equity vis-à-vis persons who are able to pay for themselves. As Lampman notes, the purpose of welfare from this perspective is essentially defensive and crisis-oriented. In its positive form, the minimum-provision mentality leads to policies that aid the truly needy, those who fall below a "means test" for eligibility. In its negative form, the minimum-provision mentality often leads to restrictive and demeaning judgments of the welfare poor—for instance, that people on welfare are lazy, are cheaters, and cannot manage their own financial affairs. As one critic has written, "There has arisen a belief that people on welfare need others to tell them how to live their lives."[5]

The second mentality, replacement of loss, is expressed in social insurance plans. Here the emphasis is on sharing loss without reference to need. In some respects, Social Security is a form of social insurance, although Social Security has large elements of public transfer as well.

The third mentality, equity, emphasizes treating people at the same economic level equally (horizontal equity) and attempting also to narrow differences across economic levels (vertical equity). This mentality is exemplified, in some respects, in the structure of the progressive income tax. The equity mentality has deep roots in religious traditions. Indeed religion has been one of the major sources of welfare equity values.[6] A well-publicized example is the Catholic Bishop's Letter on the U.S. Economy, entitled *Economic Justice for All*.[7] The letter puts explicit limits on unequal accumulation of wealth, stating that justice in the distribution of material goods requires that basic needs take priority over luxury goods. The distribution of wealth both within the United States and among nations is viewed as so disparate as to be unjust. Considerable attention is paid to the magnitude of inequality and the morality of distribution, but less attention is paid to processes of wealth creation.

The fourth mentality, efficiency of investment, does not focus on needs or equity, but on productivity, the increase in present and future output. The central issue in this mentality is a comparison of current costs with expected benefits in the future. This perspective also has deep historical roots, as John Kenneth Galbraith has described:

> Until the nineteenth century, grinding poverty had at all times and in nearly all places been the fate of all but a minority of mankind. For the relief of this poverty, nothing could be quite so important as to get more production from existing manpower and resources. Indeed, in a world where there was little unemployment, no other remedy for poverty was available given current income distribution and the considerable political discomfort and frustration that was frequently the fortune of those who advocated more equitable distribution of income.[8]

Indeed, economics as a science was born with productivity as the major focus, and economics has never much deviated from this focus. "Economists have tended to evaluate the performance of the economy in terms of efficiency and much less so in terms of distributive justice, not surprisingly since here the deepest philosophical issues are at stake."[9] Only the political creation of distributive policies has altered economic orthodoxy. Today, many debates can be summarized as a perceived trade-off between economic efficiency and equity in distribution of resources.[10] There is an assumption in these arguments (not fully supportable) that more efficiency leads to less equity, and vice versa.

As Lampman observes, the U.S. welfare system is a mixture of goals, combining each of the four mentalities described above.[11] Each goal places constraints on the others. In understanding the system, one cannot describe it simply as of one mentality or another but as a conglomeration, a mongrel system, with shifting alliances, tensions, and balances among the four basic themes.

General Characteristics of the Welfare State

There are many different ways of defining welfare policy and many different categories that may or may not be included, depending on one's viewpoint. Richard Titmuss expanded the conception of welfare policy to include *social welfare*, or direct public transfers and services; *fiscal welfare*, or tax benefits; and *occupational welfare*, or work-related benefits.[12] Titmuss pointed out that the upper classes relied mostly on fiscal welfare; the middle classes, on all three; and the lower classes, almost exclusively on social welfare. This categorization has proven to be very useful; Mimi Abramovitz[13] and many others have followed Titmuss's thinking. However, a still broader definition of welfare policy is possible. Titmuss's categories do not necessarily include the vast welfare efforts of the not-for-profit voluntary sector, which are stimulated and promoted by federal tax policies, nor do they include informal and intrafamily assistance and financial transfers.

Under the general heading *social welfare*, the United States has a two-tiered welfare system—a lower tier of targeted, means-tested, noncontributory programs for those who are unable to earn sufficient income through employment; and an upper tier of universal, non-means-tested, contributory "social insurance" or entitlement programs that are often linked to work through payroll taxes.

The lower-tier programs of means-tested transfers are targeted to those who meet certain eligibility rules. The major programs are Aid to Families with Dependent Children (AFDC), Supplemental Security Income (SSI), Food Stamps, Medicaid, various housing programs, general assistance (funded primarily at the state and local levels), Special Supplemental Nutrition Program for Women, Infants, and Children (WIC), and the Free or Reduced-Price School Lunch Program. These means-tested programs, some in the form of cash and some in the form of in-kind (noncash) services, constitute what is generally referred to as "welfare." In all cases, the coverage is intended to be minimal, and these programs altogether constitute only a small proportion of total welfare expenditures.

The upper-tier programs of non-means-tested "social insurance" benefits are, in part, linked to "earned" contributions and paid in the event of retirement, disability, or job loss. The major programs are Social Security Old Age Insurance, Disability Insurance, Medicare, and Unemployment Insurance. Despite a common misperception, non-means-tested entitlement benefits are not entirely earned. To take the major example, current recipients of Social Security retirement benefits will receive, on the average, much more than the actuarial value of their contributions (estimates vary, but most analyses find that at least half of the benefits to current retirees are not related to earnings).[14] In other words, Social Security retirees are receiving a direct income transfer, often far larger than that of an AFDC recipient, yet most Social Security recipients do not think of themselves as being "on welfare." They tend to think, incorrectly, that they have "earned" the full benefit.

The upper and lower welfare tiers differ in two key respects: the scope of benefits and stigma. To take an example, the Social Security Act has two major provisions for dependent children, AFDC and Survivors Insurance (SI). In neither case have the children themselves "earned" these benefits (SI benefits are tied to parental earnings, and AFDC benefits are means-tested). It happens that a large proportion of AFDC recipients are black or Hispanic, whereas the vast majority of SI recipients are white. SI benefits are tied to inflation, and real benefits are now almost three times more than the amount provided to AFDC children. As Senator Daniel Moynihan has observed: "We do care about some children: majority children. It is minority children—not only, but mostly—who are left behind."[15] Thus, dependent minority children are more likely to receive less benefits, and they carry the stigma of being "welfare" recipients as well.

The Size and Composition of the Grand Welfare State

In this book, welfare policy is defined as direct expenditures and tax expenditures of direct benefit to individuals in seven major categories—education, employment, social services, health care, income security, housing, and nutrition. Only federal expenditures are included. This definition does not include any federal expenditures outside of these seven categories; it does not include federal expenditures of *indirect* benefit to individuals, even though these may be substantial; it does not include federal expenditures to businesses, not even those to single proprietorships or family farmers; it does not include state, county, or municipal public expenditures; it does not include corporate welfare (other than the federal tax benefits associated with corporate fringe benefits); it does not include the vast welfare expenditures in time and money of the voluntary sector; and it does not include informal and intrafamily assistance and financial transfers.

Despite what it does not include, the definition of federal welfare policy in this book is broader than most. Typically, only direct expenditures are included, but in this book, tax expenditures are included as well. From the standpoint of the federal budget, there is no difference between a direct expenditure and a tax expenditure—each costs the government money.[16] Also, in-kind or service programs are included along with cash grants.

In the discussion that follows, the term *grand welfare state* is used to include both direct expenditures and tax expenditures to individuals in the seven welfare categories mentioned above. The two major sources of data are federal outlays as presented in the President's budget for fiscal year 1990,[17] and congressional estimates of tax expenditures in fiscal year 1990.[18] As shown in Table 4.1, the grand welfare state consists of many dozens of programs that, in fiscal year 1990, are estimated to total $775.6 billion. Of this total, $581.8 billion (75.0 percent) is in the form of direct expenditures, and $193.8 billion (25.0 percent) is in the form of tax expenditures (see Table 4.2 for a summary of the grand welfare state).

Turning to welfare categories, the largest amounts go to income security ($456.6 billion or 58.9 percent), health care ($197.5 billion or 25.4 percent), and housing ($64.8 billion or 8.4 percent). The other four categories—education, employment, social services, and nutrition—make up only 7.3 percent of the grand welfare state (Table 4.2).

Under the category of income security, by far the biggest expenditure is for Social Security Old Age and Survivors Insurance, which, at $222.4 billion, makes up about two-thirds of direct income security expenditures, and almost half of total income security expenditures (including tax expenditures). The next largest category under income security, at $48.5 billion, is the net tax exclusion of pension contributions and earnings. Other major players in this category are Civil Service Retirement, Disability Insurance, Military Retirement, the partial tax exclusion of Social Security benefits, and Unemployment Insurance. Income security for the poor is represented in far smaller amounts, mostly under SSI and AFDC.

Under health care, the largest expenditure is for Medicare, which, at a total of $97.9 billion, makes up about two-fifths of direct health expenditures and one-third of all health expenditures (including tax expenditures). Medicaid, the tax exclusion of employer-provided medical benefits, veterans medical care, and the tax exclusion of

Table 4.1

The Grand Welfare State: Estimated Federal Welfare Expenditures to Individuals, Both Direct Expenditures and Tax Expenditures, Fiscal Year 1990
(billions of dollars)

Estimated direct expenditures, fiscal year 1990

Education	
Student Financial Assistance	$6.006
Guaranteed Student Loans	3.182
Veteran Readjustment Benefits (including GI Bill)	0.451
Post–Vietnam Era Education	0.079
Subtotal	9.718
Employment	
Block Grants to States	1.799
Summer Youth Employment Program	0.701
Assistance to Dislocated Workers	0.402
Job Corps	0.741
Older Americans' Employment	0.342
Work Incentive Program	0.005
Other Training Programs	0.281
JOBS Training for Welfare Recipients	0.350
Veterans' Jobs Programs	0.002
Subtotal	4.623
Social services	
Social Services Block Grant	2.694
Rehabilitation Services	1.703
Payments to States for Foster Care	1.326
Human Development Services	2.572
Domestic Volunteer Programs	0.171
Subtotal	8.466
Health care	
Medicaid Grants	37.398
Federal Employees Health Benefits	2.779
Other Health Services	4.595
Medicare	
Hospital Insurance (less medicare premiums and collections)	52.224
Supplemental Medical Insurance (SMI)	45.833
SMI, Catastrophic (less premiums)	−0.114
Federal Catastrophic Drug Insurance	0.150
Veterans Medical Care and Hospital Services (less third-party reimbursement)	10.276
Subtotal	153.141
Income security	
Railroad Retirement	4.186
Special Benefits for Disabled Coal Miners	1.531

Income security *(continued)*

Federal Civilian Retirement and Disability	32.567
Military Retirement	21.228
Federal Employees Workers' Compensation	0.207
Federal Employees Life Insurance Fund	−0.829
Social Security	
Old Age and Survivor's Insurance	222.402
Disability Insurance	24.306
Unemployment Compensation	16.220
Income Security for the Poor	
Supplemental Security Income	12.148
Family Support Payments (AFDC)	11.180
Earned Income Tax Credit[a]	3.841
Refugee Assistance	0.287
Low Income Home Energy Assistance	1.125
Other	0.226
Income Security for Veterans	
Service-Connected Compensation (Disability)	11.226
Non-Service-Connected Compensation	3.953
Burial and Other Benefits	0.153
Supplemental for Compensation, Pensions, and Burial	0.037
National Service Life Insurance Trust Fund plus other Insurance	
Programs (less Insurance Program Receipts)	0.806
Subtotal	366.800

Housing

Subsidized Housing	13.645
Public Housing Operating Subsidies	1.652
Low Rent Public Housing	0.634
Transitional Housing and Emergency Shelter for the Homeless	0.070
Other Housing Assistance	0.167
Veterans Housing Loan Guarantee Fund	1.458
Subtotal	17.626

Nutrition

Food Stamps[b]	13.606
Child Nutrition and Other Programs	7.852
Subtotal	21.458

Total direct expenditures	581.832

Estimated tax expenditures, fiscal year 1990[c]

Education

Exclusion of Scholarship and Fellowship Income	0.500
Parental Personal Exemption for Students Age 19 to 23	0.300
Exclusion of GI Bill Benefits	0.100
Subtotal	0.900

Employment

Targeted Jobs Credit	0.300

(continued)

Table 4.1 *(continued)*

Employment *(continued)*

Exclusion of Employee Meals and Lodging	0.800
Exclusion of Benefits Provided under Cafeteria Plans	2.000
Exclusion of Rental Allowance for Minister's Home	0.200
Exclusion of Miscellaneous Fringe Benefits	3.900
Exclusion of Employee Awards	0.100
Subtotal	7.300

Social services

Credit for Child and Dependent Care Expenses	3.900
Exclusion for Employer-Provided Child Care	0.300
Subtotal	4.200

Health care

Exclusion of Contributions by Employers and Self-Employed for Medical Insurance Premiums and Medical Care	32.600
Deductibility of Medical Expenses	2.800
Exclusion of Untaxed Medicare Benefits	9.000
Subtotal	44.400

Income security

Exclusion of Untaxed Railroad Retirement System Benefits	0.400
Exclusion of Workers' Compensation Benefits	2.200
Exclusion of Special Benefits for Disabled Coal Miners	0.100
Exclusion of Cash Public Assistance Benefits	0.300
Net Exclusion of Pension Contributions and Earnings	48.500
Individual Retirement Plans	9.100
Keogh Plans	2.200
Exclusion of Premiums on Employee Life Insurance and Accident and Disability Insurance	1.900
Additional Standard Deduction for the Blind and the Elderly	1.500
Tax Credit for the Elderly and Disabled	0.100
Earned Income Tax Credit[a]	1.100
Exclusion of Untaxed Social Security Benefits	21.000
Exclusion of Veterans' Disability Compensation	1.300
Exclusion of Veterans' Pensions	0.100
Subtotal	89.800

Housing

Deductibility of Mortgage Interest on Owner-Occupied Residences	25.400
Deductibility of Property Tax on Owner-Occupied Homes	8.100
Deferral of Capital Gains on Sales of Principle Residences	10.300
Exclusion of Capital gains on Sales of Principle Residences for Persons Age 55 and Over	3.400
Subtotal	47.200

Nutrition	0
Total tax expenditures	193.800
Grand total	$775.632

Table 4.1 *(continued)*

Sources: For all the tables in chapter 4, the sources are as follows: Figures on direct budgetary expenditures are from the Office of the President of the United States, 1989. *Budget of the United States Government, Fiscal Year 1990.* Washington, DC: U.S. Government Printing Office. These are figures for budgeted outlays rather than budget authority. Figures on tax expenditures are from U.S. Congress, Joint Committee on Taxation, 1989. *Estimates of Federal Tax Expenditures for Fiscal Years 1990–1994.* Washington, DC: U.S. Government Printing Office.

Notes: In several cases, line items have been combined or rearranged from the original documents in order to fit the welfare categories in the table (e.g., a special section on expenditures for veterans in the budget has been distributed among the seven categories).

Categories in this table are limited to seven main areas of welfare spending: education, employment, social services, health care, income security, housing, and nutrition. Direct and tax expenditures are placed in these categories as carefully as possible, although sometimes the fit is not exact. Other categories might legitimately be considered part of the "welfare state" as well, such as expenditures for public infrastructure, transportation, and environmental protection. These are not included in the table. For the purposes of this discussion, the welfare state has a more narrow definition, referring to expenditures for basic needs at the individual level.

Within each of the seven welfare categories, only those expenditures and tax expenditures in which money or services are transferred directly to individuals for their personal welfare are recorded. Omitted are all categories of expenditures and tax transfers to non-individuals, even though these may promote the general welfare (e.g., aid to schools, employment services, community services block grants, health research and training, and occupational health and safety). Omitted are all transfers for agricultural purposes, even though these may make food cheaper and more readily available. Also omitted are all transfers to individuals that are not directly for their personal well-being, even though these may promote the welfare of others (e.g., tax deductions for charitable contributions and tax deductions on interest from state and local bonds).

[a] The Earned Income Tax Credit is recorded in this table in its two components: a portion that is a direct expenditure in the form of an income transfer, and a portion that is a tax expenditure in the form of foregone revenue.

[b] The entry for Food Stamps includes aid to Puerto Rico.

[c] Tax expenditures are estimated to the nearest $100 million.

Medicare benefits make up most of the remainder.

Under housing, the largest expenditure, at $25.4 billion, is for deductibility of interest on home mortgages, which makes up about two-fifths of total housing expenditures. Total tax benefits to home owners, at $47.2 billion, make up about four-fifths of all housing expenditures. The remaining one-fifth is in the form of rental housing subsidies for the poor.

Under education, the major expenditures are for student financial assistance in various forms, mostly Pell grants, for students from low-

Table 4.2

Summary: The Grand Welfare State by Major Category and Type of Expenditure, Fiscal Year 1990
(billions of dollars and percentages)

Welfare state category	Direct expenditures	Tax expenditures	Total expenditures
Education	$9.7	$0.9	$10.6
	(1.3%)	(0.1%)	(1.4%)
Employment	$4.6	$7.3	$11.9
	(0.6%)	(0.9%)	(1.5%)
Social services	$8.5	$4.2	$12.7
	(1.1%)	(0.5%)	(1.6%)
Health care	$153.1	$44.4	$197.5
	(19.7%)	(5.7%)	(25.4%)
Income security	$366.8	$89.8	$456.6
	(47.3%)	(11.6%)	(58.9%)
Housing	$17.6	$47.2	$64.8
	(2.3%)	(6.1%)	(8.4%)
Nutrition	$21.5	$0	$21.5
	(2.8%)	(0%)	(2.8%)
Total	$581.8	$193.8	$775.6
	(75.0%)	(25.0%)	(100.0%)

income families, and Guaranteed Student Loans (GSLs). Under employment, almost all direct expenditures are targeted toward the poor, whereas a somewhat larger amount of tax expenditures supports various employer-provided fringe benefits. Under social services, about two-thirds of the total is direct expenditures targeted toward the poor, and one-third is in the form of tax benefits for child care, used mostly by the middle class. Nutrition assistance is entirely in the form of direct expenditures targeted toward the poor.

The Size and Composition
of the Poor Welfare State

As indicated in the figures above, most welfare expenditures are in the form of "social insurance" or non-means-tested programs. In this section, we estimate more precisely the amount of federal welfare policy targeted toward the poor. Together, we refer to these expenditures as the *poor welfare state* (Table 4.3).[19]

Table 4.3

The Poor Welfare State: Targeted Federal Welfare Expenditures to Individuals, Fiscal Year 1990
(billions of dollars and percentages)

Welfare state category	Direct expenditures	Tax expenditures	Total expenditures
Education	$6.0	$0	$6.0
	(4.8%)	(0%)	(4.8%)
Employment	$4.6	$0.3	$4.9
	(3.7%)	(0.3%)	(4.0%)
Social services	$8.4	$0	$8.4
	(6.8%)	(0%)	(6.8%)
Health care	$37.4	$0	$37.4
	(30.0%)	(0%)	(30.0%)
Income security	$28.8	$1.4	$30.2
	(23.1%)	(1.1%)	(24.2%)
Housing	$16.2	$0	$16.2
	(13.0%)	(0%)	(13.0%)
Nutrition	$21.5	$0	$21.5
	(17.2%)	(0%)	(17.2%)
Total	$122.9	$1.7	$124.6
	(98.6%)	(1.4%)	(100.0%)

Note: When there is uncertainty on a particular budget item or tax expenditure, an effort has been made to overstate rather than understate the size of the poor welfare state. For example, in this table, a portion of the educational assistance goes to nonpoor households, as does a portion of the nutrition assistance.

Direct Expenditures

The poor welfare state, at $124.6 billion in fiscal year 1990, is made up almost entirely of direct expenditures ($122.9 billion or 98.6 percent). The only tax expenditures are under employment ($0.3 billion for the Targeted Jobs Tax Credit) and income security ($0.3 billion for exclusion of cash public assistance benefits and $1.1 billion for the tax expenditure segment of the Earned Income Tax Credit, altogether comprising only 1.4 percent of the poor welfare state).

Perhaps unexpectedly, the largest single category of the poor welfare state is not income security but rather health care. Under health care, Medicaid expenditures, at $37.4 billion, make up 30.0 percent of the poor welfare state. These expenditures go to three primary populations: the disabled; the indigent elderly, mostly those in nursing homes; and single mothers with children.

Income security is the next largest category; at $30.2 billion, it comprises 24.2 percent of the poor welfare state. SSI and AFDC combined, at $23.3 billion, make up about three-fourths of these income transfers.

Nutrition assistance, at $21.5 billion, comprises 17.2 percent of the poor welfare state. Most of this assistance is in the form of Food Stamps, but the school lunch program also accounts for a large share. (Both Food Stamps and the school lunch program serve people who are not officially poor, so this figure somewhat overstates nutrition assistance to the poor.)

Housing assistance, at $16.2 billion, comprises 13.0 percent of the poor welfare state. Most of this amount is in various types of rental subsidies targeted toward the poor.

Social services, at $8.5 billion, make up 6.8 percent of the poor welfare state. This total is in the form of social services block grants, human development services, rehabilitation services, and foster care services administered by the states. Again, not all of this money goes to the officially poor.

Education, at $6.0 billion, makes up an estimated 4.8 percent of the poor welfare state, in the form of various programs for student financial assistance. (Not all the recipients of student financial aid are poor by official standards, but exact figures on impoverished recipients are not specified. Also, a small percentage of recipients of GSLs are officially impoverished but are not included in this total. Overall, this estimate of education expenditures in the poor welfare state probably overstates the amount of aid that goes to the officially poor.)

Finally, employment, at $4.9 billion, comprises 4.0 percent of the poor welfare state. This relatively small sum flows in dribbles of direct expenditures for a large number of different employment programs, including the Summer Youth Employment Program, Assistance to Dislocated Workers, Job Corps, Older Americans Employment, and JOBS Training for Welfare Recipients.

Overall, it can be said that the bulk of the poor welfare state is directed at basic needs—health care, income security, food, and housing, which together comprise 84.4 percent of the total. On the other hand, more developmental—or human capital—expenditures in the form of social services, education, and employment account for only 15.6 percent of the total.

The Spotlight on AFDC

The annual federal expenditure for family support payments, primarily in the form of AFDC, but also including child support collection programs, was budgeted at $11.2 billion in fiscal year 1990. This amount is only 9.0 percent of the poor welfare state and only 1.4 percent of the grand welfare state. Nonetheless, in the public mind and in political debate, AFDC receives most of the attention in discussions of "welfare"—indeed, it is almost a synonym for "welfare." This rather bizarre situation might be interpreted as a benign misconception on the part of the general public (why should a program that receives only 1.4 percent of federal welfare expenditures be continually in the spotlight?), or it might be interpreted as hostility toward poor women and their children.[20] In either case, it may be useful to add a word of clarification.

AFDC provides cash aid to needy families whose children lack support due to continued parental absences, incapacitation, unemployment, or death. The majority of recipients are single mothers and their children. The average number of children in AFDC households is 2.0. In September 1988, 3.7 million families comprising 10.9 million individuals received AFDC benefits.[21]

AFDC recipients are not evenly distributed across the population. Although black and Hispanic women constitute 21 percent of all women aged fifteen to age forty-four, they constitute 45 percent of all women who head households, and 55 percent of all AFDC recipients. In 1986, 53 percent of all AFDC recipients had never been married, up from 32 percent in 1973. About 32 percent of all AFDC families live with relatives not receiving AFDC, and 5 percent live with one or more unrelated persons. The other 63 percent live in households with only AFDC recipients. Of the family situations, about half are two-generation and half are three-generation, that is, a grandparent is present.[22]

AFDC transfers are far below the poverty level. In 1987, the median state benefit for a family of three without other income was $359 per month (47.5 percent of the poverty level). The state with the lowest amount was Alabama at $118 per month (15.6 percent of the poverty level); and the state with the highest amount was Alaska at $749 per month (79.3 percent of the poverty level). Between 1970 and 1987, after adjusting for inflation, the maximum AFDC benefit level fell 31.4 percent in the median state. The vast majority of states do not have automatic cost-of-living adjustments for means-tested welfare benefits.[23]

About 85 percent of AFDC beneficiaries also receive Food Stamps, but even after including Food Stamps, families do not reach the poverty level in forty-nine states. In the median state in 1987, the maximum combined value of AFDC plus Food Stamps for a family of three was $559 per month or 74.0 percent of the poverty level. AFDC families also qualify for Medicaid, which covers many health care expenses. Health coverage greatly improves the package of benefits—indeed, it is a major reason why some families stay on AFDC—but it is difficult to argue that dollar expenditures for health care are equivalent to cash transfers for consumption. Only about 13 percent of AFDC families receive some form of rental subsidy for housing.[24]

A key feature of AFDC and several other means-tested income transfer programs is the "asset test." The asset test requires that the recipient have no more than minimal assets (usually $1,500, with home equity excluded) in order to become or remain eligible for the program. This asset test effectively prohibits recipients from accumulating savings.

The Size and Composition of the Nonpoor Welfare State

Over time, the nonpoor have successfully lodged a series of claims against the resources of the state. As Morris Janowitz has observed:

> The pattern and magnitude of allocations of the welfare state has become part of the system of inequality. . . . The emergence of the welfare state has produced a system that has as its official goals "assisting" those at the bottom of the social structure. But the long-term trend is one in which there is a diffusion of social welfare upward and throughout the social structure.[25]

At this juncture, the claims of the nonpoor, enacted into public policy in the form of nontargeted welfare benefits, comprise a total of $651.0 billion or 84.0 percent of all welfare expenditures (Tables 4.4 and 4.5). We refer to this as the *nonpoor welfare state*.[26]

Overall, the largest single category of the nonpoor welfare state is income security (mostly Social Security) at $426.4 billion or 65.5 per-

Table 4.4

**The Nonpoor Welfare State: Nontargeted Federal Welfare
Expenditures to Individuals, Fiscal Year 1990**
(billions of dollars and percentages)

Welfare state category	Direct expenditures	Tax expenditures	Total expenditures
Education	$3.7	$0.9	$4.6
	(0.6%)	(0.1%)	(0.7%)
Employment	$0	$7.0	$7.0
	(0%)	(1.1%)	(1.1%)
Social services	$0	$4.2	$4.2
	(0%)	(0.6%)	(0.6%)
Health care	$115.7	$44.4	$160.1
	(17.8%)	(6.8%)	(24.6%)
Income security	$338.0	$88.4	$426.4
	(51.9%)	(13.6%)	(65.5%)
Housing	$1.5	$47.2	$48.7
	(0.2%)	(7.3%)	(7.5%)
Nutrition	$0	$0	$0
	(0%)	(0%)	(0%)
Total	$458.9	$192.1	$651.0
	(70.5%)	(29.5%)	(100.0%)

Table 4.5

**The Poor (Targeted) and Nonpoor (Nontargeted) Welfare States as a
Proportion of the Grand Welfare State, Fiscal Year 1990**
(billions of dollars and percentages)

	Direct expenditures	Tax expenditures	Total expenditures
Poor (targeted) welfare state	$122.9	$1.7	$124.6
	(15.8%)	(0.2%)	(16.0%)
Nonpoor (nontargeted welfare state)	$458.9	$192.1	$651.0
	(59.2%)	(24.8%)	(84.0%)
Grand welfare state (total)	$581.8	$193.8	$775.6
	(75.0%)	(25.0%)	(100.0%)

cent of the total. The next largest category is health care at $160.1
billion or 24.6 percent of the nonpoor welfare state. Housing makes up
$48.7 billion or 7.5 percent of the nonpoor welfare state. The remain-
ing four categories—education, employment, social services, and nutrition—together comprise only $15.8 billion or 2.4 percent of the
nonpoor welfare state.

Unlike the poor welfare state, the nonpoor welfare state is made up of both direct expenditures and tax expenditures. Direct expenditures total $458.9 billion (70.5 percent) and tax expenditures total $192.1 billion (29.5 percent). It may be helpful to consider these separately.

Direct Expenditures

The largest category of nontargeted direct expenditures is in income security, at $338.0 billion (51.9 percent of the total nonpoor welfare state). Social Security programs (Old Age, Survivors, Disability, and Unemployment Insurance) make up about seven-tenths of this total. Railroad, civil service, and military retirement make up about one-sixth of the total, and veterans benefits make up most of the remainder.

Health care is the only other significant category of direct expenditures in the nonpoor welfare state, at $115.7 billion (17.8 percent of the nonpoor welfare state). About five-sixths of this total is in Medicare Hospital Insurance and Supplemental Medical Insurance, and about one-twelfth is in Veterans Medical Care and Hospital Services.

The remaining five categories—education, housing, employment, social services, and nutrition—together comprise only $5.2 billion in direct spending (0.8 percent) in the nonpoor welfare state. The latter three—employment, social services, and nutrition—comprise no direct expenditures at all.

As Peter Peterson, former secretary of commerce, and Neil Howe, of the Retirement Policy Institute, have observed, the huge direct expenditures to the nonpoor in income security and health care constitute a major stimulation of consumption, and little investment in human capital.[27] Most of the money goes to Social Security and Medicare for the elderly. According to Peterson and Howe, Social Security and Medicare benefits may be up to five times the actuarial value of prior contributions.

Another large portion goes to civil service and military retirement. Most of the recipients are working on other jobs and have average incomes of more than thirty-five thousand dollars. In the civil service retirement system, benefits exceed contributions and are indexed at 100 percent of the Consumer Price Index. Military personnel make no prior contributions, and many military retirees spend more years collecting benefits than they have spent in service.[28] Many pursue a second career and achieve a "triple-dip" retirement—military retirement, company pension, and Social Security.

Peterson and Howe observe that, whereas means-tested programs were the targets of debates and cuts during the 1980s, entitlements for the nonpoor were less affected, and entitlement benefits will continue to grow even if we keep current policies. These authors warn that the growth in entitlement spending puts the United States "on borrowed time." They believe that government entitlements threaten the vitality of the economy: "Americans have decided to socialize much of the cost of growing old, but very little of the cost of raising children." Eleven times more benefits go to those over age sixty-five than to those under age eighteen.[29,30]

Tax Expenditures

Although Peterson and Howe have incisively pointed out the flaws in the entitlement spending system, this is not the full story. Not all of the nonpoor welfare state is in the form of direct expenditures. Indeed, a substantial portion, $192.1 billion (29.5 percent of the nonpoor welfare state) is in the form of tax expenditures or "fiscal welfare," as Titmuss called it.[31] These expenditures are the most hidden of all; even the recipients often do not have the perception that the government is spending money on them.

Again, income security is the largest category. Nontargeted tax expenditures for income security totaled $88.4 billion (13.6 percent of the total nonpoor welfare state) in 1990. More than one-half of this amount was in tax exclusions for employer-sponsored pension contributions and earnings. About one-fourth was in untaxed Social Security benefits, and one-eighth was in tax deferments for Individual Retirement Accounts and Keogh Plans. Thus, about seven-eighths of all tax expenditures for income security go to retirement benefits, mostly for people who have incomes far above the poverty level.[32]

The next largest category is housing, where the annual tax expenditure is $47.2 billion or 7.3 percent of the nonpoor welfare state. About two-thirds of this amount is for deductibility of home mortgage interest and property taxes, and the remainder is for deferment and exclusion of capital gains on sales of principal residences.

The other significant tax expenditure is in health care, where the annual total is $44.4 billion or 6.8 percent of the nonpoor welfare state. About three-fourths of this amount is in tax exclusions for employer contributions to medical insurance, and most of the remainder is in tax exclusion of Medicare benefits. A relatively small sum, $2.8 billion, is in deductibility of medical expenses.

The remaining four categories—employment, social services, education, and nutrition—together account for only $12.1 billion in tax expenditures or 1.8 percent of the nonpoor welfare state. Most of this amount is in the category of employment, where various fringe benefits are excluded from taxes. This policy effectively acts as a wage subsidy for the nonpoor.

In looking at the various tax expenditures in the nonpoor welfare state, a prominent theme emerges—most of the tax expenditures are asset-based; that is, these nontargeted welfare benefits *directly help people accumulate financial and real assets*. The major forms in which this occurs are in tax subsidies for employer-sponsored and personally held retirement pension accounts ($59.8 billion total) and tax subsidies for home equity accumulation ($47.2 billion total). Together, these asset-based welfare programs account for $107.0 billion, well over half of all tax expenditures in the nonpoor welfare state.[33]

In total, these asset-based tax expenditures for the nonpoor are not far short of the $124.6 billion that is spent for the entire poor welfare state. As retirement pension accounts mushroom in the years ahead, it is probable that asset-based welfare expenditures for the nonpoor will exceed welfare expenditures for the poor.

It is important to note that these tax expenditures are not primarily to the wealthy, but rather substantially to the broad middle class of pension holders and homeowners. Moreover, these tax expenditures far exceed total tax expenditures to corporations, which for 1990 are estimated at $38.7 billion.[34] These figures suggest a departure from Titmuss's analysis of fiscal welfare. Contrary to populist sentiment, in the United States at the present time, fiscal welfare does not benefit the wealthy or corporations so much as it benefits the broad middle class. A large portion of this fiscal welfare is asset-based, and it is relatively hidden. Most recipients think that they have earned all the money in their retirement pension accounts and that wise investment has led to their home equity, even though these assets have been hugely subsidized by government policy.

Table 4.6

The Poor (Targeted) and Nonpoor (Nontargeted) Welfare States as a Proportion of Total Federal Expenditures, Fiscal Year 1990
(billions of dollars and percentages)

	Direct expenditures[a]	Tax expenditures	Total expenditures
Poor (targeted) welfare state	$122.9	$1.7	$124.6
	(8.4%)	(0.1%)	(8.5%)
Nonpoor (nontargeted) welfare state	$458.9	$192.1	$651.0
	(31.4%)	(13.1%)	(44.5%)
All other federal expenditures[b]	$570.0	$118.3	$688.3
	(38.9%)	(8.1%)	(47.0%)
Total federal expenditures	$1,151.8	$312.1	$1,463.9
	(78.7%)	(21.3%)	(100.0%)

[a] The figures on direct federal expenditures do not include "off budget" expenditures that have become more common in recent years.

[b] This category includes, under direct expenditures, interest on the national debt. Under tax expenditures, it includes other individual tax expenditures ($79.6 billion) plus all corporate tax expenditures ($38.7 billion).

Summary of the Poor and Nonpoor Welfare States

In sum, the poor welfare state comprises only 16.0 percent of all welfare spending to individuals, while the nonpoor welfare state comprises 84.0 percent. Regarding types of expenditures, 75.0 percent of the grand welfare state is in the form of direct expenditures and 25.0 percent is in the form of tax expenditures (Table 4.5). Almost all tax expenditures are in the nonpoor welfare state, and a large portion of these are asset-based, designed to promote individual accumulation of financial assets or real property.

As a proportion of total federal expenditures, the poor welfare state makes up 8.5 percent, and the nonpoor welfare state makes up another 44.5 percent, for a total of 53.0 percent, well over half. Looking at types of expenditures, the grand welfare state makes up slightly more than half of all direct expenditures, and over three-fifths of all tax expenditures (Table 4.6).

In general, the poor receive means-tested and stigmatized income transfers, while the nonpoor receive "social insurance" and asset accumulation subsidies. Regarding the latter, (1) tax expenditures are heavily used to promote asset accumulation; (2) asset accumulation welfare policies benefit the nonpoor disproportionately; and (3) tax expenditures have, in turn, stimulated a rapid rise in additional asset accumulation in the corporate welfare sector. Nine out of ten Fortune 1000 companies sponsor tax-deferred retirement plans such as 401(k)s, often in addition to regular pensions. As of 1989, more than $100 billion had accumulated in these accounts.[35]

Interpretation

The welfare state has been constructed in piecemeal fashion. There is no broad, integrated theoretical underpinning, nor is there a single, simplistic political explanation for its development. Rather, the welfare state embodies a bundle of different ideologies and partial political appeals. Although undirected in its formation, the welfare state nonetheless has certain systematic outcomes. Returning to Robert Lampman's four "mentalities" of welfare policy discussed at the beginning of the chapter, we can offer an assessment of the relative prominence of each theme in the current U.S. welfare state.

Minimum Provision

The welfare state in the United States, when compared with other Organization for Economic Cooperation and Development (OECD) countries, is uniquely inadequate in protection of the marginal population.[36] As shown in the above analysis, only 16.0 percent of all benefits are targeted to the poor. Robert Plotnick reports that for married couple households, all federal cash transfers reduce the official poverty rate from 10.8 percent to 9.0 percent. For single-headed households, all federal cash transfers reduce poverty from 50.9 percent to 45.2 percent. In both cases, the largest share of poverty reduction results from non-means-tested programs rather than from means-tested programs.[37] As Peterson and Howe point out, welfare expenditures of the federal government are far more a consumption-promoter for the nonpoor than a "safety net" for the poor.[38]

Replacement of Loss

Nontargeted "social insurance" makes up the bulk of the welfare state and, in this sense, the replacement-of-loss mentality has triumphed over all others. It is important to note, however, that full premiums have not been paid on most of the "insurance" benefits; that is, recipients receive far more than the actuarial value of their contributions. A large portion of the benefits to the nonpoor are straightforward income transfers. The political triumph of the nonpoor has been to promulgate the myth, even to themselves, that they receive "social insurance" while the poor receive "welfare."

Moreover, it is not widely appreciated that "social insurance" programs have redistributive features, and the redistribution does not always favor the poor. Taking the Social Security retirement system as the largest example, both the tax structure and the benefit structure have regressive elements. As Milton Friedman has observed:

> It hardly needs demonstrating that the [Social Security] tax is highly regressive, though one crucial feature of its regressivity may not be obvious. The earlier the age at which a person enters the labor market, the more years on the average he or she will pay Social Security taxes. It goes without saying that the children of the poor tend to enter the labor force at an earlier age than the children of the middle and upper classes.
>
> It is somewhat less obvious that the benefit program is also regressive. The longer the average life span of a group, the larger the subsidies it will receive on the average. Whites have a longer average life span than blacks; upper-income classes than lower-income classes.[39]

Thus, under the banner of social insurance masquerades a huge program that is, in some respects, a redistribution from the poor to the nonpoor.

Equity

Because most welfare policy consists of non-means-tested expenditures, the redistributional effects of welfare policy across class lines are small. The officially poor make up about 13 percent of the population (*after* income transfers) and targeted welfare spending accounts for only 16 percent of total welfare spending.

However, a major redistribution does occur across generations. The main effects of federal welfare policy have been the increased security of the elderly and the increased impoverishment of children. The elderly paid 10.1 percent of federal taxes in 1986 and received 68.4

percent of federal benefits. In contrast, households with children paid 41.6 percent of taxes and received 21.5 percent of benefits. Poverty among the elderly has been reduced to one in seven, due primarily to Social Security benefits, but poverty among newborn children has increased to almost one in four. The major distributional influence of all federal government policy results not from income taxation or targeted antipoverty programs but rather from the Social Security retirement program. Peterson and Howe believe that huge intergenerational transfers from the young to the old are shortsighted, the folly of which will become apparent when the baby boomers reach retirement age.[40]

Efficiency of Investment

For the most part, the welfare state does not promote economic productivity. Consumption-oriented political appeals from the nonpoor have resulted in income-oriented policies, not well integrated with the economic sector.[41] This is true in Western Europe and in many "developing" countries as well as in the United States. The welfare state as it currently exists tends to detract from economic growth, although it adds somewhat to economic stability.[42]

Inefficiency of investment in the welfare state has two dimensions —the lack of development of human capital and the lack of development of financial capital. Regarding human capital, only a very small portion of total expenditures are devoted to education, social services, and employment, categories directly related to human development and enhancement of knowledge and skills. Also, the huge intergenerational transfer from children to the elderly draws resources away from the population on which the nation's future productivity depends. Thus, the welfare state does not, for the most part, serve to develop the productive capacity of the population.

Regarding financial capital, the heavily consumption-oriented policies of the welfare state lead to large government expenditures as well as large household expenditures. The overall effect is to reduce the national savings rate, which in turn limits the amount of capital available for investment and makes capital more expensive through higher interest rates.

A significant portion (about 30 percent) of the nonpoor welfare state is devoted to individual asset accumulation through tax expenditures, primarily in home equity and retirement pensions. The massive subsidy of home equity does not directly improve the availability of investment capital because housing, from a macroeconomic perspective, is an inefficient investment. However, large sums in individually held and corporate-held retirement pension funds *do* create a pool of capital that is readily available for investment. Indeed, pension funds are today the major players in financial markets. Pension funds now own 50 percent or more of the stock in most of the large companies in the United States. This asset-accumulation aspect of the welfare state *does* substantially promote economic growth.

Conclusion

At the outset, the welfare state in America was a Keynesian creation, designed to stimulate consumer demand during economic downturns.[43] This basic macroeconomic consideration has shaped the welfare state fundamentally, and has made it income-based and consumption-oriented. However, as Morris Janowitz has observed, welfare state growth has been less and less a result of Keynesian economic policy, and more and more a result of interest group politics. The problems of the modern welfare state stem from increased demand for benefits by the nonpoor, "almost as if they are self-generating."[44] Because most of the benefits detract from, rather than add to, human capital and financial capital, there is reduced ability of the economy to increase productivity to pay for the ever-expanding benefits to the nonpoor.

Neil Gilbert has commented that rapid expansion of the welfare state between 1960 and 1980 did not include much foresight as to the nature of the welfare polices being created or their fundamental purposes.[45] There was no reasoned foundation on which either to support or to oppose the Reagan-era effort to "privatize" the welfare state, and there still is none. Neither the liberal philosophy of state-provided benefits nor the conservative philosophy of privatization offers a social philosophy that clarifies the purposes of the welfare state. Basically, the welfare state is without a rudder. It consists mostly of a conglomeration of transfers to the nonpoor that do little to help the poor, that impoverish children, that stimulate consumption, and that detract from investment.

The portion of the welfare state that is a notable exception consists of asset-based tax expenditures for the nonpoor. Government-sponsored wealth accumulation in this form is unquestionably good for individuals; they become much better able to handle their own welfare and they are more in control under these circumstances than they are when receiving income transfers. At the macroeconomic level, the accumulation of financial capital is also good for the economy as a whole. However, under current policies, the poor do not benefit from asset-based policies. An improved welfare state would promote asset accumulation among the poor as well.

Notes

1. Good overviews of the development of the welfare state are by Morris Janowitz, *Social Control of the Welfare State*. Chicago: University of Chicago Press, 1976; and Frances Fox Piven and Richard A. Cloward, *The New Class War: Reagan's Attack on the Welfare State and Its Consequences*. New York: Pantheon, 1982.

2. On results and effects of welfare policy, see Charles Murray, *Losing Ground: American Social Policy 1950–1980*. New York: Basic Books, 1984; Robert Haveman, *Starting Even: An Equal-Opportunity Program to Combat the Nation's New Poverty*. New York: Simon and Schuster, 1988; David T. Ellwood, *Poor Support: Poverty in the American Family*. New York: Basic Books, 1988; and Neil Gilbert and Barbara Gilbert, *The Enabling State: Modern Welfare Capitalism in America*. Oxford: Oxford University Press, 1989.

3. Alfred Marshall, *Principles of Economics*, eighth edition. London: Macmillan and Co., Ltd., 1920, 4.

4. Robert Lampman, *Ends and Means of Reducing Income Poverty*. Chicago: Markham Publishing Co., 1971.

5. Andrew W. Dobelstein, *Politics, Economics, and Public Welfare*, second edition. Englewood Cliffs, NJ: Prentice-Hall, 1986, 95–97.

6. Reinhold Niebuhr, *The Contribution of Religion to Social Work*. New York: Columbia University Press, 1932; and James Leiby, "Moral Foundations of Social Welfare and Social Work: A Historical View," *Social Work* 30, 1985, 323–30.

7. The Catholic Bishops' Letter was developed between 1984 and 1986; for an insightful analysis, see Marie D. Hoff, *Response to the Catholic Bishops' Letter on Economic Justice: Implications for Social Welfare*, Ph.D. dissertation, University of Washington, 1986.

8. John K. Galbraith, *American Capitalism*. Boston: Houghton Mifflin, 1952, 27.

9. Kenneth J. Arrow, "Distributive Justice and Desirable Ends of Economic Activity," in George R. Freiwel, ed., *Issues in Contemporary Macroeconomics and Distribution*. Albany: State University of New York Press, 1985, 134–56.

10. Lester Thurow, *The Zero-Sum Society*. New York: Penguin Books, 1980, 182–83.

11. Lampman, 1971.

12. Richard Titmuss, *Commitment to Welfare*. London: Allen and Unwin, 1965. Regarding occupational welfare, see Michael Sosin, *Private Benefits: Ma-*

terial Assistance in the Private Sector. Orlando: Academic Press, 1986; and David Stoesz, "Corporate Welfare: The Third Stage of Welfare in the United States," *Social Work* 31(4), 1986, 245–49.

13. Mimi Abramovitz, "Everyone Is on Welfare: 'The Role of Redistribution in Social Policy' Revisited," *Social Work* 28(6), 1983, 440–45.

14. For example, see Martha N. Ozawa, "Social Insurance and Redistribution," in Alvin Schorr, ed., *Jubilee for Our Times.* New York: Columbia University Press, 1977, 123–77; and Martha N. Ozawa, "Who Receives Subsidies through Social Security and How Much?" *Social Work* 27, 1982, 128–34.

15. Daniel Patrick Moynihan, "A Shameful Picture, in Black and White," *St. Louis Post-Dispatch*, March 22, 1988, 3C.

16. Some people object to including tax expenditures as part of federal spending. The argument goes something like this: "Taxpayers are hard-working, productive citizens, paying heavy taxes. Through the various tax deductions and exclusions, they are only getting a little deserved relief from the tax burden." Probably most Americans feel this way—I sometimes do myself. However, as shown in this chapter, relief to the nonpoor through the tax system is very great indeed. In large measure, tax expenditures to the nonpoor subvert the progressivity of the individual income tax. There is no right or wrong position on whether this is desirable. It is a matter of values and politics. If one believes that progressive taxation is a bad idea, then tax expenditures help to rectify a mistaken policy. However, if one believes that progressive taxation is desirable, then tax expenditures to individuals are equivalent to welfare benefits. The assumption in this book is that progressive taxation is desirable; therefore, tax expenditures are essentially the same as direct expenditures.

Also, this is *not* asking the question of net redistribution effects of federal policy. Robert Lampman, for example, has asked this question very effectively. He reports that the nonpoor aged are the biggest "winners" and the nonpoor nonaged are the biggest "losers" in the federal redistribution system (Robert Lampman, *Social Welfare Spending: Accounting for Changes from 1950 to 1978.* Orlando: Academic Press, 1984). In this chapter, however, I attempt only to assess spending—what benefits go to whom.

17. Office of the President of the United States, *Budget of the United States Government, Fiscal Year 1990.* Washington: U.S. Government Printing Office, 1989. The president's budget is amended by Congress and, during implementation, additional changes are made. Therefore, the amounts presented here are estimates. Budget lines may deviate during actual spending, but overall, the main outlines of welfare policy do not change very much.

18. U.S. Congress, Joint Committee on Taxation, *Estimates of Federal Tax Expenditures.* Washington: U.S. Government Printing Office, 1989.

19. The designation "poor welfare state" used in this chapter does not refer precisely to all the benefits that go to those below the income poverty line. Instead, it refers to all the benefits in means-tested programs. Most of these go to the income poor, but some do not.

20. Mimi Abramovitz, *Regulating the Lives of Women.* Boston: South End Press, 1988.

21. U.S. Department of Health and Human Services, Family Support Administration, *Quarterly Public Assistance Statistics, Fiscal Year 1988.* Washington:

U.S. Government Printing Office, 1990. At this writing, more than half of the states permit AFDC payments to families with an unemployed father present, but these families represent a small portion of total recipients (0.2 million families in September 1988). This program is known as AFDC-UP, the "UP" standing for unemployed parent. The Family Support Act of 1988 requires states to provide at least six months of AFDC coverage to two-parent families in which the principal wage earner is unemployed.

22. U.S. General Accounting Office, *Welfare: Relationships and Incomes in Households with AFDC Recipients and Others.* Washington: U.S. Government Printing Office, May 1988.

23. Isaac Shapiro and Robert Greenstein, *Holes in the Safety Net.* Washington: Center on Budget and Policy Priorities, 1988.

24. Robert Plotnick, "Directions for Reducing Child Poverty," *Social Work* 34, 1989, 523–30; Shapiro and Greenstein, 1988; and Marian Wright Edelman, *Families in Peril: An Agenda for Social Change.* Cambridge: Harvard University Press, 1987.

25. Janowitz, 1976, 77.

26. Again, the term nonpoor welfare state refers to the non-means-tested nature of the benefits. The officially poor are also eligible and receive some of these benefits, but most go to the nonpoor.

27. Peter G. Peterson and Neil Howe, *On Borrowed Time: How the Growth of Entitlement Spending Threatens America's Future.* San Francisco: Institute for Contemporary Studies, 1988.

28. Some people suggest that payments to veterans are deferred compensation and should not be considered welfare transfers. It does not seem necessary to take a position on this debate. Regardless of the rationale or explanation; the payments are being made.

29. Peterson and Howe, 1988.

30. Also, the massive transfers to farmers by way of agricultural subsidy are an unusual case of "welfare," with no relation to either prior financial contribution or level of need. As Neil Gilbert and Barbara Gilbert (1989) point out, these transfers are in the form of a complex and nearly incomprehensible labyrinth of supports, for many of which no accurate data are available. However, in 1986 in three major categories—price supports, credit subsidies, and tax expenditures—agricultural supports are estimated at $34 billion. These transfers have the effect of maintaining substantial assets in farm households, many of which, according to Gilbert and Gilbert, are in questionable need. In 1984, even after several years of "crisis" on the American farm, median farmer net worth was $141,000, compared to $33,000 for all families. Perceptively, Gilbert and Gilbert refer to farm subsides as "asset maintenance." Even though it is not assets that are directly transferred, the effect is to allow farmers to keep their landholdings and equipment and to underwrite the value of those assets indirectly by subsidizing expected income flows from the assets.

However, the comparison with social policy is not a perfect fit. Farmers may be a category of households, but they are also running a business. Farm subsidies are not only to support farm families, but also to support farm businesses. In this respect, asset maintenance of farmers might be usefully compared to asset maintenance of other businesses (depreciation allowances, capital gains exclusions, and the like).

31. See also Gilbert and Gilbert, 1989, on tax expenditures.

32. Retirement welfare policies have yet another asset-based twist. Social Security benefits allow unlimited earnings from financial assets to be excluded from calculations of Social Security benefits. But, at this writing, working poor retirees ages sixty-five through sixty-nine can earn only $9,360 before losing $1 for every $3 over the limit (there is no earnings cap for beneficiaries age seventy and above). Thus, earnings from financial assets are tax-excluded, while earnings from labor (human capital) are not tax-excluded. This policy creates a strong disincentive for retirees to work, as it was originally intended to do, but it will make less and less sense as the U.S. population ages.

33. In addition, there is another $79.6 billion in tax expenditures to individuals, some of which may contribute to asset accumulation, but not in the welfare categories defined in this discussion (e.g., $5.7 billion in exclusion of capital gains at death, $2.3 billion in exclusion of interest on state and local small issue bonds, $3.5 billion in exceptions for passive rental losses).

34. U.S. Congress, Joint Committee on Taxation, 1989.

35. For a cogent analysis, see Beth Stevens, ''Blurring the Boundaries: How the Federal Government Has Shaped Private Sector Welfare Benefits,'' Working Paper 3, Taxation, Project on the Federal Social Role. Washington: National Conference on Social Welfare, 1985.

36. Lee Rainwater, Martin Rein, and Joseph Schwartz, *Income Packaging and the Welfare State: A Comparative Study of Family Income.* Oxford: Clarendon Press, 1986.

37. Robert Plotnick, 1989, using data from U.S. Congress, Committee on Ways and Means, *Background Material and Data on Programs within the Jurisdiction of the Committee on Ways and Means: 1989 Edition.* Washington: U.S. Government Printing Office, 1989.

38. Peterson and Howe, 1988.

39. Milton Friedman, ''Social Security: The General and the Personal,'' *Wall Street Journal*, March 15, 1988, 32.

40. Peterson and Howe, 1988.

41. Ramesh Mishra, *The Welfare State in Crisis.* New York: St. Martin's Press, 1984, 102–103.

42. James O'Connor, *The Fiscal Crisis of the State.* New York: St. Martin's, 1973; and Hyman Minsky, *Stabilizing an Unstable Economy.* New Haven: Yale University Press, 1986.

43. Minsky, 1986.

44. Janowitz, 1976, 46.

45. Neil Gilbert, ''The Welfare State Adrift,'' *Social Work*, 31(4), 1986, 251–55.

5 • The Welfare Reform Debate

In important respects, the welfare state has not succeeded in mending social and economic divisions and has not developed a broad base of support. This is especially true of means-tested income transfer programs, such as AFDC. Sheldon Danziger and Robert Plotnick, in an important article, review twenty years of antipoverty policy and find that neither income transfers nor economic growth are enough to alter levels of pretransfer poverty.[1] Hence, the primary approaches of both liberals and conservatives have not succeeded in reducing poverty. Reflecting these failures, AFDC, the beleaguered symbol of "welfare," has been at the center of public debate.

The debate, however, has been narrowly circumscribed. Poverty inevitably has been defined by income levels. To be sure, a great deal of discussion has occurred around how to measure income. A major debate is about whether to include in-kind benefits, such as medical care, food stamps, and social services, in calculating income levels. However, both sides of the debate are constrained by the limitations of using income as a fixed parameter of discussion. Assets for the poor are seldom, if ever, mentioned. In this regard, it may be helpful to review the major policy perspectives.

Three broad categories of political ideology can be recognized in the United States and Western Europe. They are the conservative right, the liberal middle, and the radical left. Using more European terminology, these might be known as the far right, the social democrats, and the structural left. These three categories are by no means evenly represented in the U.S. population, and their relative prominence shifts from time to time, but they provide a useful framework for discussion of the welfare reform debate.

The Conservative Right

Among an array of conflicting ideologies in matters of welfare policy in the United States, the conservative right reflects the dominant viewpoint. The right is skeptical about public assistance and prefers compulsory work to income transfers. The right believes that an entrenched "rights concept" of welfare has established perverse incentives and "welfarism." Some conservatives speak primarily about the moral value of self-sufficiency; others focus on economic incentives; and others interweave these themes.

For the conservative right, the individual is the most important consideration in government. From this perspective, the closer decisions are made to the individual, the better the government. Local government is preferable to state government, and state government is preferable to federal government. Unregulated markets and voluntary efforts are preferred to government planning and intervention.

In its most strident form, conservative ideology is openly social Darwinist, arguing that poverty is part of the natural order of life and is, in the long run, necessary and desirable for the improvement of society. Sentiments to the contrary are viewed as softheaded and misguided. Taking a classic example, Herbert Spencer, the nineteenth century English social philosopher, commented:

> There are many very amiable people—people over whom in so far as their feelings are concerned we may fitly rejoice—who have not the nerve to look this matter fairly in the face. Disabled as they are by their sympathies with present suffering, from duly regarding ultimate consequences, they pursue a course which is very injudicious, and in the end even cruel. We do not consider it true kindness in a mother to gratify her child with sweetmeats that are certain to make it ill. We should think it a very foolish sort of benevolence which led a surgeon to let his patient's disease progress to a fatal issue, rather than inflict pain by an operation. Similarly, we must call those spurious philanthropists, who, to prevent present misery, would entail greater misery upon future generations. All defenders of a poor-law [welfare assistance] must, however, be classed amongst such. That rigorous necessity which, when allowed to act on them, becomes so sharp a spur to the lazy, and so strong a bridle to the random, these paupers' friends would repeal, because of the wailings it here and there produces. Blind to the fact, that under the natural order of things society is constantly excreting its

unhealthy, imbecile, slow, vacillating, faithless members, these unthink-
ing, though well-meaning, men advocate an interference which not only
stops the purifying process, but even increases the vitiation—absolutely
encourages the multiplication of the reckless and incompetent by offering them an unfailing provision, and *dis*courages the multiplication of
the competent and provident by heightening the prospective difficulty
of maintaining a family. And thus, in their eagerness to prevent the
really salutary sufferings that surround us, these sigh-wise and groan-
foolish people bequeath to posterity a continually increasing curse.[2]

In a reply to Spencer, Thomas Huxley, the English biologist and
cofounder of the theory of evolution, answered with equal but opposite
conviction:

It strikes me that men who are accustomed to contemplate the active or
passive extirpation of the weak, the unfortunate, and the superfluous;
who justify that conduct on the ground that it has the sanction of the
cosmic process, and is the only way of ensuring the progress of the
race; who, if they are consistent, must rank medicine among the black
arts and count the physician a mischievous preserver of the unfit; on
whose matrimonial undertakings the principles of the stud have the
chief influence; whose whole lives, therefore, are an education in the
noble art of suppressing natural affection and sympathy, are not likely
to have any large stock of these commodities left. But, without them,
there is no conscience, nor any restraint on the conduct of men, except
the calculation of self-interest, the balancing of certain present gratifica-
tions against doubtful future pains; and experience tells us how much
that is worth.[3]

This debate is hardly silenced in the late twentieth century. Modern
versions are generally couched in softer language about "dependency," but the essential social Darwinist viewpoint and its critics
form the foundation of the national ambivalence about welfare policy.

In less strident form, conservative ideology can be rather naively
paternalistic, assuming the posture of model, teacher, or noble preach-
er, as illustrated by Nelson Aldrich, Jr., in *Old Money*. Aldrich pleads
for reinvigorating traditional upper-class principles: "According to the
logic of Old Money's own values and principles, there is only one way
the class can legitimate its ascendancy over and above the riotous flood
of wanting and working that constitutes the 'hard' life of the middle
classes. That is to be a beacon, showing the more successful of those
storm-tossed strivers the way to a more gracious, edifying, and socially

responsible life.''[4] But alas, worries Aldrich, Old Money tends to be inward-looking instead of shining a beacon.

Conservatives also argue that social problems are overstated. In large measure, they say, the problem is democracy itself. Democracy has led to a series of exaggerated claims and counterclaims by interest groups that have expanded government, impoverished and paralyzed the state, and threatened capitalism. The ever-expanding claims are paid for by borrowing, slight-of-hand, or other measures that disconnect current benefits from the sacrifice of immediate payment. The final bill is deferred to future generations.[5]

Following the theme of overstating social problems, conservatives suggest that poverty is not as high as official statistics indicate. For example, Stuart Butler and Anna Kondratas conclude that the ''official measure of poverty is seriously inadequate as a basis for welfare policy.'' The definition is flawed, say these authors, because the poor achieve a nutritionally adequate diet on less than a poverty threshold income. They also argue that in-kind transfers for food and medical care should be included as household income. In place of the current income poverty line, Butler and Kondratas suggest a national consumption standard, ''defined as the income needed to buy a minimum quantity of specified goods and services,'' a ''poverty market basket.''[6]

Another portion of the right attack on welfare is on moral grounds, against the ''permissiveness'' fostered by welfare professionals and other do-gooders. To the extent that social problems are acknowledged on the right, they tend to be defined in terms of individual characteristics. Poverty is seen as a result of profligate behavior, low human capital, or lack of motivation to enter the labor market.[7] This view is variously referred to as a human capital view or a moralistic view, depending on the political persuasion of the observer. One version of the conservative perspective is offered by Lawrence Mead, who argues that, at the margin, employment is available for people who want to work, and because employment is the surest way out of poverty, the unemployed are not taking advantage of the opportunities around them.[8]

The individual-centered view by itself, however, fails to account for systematic intergenerational repetition of poverty among particular groups. In order to account for this pattern, the conservative right defines a ''culture of poverty'' with improvident values that are passed from generation to generation.[9] Often this explanation, in its portrayal of extreme intractability of poverty, borders on the biologically deterministic view of earlier day social Darwinists.

Overall, however, there is surprisingly little empirical support for the culture-of-poverty explanation. A review of the existing research on causes of poverty finds that motivational factors related to values, beliefs, and culture are weakly related to poverty; ability factors are more strongly related; and structural factors, such as economic status and race, are also more strongly related.[10]

Looking at antipoverty policy, the right identifies a "New Class" of professional helpers and managers who promote the cause of poverty for their own well-being, to the detriment of the nation as a whole. As savvy War on Poverty participants observed during the 1960s, "there is money in poverty," by which they meant that welfare policy creates a large number of jobs, and some of them are well-paying jobs with comfortable fringe benefits. According to the right, the welfare bureaucracy has no interest in moving people out of poverty.[11]

As possible solutions to poverty, conservatives focus on individuals, families, and voluntarism. Charles Murray and Nathan Glazer call for local solutions and self-help.[12] Butler and Kondratas call for better values in the family and community to eradicate the culture of poverty, and economic policies that provide incentives to work.[13]

Among conservatives, there is an almost complete oversight of the institutionalized nature of asset accumulation. Neoclassical economics suggests that individuals have different "propensities to accumulate," and this individual/motivational perspective reflects the ideology of the right. Conservatives tend to overlook the large asset transfers that are made to the non-poor in the form of mortgage interest tax deduction and retirement pension tax deferments. These large transfers are viewed as rightfully belonging to the non-poor, as if they had earned them. But similar transfers to the poor are rarely considered.

To be sure, the conservative right strongly supports the idea of savings and investment, but typically does not apply these concepts to the poor. In fact, the right usually does just the opposite. Taking a 1980s formulation of this ideology, a guiding principle of "supply-side economics" was to transfer money to the rich because the rich save and invest larger portions of their incomes. Such redistribution to the wealthy supposedly helps the impoverished because it spurs economic growth, eventually improving everyone's condition. However, this reasoning is not generally supported by economic facts. The rich did indeed become richer as a result of the 1981 tax act, but rates of saving and capital investment since 1981 have been depressed. Also, in the postwar decades, many countries with greater equality in income and wealth distribution, such as Japan and Sweden, have maintained higher ratios of investment to GNP than has the United States.

At this writing, however, a minority viewpoint is emerging on the conservative right that emphasizes empowerment of the poor through ownership. Jack Kemp, Secretary of Housing and Urban Development, is the leading figure in this movement. Secretary Kemp enthusiastically proposes the use of federal policy to promote property ownership among the poor. He sometimes uses the phrase "bleeding heart conservative" to describe his outlook. This is a decidedly different conservative voice. At this point, it is too early to tell whether Kemp's vision will substantially alter the welfare reform debate on the political right.

The Liberal Middle

The "liberal middle" covers a very large portion of the political spectrum, although in the climate of the 1980s this group found itself squeezed into a minority on the left. Although they do not often explicitly state it, liberals assume the legitimacy of a class structure and inequality. It might be said that liberals are reluctant capitalists in the sense that they believe in private ownership and market mechanisms, but they call on welfare policy to mediate some of the grosser inequalities generated by capitalism. Some mixture of planning and markets is preferred. Liberals tend to focus on the central government as the appropriate source of planning, although with the decline in federal support during the 1980s, the focus has shifted to state and local governments.

From the liberal perspective, the War on Poverty of the 1960s was not lost, but rather only half fought.[14] Marian Wright Edelman points out that many of the programs have worked very well.[15] For example, Medicaid and Food Stamps have improved child health and nutrition and lowered infant mortality. The poverty rate for those sixty-five and over plummeted from 35 percent in 1959 to 12 percent in 1984. Head Start and Job Corps are widely believed to have worked successfully.

In economic terms, liberals identify both unequal market outcomes and barriers to equal participation in the market. Therefore, the liberal paradigm comes in two basic forms: social policies that attempt to compensate for unequal effects of the market and social policies that attempt to remove barriers to equal opportunity.

The first approach—compensation for unequal market outcomes—is more common among liberals. Indeed, this is the guiding vision of the welfare state as we know it. The primary policy approach is income transfers. The assumption is that giving the poor more income makes them better off because it allows them to consume at higher levels.[16]

The second approach—promotion of equal opportunity—was a guiding vision of the War on Poverty during the 1960s. During the past twenty-five years, the concept of equal opportunity has been applied erratically, and in some areas, a backlash has occurred, such as with affirmative action. Today, the concept of equal opportunity is on the downswing, although it continues to be heard as a minority voice in the social policy debate. Taking recent examples, William J. Wilson concludes that the major source of the rise in social problems in the inner cities since the 1970s has been changes in the national economy, isolating the urban poor from viable employment opportunities.[17] Robert Haveman proposes a number of opportunity-oriented policy reforms.[18] In short, among liberals, institutional influences on poverty are sometimes recognized, usually through the theme of restricted opportunity.

Many liberals embrace some combination of the two approaches. In these cases, poverty and its possible solutions are intermittently seen in both individual and social terms. Individual suffering draws the attention of liberals, and many individual sufferings are interpreted as social issues. As C. Wright Mills puts it, liberals identify both personal troubles and public issues, whereas conservatives are less likely to interpret welfare issues as public issues.[19]

In general, liberals see more interconnections in society than do conservatives. To use a simple analogy, liberals sometimes see society as a boat. All the poor might be shoved to the back of the boat, but when the back starts taking on water, there is no advantage in sitting at the front.

Liberals have a version of the culture-of-poverty explanation. Michael Harrington talked about a "personality of poverty" that is fatalistic, does not plan ahead, does not trust others, and is pessimistic and prone to depression, and so forth.[20] This is also the view of Oscar

Lewis.[21] However, among liberals, the cause is often seen in structural terms; that is, the constraints of poverty are said to cause defeatist behaviors rather than vice versa.[22] This interpretation is sometimes called the *situation of poverty*, to distinguish it from the conservative view of individual causation.

Consistent with culture-of-poverty thinking, a reemergent theme among liberals is *case management*, known in earlier times as social casework. Case management involves a social worker in close contact with each family to help in problem solving and promotion of constructive behaviors. Following a period of de-emphasis in public policy, case management has recently become more popular.[23] At this writing, it is the latest theme in liberal policy proposals.

Another liberal theme is reminiscent of settlement house social work, such as Jane Addams's Hull House. For example, Roger Wilkins suggests turning schools into modern-day settlement houses (he does not use these words) by adding a wide range of social service programs. In Wilkins's vision, the schools would then become the central focus of community life.[24]

Among some liberals, however, a culture of poverty is not seen as the issue. They point out that there is little evidence that being on welfare increases one's dependence on public assistance.[25] The majority of children who grow up in dependent homes do not become dependent as adults, and social-psychological factors have not been shown to be either the cause or the effect of welfare recipiency. Greg Duncan and his colleagues interpret such findings as indicating a benign nature of most contact with welfare.[26] David Ellwood shows that welfare payments have not caused poverty or more single-parent families; instead, poverty is strongly related to unemployment and low wages.[27] Nonetheless, once on welfare, it is clear that single-parent families have a more difficult time in getting off welfare.[28] This speaks more to the problem of single-parent families than to a culture of poverty (see chapter 2).

Liberals today, like conservatives, propose using the states as demonstration sites or social policy laboratories, laying the groundwork for future federal policy development, just as Wisconsin did prior to the New Deal. Current welfare innovations in Wisconsin, Massachusetts, and even Mississippi are leading the nation's "welfare reform" movement. For example, in Wisconsin, a tough, mandatory standard for child support payments, including automatic wage withholding, has been implemented. This experiment is being carefully watched for application at the national level.

Nearly all the current welfare reform proposals from the liberal middle are related to work in some form.[29] For example, David Ellwood concludes that the current welfare system saps motivation to work, encourages family breakup, and isolates people from the mainstream. Ellwood suggests that policy should "make work pay" through tax credits, wage subsidies, day care support, a higher minimum wage, and the like.[30] Liberals generally would offer more choice and more support for work than conservatives, but few liberal policymakers take the position that AFDC mothers are needed more to raise children than to look for poverty-level employment.

Some liberals, accompanied by advocates from the radical left, are skeptical about the ability of the new work-oriented consensus on welfare to achieve its goals. They interpret this ideology as a deep-seated hostility to single female heads of families, who have never been accepted in American welfare policy. Work-related welfare policy represents the reemergence of that hostility.[31] From this perspective, the 1980s compromise on welfare is really more of a conservative victory because "it was achieved mainly through liberals' accepting the conservative idea that welfare can help trap people in long-term poverty."[32] The main result of the new consensus was the Family Support Act of 1988, which has a strong emphasis on work incentives.

According to some observers, this major compromise with conservatives means that liberals have abandoned the defense of the welfare state, leaving a political and intellectual vacuum. Piven and Cloward say bluntly that, during the 1980s, conservatives defined the debate, limited the perspective, and put liberals on the defensive.[33]

Whether work-related or not, the focus among liberals is decidedly on income rather than on assets. Assets of the poor are rarely mentioned. Most proposals are for more income transfers, more rent subsidies, more food stamps, and the like.

The Radical Left

At this writing, the ranks of the radical left are rapidly dwindling due to political events around the globe, most dramatically in Eastern Europe and the Soviet Union. If the left were more prominent, however, it would argue, as it always has, that large discrepancies in wealth are not an aberration, but rather a necessary and integral feature of capitalism. (Some conservatives would agree entirely; as the old saw goes, "if you go far enough left, you get right.") The fundamental viewpoint of the left is that economic conditions, particularly the distribution and use of capital, determine political, social, and ideological currents in society.

The left explicitly rejects the free functioning of markets in favor of centralized planning and decision making. Often, planning is preferred at the federal level. However, in response to the declining role of the central government in social welfare during the 1980s, more proposals for "local socialism" have arisen in the United States and Western Europe.

The traditional left view, coming from Marx and Lenin, is that the state is a political arm of the ruling class and steadfastly pursues the interests of that class. A key challenge to this interpretation is: Why are so many citizens in so many nations loyal to their country; why has nationalism been a more powerful force than class solidarity? These questions have led other Marxists to develop models of the capitalist state that are more subtle and complex, often involving the role of welfare policies.[34] Welfare policies are viewed as a device for social control through appeasement of working-class discontent. A typical view from the left is: "In general, welfare state programs represent an uneasy compromise between the demands of the economically vulnerable and the resistance of the economically powerful."[35]

From the viewpoint of the left, because the state cannot truly redistribute capital, there are contradictions in welfare capitalism and inherent limits on the size and nature of welfare programs. According to this view, the welfare state has covered up the faults of capitalism and then itself has become a problem, because it weakens the nation's capacity to accumulate an economic surplus (the typical analysis on the right and left is nearly identical in this regard). Legitimation of capitalism and accumulation of capital are seen as the two main tasks of the state. However, legitimation, in the form of welfare transfers, is in conflict with accumulation. Legitimation provides short-term stability of the system, but long-term weakness due to a shortfall in capital accumulation.[36]

There is a clear rejection of individually held capital on the left. No one has been more explicit on this point than Karl Marx, who was revolted by the idea of individually held capital; he graphically wrote that "capital comes dripping from head to foot, from every pore, with blood and dirt.''[37] From this viewpoint, capital is, above all else, the power to exploit.[38] Capital accumulation always occurs on the backs of exploited workers. It is inherently unequal and evil.

When focusing on capital and who has it, the radical left is more clear-headed than is the liberal middle about what is important, but, with reference to welfare policy, the merits of radical left thinking do not go much beyond this point.

The failure of the analysis on the radical left is that when wealth is analyzed, the focus is exclusively on the capitalist class. Generally, it is proposed or implied that wealth should be taken away from the rich, perhaps through revolution, or more moderately, through estate taxes and other direct taxes on wealth. The assumption is that the poor will have no capital until they take it away from the rich. Missing is any analysis of potential assets of the poor (other than those that might be taken away from the rich) and how such assets might be developed or maintained.

Along similar lines, the radical left, preoccupied by a perspective of conflict and class distinctions, consistently fails to recognize the importance of institutions. Thus, the institutionalized nature of asset accumulation, especially by the middle classes, is overlooked, and no attention is given to potential institutionalized asset accumulation by the poor.

Nonetheless, the left raises key questions in relation to the thinking in this book: Can capital *really* be redistributed under capitalism? Can a more democratic capitalism be achieved? For Marx, of course, the essence of capital was its domination over labor, an arrangement of production under which those with capital would consistently and systematically exploit the working class. This domination is essential to the system. If workers had more capital, they would not be a "reserve army of the unemployed," they could not be so easily exploited, and therefore, capitalists would never permit redistribution. Thus, Marxist theory poses an important question, and frankly, a great deal of historical evidence suggests that this interpretation is valid. How else, for example, is one to explain something as unsubstantiated, yet influential, as the idea of "supply-side economics"?

In response to this question from the left, it is necessary to specify the nature of modern Western economies more clearly, combining class analysis with analysis of labor markets and production, as well as knowledge of mediating institutions.[39] First, modern Western economies are not entirely capitalistic. Approximately one-third of the labor force in the United States is employed in either the public sector or the tax-supported not-for-profit sector. This huge percentage of non-private labor represents a wide range of essentially socialist mechanisms designed to accomplish what capitalistic markets do poorly (e.g., a national highway system, national defense, care of the poor) or to mediate the effects of capitalistic markets (e.g., food and drug regulations, environmental protection, protection of civil rights, assistance to the unemployed).

Second, maintaining a "reserve army of the unemployed" is less and less in the interests of capital because (1) with the expansion of the welfare state, large scale unemployment is expensive to maintain; and (2) physical labor is declining as a factor of production, while mental labor—working with the mind rather than the body—is becoming more important. Mental labor is not developed through policies that increase unemployment; mental labor must be nurtured and kept abreast of current knowledge and production processes. In short, capitalism cannot very well rely on a reserve army of unemployed thinkers.

These two developments, both relatively recent in origin, have rendered Marxism a less and less sufficient explanation of the relationship between capital and labor. Because the nature of production has changed, a different set of economic and social relationships is required for welfare capitalism. It is simply no longer in capital's interest to keep a large unemployed, uneducated population. Perhaps U.S. capitalists have not yet fully realized this tremendous change in the relationship between capital and labor, but there is little doubt that the Japanese have recognized it, and it is a major part of the explanation for their current economic success.

Conclusion

Each of the three basic positions in the welfare reform debate is useful for understanding different aspects of welfare ideology and policy. Each has its strengths and each has its shortcomings. Overall, a rigid ideological position in one particular category does not serve very well in coming to a full understanding of welfare issues and welfare policy. A more broadly-based interpretation is preferable.

What is noteworthy, however, is that *none of the major viewpoints pays attention to individually held assets of the poor*. Typical conservatives focus on assets, but only for the nonpoor;[40] liberals do not focus on assets at all; and the radical left prefers that capital be socially, rather than individually, controlled. Across the entire political spectrum, and in almost all academic studies, the lack of attention to individually held assets of the poor has been a significant oversight in the welfare reform debate.

Notes

1. Sheldon Danziger and Robert Plotnick, "Poverty and Policy: Lessons of the Last Two Decades," *Social Service Review* 60 (1), 1986, 34–51.

2. Herbert Spencer, *Social Statics*. New York: D. Appleton and Company, 1880 (first published in 1850), 353–56.

3. Thomas H. Huxley, *Evolution and Ethics and Other Essays*. New York: D. Appleton and Company, 1902 (first published in 1894), 36–37.

4. Nelson Aldrich, Jr., *Old Money: The Making of America's Upper Class*. New York: Knopf, 1988.

5. James Buchanan and Richard Wagner, *Democracy in Deficit: The Political Legacy of Lord Keynes*. New York: Academic Press, 1977. The analysis of interest group threats to capitalism has been made on numerous occasions from almost every political viewpoint; for example, on the far left by James O'Connor, *The Fiscal Crisis of the State*. New York: St. Martin's, 1973; on the nearer left by Frances Fox Piven and Richard A. Cloward, *The New Class War: Reagan's Attack on the Welfare State and Its Consequences*. New York: Pantheon, 1982; in the middle by Theodore Lowi, *The End of Liberalism*. New York: W.W. Norton, 1969; and on the right by Mancur Olson, *The Logic of Collective Action: Public Good and the Theory of Groups*. Cambridge: Harvard University Press, 1965. All these authors explicitly see democracy's entrance into economic decisions as a threat to the capitalist system. Indeed, this is one of the premiere themes in modern political economics. Overall, however, the argument is stronger and louder from the far right than from any other portion of the political spectrum.

6. Stuart Butler and Anna Kondratas, *Out of the Poverty Trap: A Conservative Strategy for Welfare Reform*. New York: Free Press, 1987. Butler and Kondratas's suggestion for a national consumption standard has many merits. Almost everyone would agree that the current income poverty definition is arbitrary. However, as Susan Mayer and Christopher Jencks point out (in "Poverty and the Distribution of Material Hardship," *Journal of Human Resources* 24, 1989, 88–114), income, by whatever standard it is measured, is not a good predictor of consumption.

7. George Gilder, *Wealth and Poverty*. New York: Basic Books, 1981.

8. Lawrence Mead, "The Logic of Workfare: The Underclass and Work Policy," *Annals of the American Academy of Political and Social Science* 501, 1989, 156–69.

9. Edward Banfield, *The Unheavenly City Revisited*. Boston: Little, Brown, 1974, 55–57.

10. Michael Morris and John Williamson, *Poverty and Public Policy: An*

Analysis of Federal Intervention Efforts. New York: Greenwood Press, 1986, 29–49.

11. This analysis is consistent with that of Herbert Gans "Positive Functions of Poverty," *American Journal of Sociology* 78, 1972, 275–89, who argues that some social groups benefit from poverty and therefore it is perpetuated.

12. Charles Murray, *Losing Ground: American Social Policy 1950–1980.* New York: Basic Books, 1984; Charles Murray, *In Pursuit of Happiness and Good Government.* New York: Simon and Schuster, 1988; and Nathan Glazer, *The Limits of Social Policy.* Cambridge, MA: Harvard University Press, 1988.

13. Butler and Kondratas, 1987.

14. Hyman Bookbinder, "Did the War on Poverty Fail?" *New York Times*, August 26, 1989, E23.

15. Marian Wright Edelman, *Families in Peril: An Agenda for Social Change.* Cambridge: Harvard University Press, 1987.

16. This assumption is questionable. For a variety of reasons, the empirical connection between income and consumption is much weaker than might be expected; see Mayer and Jencks, 1989 (also note 6 above). Therefore, income-based policy may be misguided even in its own terms, that is, it is not doing what liberals think it is doing.

17. William J. Wilson, *The Truly Disadvantaged: The Inner City, the Underclass, and Public Policy.* Chicago: University of Chicago Press, 1987; and Loïc J.D. Wacquant and William J. Wilson. "Beyond Welfare Reform: Poverty, Joblessness and the Social Transformation of the Inner City," a paper prepared for the Rockefeller Foundation Conference on Welfare Reform, Williamsburg, Virginia, February 1988.

18. Robert Haveman, *Starting Even: An Equal-Opportunity Program to Combat the Nation's New Poverty.* New York: Simon and Schuster, 1988.

19. C. Wright Mills, *The Sociological Imagination.* New York: Oxford University Press, 1959.

20. Michael Harrington, *The Other America.* New York: Macmillan, 1962.

21. Oscar Lewis, *La Vida.* New York: Random House, 1966.

22. Wilson, 1987.

23. Sar Levitan, Garth Mangum, and Marion Pines, *A Proper Inheritance: Investing in the Self-Sufficiency of Poor Families.* Washington: George Washington University, Center for Social Policy Studies, 1989; and Phoebe H. Cottingham and David T. Ellwood, eds., *Welfare Policy for the 1990s.* Cambridge: Harvard University Press, 1989.

24. Roger Wilkins, "The Black Poor Are Different," *New York Times*, August 22, 1989, Y23.

25. David T. Ellwood and Lawrence H. Summers, "Poverty in America: Is Welfare the Answer to the Problem?" Working Paper No. 1711. Cambridge, MA: National Bureau of Economic Research, 1985; Rebecca M. Blank, "How Important Is Welfare Dependence?" Working Paper No. 2026. Cambridge, MA: National Bureau of Economic Research, 1986.

26. Greg Duncan, Martha Hill, and Saul Hoffman, "Welfare Dependence within and across Generations," *Science* 239, 1988, 467–70.

27. David T. Ellwood, *Poor Support: Poverty in the American Family.* New York: Basic Books, 1988.

28. Mark Rank, "Family Structure and the Process of Exiting from Welfare," *Journal of Marriage and the Family* 48, 1986, 607–18.

29. The original notion of Aid to Dependent Children (later renamed Aid to Families with Dependent Children or AFDC) was that the problem of children in poverty was lack of resources. Beginning in 1967, the problem was redefined as a lack of employment on the part of impoverished parents. This focus on work has generally dominated the antipoverty policy debate since the 1960s.

30. Ellwood, 1988.

31. Joel Handler, "Consensus on Redirection—Which Direction," *Focus* 11(1), Spring 1988, 29–34; and Mimi Abramovitz, *Regulating the Lives of Women.* Boston: South End Press, 1988. Interestingly, from a different ideological perspective, a few conservatives also oppose workfare, not because it is anti-woman but because it is antifamily; see George Gilder, "The Collapse of the American Family," *The Public Interest* 89, Fall 1987, 20–25.

32. Nicholas Lemann, "Out of Sympathy," a review of Cottingham and Ellwood, eds., 1989, *The Atlantic Monthly*, July 1989, 91–94.

33. France Fox Piven and Richard Cloward, "The Contemporary Relief Debate," in Fred Block et al., *The Mean Season: The Attack on the Welfare State.* New York: Pantheon, 1987, 45–108.

34. See, for example, O'Connor, 1973.

35. Fred Block, Richard A. Cloward, Barbara Ehrenreich, and Frances Fox Piven, *The Mean Season: The Attack on the Welfare State.* New York: Pantheon Books, 1987, xi.

36. O'Connor, 1973.

37. Karl Marx, *Capital*, three volumes. New York: International Publishers, 1967 (originally published in German in 1867), vol. 1, 760.

38. Regarding the idea of capital as power, the Golden Rule of the Left has been stated: "The people who have the gold make the rules."

39. Ramesh Mishra, *The Welfare State in Crisis.* New York: St. Martin's Press, 1984, 176–78.

40. Again, Jack Kemp is an exception on the right because he does focus on assets of the poor.

PART II

DEVELOPMENT: WELFARE AS ASSETS

6 • The Nature and Distribution of Assets

As Alexis de Tocqueville observed more than 150 years ago, money and material goods are central to the culture of the United States.[1] As a nation, we are preoccupied with wealth and those who have it. Each year *Forbes* magazine publishes a list of the richest Americans. This list is certain to make the front page of daily newspapers and is discussed on morning talk shows. Overwhelmed by so many zeros, most of us have a difficult time distinguishing between millions and billions—they might as well be zillions—but we pay a great deal of attention to who has these millions and billions of dollars. A disproportional number of television shows are about the rich and ultrarich. On the newsstand we find a magazine called *Money*, but none called *Values*. The American dream is not to be born common and become noble, nor to be born ignorant and become smart, but to be born poor and become rich. It is a dream about financial wealth.

Another nineteenth-century observer, the German sociologist Max Weber, provided a useful foundation for understanding U.S. values and beliefs about economic and social life. According to Weber's well-known analysis, the spirit of capitalism is historically entwined with the Protestant Ethic.[2] During the Middle Ages, wealth and spirituality were seen by the Church as incompatible. The traditional Christian orientation to property was framed in terms of stewardship. However, with the rise of Protestantism and capitalism in Europe, this outlook was profoundly altered. Under Protestantism, hard work and the accumulation of wealth were seen not only as serving the individual, but also as serving society and God. The pursuit of personal wealth became imbued with the goodness of the Lord. Assets were sanctified and traditional Christian imagery was adapted to financial affairs—

wealth became an anchor in the storm, a growing tree, the wellspring, the rock.

When I was a boy growing up in a small midwestern town during the 1950s, my family regularly attended the First Methodist Church, and I heard these ideas often. I remember one incident in particular when I was very young, perhaps five or six years old, possibly it was during a session of Vacation Bible School. The teacher had a "felt board" on which she placed colorful cutouts to tell stories. On this particular day she told us about the house upon the sand and the house upon the rock. She said that the story was about saving money, and that saving money was how to build a house upon the rock. Two houses were placed on the felt board. A dark cloud appeared. Lightning flashed. The wind blew. The house upon the sand collapsed—the little felt cutout fell un-Christian-like to the floor. But the house upon the rock, where the money was saved, stood firmly through the storm.

Over time, the Christian basis for morality associated with capitalism has somewhat diminished. To an extent, the spirituality of capitalism has shifted to the products of capitalism themselves and the worship of entrepreneurs. An example of entrepreneur worship is George Gilder's best-selling book, *Wealth and Poverty*.[3] Such exuberant adoration for money-makers, detached from the religious basis of capitalism, is a relatively recent development. Even fifty years ago it would have been unseemly. But Weber saw the change coming long before. In his words, "Wealth and materials have gained an increasing and finally inexorable power over the lives of men as at no previous period in history. . . ."[4]

The focus of all this attention is not merely money, but the accumulation of money, which we typically call wealth or assets. Assets are the *stock* of wealth in a household or other unit. A moment to examine this concept may be helpful. According to the *Oxford English Dictionary*, the origin of the English usage for the word asset is found in the Anglo-French law phrase *aver assetz*, which means "to have sufficient," referring to the meeting of certain claims. The term was first used in the context of settling debts in an estate. Current usage is often in the plural, assets, and applies to current holdings and related claims against those holdings (liabilities), as illustrated in the structure of an accounting balance sheet. When all liabilities have been claimed against assets, the remainder is referred to as net assets or net worth, or "equity" in the case of a business. These concepts can apply to any level of economic organization, from an individual to an entire nation, or even the world. Our concern here, however, is centered on the welfare of individuals and families; therefore we focus on personal or self claims that remain in personal balance sheets after other claims are exercised. It is in this individualistic and household sense that assets are considered in this book.

Because this topic is so important in our culture, we have created dozens of words to talk about it. The word *assets* has many synonyms. These include words such as belongings, bounty, capital, coffers, cushion, equity, estate, fortune, goods, holdings, inheritance, investment, means, ownership, principal, property, possessions, resources, riches, savings, security, stake, stock, substance, sum, surplus, treasure, valuables, and wealth, as well as the word *money* and its many slang terms, including bread, bills, booty, bucks, cash, currency, dinero, dollar, dough, loot, lettuce, lucre, moolah, pesos, shekels, and wherewithal, to name only a few. To put this long list of synonyms in cultural perspective, the number of different terms we use for financial matters may be exceeded only by the number of different terms we use for sexuality, and even then it would be a close contest.

In this book, I prefer to use the accounting term, assets. In part, this choice is made because assets is a more precise term than many of the others, and can be more clearly distinguished from the term income. Income refers to flows of money, goods, or services, while assets refer to stocks of wealth or accumulations. However, some of the synonyms for assets listed above suggest that an asset is more than just an accounting idea. Some of the synonyms have distinct social and psychological content—for example, the words cushion, security, and stake—and these words become clues for exploring the effects of assets in individual and family lives (a discussion to which we turn in chapter 8). At present, our attention is given to what assets are and how they are distributed.

The Relationship of Income and Assets

Income and assets are closely associated ideas. Income can be saved to accumulate assets, creating a storehouse for future consumption. In turn, many assets generate flows of income. Indeed, most neoclassical economists would not make much of a distinction between income and assets. The common perspective is that both income and assets repre-

Figure 6.1. **The Relationship of Income and Assets: Two Continua with an Area of Similarity**

Income			Assets		
		Area of Similarity			
			Fully restricted assets	Partially restricted assets	Unrestricted assets
Unstable income	More stable income	Entitlement income			
Stability ⟶			⟵		Restrictiveness

sent potential for consumption. However, this viewpoint seems at odds with our experience in everyday life. Even the most unimaginative accountant knows that there are very important differences between income and assets, as does the entire business world. To take one illustration, a company with weak income flows but substantial net assets is quite different from a company with strong income flows but few net assets. When pressed on this point, even neoclassical economists agree that it is better to have assets than an equivalent expectation of income flows because the current possession of assets allows more choice and flexibility.

However, economists are correct in their perception that the line between income and assets is not as clear-cut as an accountant would sometimes draw it. Instead, it might be better to think of income and assets along two continua that have an area of similarity (see Figure 6.1). Income is on the left continuum, and assets are on the right continuum. The key dimension for income is stability, and the key dimension for assets is restrictedness. Income and assets almost meet in the middle, where the difference is blurred—a stable entitlement income is, in some respects, similar to a fully restricted asset.

Let us look first at income. On the far left side of the continuum is unstable or irregular income, such as intermittent labor income or irregular business income. Moving toward the right, the next entry on the continuum is stable income, such as income from regular employment. Still further to the right is entitlement income. Entitlement income, from private or public sources, is the most stable of all because it is protected as a legal right. An entitlement is typically for a specific purpose (retirement, disability, dependency, or other). A key characteristic of an entitlement is that *the underlying financial assets are never individually held and controlled.* Indeed, in the case of most public sector entitlements, there are no underlying financial assets, but rather a system of promises for payments out of future revenue flows. Thus, although legally stable, entitlements are to some extent vulnerable to loss. For example, some companies go bankrupt prior to meeting their pension obligations, and it is by no means clear that the Social Security retirement system will be able to fulfill its projected benefit levels when the baby boom generation retires in the next century.

Crossing the gap to the assets continuum, the first entry is fully restricted assets. These are assets that are individually held, but the individual cannot take direct possession of the underlying assets, such as in the case of an annuity retirement plan. In this regard, a fully restricted asset is similar to an entitlement—both are legal guarantees and can generate a flow of income for a specific purpose. However, the key difference is that the underlying assets of an entitlement, if they exist at all, are not individually held, whereas the underlying assets of an annuity plan *are* individually held. This difference is critical from the standpoint of the recipient. The sense of personal control on the part of the individual is greater in an annuity plan than in an entitlement plan.

Moving to the right, the next entry on the assets continuum is partially restricted assets. In this case, assets are designated for specific purposes and the individual does not have unencumbered access. Restrictions generally derive from particular tax treatments. A good example is an Individual Retirement Account (IRA), which is designated for retirement purposes. In an IRA, the individual completely controls the underlying assets, but the money cannot be used for other purposes unless the individual is willing to pay a penalty amount—10 percent of the withdrawal in this case. Somewhat similar to IRAs are defined-contribution retirement plans, wherein the funds are held in individual accounts, investment decisions are controlled to some extent by the individual, and the money is usually available only for retirement. However, under certain conditions—hardship, medical bills, or education—the underlying assets may be available prior to retirement. Another type of partially restricted asset is home equity. This asset enjoys tax benefits in several forms, including income tax deductions for mortgage interest and property taxes, and deferment and exclusion of capital gains. Tied to these benefits, certain restrictions are imposed on selling the home without paying additional taxes. It is in this category of partially restricted assets that most American households have accumulated most of their assets, greatly assisted by tax expenditures (see chapter 4).

Finally, at the far right side of the continuum are unrestricted assets, individually held, which have no special legal constraints on how they are invested, when the money is available, or for what purposes it is available. This category represents investments in all manner of financial securities, real property, and other assets. As shown later in this chapter, unrestricted assets, particularly in the form of capital wealth, are greatly skewed in distribution toward the rich. Most of the population holds only a small amount of unrestricted assets.

Definitions and Types of Assets

Assets are not things in themselves, nor are they the possession of things. More precisely, assets are rights or claims related to property, concrete or abstract. These rights or claims are enforced by custom, convention, or law.[5] "Private property is then a person's socially enforceable claim to use, or to exclude others from the use of, or to receive the benefits of, certain rights."[6] As R.H. Tawney observed:

> Property is the most ambiguous of categories. It covers a multitude of rights which have nothing in common except that they are exercised by persons and enforced by the State. Apart from these formal characteristics, they vary indefinitely in economic character, in social effect, and in moral justification. They may be conditional like the grant of patent rights, or absolute like the ownership of grounded rents, terminable like a copyright, or permanent like a freehold, as comprehensive as sovereignty or as restricted as an easement, as intimate and personal as the ownership of clothes and books, or as remote and intangible as shares in a goldmine or rubber plantation.[7]

Assets comprise capital for investment which, in turn, generates future flows of income. Whether current asset holdings increase in real value over time depends on successful investment. Money under the mattress will not do the job. Capital is not just money, but money *in action*. Capital is the continuous retransformation of money into production and back into money. In other words, capitalism is a process.[8]

The Spanish term for assets, *activos*, captures this meaning of the word.[9]

Conceptually, there are several ways to cut the asset pie. Assets can be divided into individual versus social, little versus big, or other dichotomies. For the purposes of this discussion, a useful distinction is tangible versus intangible. Each type of asset can be categorized (as in all matters of categorization, debatably) as either tangible or intangible. In addition, each type of asset can be viewed as generating a particular form of earnings.

Tangible Assets

Tangible assets are legally held and include physical property as well as rights that function in much the same way as physical property. These can be thought of in eight principal categories, as follows:

1. *Money savings, with earnings in the form of interest.* This category includes all cash, savings accounts, checking accounts, and money market instruments.

2. *Stocks, bonds, and other financial securities, with earnings in the form of dividends, interest, and/or capital gains (or losses).* Stock ownership in the current business world is really more a form of lending than owning, because for the vast majority of shareholders, stock ownership provides no genuine decision-making power—modern companies are run by managers who are often far removed from responsibility to "owners." In this light, stocks are more like bonds. Regardless, all such securities can be viewed as claims on the property of private or public corporations.

3. *Real property, including buildings and land, with earnings in the form of rent payments plus capital gains (or losses).* For most people, the key asset in this category is equity in an owner-occupied house.

4. *"Hard" assets other than real estate, with earnings in the form of capital gains (or losses).* In this category are non-interest-bearing assets such as precious metals, jewelry, art, fine furniture, and all collectibles.

5. *Machines, equipment, and other tangible components of production, with earnings in the form of profits on the sale of products plus capital gains (or losses).* This is the category closest to "capital" in the production sense and it is directly owned by only a small portion of

the population, although many more participate indirectly through stock ownership, primarily through pension plans.

6. *Durable household goods, with earnings in the form of increased efficiency of household tasks.* In some respects, durable household goods are, for the household sector, analogous to machines and equipment in the business sector—both require the expenditure of financial capital, both are intended to increase efficiency, and both have long-term but not indefinite usefulness.

7. *Natural resources, such as farmland, oil, minerals, and timber, with earnings in the form of profit on sale of crops or extracted commodities plus capital gains (or losses).* Prior to the industrial revolution, a large portion of the nation's total wealth was in the form of small landholdings, widely distributed. Land and natural resources make up a much smaller proportion of total wealth today, and the distribution has greatly narrowed.

8. *Copyrights and patents, with earnings in the form of royalties and other user fees.* This category of "intellectual property" is listed, somewhat arbitrarily, under tangible assets because copyrights and patents are protected by explicit legal rights.[10]

Intangible Assets

Intangible assets are more nebulous, not legally held, and often based imprecisely on individual characteristics or social and economic relations. At least six categories of intangible assets can be identified, as follows:

1. *Access to credit (other people's capital), with earnings depending on the use of the credit (the nature of the investment).* Access to credit cannot be precisely defined, but it is certainly not distributed evenly. Access to credit is largely related to possession of other forms of assets. As the infamous Rule of Borrowing states: "To him that hath shall be lent." Joseph Schumpeter saw credit, not money, as the basis of capitalism: "Capitalism is that form of private economy in which innovations are carried out by means of borrowed money, which in general, though not by logical necessity, implies credit creation."[11] Schumpeter focused on the use of credit by entrepreneurs in stimulating innovation and economic growth.

2. *Human capital, which is generally defined as intelligence, edu-*

cational background, work experience, knowledge, skill, and health, but might also include energy, vision, hope, and imagination, with earnings in the form of salary or other compensation for work, services, or ideas provided. The recognition of human resources as the primary wealth of nations is not new; it was a common theme among mercantilist economists.[12] Modern approaches are more quantitative and more theoretically rigorous. Gary Becker of the University of Chicago is sometimes considered the father of modern human capital theory. Becker calculates that most of the nation's wealth is embodied in skills and training that generate present and future earnings. This human wealth, according to Becker, constitutes 75 percent or more of the United States' total wealth, the rest consisting of corporate capital, capital in unincorporated businesses, housing, consumer durables, government capital, and cash. The Commerce Department estimates total U.S. nonhuman wealth at about $15 trillion in 1989, which would make human capital worth close to $45 trillion by Becker's estimate. Whether or not this is precisely accurate, human capital is probably the most important form of capital in the world economy.[13]

3. *Cultural capital, in the form of knowledge of culturally significant subjects and cues, ability to cope with social situations and formal bureaucracies, including vocabulary, accent, dress, and appearance, with earnings in the form of acceptance into rewarding patterns of associations.* Pierre Bourdieu has proposed this idea as a basis for social organization.[14] Cultural capital is somewhat similar to human capital, but it is not oriented toward capabilities so much as toward appearances and behaviors. In short, it is the ability to know and practice the values and behaviors of the dominant group. I refer to this as the *management of appearances*, the behavioral underpinnings of acceptance. Bourdieu has incisively argued that reading and adapting to cues on taste, style, and behavior are central to all social and economic relationships.[15] Obtaining a good job depends not only on education and ability, but on presenting the correct appearance and saying the right words to the right person in the right tone of voice. Some people instinctively manage appearances perfectly, while others fail to read the cultural environment and are hopelessly off cue and inappropriate. For example, one study suggests the idea of cultural capital as a competing view, perhaps stronger than human capital, in explaining schooling success.[16]

4. *Informal social capital in the form of family, friends, contacts*

and connections, sometimes referred to as a "social network," with earnings in the form of tangible support, emotional support, information, and easier access to employment, credit, housing, or other types of assets. Recently, the concept of social capital has been more formally developed by Mark Granovetter[17] and James Coleman,[18] who suggest that informal social relationships can be critical in creating the potential for individual social and economic activity. Informal social capital comes in various forms and serves different purposes for different groups. The well-to-do tend to be well connected, which means that they have easier access to scarce goods, services, and opportunities. On the other hand, the very poor may depend on a social network for survival. As Carol Stack has demonstrated in her classic study, *All Our Kin*, the trading of goods and services in a network pervades the social-economic life of the urban poor.[19] Trading refers to the offering of goods or services with the intent to obligate. It is, in one sense, a contractual relationship, based on offer and acceptance, with enforcement of the obligation left to kinship or community pressure. In some respects, this pattern of trading is analogous to a social insurance institution for a poor person, allowing her to call on others for assistance because she has paid her premium by having supplied goods or services in the past.[20]

5. *Formal social capital, or organizational capital, which refers to the structure and techniques of formal organization applied to tangible capital, with earnings in the form of profits through increased efficiency.* For example, John Tomer describes organizational relations and capabilities as organizational capital.[21] Such capital is widely held to explain the success of business organizations in Japan. Unfortunately, social capital in organizations tends to be overlooked in the United States, where the stronger orientation is toward the individual. Most economic analyses, which dominate discussions of wealth and productivity, do not focus on organizational interactions.[22]

6. *Political capital in the form of participation, power, and influence, with earnings in the form of favorable rules and decisions on the part of the state or local government.* Mortimer Adler includes as a form of wealth the political climate, including justice, civil peace, liberty, and security of life and limb.[23] Some individuals enjoy more of this political capital than do others. In many cases, political capital is viewed as intimately connected with financial capital. Karl Marx believed that financial capital was the source of political power. Con-

versely, Frances Fox Piven and Richard Cloward suggest that political power in democratic states has led to greater economic power for the poor.[24]

The types of tangible and intangible assets listed above are somewhat arbitrary. They could be revised, emphasizing one type more than another; some categories might be combined; others might be added. One can imagine, for example, other types of assets in the form of traditional values, spiritual enlightenment, charismatic appeal, and even physical attractiveness.[25] Indeed, as in the case of most typologies, it is possible to see almost everything through this lens. However, the meaning of the original construct tends to become obscured in the process. It is therefore preferable, in the context of a given discussion, to limit the meaning of the focal term, as we will do in the case of assets. But first, let us turn to a note on the fluidity of assets.

Fluidity of Assets

Types of assets shift over time. The categories are not as rigidly bounded as they might appear in a typology. Instead, different types of assets are interconnected, intertwined, fluid, and synergistic. This can be illustrated by example. Because it is sometimes easier to see key relationships in unfamiliar settings, let us briefly examine a small village in a developing nation (this is actually where the idea of asset fluidity first became apparent to me).

Benito Juarez is a small pueblo in the Sierra Madre del Sur of Oaxaca in southern Mexico. By the standards of an industrial nation, the community is very poor. However, the people of Benito Juarez have been exceptionally successful in organizing themselves into a highly functional community. They have saved and invested both the time (human capital) and the money (financial capital) to create relatively productive agriculture and forestry. They also have planted fruit trees and have learned to build furniture (natural resources, formal social organization, and business equipment). As a result, they are relatively well off; they live at a higher standard of living than do their neighbors in nearby communities. They also have good medical care (contributing to human capital), in large part because the federal health program places a very capable doctor in Benito Juarez—villagers complain (political capital) when they do not have a good doctor. Most of the people now boil their water, and gastrointestinal illness has been almost entirely eliminated (contributing to human capital). A healthier community allows more hours to be devoted to the development of schools, roads, agricultural improvements, and housing in the community (real property and physical capital in the from of infrastructure). Due partly to Benito Juarez's success, the village has attracted some attention from outside the immediate region (informal social capital). For example, an architect took an interest in the village and she raised money (financial capital) and designed a children's nursery, greenhouse, and improved sanitary facilities, which the villagers constructed (buildings and real property, which contribute directly to human capital in the form of health and education). Connections with Israeli friends (more informal social capital) led to training in construction of an Israeli-designed stove which uses local materials, cooks more efficiently, produces less smoke, and uses less firewood. Many of the villagers now use these improved stoves (better durable goods). A visitor to Benito Juarez can see these dynamic interconnections of various types of assets at work.

Although the nature of the assets may vary from one place and time to another, similar asset fluidity and synergism occur in all situations. Some of these interconnections are described as explicit theoretical propositions in chapter 8, where financial assets are viewed as having a number of specific welfare effects. Consistent with the discussion here, many of these welfare effects could be thought of as assets in different forms.

The Definition of Assets in This Book

As noted above, assets can be a very broad idea. The concept of assets has been applied to nearly everything of any conceivable value, concrete or abstract, including personal, social, cultural, and political characteristics, as well as all categories of tangible wealth. The wide-ranging literature on this topic comes from accounting, economics, sociology, political science, and philosophy. There is no single correct definition of assets. The appropriate definition depends on usage in a particular context.

Regarding the theory and policy proposals in the current discussion, the usage is limited to tangible assets, primarily financial assets (money savings and financial securities) for two reasons. First, through this limitation, theoretical speculations can be tied more directly to traditional economics, thus grounding the theory in somewhat known and accepted footing. Second, on the more practical side, focusing on financial assets is what social policy can do best and with the least bureaucracy. Thus, the policies proposed in later chapters (see chapters 9, 10, and 11) would facilitate accumulation of financial assets. However, because assets are often fluid and synergistic, the intent of the policy is to stimulate development of other types of assets, such as human capital, in the form of education, and real property, in the form of housing equity.

The Pattern of Asset Distribution

Scarcity of Data

The debate among economists who study assets is heavily theoretical. Indeed, portions of the debate are oddly contorted, removed from intuitive perceptions of reality. The reason, says Robert Haveman, is that regular, systematic data on asset distributions are not available.[26]

It is not entirely clear why a systematic asset data base has never been collected. One reason is that accurate figures on assets are difficult to obtain in survey research many individuals simply do not know the scope and nature of their financial holdings. A second reason is that many people, perhaps especially the wealthy, tend to avoid public scrutiny of their wealth. A third reason is that there are few advocates for the collection of asset-based data, and most of these advocates are academic researchers and theorists with limited political influence. Partly for these reasons, and perhaps others, most data collection in the study of inequality is income-based rather than asset-based.

Only a few inequality analysts have questioned the usefulness of income-based data, or considered the possibility that some other measure of inequality might shed a different, and perhaps more useful, light on the issues. Early exceptions are Burton Weisbrod and W. Lee Hanson, and Marilyn Moon,[27] who suggest a combined income and net worth approach to measuring economic welfare. Recent contributions have been made by Susan Mayer and Christopher Jencks,[28] who suggest measuring consumption directly; and Edward Wolff[29] and Daniel Radner,[30] who suggest combining income and asset measures.

Fortunately, however, selected studies, several intermittent surveys, and the work of a handful of key researchers—people such as Robert Lampman, James D. Smith, and Edward Wolff—do provide at least a minimal understanding of how assets have been distributed in the United States. To this information we now turn.

Historical Trends

The settlement of the American frontier began with a relatively egalitarian distribution of wealth. As time passed, selected families consolidated their wealth and inequalities grew larger.[31] This pattern probably continued in most regions of the country until industrialization began.

As factories began to appear on the eastern seaboard of America, Karl Marx wrote that industrialization leads inevitably to "immiserization of the proletariat" and greater inequality. On the other hand, one hundred years later and with the benefit of hindsight, Simon Kuznets suggested that industrialization leads eventually to reduced economic inequality.[32] Evidence indicates that Kuznets was more nearly correct than was Marx. A study of data from sixty-six nations is generally consistent with Kuznets's view.[33] Overall, the trend in industrial societies has been toward decreasing concentrations of wealth.[34]

With industrialization, workers in industrial economies have produced much larger surpluses than have workers in agricultural societies. Simultaneously, concentrations of wealth have been reduced, possibly because industrial workers have greater skills and thus more bargaining power.[35] From a different perspective, access to political rights in democratic states, over time, may have altered access to economic rights—that is, the rich may have had a portion of their wealth voted away.[36]

In a major international study, the most thorough to date, a key finding is the gradual but persistent improvement in the degree of wealth equality among households during the twentieth century. This conclusion is based primarily on data for Sweden, the United Kingdom, and the United States, the countries for which the best time-series information is available. In Sweden, the share of household wealth held by the top 1 percent fell from 50 percent in 1920 to 21 percent in 1975. In the United Kingdom, the share of the top 1 percent fell from 61 percent in 1923 to 23 percent in 1980. In the United States, the share of the top 1 percent fell from 36 percent in 1929 to 19 percent in 1976.[37]

The types of U.S. household assets have also changed over time. In 1900, unincorporated business assets accounted for 34.6 percent of all household assets, but pension reserves were still zero. By 1988, unincorporated business assets had declined to 7.6 percent, and pension reserves had reached 14.5 percent. Housing assets rose to a century high 20.6 percent by 1988.[38]

Short-term fluctuations are somewhat less certain. Looking at several data bases from 1962 to 1983, Edward Wolff concludes that inequality in U.S. household net worth remained about the same between 1962 and 1973, declined "rather substantially" between 1973 and 1979, and then increased "quite sharply" between 1979 and 1983. In 1983, wealth inequality was about the same as it had been in 1962.[39] Much has been made in the media about an apparent "reversal" of the historic pattern of U.S. wealth distribution, with greater inequality arising during the 1980s.[40] However, to the extent that this pattern exists, it is more likely a short-term fluctuation than a historic reversal.

The Current Pattern of Asset Distribution

Despite the long-term trend toward greater asset equality, huge differences in household wealth remain. In general, the pattern of asset distribution is related to the pattern of income distribution; that is, those with low incomes tend to have few assets and those with high incomes tend to have many assets. However, asset distribution is much more unequal than is income distribution. To summarize very simply, the richest 5 percent of Americans receive about the same income as the bottom 40 percent, but the richest 1 percent own more assets than the bottom 80 percent.

It may be helpful to look at asset distribution statistics in some detail. The only way to do this is to present the relevant figures and tables. At times, the numbers and terminology become a little thick, and it may seem like slow going over the next several pages. A bit of persistence on the part of the reader might be required. Hopefully, the effort will pay off in an improved understanding of who owns what assets in the United States.

According to data from the Survey of Income and Program Participation (SIPP), reported by the U.S. Bureau of the Census, in 1984,

Table 6.1

Distribution of Household Net Worth, 1984

Household net worth*	Percentage of households
Zero or negative	11.0
$1 to $4,999	15.3
$5,000 to $9,999	6.4
$10,000 to $24,999	12.4
$25,000 to $49,999	14.5
$50,000 to $99,999	19.3
$100,000 to $249,999	15.3
$250,000 or more	5.9

Source: U.S. Bureau of the Census, 1986. "Household Wealth and Asset Owner-ship, 1984." *Current Population Reports, Household Economic Studies*, Series P-70, no. 7. Washington, DC: U.S. Government Printing Office, using data from the 1984 supplement to the Survey of Income and Program Participation (SIPP).

*Household net worth in this survey does not include equities in pension plans, or cash value of life insurance policies, jewelry, or home furnishings.

median household net worth in the United States was $32,670 (not including equities in pension plans or cash value of life insurance policies, jewelry, or home furnishings).[41] Equity in a home accounted for a remarkable 41 percent of all household net worth in the country. Other significant proportions were in interest-earning assets (17 percent), businesses (10 percent), rental property (9 percent), stocks (7 percent), and vehicles (6 percent). In 1984, 11.0 percent of households had zero or negative net worth, and 5.9 percent had net worth in excess of $250,000 (Table 6.1).

Assets are very unevenly distributed by race. According to the Census Bureau, in 1984 the median white household had a net worth of $39,135. This figure was eight times higher than the $4,913 net worth of the median Hispanic household, and twelve times higher than the $3,397 net worth of the median black household. Whereas only 8.4 percent of white households reported zero or negative net worth, 23.9 percent of Hispanic households reported zero or negative net worth, as did 30.5 percent of black households.[42]

Table 6.2 illustrates the overall pattern of asset distribution in 1983, based on the Federal Reserve Board's Survey of Consumer Finances (SCF). The top 20 percent of the population held 74.7 percent of the assets, nearly three times more than the bottom 80 percent held. The

Table 6.2

Total Household Wealth Distribution, 1983

Portion of population	Percentage of wealth
Bottom 20 percent	0.1
Fourth 20 percent	3.0
Middle 20 percent	6.9
Second 20 percent	14.2
Top 20 percent	74.7
Top 5 percent	49.1
Top 1 percent	28.3

Source: Wolff, Edward N., 1987. "Estimates of Household Wealth Inequality in the U.S., 1962–1983," *Review of Income and Wealth* 33 (3): 231–42, using data from the 1983 Federal Reserve Board's Survey of Consumer Finances (SCF), adjusted estimates.

top 5 percent held 49.1 percent of all assets, and the top 1 percent held 28.3 percent.

The picture of asset distribution is enhanced by looking at types of wealth. Wolff reports Gini coefficients for adjusted 1983 SCF wealth estimates.[43] Gini coefficients are measures of inequality, where 0 equals complete equality and 1 equals complete inequality.[44] Wolff's figures are as follows: The Gini coefficient for all wealth is 0.72; fungible wealth (defined as total wealth minus consumer durables and household inventories) is 0.80; financial wealth (defined as fungible wealth minus owner-occupied housing equity) is 0.91; and capital wealth (defined as financial wealth minus cash savings and cash surrender value of pension funds and insurance) is 0.94. As a rough summary of these statistics, it can be said that asset inequality increases rather sharply when housing and consumer goods are not taken into consideration.

As illustrated in Table 6.3, the distribution of capital wealth (primarily nonpension stocks and bonds, and nonowner-occupied real estate) in 1983 was as follows: The top 20 percent held 95.1 percent of all capital wealth; the top 5 percent held 78.6 percent; and the top 1 percent held 49.9 percent. Thus, possession of capital wealth (other than indirect capital wealth in pension and insurance funds) is highly concentrated—most households have little or no capital wealth, and a few households have a great deal.

Table 6.3

Distribution of Capital Wealth, 1983

Portion of population	Percentage of wealth*
Bottom 20 percent	0.0
Fourth 20 percent	0.1
Middle 20 percent	0.4
Second 20 percent	4.4
Top 20 percent	95.1
Top 5 percent	78.6
Top 1 percent	49.9

Source: Wolff, Edward N., 1987. "Estimates of Household Wealth Inequality in the U.S., 1962–1983," *Review of Income and Wealth* 33 (3): 231–42, using data from the 1983 Federal Reserve Board's Survey of Consumer Finances (SCF), adjusted estimates.

*Capital wealth consists primarily of non-pension-fund stocks and bonds, nonowner-occupied real estate, "hard" investment assets such as precious metals and collectables, and cash equivalents (cash, savings, and money market accounts).

This picture is corroborated by another study of the 1984 SIPP data. Melvin Oliver and Thomas Shapiro report that 34 percent of American households have zero or negative net financial assets (defined as "those assets normally available for use," and not including equity in homes or automobiles). For white households, 30 percent have zero or negative net financial assets; and for black households, the figure is a remarkable 67 percent. Among single-parent households, 68 percent have zero or negative net financial assets.[45] For these millions of American families, there is no financial backup whatsoever on a day-to-day basis. When the household income stream is interrupted, there is an immediate financial crisis.

Assets of Income-Poor and Income-Nonpoor Households

Although the following figures are in some respects misleading, it is useful to look at asset holdings of income-poor and income-nonpoor households.[46] Data in Table 6.4 are from a detailed study employing the 1983 SCF data.[47] According to these figures, the mean or average wealth of income-poor households was $35,719, about one-sixth of the mean wealth of $232,270 among income-nonpoor households (unlike

Table 6.4

Mean Wealth of Income-Poor and Income-Nonpoor Households, 1983
(percentages)

	Poor	Nonpoor
Housing equity	$12,021	$43,403
	(33.7%)	(18.7%)
Pension wealth*	$5,517	$69,208
	(15.4%)	(29.8%)
Marketable net worth other than housing equity and pension wealth	$18,181	$119,659
	(50.9%)	(51.5%)
Total	$35,719	$232,270
	(100.0%)	(100.0%)

Source: Adapted from Wolff, Edward N., 1990. "Wealth Holdings and Poverty Status in the U.S.," *Review of Income and Wealth* (unpublished at this writing), based on an earlier draft presented at the 20th General Conference of the International Association for Research on Income and Wealth, in Roca di Papa, Italy, August 1987.

*Pension wealth does not include Social Security retirement benefits; pension wealth is calculated as the present value of expected benefits with a net discount rate of zero.

the SIPP data reported above, these figures include all assets plus Social Security entitlement benefits).

However, the mean figures do not capture the whole picture. As with the population as a whole, assets in both income-poor and income-nonpoor families are unevenly distributed. In 1983, the Gini coefficient for net worth of all income-poor families was 0.60; and for income-nonpoor families it was 0.63. Among both the income-poor and the income-nonpoor groups, the top 20 percent held 67 percent of the assets. Indeed, the mean marketable net worth of the top 10 percent of income-poor families was an astounding $202,000—a figure which raises questions about the usefulness of income poverty statistics. On the other hand, most of the income poor in 1983 had hardly any net worth at all.[48]

This can be illustrated by comparing mean (average) and median (midpoint) fungible wealth. Fungible wealth is marketable net worth less household durables and inventory. The logic of the concept of fungible wealth is that it is the wealth *available for use*, omitting items that are sunk costs. In 1983, the mean fungible wealth of the income poor was $21,139, but the median fungible wealth was only $797.[49] In other words, half of the income poor had a marketable net worth of

Table 6.5

Median Net Worth by Monthly Household Income Level and Race, 1984

	Total	White	Hispanic	Black
Less than $900	$5,080	$8,443	$453	$88
$900 to $1,999	24,647	30,714	3,677	4,218
$2,000 to $3,999	46,744	50,529	24,805	15,977
$4000 or more	123,474	128,237	99,492	58,758

Source: U.S. Bureau of the Census, 1986. "Household Wealth and Asset Owner-ship, 1984." *Current Population Reports, Household Economic Studies*, Series P-70, no. 7. Washington, DC: U.S. Government Printing Office.

less than $797 if household goods were not taken into consideration. This is not much of a cushion against hard times.

SIPP data on median net worth by household income corroborate this picture. In 1984, for households with less than $900 in monthly income, the median net worth was only $5,080 overall, only $453 for Hispanics, and a paltry $88 for blacks (Table 6.5). Thus, low-income minorities are much less likely than are low-income whites to hold any assets at all.[50]

Home Equity

According to SIPP data for 1984, across the entire population, home ownership accounted for 41.3 percent of total net worth (not including equity in pension plans, life insurance policies, jewelry, or home furnishings). During that year, 64.3 percent of U.S. households owned their own home. Home ownership was associated with a huge difference in household net worth. In 1984, the median net worth of home owners was $63,253, but the median net worth of renters was only $1,921.[51]

In 1983, according to SCF data, 67.6 percent of the income nonpoor lived in owner-occupied housing, as did a surprising 38.3 percent of the income poor. Mean net equity in owner-occupied housing for the income-nonpoor was $43,403, and for the income poor it was $12,021 (Table 6.4). Housing equity made up 18.7 percent of total wealth in nonpoor households, and 33.7 percent of total wealth in poor households. Thus, fewer of the income-poor own their homes, but the limited wealth that *some* of the income-poor hold tends to be in owner-occupied housing.

This housing wealth of the income poor is unevenly distributed. More than 60 percent of the income poor have no housing equity at all. By age, 62.6 percent of the elderly poor, but only 30.0 percent of the nonelderly poor, were home owners in 1983. By geographical location, 48.2 percent of the rural poor; 40.8 percent of the suburban poor; and only 23.9 percent of the urban poor were home owners.[52] Thus, equity in poor people's housing is disproportionately found among the elderly and in rural areas. Young urban families who are income-poor are much less likely to be home owners.

Pension Assets

In 1983, according to SCF data, for those above the income poverty line, mean pension wealth was $69,208. For those below the income poverty line, mean pension wealth was $5,517 (Table 6.4; Social Security entitlement benefits not included). Pension wealth made up 29.8 percent of total wealth in nonpoor households and 15.4 percent of total wealth in poor households.[53]

Possession of pension assets is also strongly associated with possession of other types of assets. According to SIPP data, among income-poor households, those not covered by an employer-provided pension plan have roughly one-third as much net worth ($12,898 versus $38,176, exclusive of the pension plan) as do income-poor households that are covered by an employer-provided pension plan.[54]

Assets of the Welfare Poor

Detailed studies of assets of the welfare poor (means-tested welfare recipients) are rare. Asset limits for eligibility for public assistance effectively curtail asset accumulation. Housing equity and tools of a trade are sometimes excluded from asset limits, but all liquid assets, such as bank accounts, stocks, and bonds count toward the limit. For example, in a study of Food Stamp recipients versus nonrecipients based on the 1979 spring wave of the SIPP, nearly half the Food Stamp recipients had no countable assets at all; 91 percent had $500 or less.[55] Because Food Stamp eligibility extends higher on the income scale than does AFDC eligibility, it is likely that AFDC families, on average, hold even fewer assets.

Summary and Interpretation

As illustrated in this chapter, nearly 50 percent of all household assets (not including Social Security entitlement benefits) are in the form of owner-occupied housing and retirement pensions. Asset accumulation in these forms is facilitated directly and substantially by tax policy (see chapter 4). Moreover, because capital wealth is so concentrated (Table 6.3), the average figures are highly misleading. Most U.S. households have little or no capital wealth and hold the bulk of their net worth in housing equity and pensions. Also, as discussed in chapter 7, a large portion of total household assets is inherited—estimates vary between 20 percent and 80 percent.

Altogether, it seems reasonable to estimate that housing equity, pensions, and inheritance account for somewhere between 50 percent and 90 percent of all household net worth in the United States (the exact figure is probably closer to the top of this range). These asset accumulations are greatly facilitated by tax expenditures (see chapter 4) and by tax-free intergenerational transfers.

In other words, asset accumulations are primarily the result of institutionalized mechanisms involving explicit connections, rules, incentives, and subsidies. Certain screening processes—especially parentage, type of employment, and level of income—determine whether or not individuals have an opportunity to benefit from institutionalized asset accumulation. Once at the "door" of institutionalized asset accumulation, the rules of the game strongly influence subsequent accumulation.

Notes

1. Alexis de Tocqueville, *Democracy in America*. Garden City, New York: Anchor Books, 1969 (originally published in 1835).

2. Max Weber, *The Rise of the Protestant Ethic and the Spirit of Capitalism*. New York: Charles Scribner's Sons, 1958 (originally published in 1904–1905).

3. George Gilder, *Wealth and Poverty*. New York: Basic Books, 1981.

4. Weber, 1958, 170, 181–92.

5. C. B. MacPherson, ed., *Property: Mainstream and Critical Positions*. Toronto: University of Toronto Press, 1978.

6. Lars Osberg, *Economic Inequality in Canada*. Toronto: Butterworths, 1981, 165.

7. R.H. Tawney, "Property and Creative Work," in C. B. MacPherson, ed.,

Property: Mainstream and Critical Positions. Toronto: University of Toronto Press, 1978, 135–51 (originally published in 1920).

8. Robert L. Heilbroner, *The Nature and Logic of Capitalism.* New York: W.W. Norton, 1985, 36–37.

9. What is defined as an asset, or capital, is not some immutable characteristic, but rather a social construction. This was perhaps best said by Marx: "A cotton-spinning jenny is a machine for spinning cotton. It becomes *capital* only in certain relations. Torn from these relationships it is no more capital than gold in itself is *money* or sugar the price of sugar . . ." (Karl Marx, *Wage Labour and Capital,* in *Selected Works in Two Volumes.* Moscow: Foreign Languages Publishing House, 1950, vol. 1, 83). In other words, capital is an artifact of the economic and social system of which it is a part. To take another example, the very worst major league baseball team is worth tens of millions of dollars, but a team of poetry readers, although the best in the world, is worth next to nothing. One can imagine a society in which this relationship is reversed (although, without professional baseball, who would want to live there?).

10. Still other categories of tangible assets are possible. One of these might be *special rights, entitlements, and other legal commitments for particular purposes from public or private entities to individuals or families, with earnings as money, goods, or services.* In the public sector, this would include welfare state transfers such as Social Security Old Age Insurance, AFDC, Medicare, Medicaid, and Food Stamps. Counterparts in the private sector include defined-benefit private pension arrangements and private health care plans.

Another possible category of tangible assets is *general rights, in the form of socialist provision, of highways and other transportation facilities, water and sanitation systems, military protection, education, recreational facilities and so forth, with earnings in the form of state provided services available to all.* These are often called *public goods.* In a nation such as the United States, dominated by capitalist ideology, government provision of essential services is sometimes seen as a necessary evil rather than as a general right or general asset, but for individuals and households, these general rights can nonetheless be viewed as assets.

In both of these cases, however, the element of individual control of the asset is missing (see discussion above on the difference between income and assets). Therefore, for the purpose of this discussion neither entitlements nor socially provided goods and services are included in the definition of assets.

11. Joseph Schumpeter, *Business Cycles: A Theoretical, Historical, and Statistical Analysis of the Capitalist Process.* New York: McGraw-Hill, 1939, vol. 1, 223.

12. Paul McNulty, *The Origins and Development of Labor Economics.* Cambridge, MA: MIT Press, 1980, 192.

13. The concept of human capital has been sharply criticized from the left, especially when the theory moves away from the more concrete ideas of education and skills and into the fuzzy world of cultural characteristics (see the description of cultural capital). In this case, the nefarious image of "cultural determinism" is raised (for a critique, see Stephen Steinberg, "Human Capital: A Critique," *Review of Black Political Economy* 14(1), 1985, 67–74. Steinberg is especially critical of the work of Thomas Sowell, *Ethnic America.* New York: Basic Books, 1981). However, even Karl Marx recognized human beings as liv-

ing capital. The difference between the right and left political views is not so much whether human capital exists, but rather how it comes to be formed, valued, utilized, and compensated.

14. Pierre Bourdieu, "Cultural Reproduction and Social Reproduction," in Richard Brown, ed., *Knowledge, Education and Cultural Change*. London: Tavistock, 1973.

15. Pierre Bourdieu, *Distinction: A Social Critique of the Judgement of Taste*. Cambridge, MA: Harvard University Press, 1984.

16. George Farkas, Robert Grobe, and Daniel Sheehan, *Human Capital or Cultural Capital*. Hawthorne, NY: Aldine de Gruyter, 1990.

17. Mark Granovetter, "Economic Action and Social Structure: The Problem of Embeddedness," *American Journal of Sociology* 91, 1985, 481–510.

18. James S. Coleman, "Social Capital in the Creation of Human Capital," *American Journal of Sociology* 94, 1988, S95-S120.

19. Carol B. Stack, *All Our Kin*. New York: Harper and Row, 1974.

20. Indeed, the prominence of informal social capital (family and friendship networks) has been offered as an explanation of the family patterns of poor urban blacks:

> We believe that the poor Black urban family has not developed along the nuclear pattern partly because of the need to provide an alternate system of economic security. We find that various domestic networks of cooperative support sustain and socialize the family members. The membership in domestic networks is based largely on kinship, including that of the father of the children. (Carol B. Stack and Herbert Semmel, "Social Insecurity: Welfare Policy and the Structure of Poor Families," in Betty Reid Mandell, *Welfare in America: Controlling the "Dangerous Classes."* Englewood Cliffs, NJ: Prentice-Hall, 1975, 89–103)

21. John F. Tomer, *Organizational Capital*. New York: Praeger, 1987.

22. Oliver Williamson and other institutional economists who study organizations are notable exceptions. For example, see Oliver Williamson, *The Economic Institutions of Capitalism*. New York: Free Press, 1985.

23. Mortimer Adler, *A Vision of the Future*. New York: Macmillan, 1984, 45–46.

24. Frances Fox Piven and Richard Cloward, *The New Class War: Reagan's Attack on the Welfare State and Its Consequences*. New York: Pantheon, 1982.

25. A delineation of various types of capital is similar, in some respects, to a delineation of various types of power.

26. Robert Haveman, "Conclusion," in Denis Kessler and André Masson, eds., *Modelling the Accumulation and Distribution of Wealth*. Oxford: Clarendon Press, 1988, 323–28.

27. Burton A. Weisbrod and W. Lee Hanson, "An Income-Net Worth Approach to Measuring Economic Welfare," *American Economic Review* 8, 1968, 1315–19; and Marilyn Moon, *The Measurement of Economic Welfare*. New York: Academic Press, 1977. The standard treatment of assets in these formulations is as a storehouse of potential consumption. Among welfare policy analysts, assets have not been viewed as having welfare effects other than consumption.

28. Susan Mayer and Christopher Jencks, "Poverty and the Distribution of Material Hardship," *Journal of Human Resources* 24(1), 1989, 88–114.

29. Edward N. Wolff, "Wealth Holdings and Poverty Status in the U.S.,"

Review of Income and Wealth, 1990 (in press at this writing, based on a paper presented at the 20th General Conference of the International Association for Research on Income and Wealth, in Roca di Papa, Italy, August 1987).

30. Daniel Radner, "Assessing the Economic Status of the Aged and Non-aged Using Alternative Income-Wealth Measures," *Social Security Bulletin* 53(3), 1990, 2–14.

31. James Kearl, Clayne Pope, and Larry Wimmer, "The Distribution of Wealth in a Settlement Economy: Utah, 1850–1870," *Journal of Economic History* 40, 1980, 477–96.

32. Simon Kuznets, "Economic Growth and Income Inequality," *American Economic Review* 45, 1955, 1–28.

33. M.S. Ahluwalia, "Income Inequality—Some Dimensions of the Problem," in H. Chenery et al., *Redistribution with Growth.* London: Oxford University Press, 1976, 3–37.

34. John Angle, "The Surplus Theory of Social Stratification and the Size Distribution of Personal Wealth," *Social Forces* 65, 1986, 293–326; and Robert Lampman, *The Share of Top Wealth-Holders in National Wealth, 1922–1956.* Princeton, NJ: Princeton University Press, 1962.

35. Gerhard Lenski, *Power and Privilege: A Theory of Social Stratification.* New York: McGraw-Hill, 1966.

36. Piven and Cloward, 1982.

37. Edward N. Wolff, ed., *International Comparisons of the Distribution of Household Wealth.* Oxford: Clarendon Press, 1987.

38. Data on changing forms of assets over time are from Edward N. Wolff, "Trends in Aggregate Household Wealth in the U.S., 1900–1983," *Review of Income and Wealth* 35(1), 1989, 1–29; and Wolff and the U.S. Federal Reserve Board, cited in "Changing Profile," *Wall Street Journal,* October 20, 1989, R27.

39. Edward N. Wolff, "Estimates of Household Wealth Inequality in the U.S., 1962–1983," *Review of Income and Wealth* 33(3), 1987, 231–42.

40. The 1983 study sponsored by the Federal Reserve and other federal agencies received a great deal of publicity in 1986 when the results were first published, because it showed that wealth had become much more concentrated. However, there was an error in data collection. One respondent's assets were recorded as $200 million rather than $2 million, which illustrates the hazards of survey research even when dealing with something as quantifiable as money. The corrected data showed not much change in wealth distribution (James D. Smith, "Wealth in America," *ISR Newsletter,* published by the Institute for Social Research, University of Michigan, Winter 1986–87, 3–5; see also Paul Blustein, "Share of Wealth Held by U.S. Richest Rose Only Slightly, According to Revised Data," *Wall Street Journal,* August 22, 1986, 2, citing a 1986 report by the Joint Economic Committee of Congress).

41. 1983 and 1984 are the latest years for which published data on asset distribution are available. However, the asset distribution changes only gradually from year to year and therefore the picture presented is not far from the current distribution (U.S. Bureau of the Census, "Household Wealth and Asset Ownership, 1984," *Current Population Reports, Household Economic Studies,* Series P-70, no. 7. Washington, D.C.: U.S. Government Printing Office).

42. Ibid.

43. Wolff, "Estimates of Household Wealth Inequality in the U.S., 1962–1983," 1987.

44. The Gini coefficient is perhaps the most widely reported measure of inequality other than percentages. The Gini coefficient varies from perfect equality (0.0) to perfect inequality (1.0). It can be understood by thinking in terms of a graph with two axes. If percentage of household income is plotted on one axis, and percentage of households is plotted on the other, then a diagonal line from the lower left to the upper right would represent perfect equality. However, if the distribution is unequal, the line would sag in a curve below the diagonal (known as the Lorenz curve). The more unequal the distribution, the greater the sag in the curve. The Gini coefficient is calculated as two times the total space between the diagonal and the curved distribution line, compared to all the space on the graph. Gini coefficients for household income are typically around 0.4, while Gini coefficients for household wealth tend to be between 0.7 and 0.9. The Gini coefficient, although simple and useful, has several shortcomings; for comment and critique, see F.A. Cowell, *Measuring Inequality*. Oxford: Philip Allan Publishers, 1977.

45. Melvin Oliver and Thomas Shapiro, "Wealth of a Nation: A Reassessment of Asset Inequality in America Shows at Least One Third of Households are Asset-Poor," *American Journal of Economics and Sociology* 49, 1990, 129–51.

46. The definition of income poverty is the official one; see chapter 2 for a description.

47. Wolff, 1990.

48. Ibid.

49. Ibid.

50. U.S. Bureau of the Census, "Household Wealth and Asset Ownership, 1984," 1986.

51. Ibid.

52. Wolff, 1990.

53. U.S. pension funds, at this writing, control about $2.6 trillion in total assets. They own about 18 percent of all common stock and about 27 percent of all corporate bonds in the United States. Typically, these funds own one-half or more of the equity of larger companies. Thus, corporate America is rapidly becoming controlled by pension funds. Some observers interpret this as a source of financial stability. Others point out that, although ownership of pension funds is nominally distributed among millions of Americans, management of the funds is in relatively few hands. In this sense, stock ownership is growing more concentrated. Peter Drucker ("A Crisis of Capitalism," *Wall Street Journal*, September 30, 1986) worries that the investment horizon of pension funds tends to be short term, contributing to "speculator's capitalism."

54. U.S. Bureau of the Census, "Household Wealth and Asset Ownership, 1984," 1986.

55. U.S. Department of Agriculture, Food and Nutrition Service, "Assets of Low Income Households: New Findings on Food Stamp Participants and Nonparticipants," unpublished report to the Congress, 1981.

7 • Inheritance of Asset Inequality

Are children of the poor likely to remain poor and children of the rich likely to remain rich? Evidence on intergenerational transmission of inequality is mixed. According to some observers, the inheritance of inequality, in both capitalist and socialist societies, is one of the strongest research findings in social science.[1] From this perspective, the best predictor of socioeconomic status is the socioeconomic status of one's parents. Although there are many individual exceptions, social class tends to be passed from generation to generation except in extraordinary circumstances, such as revolutions, major migrations, or large-scale institutional interventions.[2] John Brittain observes:

> It is well known that the degree of inequality of income and other measures of economic success achieved by individuals has persisted over time at a high and rather stable level. Through New Deal, Fair Deal, New Society, Great Society, and the War against Poverty, the relative gap between rich and poor in America has remained substantially impervious to egalitarian public policy.[3]

Brittain goes on to say that the forces of *intergenerational* inequality, particularly the advantages and disadvantages conferred by family of origin, account for as much as two-thirds of the variation in some measures of subsequent success. These effects are so strong, says Brittain, that they overwhelm the redistributive effects of public policy. Intergenerational persistence of income inequality has been noted by many social scientists, including David Ellwood[4] and Lee Rainwater.[5]

Indeed, class inheritance is sometimes said to be so universal that it is as close to a law as is any other relationship in social science. This is sometimes dryly referred to as the Law of the Haves, which is stated simply: "The Haves have it." As Billie Holiday sings, "Them that's got shall get,/ Them that's not shall lose." In America we are sometimes reluctant to believe that opportunity is unequally available, but much of the evidence indicates that the Haves have an easier time achieving socioeconomic success than do the Have-Nots.

However, the Law of the Haves is not carved in stone, and it is not impervious to the changing tides of history. The rise of capitalism and industrial society has been accompanied by increased rates of social mobility. Indeed, Ralf Dahrendorf regards this increase in social mobility as one of the key features of industrial society.[6] Social mobility has, to some extent, blurred the boundaries between classes, and transformed class conflict into individual competition. Also, says Dahrendorf, the achievement of citizenship rights and access to political power has led to greater economic equality.

Increased social mobility has led to a mixed pattern of research results in intergenerational inequality. Among the authors of major studies, Peter Blau and Otis Dudley Duncan find a weak influence of socioeconomic background on chances of success, but a strong effect of educational attainment independent of family background.[7] In contrast, Samuel Bowles finds a stronger family background influence and a weak independent effect of education.[8] Christopher Jencks finds a strong effect from neither, suggesting that economic success is more random or unexplained.[9]

Income inequality is known to be quite dynamic, even within a period of a few years. Using large-scale survey evidence from the Panel Study of Income Dynamics, Greg Duncan finds that from 1971 to 1978, about 52 percent of the families who started off in the top quintile shifted to a lower bracket, and 45 percent of those in the bottom quintile moved up. In all, Duncan reports, nearly one out of four families moved at least two quintiles. Family income mobility "is pervasive at all levels." Income poverty is found to be largely transitory: "Only a little over one-half of the individuals living in poverty in one year are found to be poor in the next."[10] If income poverty is this dynamic, then children of the income poor have a good chance of not being poor themselves.

Thus, the picture of intergenerational inequality, at least in relation to income, is somewhat mixed. Assets, however, have a more stable, long-term character and are not quite as dynamic from one generation to another.

The Inheritance of Asset Inequality:
The Academic Debate

Of all the forms of influence of parents on their children, financial wealth is the easiest to transmit and perhaps the easiest to measure as well. The pattern of inherited assets is fairly clear, especially among the wealthy. Although wealth is taxed at death, there are numerous pathways around the tax laws and great family fortunes continue for generations.[11] Lester Thurow concludes that "approximately half of all great wealth is inherited."[12]

However, there is an active debate concerning the proportion of wealth that is inherited in the general population. This debate is closely tied to theories and empirical evidence about savings and bequests. The notion that people save and consume following a life cycle model (known as the life cycle hypothesis or LCH) was proposed by Franco Modigliani and Richard Brumberg; this model suggests that people save primarily for consumption and to buffer uncertainty during retirement, and not in order to make bequests.[13] A general consensus on this viewpoint was altered by Kotlikoff and Summers, who concluded that the bulk of wealth accumulation, about 80 percent, was due to intergenerational transfers.[14] Modigliani continues to argue that the percentage of intergenerational transfer is closer to 20 percent. The debate remains lively.[15,16]

Much of the discrepancy between the two viewpoints rests on how "wealth" and "wealth accumulation" are defined. A major difference is that Modigliani assumes that income from inherited wealth is part of lifetime income rather than part of inheritance. Kotlikoff and Summers assume the opposite. Modigliani's position on this matter seems rather odd. If the son or daughter of a millionaire inherits a fortune, why would not the earnings from that fortune—or at least the portion of earnings that is equivalent to a market rate return—be attributed to the original inheritance? It would be a little misleading to say that the son or daughter is responsible for all of the earnings on the parent's fortune.

Thurow points out that the pattern of inheritances is not what would be predicted by the consumption-oriented LCH. In general, says Thurow, it is difficult to find points where individuals begin to deaccumulate their wealth in later years.[17] David Wise points out that most personal "savings" are in the form of housing, pension plans, and

IRAs, and that much of this wealth is not de-accumulated during retirement.[18] Also, says Thurow, too much wealth is accumulated in some households to be consistent with the LCH. Sometimes accumulations are far more than could conceivably be spent; and large fortunes are passed from generation to generation.[19] The natural conclusion, now accepted by many economists, is that people save to benefit their children as well as themselves.[20]

The Role of Institutions

As the saying goes these days, the playing field is not level. But what causes the tilt? What causes the pattern of wealth distribution to be replicated from generation to generation? Neoclassical economists, such as Modigliani, downplay inheritance and social relations and focus on "accumulation behavior," as if individuals save as autonomous actors in an unstructured socioeconomic world. However, it is unlikely that diligence and parsimony alone are responsible for individual prosperity. In my experience, hard work and frugality are found among the poor at least as often as they are found among the rich. Other factors undoubtedly play a role in wealth accumulation, perhaps especially the structure of social and economic relations, sometimes called institutional factors:

> Institutions provide the framework within which human beings interact. They establish the cooperative and competitive relationships which constitute a society and more specifically an economic order. When economists talk about their discipline as a theory of choice and about the menu of choices being determined by opportunities and preferences, they simply have left out that it is the institutional framework which constrains people's choice sets. Institutions are in effect the filter between individuals and the capital stock and between the capital stock and the output of goods and services and the distribution of income.[21]

Institutions consist of formal and informal socioeconomic relationships, rules, and incentives, including the organization of capitalist enterprises and voluntary associations, and all the laws, procedures, and agents of the state that affect organizations and households. Many of these institutional arrangements affect asset accumulation and the transmission of assets across generations.[22]

Related to wealth accumulation and transmission is the tax system, one of the key institutional parameters. Progressive income taxation, intended as a means of property distribution since the 1920s, has not accomplished its objective. Indeed, the rich often pay less taxes than do working people. This unequal situation became more so during the 1980s. The Congressional Budget Office has found that from 1980 through 1989, the poorest 20 percent of Americans saw their real income drop 3 percent and their net federal tax rate go up 16 percent; but the richest 20 percent had a 32 percent increase in their income and a 5 percent cut in their net federal tax rate.

The pattern of taxation, year after year, has a tremendous influence on wealth accumulation. In general, tax laws often work to maintain or increase a high concentration of wealth in a small proportion of the population. Looking at different groups among the rich—the poor-rich, middle-rich, and rich-rich—research finds that the middle-rich pay the most taxes, while the rich-rich, for the most part, avoid taxation. The charitable deduction became so widely used in the 1960s and 1970s that those with wealth over $10 million paid a lower proportion of their gross income in taxes than did those with only $1 million or $2 million in gross income.[23]

Not only the wealthy are affected by favorable tax laws. As pointed out in chapter 4, tax expenditures to support home ownership and retirement pension accumulations are substantial, directly benefiting at least two-thirds of U.S. households. In contrast, non-homeowners and employees without retirement benefits do not participate in these major forms of institutionalized asset accumulation.

Patterns of Accumulation
and Transmission of Assets

As suggested above, patterns of asset accumulation and transmission are quite different for different groups in society. For discussion purposes, let us consider four economic strata: the wealthy, the middle class, the working poor, and the welfare poor.

The Wealthy

For the wealthy, assets are far more important than income. Children in wealthy households learn about investment and accumulation as they grow up, around the dinner table, on the tennis court. In addition, needless to say, wealth generates power, and power generates privileges conducive to accumulation of still greater wealth. Such privilege takes many forms, the most common of which are access to other people's capital, access to critical information, oligopolistic or monopolistic control of markets, and favorable business and investment tax laws. Thus, the wealthy maintain their assets and pass them along to their children, not entirely through superior intelligence, particular character traits, or hard work, but also through elaborate structures of information, associations, procedures, and favorable rules. When there is a difficulty to overcome, "phone calls are made." In short, the wealthy operate within privileged relationships and institutions, both public and private, that facilitate asset accumulation, and the process tends to be intergenerational. As pointed out above, the majority of wealthy people in the United States have inherited their wealth. Occasionally, an offspring squanders the family fortune, but this is not the common pattern.

The generation-to-generation transmission of old money is described by an insider, Nelson Aldrich, Jr., who details the initiation rites of the rich.[24] First comes boarding school where a "fierce indoctrination in the spirit of performance gives rich kids the sense that they are accomplishing something on their own." (It might be said that a child of old money, although born on third base, learns to think that he hit a triple.) Boarding school is followed by an "epic confrontation with nature," through the military, the Central Intelligence Agency, or perhaps the Peace Corps. Following these initiations, the offspring of old money are ready to assume their places on corporate boards, as patrons of the arts, and a few in public service.

The Middle Class

The middle class does not think about assets in the same way the rich do. Income is a more dominant idea. Today, this group is made up primarily of professionals and managers who did not grow up surrounded by large family assets. However, most did grow up with parents who owned a home, planned ahead, and valued education and achievement. Among the middle class, both income and consumption are substantial, while ordinary savings and investment (outside the protection of tax privilege) are surprisingly limited.

Nonetheless, the middle class has significant access to two important forms of asset accumulation—home ownership and retirement pensions.[25] Mortgage interest tax deductions and tax-deferred retirement plans have facilitated the bulk of asset accumulation in most households. Members of the middle class, because their incomes support larger homes and greater retirement plan contributions, have benefited substantially from these arrangements. The scope of federal subsidy should not be underestimated—federal tax expenditures for home-mortgage tax deductions alone are more than twice the federal expenditures for Aid to Families with Dependent Children (AFDC). Thus, the middle class accumulates its wealth, not so much through superior individual investment, but through structured, institutionalized arrangements that are in many respects difficult to miss (see chapter 4 for an analysis of tax expenditures for home mortgages and retirement pensions). Some few people do manage to lose it all through profligacy or an ill-advised investment, but they are the exception rather than the rule.

It is important to emphasize that these institutionalized arrangements provide tremendous access and incentives to accumulate assets. People participate in retirement pension systems because it is easy and attractive to do so. This is not a matter of making superior choices. Instead, a priori choices are made by social policy, and individuals walk into the pattern that has been established.

These institutional arrangements have a reality of their own above and beyond a choice among financially equivalent alternatives. This can be demonstrated by the following thought experiment. Suppose, in my personal case, over the past ten years, that the matching contribution from the university and tax deferment for my retirement pension had not been granted to me, but in their place was an equivalent compensation in higher salary (this would have amounted to several thousand dollars per year). What would my family have done with the money? Would we have put it into a retirement account? Would we have saved it in any form? Very likely the answer to both questions is no. We would have seen it as part of our income flow and, with two young children, student loan payments, car payments, a mortgage, and house repairs, we would have spent it to pay the bills. In this regard, we are probably not a great deal different from many other families. Without a structure to facilitate asset accumulation, much of it simply would not occur.

The Working Poor

The working poor are not so fortunate. Income is more limited, employment is less stable, and the majority of this group does not manage to purchase a house or accumulate significant balances in retirement pension accounts. In most cases, retirement pensions are not available at the workplace, and in the absence of institutionalized asset accumulation schemes, little is saved. Working-poor families have little cushion to protect them from poverty when a job loss, divorce, major illness, or other life crisis strikes. It is members of this group, without assets, who slip into hardship and public assistance, then work their way out again, accounting for the "dynamic" nature of welfare recipiency in the United States. Without assets, children in these families are less likely to plan for the future and less likely to undertake a college education, perpetuating lower incomes and intergenerational finances removed from asset accumulation.

At this point, the question of preferences and choice might again arise from neoclassical economists. The argument is that if the working poor preferred to save their income and invest, they would choose to do so. This is all very well in textbooks, but in reality, working-class families are influenced by several sets of institutional constraints. The first and most important is the absence of asset accumulation schemes, principally retirement pensions, through the workplace.

A second constraint, regarding especially home ownership, is institutional barriers to credit. Studies have shown that owning a home is, on the average, less expensive than renting,[26] but many of the working poor are not able to accumulate a down payment to make home ownership possible. Theoretically, the working poor could borrow against their future income streams, but liquidity constraints, stemming from the uncertainty of lenders, prevent the extension of credit even when the working poor might be a good risk.

A third type of constraint on pure choice is so-called positional effects or expectations associated with the context of social interaction. For example, it may be that a poor person today has a higher real standard of living today than a middle-class person of one hundred years ago; however, the poor person today functions within her or his context, which has a different set of expectations. These expectations are not simple preferences; they are not arbitrary; they are the reality of a particular society at a particular point in history. For example, one hundred years ago the average person did not have running water or electric lights, much less a telephone. However, today these are not preferences, they are *the way things are*. If a working-poor person wanted to save money by doing without running water, it would not be a realistic choice. The health department would not permit it. Nor, for that matter are giving up a telephone and a car realistic choices. In our society, for most people, it is very difficult to hold down a job without a telephone and a car. In addition, a certain quality of clothing and appearance is expected. In other words, the institutional context of employment *requires* a certain level of consumption, which places real limits on savings. These and other institutional constraints effectively prevent accumulation of assets in most working-poor households.

The Welfare Poor

The welfare poor are in still worse shape. For those receiving public assistance, not only is asset accumulation not encouraged, it is not permitted. Households that receive AFDC transfers cannot own more than a trivial amount of assets, other than home equity, in order to qualify and remain eligible for income transfers. The following newspaper account illustrates the point:

MILWAUKEE —A penny saved is a penny earned. Usually.

Take the case of Grace Capitello, a 36-year-old single mother with a true talent for parsimony. To save on clothing, Ms. Capitello dresses herself plainly in thriftstore finds. To cut her grocery bill, she stocks up on 67-cent boxes of saltines and 39-cent cans of chicken soup.

When Ms. Capitello's five-year-old daughter, Michelle, asked for "Li'l Miss Makeup" for Christmas, her mother bypassed Toys "R" Us, where the doll retails for $19.99. Instead, she found one at Goodwill—for $1.89. She cleaned it up and tied a pink ribbon in its hair before giving the doll to Michelle. Ms. Capitello found the popular Mr. Potato Head at Goodwill, too, assembling the plastic toy one piece at a time from the used toy bin. It cost her 79 cents, and saved $3.18.

Ms. Capitello's stingy strategies helped her build a savings account of more than $3,000 in the last four years. Her goal was to put away enough to buy a new washing machine and maybe one day send Michelle to college. To some this might make her an example of virtue in her gritty North Side neighborhood, known more for boarded-up houses than high aspirations. But there was just one catch: Ms. Capitello is on welfare—$440 a month, plus $60 in food stamps—and saving that much money on public aid is against the law. When welfare officials found out about it, they were quick to act. Ms. Capitello, they charged, was saving at the expense of taxpayers.

Last month, the Milwaukee County Department of Social Services took her to court, charged her with fraud and demanded that she return the savings. . . .

Finally her day in court arrived. At first, Circuit Court Judge Charles B. Schudson had trouble figuring out Ms. Capitello's crime. To him, welfare fraud meant double dipping: collecting full benefits and holding down a job at the same time.

After the lawyers explained the rules about saving money, he made it clear that he didn't think much of the rules. "I don't know how much more powerfully we could say it to the poor in our society: Don't try to save," he said. Judge Schudson said it was "ironic" that the case came as President Bush promotes his plan for Family Savings Accounts. "Apparently, that's an incentive that the country would only give to the rich."[27]

Naturally, the logic of the no-savings-on-welfare rule is that taxpayers should not support families that have their own resources. However, the self-defeating nature of the policy is apparent. Without the possibility of asset accumulation, families tend not to plan for a better future and do not accumulate a cushion that might sustain them during a climb out of poverty. Without a positive future orientation, it is also painfully apparent why so many children from such families find themselves in poverty as adults.

Moreover, institutions for saving, by and large, no longer serve the poor. During the early part of this century, the poor often had savings accounts. For example, we can recall the Penny Savings Bank of New York, and its successor, the Dime Savings Bank, which still exists, but no longer seeks deposits of dimes. Today, most banks and savings and loans have left poor neighborhoods. The ones that remain are not very interested in small depositors.

Even in my neighborhood, the savings and loan is not very receptive to small accounts. I have noticed that the teller sometimes seems to resent the deposits of fifteen or twenty wrinkled dollar bills that my children have diligently saved, and bring to her with pride and a sense of importance. She acts as if these small deposits are a nuisance. I cannot help but think that there is something wrong with the teller's attitude that is of far greater significance than its possibly negative effect on the savings habits of my children. A nation that does not encourage small savers has a questionable future (see chapter 12).

In summation, certain institutions tend to promote asset accumulation; others tend to block asset accumulation; and still others tend to draw down existing assets. Most of the institutions with which the poor interact in their daily lives fall into the categories of blocking and drawing down asset accumulations. Very few institutions encourage and promote asset accumulation by the poor.

Assets and African-Americans

Why have blacks, on the average, been less able than whites to accumulate assets? The most obvious answer is that blacks have always earned less than whites, and, over the years, these earnings shortfalls have resulted in less savings, less investment, and less transfers to succeeding generations. Over time, less income can result in vast differences in asset accumulation. In addition, however, there is another dimension to the explanation: social and economic institutions have systematically restricted asset accumulation among blacks.

The Historical Record

Historical information on asset holdings of African-Americans is scanty. Historians and social scientists have not focused very much on assets in describing or explaining black social and economic successes and failures. Nonetheless, the rough outlines of asset accumulation among African-Americans can be sketched.

Most fundamentally, the ancestors of most African-Americans were brought to these shores as economic property, with no rights to any assets—not even their own bodies. The institution of slavery expunged all legal support for ownership within the enslaved black community, and secondarily, mitigated strongly against the development of a culture of property ownership.[28]

However, during the antebellum period, free blacks, in pockets of the South and in some Northern cities, did own property.[29] A few were wealthy. The total value of property owned by free blacks in 1860 has been estimated at $50 million.[30] This figure leads Thomas Sowell to conclude: "Among the few rights [of free blacks] not abrogated in the antebellum period was the right to property.''[31] Thus, a culture of ownership did develop among free blacks, but Sowell's conclusion is overstated. Free blacks certainly were not as free as whites to own whatever they wanted. In particular, the historical record suggests that, outside of agriculture and service businesses, the ownership of productive capital was quite limited.[32] Free blacks may have had some money, but there is little evidence that they acquired a stake in America's developing industrial capacity. Instead, their assets, like their social relations, were quite segregated.

Sowell illustrates this very well in his description of black colleges, which served the free black elite:

> Negro colleges were geared to serving the social elite. . . . The education at such colleges was . . . neither "practical" nor "intellectual." Rather, the campus was a setting for elaborate and costly social activities for those who could afford them. . . . In short, one of the major institutions for economic advancement in the case of other minorities was devoted to entirely different purposes in the case of the American Negro.[33]

Sowell attributes the social character of black colleges to self-interest and indulgence of the black elite. He paints a picture of rich, light-skinned blacks socializing in a country club atmosphere, insensitive to the struggles of the black masses. To the extent that this portrayal is accurate, Sowell does not ask the next question: Why? In part, the answer is that black colleges focused on social affairs because America's industrial and occupational structure was not open to them.

In any case, antebellum free blacks were a small minority. The real story of African-Americans is far removed from comfortable social gatherings at black colleges. The central experience of blacks in America has been the brutal experience of slavery and its long-lasting aftermath, most particularly in terms of limited property ownership.

Following the Emancipation Proclamation, there was widespread talk of redistribution of Southern property to freed blacks in the form of "forty acres and a mule." Although never an official promise, the hope of forty acres and a mule was widely shared among freed slaves. The property was never delivered, and other scattered efforts to distribute land to blacks in the South were also squashed.[34]

In the late 1860s, Sojurner Truth proposed massive relocation of blacks from the South to the plains states. "In her view, no black political solution was possible without a general reallocation of land. . . . she urged her people to buy land and to develop a sufficient economic base from which to wage their various struggles for social and political justice."[35]

In his last Sunday sermon, Martin Luther King pointed out that European pioneers who settled the West and Midwest received free land and later, low-interest loans to mechanize farms. At about the same time, King noted, the Emancipation Proclamation freed the slaves without making any serious effort to assist them in becoming property owners. Earlier, reflecting on this differential application of social policy, W.E.B. Du Bois suggested that, if the promise of land to freed blacks had been kept, it "would have made a basis of real democracy in the United States."[36]

The Freedmen's Bureau was established to promote black social welfare and, supposedly, land ownership. But whites in the South systematically denied blacks the opportunity to purchase land. Southern banks denied blacks the right to make deposits, much less obtain loans for land or housing.

One major institution, the Freedman's Bank, did facilitate and encourage savings among blacks for land and home purchases. As Frederick Douglass commented:[37]

> The history of civilization shows that no people can well rise to a high degree of mental or even moral excellence without wealth. A people uniformly poor and compelled to struggle for barely a physical existence will be dependent and despised by their neighbors, and will finally despise themselves. While it is impossible that every individual of any race shall be rich—and no man may be despised for merely being poor—yet no people can be respected which does not produce a wealthy class. Such a people will only be the hewers of wood and the drawers of water, and will not rise above a mere animal existence. The mission of the Freedman's Bank is to show our people the road to a share of the wealth and well being of the world.[38]

The Freedman's Bank increased black savings and purchases of both agricultural and residential property. However, patterns of institutional racism eventually undermined its financial integrity. The board of directors was controlled by whites. Highly questionable no-interest loans from the bank to white companies put the bank in a precarious financial position. Frederick Douglass, in reference to these and other self-serving financial transactions by whites, recalled the German proverb: "They who have the cross will bless themselves." In its weakened financial condition, the Freedman's Bank did not withstand the economic panic of 1873 and failed in 1874. Thousands of working blacks lost their small savings and were never repaid. Following this catastrophic episode, many blacks were reluctant to trust banks again. Thirty years later, Du Bois observed:

> Then in one sad day came the crash,—all the hard-earned dollars of the freedmen disappeared; but that was the least of the loss,—all the faith in saving went too, and much of the faith in men; and that was a loss that a Nation which to-day sneers at Negro shiftlessness has never yet made good. Not even ten additional years of slavery could have done so much to throttle the thrift of the freedmen as the mismanagement and bankruptcy of the series of savings banks chartered by the Nation for their especial aid.[39]

Later still, Booker T. Washington, a promoter of black-owned businesses, and hardly a radical, noted the lingering shadow of the Freedman's Bank failure:

> When they found that they had lost, or been swindled out of all their little savings, they lost faith in savings banks, and it was a long time after this before it was possible to mention a savings bank for Negroes without some reference being made to the disaster of the Freedman's Bank. The effect of this disaster was the more far-reaching because of the wide extent of territory which the Freedman's Bank covered through its agencies.[40]

Following the failure of the Freedman's Bank, black land ownership did not increase as rapidly for the remainder of the nineteenth century. In addition to the problem of financing, titles to black landholdings in the South were often under a legal cloud, and land in the North was virtually not available to blacks at all. "The tragedy of Reconstruction [was] the failure of the black masses to acquire land, since without the economic security provided by land ownership the freedmen were soon deprived of the political and civil rights which they had won."[41]

Restrictions on business ownership were also severe. Many Southern states enacted legal restrictions on black businesses in general, particular types of black businesses, location of black businesses, or percentage of ownership by blacks. For example:

> In late 1865 many Southern states passed "Black Code" regulations declaring that any Black man who did not have an employer was subject to arrest as a "vagrant." Working independently for themselves, some Black artisans were fined, jailed, and even sentenced to work as convict laborers. South Carolina's legislature declared in December 1865, that "no person of color shall pursue or practice the art, trade, or business of an artisan, mechanic, or shopkeeper, or another trade employment or business . . . on his own account and for his own benefit until he shall have obtained a license which shall be good for one year only." Black peddlers and merchants had to produce $100 annually to pay for the license, while whites paid nothing.[42]

With barriers to property ownership, the social situation of African-Americans deteriorated. The post-Reconstruction period was brutally oppressive. Mob violence and public lynchings became acceptable. As Ida B. Wells found in her research on lynchings, the threat of public torture and death were used to intimidate blacks who began to accumulate property and wealth. This was especially true in the case of business property that might compete with white-owned enterprises.[43] Black business ownership remained uncommon in both the South and the North.

Nonetheless, black ownership of land gradually increased in the south.[44] By 1900, 25 percent of black Southern farmers, some 193 thousand families, owned their own land, averaging twenty-seven acres in the South Atlantic region to forty-eight acres in the South Central region.[45] This land ownership and family farming provided, in most cases, a very meager existence. But it was a huge step beyond the peonage of sharecropping or tenant farming; landowning provided a degree of dignity for Southern blacks.

The Twentieth Century

One of the unanswered questions of modern sociology is: Why have African-Americans been left behind while many European immigrant groups have advanced during the twentieth century? One thesis, reflecting the individualistic ideology that is dominant in the United States, is that blacks have not worked hard enough, or have not been capable enough, or both. A second thesis is more social, focusing on patterns of racial discrimination in education, employment, and housing. A third thesis is political, arguing that a group's movement to middle-class status is a function of protection within a political system that guarantees civil rights and electoral participation. A fourth thesis relies on an income-based economic analysis, looking at levels of income and employment earnings. Finally, a fifth thesis suggests that social and economic advancement is based primarily in patterns of property ownership or asset accumulation. Although the "true" explanation is undoubtedly complex, the last thesis, asset accumulation, is the perspective taken in this book.

In this regard, patterns of land-wealth acquisition have continued to restrict blacks throughout the twentieth century. Most agricultural land owned by blacks in the South was sold as small family farming became less viable and blacks migrated to Northern cities. The number of black-owned farms increased until it totaled 218 thousand in 1910, and then remained steady until 1920. After 1920, the number of black-owned farms began to drop, falling to 182 thousand in 1930, and to 173 thousand in 1940.[46] During this period, many blacks moved to industrial jobs in the North, even though trade unions remained hostile to blacks. Black business ownership in the North was limited due to the necessity of relying, in most cases, on a totally black clientele, and to difficulties in obtaining credit.[47]

In the North, the majority of blacks were urban, and home ownership expanded. In 1890, 19 percent of all U.S. blacks owned their homes; this figure reached 38 percent by 1960.[48] However, racial discrimination in housing kept black property values low, limiting asset accumulation. These institutionalized limits to housing appreciation have been a major barrier to wealth equality. Housing equity is often the first form of significant wealth accumulation in a household and it is eventually translated into other types of financial assets and human capital.[49] Without a beginning in housing equity, other forms of asset accumulation are less likely.

Restrictions on accumulation of housing equity continue to plague blacks to the present day. A study of 10 million mortgage loan applications submitted between 1983 and 1988 to all savings and loan associations in the United States found that blacks are rejected more than twice as often as whites when they apply for home loans at these institutions. In addition, blacks withdraw applications more often and get no decision more often. In much of the country, high-income blacks are rejected at the same rate as low-income whites. "Redlining" of poor neighborhoods has persisted, and may have grown worse in the 1980s.[50] Thus, continuing patterns of institutionalized racism in lending practices have had a direct negative impact on accumulation of black wealth.

It is not clear that the civil rights movement has been helpful in changing this pattern of asset accumulation. According to some interpretations, the major effect of the civil rights movement was that middle-class blacks moved out of central cities into segregated, middle-class suburbs, leaving poor blacks behind.[51] By other accounts, the black middle class simply shrunk in size—more black households became poor, and, due to racial segregation in residential housing, black poverty became more concentrated.[52] In either case, it is questionable that the process has led to an increase in black wealth. Housing, even for middle-class blacks, has remained substantially segregated. Because whites are reluctant to move into neighborhoods that are as little as 20 percent black, the number of buyers for houses in these neighborhoods is low. Over time, fewer buyers means lower prices. Therefore, even middle-class housing does not appreciate at nearly the same rate for blacks as for whites.[53]

Since the beginning of the civil rights movement, the rate of black and other minority home ownership, relative to that of whites, has not improved very much. In 1960, the home ownership rate was 38.4 percent for blacks and other minorities, and 64.4 percent for whites, a ratio of 0.60. By 1985, the home ownership rate was 42.8 percent for blacks and other minorities, and 66.8 percent for whites, a ratio of 0.64. This pattern of slight improvement reflects a long-term, albeit uneven, historical trend. There have been periods when inequality in home ownership narrowed much more quickly. For example, between 1940 and 1950, the ratio of minority-to-white home ownership improved from 0.52 to 0.61. Looking at these statistics, it would appear that World War II did much more for black and other minority home ownership than did the civil rights movement.[54]

In addition, according to one interpretation, before the civil rights movement blacks owned many central-city service businesses—hotels, barber shops, restaurants, grocery stores, laundries, automotive repair shops, funeral parlors, insurance companies, and small banks. Of necessity in a prejudiced society, blacks had to own these businesses or they would not have had access to the services.[55] With integration, middle-class blacks moved to the suburbs and abandoned these businesses. However, because of continuing patterns of discrimination, there is not much evidence that blacks successfully reopened businesses outside the central city. Instead, they moved into management, the professions, and government employment. Thus, the positive effect of the civil rights movement on black business ownership may have been limited.[56]

Limited assets and barriers to asset accumulation are major reasons why poor blacks remain segregated in central cities. If there is a culture of poverty, in my view, it is fundamentally asset-based. Slavery robbed blacks of the right to property and prevented their assimilation into the American culture of property ownership. Following slavery, institutions to facilitate and promote black wealth accumulation did not develop successfully. Indeed, to a large extent, social prejudice and banking institutions have systematically blocked asset accumulation among blacks.

This applies not only to poor blacks but to middle-class blacks as well. As a proportion of total wealth, income-producing assets tend to be far lower for blacks than for whites, even controlling for income levels. Middle-class blacks are less likely than are middle-class whites to own stocks and bonds, real property, or businesses.[57]

As reported in the preceding chapter, African-American households owned, on the average, only one-twelfth of the assets of white households in 1984 (not including pension funds, household effects, or the cash value of life insurance policies). Of these amounts, 75.8 percent of all black assets were in the categories of owner-occupied housing and motor vehicles, non-income-producing assets. For whites, the same figure was only 46.4 percent. The largest category of income-producing assets for blacks was rental real estate, which accounted for 12.4 percent of all black assets in 1982, larger than the 8.6 percent for whites. In all other income-producing categories—interest-bearing accounts, stocks and mutual funds, business property, other real estate, U.S. savings bonds, and IRA or Keogh accounts—blacks were significantly behind whites in proportion of assets.[58]

Only about 1.3 percent of U.S. blacks owned businesses in 1982, the lowest percentage of any minority group, compared to a 6.4 percent ownership rate for the population as a whole. Black business owners were more likely to be involved in services, transportation, and retail trade, and less likely to be involved in agriculture, mining, wholesale trade, and finance. Only 11.4 percent of black-owned businesses had any employees at all, by far the lowest percentage of any minority group. In 1982 the average black-owned business had total annual sales of just $37,000, which was about one-half the sales of the average Asian or Hispanic business, and one-twelfth the sales of the general business population. All minority-owned businesses—including those of blacks, Hispanics, and Asians—accounted for only 0.7 percent of total U.S. business sales in 1982.[59]

For blacks, business financing barriers are more difficult to overcome, and racial discrimination continues to limit white patronage of black businesses. Yet, without income-producing assets,

> affluent blacks exist upon a much shakier ground, which can be knocked from under them at the whim of an angry boss or a sudden downturn in the economy. Furthermore, the lack of investments forestalls a generation-by-generation growth of wealth, with each new black middle class being virtually created from scratch.[60]

Conclusion

Never in the history of the United States have blacks had equal access to institutions that facilitate savings, investment, credit, business opportunity, or ownership of property. Although there has been improvement in some areas over time, the rate of black property ownership, especially for income-producing property, remains distressingly low.

In retrospect, we can identify several lost opportunities that might have begun to set right the severe inequality of asset distribution in the course of African-American history. These lost opportunities include the post–Civil War failure to deliver on the promise of forty acres and a mule; the failure to establish an honest banking system to serve freed blacks; the failure of the 1960s civil rights movement and resulting public policy to reshape, to any significant extent, patterns of property ownership; and the continuing failure to integrate residential real estate. It seems very likely that until asset distribution becomes more equal across the races, high rates of black poverty and hardship, racial division and strife, and massive loss of economic and social potential will continue to burden the nation.

Notes

1. Charles E. Hurst, *The Anatomy of Social Inequality*. St. Louis: C.V. Mosby, 1979.

2. One striking example of a large-scale institutional intervention was the GI Bill following World War II, which enabled a generation of returning soldiers to achieve academic and occupational success beyond their class of origin.

3. John A. Brittain, *The Inheritance of Economic Status*. Washington: Brookings Institution, 1977, 5–6.

4. David T. Ellwood, "Understanding Dependency: Choices, Confidence, or Culture?" a paper prepared for the U.S. Department of Health and Human Resources, Center for Human Resources, Brandeis University, 1987.

5. Lee Rainwater, "Class, Culture, Poverty, and Welfare," report prepared for the U.S. Department of Health and Human Resources, Harvard University, 1987.

6. Ralf Dahrendorf, *Life Chances: Approaches to Social and Political Theory*. Chicago: University of Chicago Press, 1979.

7. Peter M. Blau and Otis Dudley Duncan, *The American Occupational Structure*. New York: John Wiley & Sons, 1967.

8. Samuel Bowles, "Schooling and Inequality from Generation to Generation," *Journal of Political Economy* 80, 1972, pp. S219-S251.

9. Christopher Jencks et al., *Inequality: A Reassessment of the Effect of Family and Schooling in America*. New York: Basic Books, 1972.

10. Greg Duncan, *Years of Poverty, Years of Plenty*. Ann Arbor: Survey Research Center, 1984.

11. James D. Smith and Stephen D. Franklin, "The Concentration of Personal Wealth, 1922–1969," *American Economic Review* 64, 1974, 162–67.

12. Lester Thurow, *Generating Inequality: Mechanisms of Distribution in the U.S. Economy*. New York: Basic Books, 1975, 197.

13. Franco Modigliani and Richard Brumberg, "Utility Analysis and the Consumption Function: An Interpretation of Cross-Section Data," in Kenneth K. Kurihara, ed., *Post-Keynesian Economics*. New Brunswick, NJ: Rutgers University Press, 1954.

14. Laurence Kotlikoff and Lawrence Summers, "The Role of Intergenerational Transfers in Aggregate Capital Accumulation," *Journal of Political Economy* 89, 1981, 706–32.

15. Denis Kessler and André Massson, eds., *Modelling the Accumulation and Distribution of Wealth*. Oxford: Clarendon Press, 1988.

16. The evidence on intergenerational transfers still depends on how one counts. For example, Laurence Kotlikoff (*What Determines Saving?* Cambridge, MA: MIT Press, 1989, xi) concludes: "U.S. wealth accumulation is primarily the consequence of intergenerational transfers as opposed to life cycle saving for retirement." Another study finds that only 15–20 percent of all household wealth comes from inheritances, and another 5–10 percent comes from gifts, for a total of 20–30 percent overall. The top 10 percent of the income distribution received 40–60 percent of their wealth from gifts and inheritances, and this group received 82 percent of the value of all inheritances. The other 90 percent of the income

distribution received less than 10 percent of their wealth from gifts and inheritances; about 85 percent of this group received no gifts or inheritance at all, or had less than one thousand dollars in assets (Michael Hurd and Gabriela Mundaca, "The Importance of Gifts and Inheritances among the Affluent," NBER working paper no. 2415. Cambridge, MA: National Bureau of Economic Research, 1988).

17. Thurow, 1975, 136.

18. David T. Wise, "Saving for Retirement: The U.S. Case," a paper presented at a conference. Cambridge, MA: National Bureau of Economic Research, 1988.

19. Thurow, 1975.

20. Thurow questions whether the pattern of intergenerational transfers supports the conclusion about the desire to benefit children through bequests. The pattern of asset transfers after death suggests that parents are interested only in their children's future consumption rather than present consumption. Thurow (1975, 139) reasons that if parents were interested in children's present consumption, they would transfer assets before death as well. Therefore, there must be some other motive for asset accumulation. Thurow decides that the motive is power. Other explanations exist as well, such as security and stability (see chapter 8 for an explication of effects of asset accumulation other than consumption).

21. Douglass North, *Structure and Change in Economic History.* New York: W.W. Norton, 1981, 201.

22. For example, consistent with the institutional perspective, Alan Blinder ("Inequality and Mobility in the Distribution of Wealth," *Kyklos* 29, 1976, 607–38) questions the assumption of perfect markets in wealth accumulation, as do Kessler and Masson (1988). To take one classic example, Martin Feldstein ("Social Security, Induced Retirement and Aggregate Capital Accumulation," *Journal of Political Economy* 82, 1974, 905–26) examines the effects of Social Security, a major social institution, on retirement savings. He finds that Social Security reduces personal retirement savings by 30–50 percent.

23. Carole Shammas, Marylynn Salmon, and Michael Dahlin, *Inheritance in America: From Colonial Times to the Present.* New Brunswick, NJ: Rutgers University Press, 1987, 144.

24. Nelson W. Aldrich, Jr., *Old Money: The Making of America's Upper Class.* New York: Alfred A. Knopf, 1988.

25. Pension fund assets are more flexible than they might at first appear. The IRS has permitted "hardship" withdrawals from 401(k) plans, but until 1988 had never established guidelines for hardship. The IRS has now taken a "hard line" on 401(k) hardship withdrawals, but this hard line permits the following: medical expenses for the employee, spouse, and dependents; the down payment on the employee's principal residence; a payment to prevent eviction from or foreclosure on the employee's principal residence; and the payment of the next term's tuition for college or other post–high school education for the employee, spouse, or children. Moreover, employers may broaden this list of options by considering each employee withdrawal on its own merits, a "facts and circumstances" approach.

26. Paul Leonard, Cushing Dolbeare, and Edward Lazere, *A Place to Call*

Home: The Crisis in Housing for the Poor. Washington: Center on Budget and Policy Priorities and Low Income Housing Information Service, 1989.

27. Robert L. Rose, "For Welfare Parents, Scrimping Is Legal, But Saving Is Out," *Wall Street Journal,* February 6, 1990, A1 and A10.

28. A counterpoint is that black slaves in America did not have a cultural background in Africa that emphasized individual property rights. African cultures were more communal and less materialistic; for example, see Imamu Amari Baraka, *African Congress: A Documentary of the First Modern Pan-African Congress.* New York: William Morrow, 1972.

29. John Hope Franklin, *From Slavery to Freedom.* New York: Vintage Books, 1969, 223–25.

30. E. Franklin Frazier, *Black Bourgeoisie.* New York: Collier Books, 1962, 35.

31. Thomas Sowell, *Race and Economics.* New York: Longman, 1975, 40.

32. J.H. Harmon, Jr., Arnett Lindsey, and Carter G. Woodson, *The Negro as a Business Man.* College Park, MD: McGrath Publishing Company, 1929.

33. Sowell, 1975, 43.

34. Claude F. Oubre, *Forty Acres and a Mule: The Freedmen's Bureau and Black Land Ownership.* Baton Rouge: Louisiana State University Press, 1978.

35. Manning Marable, *How Capitalism Underdeveloped Black America.* Boston: South End Press, 1983, 79–80.

36. W.E.B. Du Bois, *Black Reconstruction.* Cleveland: Meridian Books, 1968 (originally published in 1935), 602.

37. For the account of the Freedman's Bank, I have relied substantially on Carl R. Osthaus, *Freedmen, Philanthropy, and Fraud: A History of the Freedman's Savings Bank.* Urbana: University of Illinois Press, 1976; and Oubre, 1978.

38. Frederick Douglass, *New National Era,* June 25, 1874, cited in Osthaus, 1976, 197.

39. W.E.B. Du Bois, *The Souls of Black Folk.* Greenwich, CT: Fawcett Publications, 1970 (originally published in 1903), 39.

40. Booker T. Washington, *The Story of the Negro.* New York: Doubleday, Page & Co., 1909, vol. 2, 214.

41. Oubre, 1978, 197.

42. Marable, 1983, 142–143.

43. Ida B. Wells-Barnett, *On Lynchings.* New York: Arno Press, 1969 (sections originally published in 1892, 1894, and 1900).

44. Robert Higgs, "Accumulation of Property by Southern Blacks before World War I," *American Economic Review* 72(4), 1982, 725–37; and Robert Margo, "Accumulation of Property by Southern Blacks before World War I: Comment and Further Evidence," *American Economic Review* 74(4), 1984, 768–76.

45. August Meier and Elliott Rudwick, *From Plantation to Ghetto,* third edition. New York: Hill and Wang, 1976, 176–77; and Oubre, 1978, 197–98.

46. Meier and Rudwick, 1976, 176–77. Ownership of agricultural land by African-Americans has continued to decline, by one estimate at the rate of 350,000 acres per year; see Johnson Y. Lancaster, "African-American Farmers on Verge of Extinction," *St. Louis American,* May 3–9, 1990, 1.

47. Ibid., 183–84.

48. *The Negro Handbook*. Chicago: Johnson Publishing, 1960, 289.

49. R.S. Browne, "Wealth Distribution and Its Impact on Minorities," *The Review of Black Political Economy* 4(4), 1974, 27–37; and W.P. O'Hare, *Wealth and Economic Status: A Perspective on Racial Inequality*. Washington: Joint Center for Political Studies, 1983; see also John C. Henretta, "Race Differences in Middle Class Lifestyle: The Role of Home Ownership," *Social Science Research* 8, 1979, 63–78.

50. Reported in Bill Dedman, "Lending Gap Tied to Race," *St. Louis Post-Dispatch*, January 22, 1989, 1A and 12A. The study was carried out by Charles Finn and journalists from the *Atlanta Journal-Constitution* based on data collected over a period of several years by the Federal Home Loan Bank Board as a result of a civil rights suit, but never before analyzed. No official report was published from this study. For a similar study in Boston, see Charles Finn, *Mortgage Lending in Boston Neighborhoods, 1981–1987*. Boston: Boston Redevelopment Authority, 1989.

Related to this, social scientists have tended to overlook the role of asset accumulation and asset de-accumulation as a factor in the social and economic progress of blacks in America. To take one example, sociologist Stanley Lieberson wrote *A Piece of the Pie: Black and White Immigrants Since 1880* (Berkeley: University of California Press, 1980). Lieberson asks the question why blacks are not like the "new European" groups who have managed to make economic and social progress. Despite the suggestive title, assets are not a focus of inquiry in the book.

51. William J. Wilson, *The Truly Disadvantaged: The Inner City, the Underclass, and Public Policy*. Chicago: University of Chicago Press, 1987.

52. Douglas Massey and Mitchell Eggers, "The Ecology of Inequality: Minorities and the Concentration of Poverty, 1970–1980," *American Journal of Sociology* 95(5), 1990, 1153–88.

53. For example, in 1989 *Money* magazine commissioned Dataman Information Services Inc., an Atlanta firm that tracks housing prices, to provide sales data by zip code in three cities. Predominantly white and predominantly black areas were then matched by income levels. A consistent pattern of significantly lower appreciation of housing values in black neighborhoods was found (Walter L. Updegrave, "Race and Money," *Money*, December 1989, 152–72).

54. Calculations based on data from U.S. Bureau of the Census, *Statistical Abstract of the United States: 1989*, 109th edition. Washington: U.S. Government Printing Office, 1989.

55. Marable, 1983.

56. Data to corroborate the interpretation of limited increases in black business ownership from the 1960s to the 1980s are apparently non-existent. Jules Lichtenstein, Chief of Applied Policy, Small Business Administration, reports that reliable comparative data are not available.

57. Billy J. Tidwell, "Black Wealth: Facts and Fiction," in National Urban League, ed., *The State of Black America 1988*. Washington: National Urban League, 1988, 193–238; and Francine D. Blau and John W. Graham, "Black/White Differences in Wealth and Asset Accumulation," Working Paper No. 2898. Cambridge, MA: National Bureau of Economic Research, 1989.

58. U.S. Bureau of the Census, *Household Wealth and Asset Ownership, 1984*, Current Population Reports, Household Economic Studies, Series P–70, No. 7. Washington: U.S. Government Printing Office, 5.

59. U.S. Small Business Administration, *The State of Small Business*. Washington: U.S. Government Printing Office, 1987, 223–70.

60. Chester L. Blair, "Increasing Black Wealth," *St. Louis American*, January 4–10, 1990, 4A, reprinted from the *Pittsburgh Courier*.

8 • Toward a Theory of Welfare Based on Assets

The question is: What constitutes welfare (well-being) under the social and economic conditions of welfare capitalism?[1] The thesis of this book is that the answer lies, in part, in accumulation of assets—not income alone, but assets as well. Therefore, a dynamic welfare theory that incorporates the economic and behavioral effects of asset accumulation is perhaps required. Because such a theory does not already exist, the purpose of this chapter is to attempt, in a preliminary way, to construct it.[2]

Springs and Ponds

A respected friend and economist read one of my early papers on asset-based welfare policy. He responded that although asset-based welfare is an interesting idea, in his opinion, it probably would not turn out to be very useful. My colleague went on to reason as follows:

> Both flows and stocks (income and assets) are important, but nothing about inequality or poverty *turns* on the distinction. I can make this clear by an example. Is a spring or a pond more valuable as a source of water? Water is clearly what is important. Likewise, *command over resources* is what is important regarding poverty and inequality.

On the face of it, this sounds sensible—incisive and challenging words from a thoughtful person. This is the standard perspective of neoclassical economics, wherein assets are assumed to be stored income, representing potential for consumption, but nothing more. In this sense, income and assets are seen as different forms of the same thing—financial resources—and one can be made equivalent to the other. But let us take a closer look at the analogy. Which is more valuable as a source of water, a spring or a pond? Are they really only different forms of the same thing?

Having grown up in Kansas and worked for a while in rural Arkansas, I have spent some time on farms, and I know a little about springs and ponds. If springs are very large and very reliable (that is, do not give out during dry weather), then farmers may rely on such springs. But such springs are quite rare. Smaller springs are more common. Typically, these smaller springs have small flows of water, sometimes seasonal in output, perhaps drying up altogether during July and August. But farmers know how to use small and irregular springs—they build ponds to store the water, making it available year-around. Thus, for most farmers who are lucky enough to have a spring, the question really is not spring versus pond, but spring *and* pond. Many other farmers, of course, have no spring at all, but build ponds to catch rain water. Thus, whatever the source, small and irregular flows of water are captured and held for future use. True, all of the water initially comes from the flows. But without the pond (the stock of water), farmers are at the mercy of unreliable flows; they have no command over resources across an extended period of time. Thus, over the long term, flows and stocks (income and assets) play *complementary* roles. It is not a matter of choosing one or the other. Rather, it is a matter of balancing one with the other.

In this analogy, command over resources across time has several desirable consequences. The first and most obvious is to smooth uneven flows of water so that water is available in the pond even when it is not flowing from the spring or from rainfall. A second consequence is that, with water always available, farmers spend far less time and effort locating and hauling water for livestock; the whole process of watering animals is easier. Note that this is not simply a matter of being able to water the animals, but how much energy and effort it takes to do so. (For example, during the dust-bowl years of the 1930s, the wells dried up on my grandparents' farm and the family had to haul water in a horse-drawn wagon for their livestock for several months. This activity took many hours each day.)

Third, with readily and consistently available water, farmers can plan for the future. Were they totally at the mercy of the weather, farmers would be very cautious in expanding the herd or taking any risk, and they would at times have no control over when to sell. (For example, during the drought of the summer of 1988 in the Midwest—in some areas the driest summer in more than fifty years—many farmers were forced to sell their cattle because they could not properly feed and water them. With so much beef on the market, prices at livestock auctions were greatly reduced. Many farmers lost money selling at these prices, but they had no choice.) But if farmers control water resources, they can hold the cattle and wait until prices are higher. With water available, they can calculate and carry out a long-term strategy.

Fourth, due to increased predictability, farmers feel a greater sense of personal control. In an occupation that is sometimes like a poker game, the farmers hold some of the aces. With uncertainty and risk reduced, they are more likely to maintain and expand assets. This retention and increase in assets also leads to the enhanced social position of "successful farmer" and to greater social standing in the community. Very often this social influence is also transformed into increased political participation. With greater assets, farmers are more likely to engage in the political activities necessary to protect and enhance those assets.

Welfare Effects of Assets in Households

If the springs and ponds analogy above has merit, then a theory of social welfare based on assets should be explored. To be successful, this theory would specify and begin to demonstrate economic, social, and psychological outcomes *in addition to potential consumption* that constitute welfare benefits of assets. As previously discussed, income-based welfare policy assumes that the level of household income (as a proxy for consumption) is equivalent to "welfare." I have argued that this income and consumption perspective is inadequate. But if assets create welfare effects beyond consumption, what are these effects? What do assets do for individuals and families that income does not do?[3]

The preliminary theory presented here has two principal features. First, it views household financial welfare as a long-term, dynamic process rather than as a cross-sectional financial position at a given time. Assets capture this long-term, dynamic quality better than income because assets reflect lifetime financial accumulation. Second, the theory proposes that more than consumption is involved in house-

---

Figure 8.1. **Welfare Effects of Assets**

- Improve household stability
- Create an orientation toward the future
- Stimulate development of other assets
- Enable focus and specialization
- Provide a foundation for risk taking
- Increase personal efficacy
- Increase social influence
- Increase political participation
- Enhance the welfare of offspring

---

hold financial welfare, possibly much more. In other words, according to this viewpoint, assets yield important effects beyond consumption.[4]

In the following discussion, a number of theories and sources of data from psychology, sociology, and economics are borrowed and incorporated into an asset-based welfare theory. On occasion, an observation, a story, or a bit of reasoning is added to the analysis. As with most new ideas, the major theoretical problem is not that no theory exists, but rather that various pieces of theory and evidence have not previously been put together in a way that illuminates the new idea. This chapter attempts to make some of these conceptual connections regarding the welfare effects of assets.

The suggestion here is that assets have a variety of important social, psychological, and economic effects. Simply put, people think and behave differently when they are accumulating assets, and the world responds to them differently as well. More specifically, assets improve economic stability; connect people with a viable, hopeful future; stimulate development of human and other capital; enable people to focus and specialize; provide a foundation for risk taking; yield personal, social, and political dividends; and enhance the welfare of offspring (Figure 8.1).

These nine welfare effects of assets are presented here as propositions. Each proposition is based on established theory and evidence. However, the extent to which each proposition is true, and under what circumstances, and possible interrelationships among the propositions, are not specified at the present time. In the future, specific empirical questions should be raised and research designed to answer those questions. For now, we take a closer look at the propositions.

Assets Improve Household Stability

In terms of household stability, the principal role of assets is to cushion income shocks that occur with major illness, job loss, or marital breakup. These events, when they occur in families near the income poverty line, throw many families into income poverty. Assets cushion income shocks by providing resources to bridge income shortfalls. When assets are present, the family is less likely to fall into chaos, and more likely to maintain social and economic equilibrium until sufficient income can be reestablished.

Let us take the most common type of income shock—the loss of a regular job. When unemployment strikes, the family first relies on unemployment insurance if it is available. (At this writing, only about one-third of all unemployed people receive unemployment insurance, and those who receive it are not those with the greatest needs.) When unemployment insurance runs out, the family turns to primary assets, first spending accumulated savings, then cash from the sale of insurance policies, and later cash from sale of the family car or home. When primary assets are exhausted, the family typically turns to various forms of borrowing from relatives, thereby accumulating liabilities (negative assets), financial or personal. These include loans from parents or other family members, and eventually moving into the residence of other family members. In this way, many families ride out the transition to new employment. Those with limited primary and secondary resources become economically desperate much faster. Moreover, because economic worries are a major contributor to a cluster of psychological and social problems associated with unemployment, the family is also more likely to bear the wounds of mental depression, rage, marital breakup, child and spouse abuse, alcohol and drug use, and so forth.[5]

Looking at this issue through the lens of neoclassical economics, people theoretically try to consume at a level in accordance with their ''permanent income'' (expected lifetime income). This tendency smooths short-term ups and downs in income. When people have less income, they spend from accumulated assets, borrow against assets, or borrow against future income.[6] However, when assets are not present, liquidity constraints (lack of readily available and fairly priced credit) often prohibit borrowing against future income.

What is the nature of these liquidity constraints? Capital markets (credit markets) have imperfect information about borrowers and may refuse to lend even when borrowers are good risks.[7] Another way of looking at this is that capital markets function much less perfectly in evaluating human capital than in evaluating financial capital. Even though someone may have the educational background and skills required to earn a solid income, capital markets may not accurately value this human capital. This is a problem of asymmetric information—the borrower may have more accurate information about the risk of the loan than does the lender. The lender asks for a premium to cover the perceived risk. Therefore, when credit is available at all, it is often paid for at a premium because of this imperfect information and imperfect valuation. Thus, when assets are not accumulated ahead of time, borrowing is, in most households, an added real cost. This added cost, in itself, can be enough to make a marginal borrower ineligible for a loan.

Financial assets reduce imperfections in credit market information because they are more easily valued. Also, financial assets can be collateralized. Equity in housing, for example, although often considered illiquid, may be flexibly used in times of emergency, or used simply to enhance one's standard of living. The rapid rise in home equity credit lines is one example of using housing assets at relatively low—and tax-benefited—costs for the credit.

A related concept is path dependence. This dynamic concept suggests that economic welfare depends not only on total lifetime income but on how one proceeds through the income flow. In other words, welfare depends, to some extent, on the path one has taken to arrive at his or her present position. Applying this idea to household income shocks, a household with sharp income fluctuations may not be in the same financial position as a comparable household that has enjoyed stable income, even though the total income for both households is the same. Instability can lead to liquidity constraints, and under these circumstances, even temporary shortfalls can lead to large problems. For example, during an income shock, a house might have to be sold for a loss in a depressed housing market, a previously sound credit rating might be ruined, or a child's education might be interrupted. Susan Mayer and Christopher Jencks report that the effects of an income shortfall greatly depend on the sequence (or path) of affluence and poverty: "Past affluence provides some cushion against the effects of current poverty; future affluence provides none."[8]

Assets Create an Orientation toward the Future

When human beings are secure in the present, they tend to look toward the future. For most people, it is not so much today that matters, but tomorrow, the dream, the chance, the hope of improvement. There is great individual variation, but in general, people look ahead. In this respect, human beings are more teleological than most modern psychological theory recognizes.

Permit me to recount a story: I was fortunate to attend a presentation, in 1976, by the Argentinian writer and Nobel laureate, Jorge Luis Borges. Old, frail, and blind, the famous author was asked which of his many stories, novels, poems he liked best. Borges thought for a moment, and surprisingly said, ''I like only a couple of the short stories and one poem. All the rest are not any good at all, a waste of time.'' The audience was shocked at his reply. The room was totally silent. Having created the desired effect, a great smile came over Borges's face, and he said, ''But I'm very fond of my future work.''

Of course, Borges's strong orientation toward the future had much to do with his enormous literary productivity. Future orientation is a key element in achieving success. Olympic athletes imagine themselves competing in a future event at the peak of their abilities. Without orientation toward the future, hope does not thrive, visions are not created, plans are not made, and struggle and sacrifice are not undertaken. Future orientation is common among successful people, and not so common among those who are not successful.

Middle-class people, on average, have stronger future orientations than do lower-class people. The poor tend to be oriented toward the present, and tend not to work toward long-term goals.[9] Why is this so? Explanations differ. The conservative right says the problem is values. According to this perspective, until values are changed, nothing can improve, and values are changed only by individuals and families. The progressive left, on the other hand, says that it is impossible to think about tomorrow when there is not enough food on the table today. Without sufficient food, housing, medical care, and other basic necessities, people are not free to look ahead and plan for a better tomorrow. Unfortunately, neither of these explanations is entirely satisfactory. Let us explore the issue further, beginning with a well-publicized news story.

In 1980, Eugene Lang, a multimillionaire industrialist, gave a commencement address to sixty-one sixth graders in Harlem. Most were black or Hispanic. Most were poor. The high school dropout rate in the area was 50–75 percent, and almost no one went to college. Lang told the sixth graders that if they stayed in school, he would pay their college tuition. In 1985, all fifty-two students remaining in the New York area had stayed in school and many were doing well enough to qualify for college. Almost all of these students graduated from high school. In 1988, about half of the original group were enrolled in college. (A number of others enrolled in college, did not do well, and quit—possibly due to the inferior quality of their high school education.) Although not a perfect success, the record of educational achievement in this experiment is nothing short of remarkable.[10]

Why did the program succeed? Several students explicitly said they thought that Lang's concept had worked because many children in the neighborhood had, in the past, put ideas of college out of their minds at an early age, thinking that it was a luxury beyond their reach. But with a guarantee of college, the students and their families began to think and behave differently.

Apparently, even the most poor and disadvantaged young people respond constructively to future possibilities when they *have* possibilities. This observation relates to the concept of life chances developed by Max Weber[11] and Ralf Dahrendorf.[12] The Lang experiment confirms that life chances (structural limitations and opportunities) are very real. In this regard, the values-only perspective of the conservative right appears to be inadequate (Lang did not tell the sixth graders that they needed better values; he told them that they could go to college if they wanted to do so—he promised them a future asset). But why did the students respond? How do life chances get inside of people's heads and express themselves in particular actions? Specifically, how are structural opportunities translated into future-oriented behavior? On this key question, the progressive left has made little progress.

The proposition here is that orientation toward the future begins in part with assets, which in turn shape opportunity structures, which in turn are quickly internalized. This process might be called the construction of future possibilities. Whole life chances, life courses, are assessed, integrated, and fixed at an early age unless something out of the ordinary breaks the pattern.

For example, it can be convincingly argued that high rates of high school dropout result from teenage perceptions of futures with too few possibilities. Impoverished young people, regardless of race, tend to drop out of school because they do not believe that they will be able to go to college, and they do not believe that finishing high school will make much difference in their life chances.[13] Many urban teenagers who use crack and other drugs say matter-of-factly that they have nothing to live for, do not care if they die, and just want to have a good time today.

Just as negative expectations about the future have negative effects on behavior, positive expectations have positive effects. Turning to the problem of adolescent pregnancy, columnist William Raspberry perceptively comments on a National Academy of Sciences report:

> Youngsters who believe that they have a bright future ahead of them find it easier to make positive decisions, easier to resist peer pressure, easier to make the sacrifices necessary for academic excellence and easier to say no to drugs, sex and other future-threatening temptations. . . . our major task is to see to it that our children have, and know that they have, an opportunity for a decent, fulfilling life. We have to help them understand that, to a far greater extent than many of them imagine, they have the capacity to create their own success. What they need, in short, is not merely the means for avoiding pregnancy but a reason for doing so.[14]

It has become clear that adolescent pregnancy is not always a "mistake." Some adolescent boys use pregnancy to establish identity and manhood. Some teenage girls *choose* pregnancy because, within their limited set of opportunities, pregnancy and motherhood provide a definition of adulthood and independence. In other words, as they see the world, pregnancy is a positive choice. The large racial difference in adolescent pregnancy and unmarried motherhood may be, in part, explained by this. A study of "locus of control" among pregnant teenagers reports that pregnant white teens generally have an external locus of control, while pregnant black teens have an internal locus of control.[15] In other words, pregnant white teens are more likely to be influenced by others, but pregnant black teens are choosing pregnancy. This interpretation is supported by data on abortions. Black teens, on the average, have more pregnancies than white teens, but black teens have fewer abortions.[16] A reasonable interpretation is that black teens see pregnancy as a legitimate path to adulthood. They are responding to a limited set of options.

One of the chief psychological tasks of adolescence is gaining independence from parents. Children from middle-class backgrounds may use college as the mechanism for fulfilling this task. But lower-class adolescents do not necessarily view education and economic independence as phases of maturation that precede parenthood.[17] This interpretation is supported by the fact that women who plan to finish high school and go to college are much more consistent users of birth control than those who have no future educational plans.[18] Thus, lower-class teens have a different idea about growing up and becoming mature. For black teens especially, the "normal" progression of entering the labor market and then moving on to childbearing is often reversed.

How are such ideas constructed? From whom, what, where, when, and how does a particular view of the future develop? To begin to answer these questions, it is helpful to turn to cognitive psychological theory.[19]

Information reception begins at birth, and the effects of information are cumulative. But information does not accumulate randomly. Only salient information, that is, information that is considered to be relevant, is received. All the rest goes by unreceived, quite literally as if it did not exist.

Environmental limitations, particularly early in the life cycle, restrict development of the cognitive structure, limiting opportunity for later learning. For example, if the concept of "asset accumulation" is not part of the household environment—as it is not in many poor households—then nothing is learned about this idea.

Elaboration of salient information is developed through attributions of causality in the environment.[20] In other words, people pay attention to events and information that they believe are the causes of things that matter to them. People do this because they are trying to understand and control their environments in order to increase their safety and well-being.[21]

Salient information leaves memory traces in the brain and facilitates development of categorical structures, or schemata, which influence the perception and interpretation of subsequent similar information. Schemata are cognitive structures, or general expectations—in a scientific framework, hypotheses and theories—about the way the world functions.[22] Schemata are used to simplify the person's understanding of the social world, allowing the person to focus on what she or he considers to be the most relevant features of that world. Once formed, schemata are strong and resistant to change.[23] But new information sometimes changes schemata, literally creating new structures of knowledge. This in turn may change both the salience and the meaning of subsequent information.

Thus, schemata serve as templates or filters for subsequent information. The extent to which information is useful to a particular individual depends on whether his or her cognitive structure can recognize and apply the information to advantage. Given a certain cognitive structure, some information becomes meaningful or consequential and some does not. The total network of schemata can be considered an individual's personalized view of the world, his or her own theory of reality.[24]

Thus, a teenage female who has spent fifteen or sixteen years growing up in an environment that provides few options to poor families, few life chances, tends to develop a set of cognitive schemata that recognizes only those limited opportunities. If the only schema for maturity she has known is to grow up and have children, it is actually quite difficult for her to even *perceive* information about other options. This information has no place to fit into her brain: it goes right by.

How do assets relate to cognitive theory? When assets are present, the concept of assets becomes a meaningful schema. Assets alter the reception of information. To put it plainly, when assets are present, people begin to think in terms of assets. For example, if a young mother owns her own home, she begins to pay more attention to real estate values, property taxes, the cost of maintenance, and so forth. If she has a certificate of deposit, she is more likely to pay attention to interest rates and what makes interest rates go up and down. If she owns twenty-five shares of IBM stock, she is more likely to pay attention to news about IBM, the computer business in general, the stock market, and alternative investment options. Note that *it is the assets themselves that create this effect* (as opposed to educational programs or exhortations toward better values). Assets create a cognitive reality, a schema, because assets are concrete and consequential. All this can be said very simply: Assets matter and people know it, and therefore, when they have assets, they pay attention to them. If they do not have assets, they do not pay attention.

Assets are, by nature, long term. They financially connect the present with the future. Indeed, in a sense, assets *are* the future. They are hope in concrete form. Eugene Lang offered the Harlem sixth graders a future asset—college tuition—and they responded literally as if they had been given a future. Thinking about management and use of assets automatically results in long-term thinking and planning. If people are to believe in a viable future, there must be some tangible link between now and then. In very many situations, assets are that link.

Assets Promote Development of Human Capital and Other Assets

Owning financial assets, for most people, is an educational process. People pay attention to the investment, manage it, make some successful decisions, make some mistakes, seek out information, and throughout this process, gain a greater financial knowledge and sophistication. With this experience, people are likely to display greater interest, greater effort, and greater success in additional financial endeavors. This added effort, on the average, leads to increased income and accumulation of assets.

In this way, financial capital stimulates the development of human capital. The traditional assumption of human capital theorists is that the process of personal economic development begins with human capital, that is, that individuals improve themselves and then they become financially better off. But it is not a one-way street. A main point of this book is that tangible assets also stimulate people to improve themselves.

In a study of U.S. blue-collar workers, sociologist David Halle finds that property in the form of home ownership is a rarely questioned goal, and when achieved, is seldom regretted. Home ownership, for blue-collar workers, is the most important way of saving and accumulating wealth. Halle notes that purchasing the first home is a large hurdle, and many workers are willing to make big sacrifices to get started. "A man can work overtime or take a second job; his wife can work; they can postpone having children for several years; they can avoid paying rent during the first stage of marriage by living with parents or close kin. . . ."[25] All of these can be seen as unusual efforts to build capital for the sake of a future asset.

Owning concrete assets, such as land, durable goods, and housing, also promotes the productivity, care, and maintenance of those assets. This ancient and oft-repeated lesson was learned by Europeans on these shores at the Jamestown colony. At the outset, the Virginia Company required all Jamestown employees to contribute the fruits of their labor to a common storehouse, from which the goods were distributed according to need. However, after several years of near starvation, the company abandoned this policy and gave each settler a three-acre garden. Private ownership caused a boon in productivity. Food shortages were no longer a problem.[26] At this writing, a similar scenario, on a very large scale, is being attempted in Eastern Europe and the Soviet Union.

A fruitful area of social science research in recent years has been the study of household time use. In a study comparing time use of the lower and middle classes, one striking conclusion is that members of middle-class households not only enjoy more stable employment income, but are also more likely to work in non-employment activities to better the household financial position, such as home remodeling and improving skills.[27] In other words, the presence of higher income and assets is associated with increased nonlabor market productivity. A partial explanation of these results is that those with assets have assets to protect, see a more positive future, and consequently are more willing to spend time and energy improving their condition. Thus, assets not only permit the acquisition of better goods, but also encourage maintenance of existing goods.

One promising line of thinking in explaining informal economic activity is the "new household economics," an extension of neoclassical economics to nonfinancial matters within the household.[28] The new household economics recognizes economic choices in apparently non-economic matters.[29] The theory has not yet been used to explain the effects of assets in household maintenance and improvement decisions. Nonetheless, there is in this theory a view of "investment" in a broad sense that may prove useful in understanding these activities. Actually, in a commonsense way, asset maintenance and improvement effects are very clear. They are sometimes called "sweat equity." Why does a young mother spend two weekends putting a new tile floor in her kitchen? In part to enhance the value of her property. Would she undertake this project if she rented (did not own) the house? Unlikely.

Assets Enable Focus and Specialization

Let us begin this point by analogy. Adam Smith in *The Wealth of Nations* recognized that in industry, accumulation of capital did not follow, but logically preceded, specialization of labor:

> A weaver cannot apply himself entirely to his peculiar business, unless there is beforehand stored up somewhere, either in his own possession or in that of some other person, a stock sufficient to maintain him, and to supply him with the materials and tools of his work, till he has not only compleated, but sold his web. This accumulation must, evidently, be previous to his applying his industry for so long a time to such a peculiar business.[30]

In Smith's day, households were typically units of production, either as farms or as small manufacturers. Today, households tend not to be units of production, but the dynamics of capital accumulation and specialization are similar. Accumulation of household assets enables focus and specialization. In poor households, people spend their time in a wide diversity of tasks because they do not have sufficient assets to enable greater focus and specialization. The reasons are twofold: First, assets are needed in advance of income flows to purchase the tools and skills for specialization. Second, without assets, there are no resources to pay others for required goods and services while one specializes. Consequently, short-term and odd jobs are undertaken for additional income, even though these jobs are often unrelated to specialized career advancement. Overall, it is exactly as Adam Smith suggested—without assets, "a weaver cannot apply himself entirely to his peculiar business," and a poor person cannot specialize enough to get ahead.

For example, living in rural Arkansas a number of years ago, in a very poor county, I was impressed by a couple of things. First, in situations of poverty, a large number of things go wrong. Poverty generates a sort of continual chaos. Things are always breaking down; every transaction seems to be complicated. Second, individuals necessarily respond to most of these problems on their own. A single individual is farmer, gardener, rancher, veterinarian, horse trainer, carpenter, electrician, welder, auto repair person, cook, housekeeper, and single parent of six children. (In this case, I am speaking about a particularly capable woman, but there are many others like her, both male and female.) All of these skills and activities are required just to get by. One might imagine that a person with so many skills, and who is very hardworking, would be wealthy. But this is not so. These varied tasks are undertaken because the individual has no resources to pay others to do them. In poor households, people tend to be Jills and Jacks of all trades. The resulting set of skills may be admirable, even remarkable, and the person may be, in this sense, well rounded. But she or he is not likely to be wealthy. Generation of wealth requires focus and specialization of knowledge and skills.

The same principle applies to paid labor activity. Poor people, because they have no choice, make decisions for short-term income that are not in their long-term career interests. Many people forego opportunities for specialized education and training because they have to feed their families. In economic terms, specialization yields a division of labor and comparative advantage, but asset-poor households do not have much opportunity to develop a comparative advantage.

It is also my perception that these dynamics are all but invisible to people who have assets. When sufficient assets are present, freedom to focus is taken for granted. Because of this, those who have assets may not correctly interpret patterns of behavior among those with no resources. Many behaviors labeled "culture of poverty" are, in my opinion, better explained by financial inability to focus and specialize. Apparently non-directed behavior can often be understood as survival activity in the presence of no resources and, consequently, no ability to focus and specialize.

Assets Provide a Foundation for Risk-Taking

Related to focus and specialization, assets also provide a foundation for risk taking. The conceptual base that underlies this thinking is portfolio theory.[31] Portfolio theory deals with the construction of optimal portfolios by rational risk-averse investors.

With more assets, a household can more effectively diversify its holdings. This is true because, for a household with few assets, transaction costs for multiple investments are too high. For example, it is inefficient to buy and sell odd lots of common stocks. Diversification, when it can be done efficiently, increases returns. In other words, with diversification, one can obtain a higher return for a given level of risk. Harry Markowitz called these "efficient portfolios" (see note 31). Also, diversification protects against negative consequences of taking a loss, and therefore permits greater freedom for risk taking in the search for larger gains. Simply put, with more assets, the ability to take risks with a safety net is increased.

Of course, the concept of risk taking has more than purely financial applications. When the level of security is increased, from assets or any other source, the ability to take psychological and social risks is also increased. When there is something to fall back on, people behave differently. A good example of this is the tenure system in universities. Tenure is a promise of a lifetime job. It is a very large financial, as well as professional, asset. Anyone familiar with this system has seen the rather cautious behaviors of pre-tenure faculty members, and the more independent behaviors of the same faculty members after they have received tenure.

Assets Increase Personal Efficacy

Assets also increase personal efficacy. This feature of assets was recognized by Adam Smith[32] and many others, including the nineteenth century sociologist William Graham Sumner. Sumner wrote a very popular social Darwinist tract entitled *What the Social Classes Owe to Each Other* (his answer was: not much). However, Sumner did correctly see the critical role of capital in determining well-being:

> Undoubtedly the man who possesses capital has a great advantage over the man who has no capital, in all the struggle for existence. Think of two men who want to lift a weight, one of whom has a lever, and the other must apply his hands directly; think of two men tilling the soil, one of whom used his hands or a stick, while the other has a horse and a plough; think of two men in conflict with a wild animal, one of whom has only a stick or a stone, while the other has a repeating rifle; think of two men who are sick, one of whom can travel, command medical skill, get space, light, air, and water, while the other lacks all these things. This does not mean that one man has an advantage against the other, but that, when they are rivals in the effort to get the means of subsistence from Nature, the one who has capital has immeasurable advantages over the other. . . . The man who has capital has secured his future, won leisure which he can employ in winning secondary objects of necessity and advantage, and emancipated himself from those things in life which are gross and belittling. . . . The maxim, or injunction, to which a study of capital leads us is, Get capital.[33]

This idea of strength, control, and security coming from assets has been recently noted by Senator Daniel Moynihan. The very week that his income-based welfare reform bill, the Family Support Act, had become law, he made the following observation about assets:

> We make a great fuss over regular income—partly because we measure it precisely (thanks to the income tax) and partly because it is what most of us live on. In reality, regular income is a sometime thing. It bounces around, especially at lower levels. Wealth—real estate, stocks, bonds, and capital assets—endures. . . . It can be used to nurture children for whatever success is said to require, be it tuition or orthodontia. Wealth is an insurance policy that gives not only physical but psychological comfort to a developing child.[34]

In other words, assets allow greater prediction and control.[35] They serve as a counterweight to learned helplessness and vulnerability. Also, assets provide flexibility. There is no need to occupy oneself in the exercising of financial assets the way one must with human capital. More time and energy is available for other endeavors.[36]

When Lester Thurow identifies "economic power" as a motive for asset accumulation, he is perhaps talking about personal efficacy. He concludes that people leave large bequests, rather than consuming the wealth or transferring the wealth to children before death, "simply because there is no way to enjoy economic power until death without leaving a fortune after death. . . . To give up economic power within the family is to give up one's status and station. Few individuals are willing to give up their economic power even vis-à-vis their own children."[37]

To take one concrete example of control and empowerment effects of assets in welfare policy, we can look at retirement pension plans. Personally held assets yield greater choices at retirement. Social Security, an entitlement to retirement income at a certain age, has tremendous effects on the average age of retirement; that is, people tend to retire when Social Security is available. In addition to Social Security, about 50 percent of U.S. workers are now covered by some type of private pension plan, and about 75 percent of these private pensions are defined-benefits plans (defined-benefit means that the company controls when and how much retirement income the worker receives). Defined-benefit pension plans have even larger effects on retirement decisions than does Social Security. In other words, defined-benefit plans tend to limit retirement choices because, under defined-benefit plans, there are large incentives *not* to retire until a certain age, and then large incentives *to* retire when that age is reached. On the other hand, defined-contribution pension plans, in which the worker controls the underlying assets, have much smaller retirement effects (i.e., workers have greater choices). Workers with defined-contribution plans are more likely to retire before the age of sixty and also more likely to work beyond the "normal" retirement age of sixty-two or sixty-five. Defined-contribution plans, because the workers control the assets, give workers greater choices about when to retire, and empirical evidence indicates workers take advantage of these greater choices.[38] Employers use defined-benefit plans as a "stick" to get older workers to retire, but they cannot do the same with defined-contribution plans.[39] The key difference is *who controls the assets.*

Assets Increase Social Influence

Some ninety years ago, Thorstein Veblen, in his classic book, *The Theory of the Leisure Class*, recognized that wealth accumulation serves social purposes far beyond economic necessity. Veblen saw wealth accumulation as a function of "pecuniary emulation," the seeking of social influence through accumulation of money, a pursuit without end:

> If, as is sometimes assumed, the incentive to accumulation were the want of subsistence or of physical comfort, then the aggregate economic wants of a community might conceivably be satisfied at some point in the advance of industrial efficiency; but since the struggle is substantially a race for reputability on the basis of an invidious comparison, no approach to a definitive attainment is possible.[40]

In other words, assets yield not only economic well-being, but also social status effects. This proposition seems so true to us today that it would be difficult to find a person who disagreed. As Veblen went on to describe, these social status effects are achieved in part through displays of wealth in "conspicuous leisure" and "conspicuous consumption."

Adam Smith, in *The Wealth of Nations*, saw the social influence effects of assets in more direct terms, observing that capital has "a certain command over all the labor, or over all the produce of labor, which is then in the market."[41] Responding to Smith, Karl Marx also recognized the "command" of capital. In Marx's thinking, capital is power, and the love of power is the driving force in capital accumulation. For observers on the left, the drive for prestige and distinction, evidenced through prestige goods, is a drive for power: "Wealth is therefore a social category inseparable from power."[42]

Alexis de Tocqueville, looking at the United States in the early part of the nineteenth century, believed that wealth played a stronger role in democratic nations than in aristocracies:

> Men living in democratic times have many passions, but most of these culminate in love of wealth or derive from it. That is not because their souls are narrower but because money really is more important in such times.
>
> When every citizen is independent of and indifferent to the rest, the cooperation of each of them can only be obtained by paying for it; this indefinitely multiplies the purpose to which wealth may be applied and increases its value.
>
> When the prestige attached to what is old has vanished, men are no longer distinguished, or hardly distinguished, by birth, standing, or profession; there is thus hardly anything left but money which makes very clear distinctions between men or can raise some of them above the common level. Distinction based on wealth is increased by the disappearance or diminution of all other distinctions.
>
> In aristocratic nations money is the key to the satisfaction of but few of the vast array of possible desires; in democracies it is the key to them all.[43]

Several important sociological studies have focused on the connection between wealth and social influence.[44] Among modern economic theorists, Anthony Shorrocks explicitly suggests that a major function of wealth is to increase social influence.[45] Denis Kessler and André Masson develop the idea of K-wealth, which includes assets held mainly for economic returns, social power, and transmission to future generations. As these writers observe, K-wealth is considerably more concentrated than is S-wealth, which is for consumption and short-term precaution. K-wealth is controlled primarily by the upper class.[46] Long before, Adam Smith drew much the same distinction between two types of wealth.[47] In the first systematic U.S. study of attitudes toward property, the sociologist and investor Alfred Winslow Jones found that the public makes a similar distinction.[48] The public view of property rights differs depending on the nature of the property—corporate property is not considered to be as rightfully held as personal property.

Assets have other important social effects as well. Assets can buy social capital in the form of contacts, networks of protection, information, resources, and so forth. As discussed in chapter 7, in a wealthy family, "phone calls are made" to open doors, bend rules, and move to the head of the line.

Another important social effect of assets, perhaps the most important, is that assets provide backup in negotiations. With assets, people have more options and are less likely to be "pushed around." In part, this means that people are less likely to make bad decisions based on short-term constraints.

Paradoxically, people who hold assets may not see their own influence and the freedom of decision it offers. John Kenneth Galbraith, in a discussion of wealth, has recognized this naive quality of social power:

> A decision which one is free to make rarely impresses one as an exercise of power. To the extent that it makes any impression at all it is likely to seem a rather obvious exercise of intelligence. A decision on which one is blocked by the authority of another is a very different matter. It is bound to make a deep impression. The impression will also, normally, be one of arbitrary or egregious misuse of power. This is why we live in a world of constant protests against the authority of others and of replies which reflect a deep and usually genuine content of injured innocence.[49]

Thus, in certain respects, those who control assets may be the last to acknowledge the influence that assets bestow. One cannot help but wonder if this impairment of vision has anything to do with the almost complete absence of asset-based welfare policies for the poor.

To summarize the social function of assets very clearly, assets often make the difference between an inferior and a superior position in social interactions. Poor people, without assets, are more often in inferior positions, as society expects them to be. Wealthy people, with assets, are more often in superior positions, once again as society expects them to be. Despite the "common man" rhetoric of American culture, almost everyone understands that, most of the time, it is more comfortable to be in the superior position.

Assets Increase Political Participation

Thomas Jefferson extolled the political stability of a nation of small farmers, believing that widespread property ownership guaranteed an active and involved citizenry. Indeed, access to political participation was constructed around landownership. This situation gradually changed, but when Tocqueville visited America in 1830, land, financial capital, or taxpaying on property was still required by law for exercising the right to vote in Massachusetts, Rhode Island, Connecticut, New Jersey, South Carolina, Maryland, Tennessee, Mississippi, Ohio, Georgia, Virginia, Pennsylvania, Delaware, and New York.[50] The direct connection between property holding and voting basically ended by 1860;[51] however, remnants still remain in the voter registration process. In the absence of automatic registration, home owners are more likely to vote in elections than are people who do not own their homes. And when one looks at the shocking amount of capital required to run a successful political campaign, it is clear that the role of assets in political participation is very much with us.

People with assets have both greater incentives and greater resources to participate in the political process. Wealth leads to a greater effort to protect property, and ultimately, to greater political participation. Related to the latter point, John Kenneth Galbraith has perceptively argued that the redistribution of wealth in industrialized nations has been a primary cause for the development of middle-class-oriented welfare state policies.[52] People with assets become politically active in protecting those assets, which leads to social policy development.

It is also true that increased household assets tend to lead, for better or worse, to greater commitment to the status quo. Galbraith observes: "It is simply a matter of arithmetic that change *may* be costly to the man who has something; it cannot be so to the man who has nothing. There will always be a high correlation between conservatism and personal well-being."[53]

Again, the observant Tocqueville noticed this relationship. He believed that democracy leads to greater distribution of wealth, and with wealth distribution comes political stability, because small property owners are "eager and restless" in protecting and increasing their stake:

> Not only do men in democracies feel no natural inclination for revolutions, but they are afraid of them.
>
> Any revolution is more or less a threat to property. Most inhabitants of a democracy have property. And not only have they got property, but they live in the conditions in which men attach most value to property.
>
> If one studies each class of which society is composed closely, it is easy to see that passions due to ownership are keenest among the middle classes. . . .
>
> Hence the majority of citizens in a democracy do not see clearly what they could gain by a revolution, but they constantly see a thousand ways in which they could lose by one.[54]

In contrast, those who are propertyless have no such commitment to the status quo. For example, at this writing, there is public disorder in Great Britain in protest of a new tax on government services, replacing real estate taxes on homes. As a result of this policy change, millions of poor British households will be worse off, and home owners will be better off. The propertyless have reacted by rioting:

> Sociologists, experts on public order and politicians now say the violence was largely the work of a small group of unemployed young men who are generally homeless and penniless.
>
> Whether operating as revolutionary groups or on their own, they are viewed as part of an embittered class of young people with little stake in the new Britain. . . .[55]

Sometimes the phrase "property-owning democracy" is used to indicate the almost implicit political stability that ownership of assets—a stake in the system—seems to generate. Today in the United States, it is not only real estate and personal property that enhance political stability but also substantial assets in retirement pension accounts, which many middle-class Americans have accumulated.

Assets Increase the Welfare of Offspring

Related to future orientation, assets also increase the welfare of offspring. Assets provide an intergenerational connection that income and consumption cannot provide. For a parent, this may be a more important welfare effect than the parent's own well-being. The welfare of offspring is, after all, a form of immortality. Indeed, it is the only realistic and tangible form of immortality available to the vast majority of the population. And the pull of immortality is strong.

As described in chapter 7, the cumulative tendency of assets has important intergenerational welfare effects. Beginning life with some financial assets in the household is a tremendous advantage. As the old saying goes, "Some people stand on their own two feet, but some stand on their parents' shoulders." Franco Modigliani and Richard Brumberg, among the most consumption-oriented economic theorists, allow for the possibility that one motive of asset accumulation is to leave an estate to one's heirs.[56] Anthony Shorrocks states explicitly that one of the purposes of asset accumulation is transmission of advantages to future generations.[57] Accumulation of assets for this purpose has also been recognized by Lars Osberg.[58] Some wealth researchers suggest that the desire to make bequests and other intergenerational transfers is the *primary* reason for saving in the United States. Astoundingly, Laurence Kotlikoff finds that "If it could be enforced, a law that prohibited all intergenerational transfers could well reduce U.S. wealth by as much as 50 percent in the long run."[59]

An interesting observation related to this point is that reverse annuity mortgages (RAMs), a financial innovation developed during the late 1980s, have been highly unpopular. RAMs were introduced so that older people might be able to live off their housing equity, but older people apparently do not want to reduce their housing equity. There is presently almost no market for RAMs.[60] A likely explanation for the unpopularity of RAMs is the individual's desire to hold assets for the purpose of leaving bequests to offspring.

The Utility of Holding Assets

As noted in chapter 3, the theoretical model underlying most welfare programs for the poor is income-based. This model is almost entirely taken for granted, never explicitly stated. The model is highly influenced by a neoclassical economic perspective, which suggests that consuming more (more food, more housing, more recreation, more of whatever) is preferable to consuming less. The assumption is that people consume in ways that maximize utility. In other words, people spend their money, across time, in order to obtain as much consumption and leisure benefit as possible (either now or in the future). This consumption and leisure are assumed to have welfare benefits. Indeed, in this model, consumption and leisure are the only welfare benefits, that is, the level of consumption (of goods as well as leisure) is taken to be equivalent to the level of welfare.

In this conceptualization, savings and wealth accumulation serve no purpose other than to distribute consumption across the life path to maximize utility: "The level of savings actually achieved by anyone represents the outcome of the conflict between his desire to improve his current standard of living and his desire to obtain future welfare by saving."[61] Therefore, saving "has no direct utility but is only the means through which resources are carried back and forth to enforce the chosen consumption path."[62]

In many senses, the assumption that consumption equals utility is appealing, concise, and true by definition. When people do not have sufficient food, shelter, or medical care, they need more of it. On the other hand, it is a rather narrow vision. A consumption-only view of human welfare does not adequately reflect the complexities of human psychology, social life, or even economic behavior.[63]

Economic utility has always been a subject of considerable debate. Amitai Etzioni offers a review and discussion of various critiques of utility theory.[64] To take one criticism among many, Lester Thurow turns to "economic power" as an alternative motive for asset accumulation, and he concludes: "The net result of a desire for economic power is an accumulation of wealth and a transmittal of wealth that is irrational from the point of view of simple consumption economics."[65]

The theoretical propositions presented in this chapter, if they hold up to scrutiny, might warrant a reconsideration of a consumption-only view of economic utility. In other words, it may be that nonconsumption is not always nonutility. The thinking and evidence in this chapter suggest that nonconsumption (in the form of saving and asset holding) has, in and of itself, welfare effects quite apart and distinct from consumption, and perhaps no less important. If this is the case, some notion of the utility of savings and investment (beyond the utility of potential consumption) would be a worthwhile theoretical development.

Asset Sufficiency or Threshold

If assets indeed have the welfare effects suggested above, then an important issue related to asset-based welfare is sufficiency of asset accumulation. How much accumulation is necessary to achieve welfare effects? Is it appropriate to think in terms of some sufficient amount of assets?

The effect of household assets in generating welfare effects may not be perfectly linear. A more accurate picture might be that welfare effects of assets are lumpy or notched. In other words, it is possible that quanta or thresholds of assets are necessary to yield bundles of welfare effects. For example, considering household durable goods, one threshold might be the amount of resources required to purchase a washing machine, avoiding time-consuming and expensive trips to the laundromat. In financial affairs, a critical threshold might be the amount of resources necessary to maintain a checking account efficiently. Moving up the resource ladder, a critical threshold might the amount necessary to purchase residence in a "good" neighborhood with better schools and better public services. Overall, it is possible that some level of assets might allow the family to "take off" economically, socially, and psychologically, a hypothesis similar to international development theories based on a threshold of economic accumulation.[66] This might be thought of as a "virtuous circle," where possession of a certain amount of assets yields a bundle of welfare effects, which in turn facilitate accumulation of still more assets. Commonly stated, this is one version of "the more you have, the more you get" principle.

In reverse, if assets are diminished, bundles of welfare effects are withdrawn, leading to inability to cope, still fewer assets, and so on in a downward spiral. This is perhaps a useful way to look at the "vicious circle" of poverty. Instead of treating the vicious circle of poverty as a vague cultural matter, we might better understand it in more concrete terms—as a function of welfare effects of household assets.

Venturing further afield, a related theoretical question is the possibility of dynamism and curvilinearity between assets and welfare effects. Recent developments in theoretical physics, which go under the heading of "chaos," suggest, among other things, that small inputs in dynamic, nonlinear systems can have large effects. These effects, over time, may appear to be random, but in fact may be ordered.[67] In financial structures of households, it is conceivable that behavioral effects of asset accumulation might be understood as dynamic, curvilinear processes. A key asset at a key point in time, such as college tuition or seed capital for starting a new business, might have huge future impacts. Or, to borrow the idea of fractals, it is possible that a pattern of asset accumulation at one scale is reproduced at a higher scale; the pattern may have a reality of its own, recreating itself. Unfortunately, the development of both theory and measurement in the social sciences is a long way from exploring such possibilities.

Expectations of Permanent Assets

Another interesting idea is the possibility of permanent assets. This requires a brief explanation: In 1957, Milton Friedman proposed a theory of consumption built on the concept of permanent income, which he defined as the "income to which consumers adapt their behavior," as opposed to recorded income. Permanent income is more or less related to expectations of lifetime income. According to Friedman, permanent income is not readily measurable but "must be inferred from the behavior of the consumer units."[68] He also proposed a related idea of permanent consumption. Friedman suggested that people's consumption behavior is guided not by recorded income, but by permanent income.[69]

In order to understand Friedman's concept, it is helpful to turn to Franco Modigliani's theory of savings, which he began to develop in the early 1950s. The accepted view at the time was that the proportion of income saved by a household, or a nation, was directly related to current income. But empirical evidence did not cooperate in affirming the theory. Modigliani and Richard Brumberg suggested, instead, that savings be viewed as a difference between current income levels and a rate of consumption approximately equal to the average flow of resources over an entire life, a perspective that has since become known as the life cycle hypothesis (LCH). Thus, LCH is based on expectations of future resource flows, and is a far more elaborate view of human psychology than is traditional microeconomics.[70] Friedman, of course, was influenced by Modigliani in developing the concepts of permanent income and permanent consumption.

Borrowing from Modigliani and from Friedman's permanent income concept, can we construct a definition of *permanent assets*? Permanent assets would be the expected accumulation of assets over a lifetime. (Standard neoclassical theory would say that a distinction between lifetime income and lifetime assets is meaningless, that both are part of lifetime resources available for consumption. The suggestion here is that the two might be separated with interesting results.) If, in fact, people have such expectations about asset accumulation, and these expectations influence behavior, then permanent assets might be a more relevant theoretical concept than actual (recorded) assets in determining the psychological and behavioral effects of asset accumulation. In other words, welfare effects of assets may occur in relation to people's expectations of assets in the future rather than to their expectations of actual assets at present. If so, it may well be that the process of asset accumulation is, in this respect, more important than the result.

To carry these thoughts a step further, if asset accumulation is understood as a dynamic process, then even the idea of permanent assets may be unnecessarily static. A better theoretical construction might be "unbounded assets." In other words, the idea of some anticipated fixed amount of lifetime assets might give way to the idea of unbounded accumulation, changing possibilities, emerging choices, and greater creativity. This concept, however, begins to sound slightly spiritual. (I remind myself of George Gilder's descriptions of entrepreneurship.[71]) Whether such limitless notions actually guide economic behavior, or for whom, and under what circumstances, is far from established. For the moment, these ideas remain unexplored.

Alternative Explanations

Regarding the construction of the above theoretical propositions on welfare effects of assets, two alternative explanations must be considered. The first is that income, if sufficient and stable, might have the same welfare effects as assets; and the second is that certain types of behaviors might lead to asset accumulation, rather than vice versa. In both cases, there is some truth to the alternative explanations. The point to be made here is not that these alternative explanations are wrong; only that they are not the whole truth, as is frequently assumed.

Does Income Have the Same Effects as Assets?

As mentioned previously, accepted wisdom in neoclassical economics holds that income and assets are two forms of the same thing—potential for consumption; and this consumption is considered the sole definition of individual well-being or welfare. From this perspective, an income stream would generate welfare effects similar to a pool of existing assets (this is the springs-are-the-same-as-ponds idea discussed at the beginning of the chapter).

Although neoclassical economics tends to focus only on consumption, it is conceivable that income generates welfare effects other than consumption, and that these are essentially the same as the effects of asset accumulation.[72] The most likely examples: Personal efficacy might result from high income as much as from asset accumulation. Social influence might result from consumption as much as from accumulation (the social influence of consumption was Thorstein Veblen's primary theme). Political participation might be activated to protect income streams as much as to protect assets. Similar arguments—some stronger than others—could be offered against each of the nine propositions presented in this chapter.

Applying this thinking to welfare policy, we can hypothesize that income benefits from the federal government, if they reached a high enough level and were firmly guaranteed (as in some Scandinavian countries), might yield essentially the same welfare effects as individually held assets.

Plausible as this alternative explanation might be at first glance, it does not hold up very well to further scrutiny. As pointed out above, liquidity constraints and problems of path dependence can create quantitatively different financial outcomes between a flow of income and an equivalent stock of wealth. If a family cannot draw on future income during a crisis, permanent financial loss can occur.

In general, the welfare effects of income are different from the welfare effects of assets because of the element of *individual control*. An income stream from the government does not put much control in the hands of the recipient, no matter how guaranteed and secure the income. The example of retirement income discussed above indicates that a major effect of Social Security is to induce individuals to retire at a particular age. On the other hand, a major effect of defined-contribution pension plans, where the underlying assets are controlled by individuals, is to create greater variation in the age of retirement; it varies according to individual choice. This research finding is consistent with common sense: personally, I have a great interest in the retirement assets I control. I believe, in a concrete way, that I can invest these funds and use them to shape my well-being and expand my choices during my older years. On the other hand, I give almost no thought to Social Security retirement benefits; I am not even sure such benefits will be there when I retire, or if they are, to what extent.

This element of individual control has far-reaching effects. A few years ago I had the opportunity to visit Sweden, to attend a meeting on social welfare and employment policy. To my great surprise, one of the most prominent (informal) themes of discussion among Swedish welfare scholars was that life in Sweden, while very secure, was also dull and without sufficient challenge (this is not what we typically read in scholarly books about Sweden's welfare state). Everything was taken care of "from cradle to grave"; no one was desperately in need; but individuals had little control over the implementation and use of their vast state-provided welfare resources. Many of life's challenges and choices had been taken out of their hands. The Swedes felt taken care of, and were glad of it, but they did not feel empowered. If the state-provided income stream—in both money and services—yielded the welfare effects described in this chapter, they were, in many cases, thin and hollow versions of these effects due to the absence of individual control.[73]

One might argue that the empowerment generated by individual control of assets is only an arbitrary interpretation, a psychological construction shaped by a culture of capitalism. However, a recent study comparing the United States, Japan, and Poland—three nations in very different political and economic circumstances—suggests that the psychological effects of asset control are strong cross-nationally. This study reports that men who own and control productive assets place a higher value on self-direction for their children, are more self-directed themselves, and are more intellectually flexible. Moreover, these effects are strong after controlling for levels of income and education.[74] Thus, assets appear to have psychological effects that are, at least to some extent, independent of income and independent of national culture.

Taking a broader interpretation of culture, one might argue that all three countries—the United States, Japan, and Poland—reflect the values and culture of Western industrial capitalism, regardless of historical differences or differences in political regimes. To some extent this is undoubtedly true. I would not, at this point, suggest that the preference for control of assets is fundamental to human nature, more basic than cultural influences, although it may be.[75]

However, even if the preference for individual control of assets is only cultural, it assuredly shapes people's perceptions and their well-being. Especially for the United States, the culture is highly individual-istic and capitalistic; individual control is highly valued. In this envi-ronment, the control afforded by asset accumulation yields a quality of welfare effects that is, in all probability, not achievable by an equiva-lent stream of income, no matter how regular.

Do Behaviors Lead to Assets?

Instead of assets leading to desirable behavioral characteristics, per-haps it is the other way around. Perhaps behavioral characteristics lead to assets. This, of course, is the basic argument of the conservative right, human capital theory, and of most individual-level explanations of wealth and poverty.[76] One conservatively oriented scholar, com-menting on an earlier version of my ideas on asset-based welfare, provides an example of this viewpoint:

> You argue, in essence, that to give assistance to the poor partly in the form of assets would change their behavior. They would become more forward-looking because they would have a greater stake in the system. I don't believe that. There are already sufficient incentives to be for-ward-looking, yet the poor hurt themselves with improvident behavior. That is the whole problem they pose.

Existing evidence is not perfect, but the majority of studies have yielded evidence contrary to this viewpoint. Structural-economic vari-ables consistently explain the persistence of poverty better than attitudinal variables.[77] Longitudinal data provide the best test of such hypotheses, and some of the best longitudinal data are in the Panel Study on Income Dynamics (PSID). PSID data overwhelmingly con-firm the unimportance of attitudes in shaping financial success. Re-porting on three key attitudes—achievement motivation, sense of personal efficacy, and orientation toward the future—Greg Duncan finds no relationship between any of these attitudes and later economic status (as measured by earnings and income). He goes on to say:

> The mass of negative evidence extends far beyond these tests. We have repeatedly performed such tests over different time periods, with differ-ent concepts of change in economic status (including climbing out of poverty) and for many different subgroups in the population. We find

almost no evidence that initial attitudes affect subsequent economic success.[78]

Based on these results, there is little empirical reason to believe that attitudes affect asset accumulation rather than vice versa.

However, the PSID is only a single set of data, and negative findings, in themselves, do not rule out a theory, especially if the theory has only vaguely specified variables at the outset. Working with data in the National Longitudinal Survey (NLS), Paul Andrisani does find relationships between attitudes and subsequent economic outcomes.[79]

In addition, because the economic measures used in most studies are income-based, questions regarding relationships between attitudes and assets remain open. A notable exception is the study of the effects of class position on psychological functioning in the United States, Japan, and Poland, reported above. These researchers find that ownership and control of productive assets leads to psychological orientation more than the other way around.[80] Hopefully, additional studies can address this question in the future.

In the meantime, it is reasonable to assume that the relationship, to a certain extent, works both ways, that is, the presence of assets influences behavior and behavior influences the accumulation of assets. In the absence of more definitive knowledge, this would seem to be a sensible middle-ground interpretation.

Models of Welfare

Having suggested that assets have important welfare effects, the next step is to incorporate this thinking into conceptualizations of how financial welfare actually functions. To do so, it may be helpful to model sources of financial support, the form of the support, and the short-term and long-term effects of support in different forms. In this endeavor, it is useful to think separately about existing models of welfare for the nonpoor and the poor, and then finally to turn to a model for the poor that would incorporate assets. Some notes on the models follow:

1. The models identify only two groups in society—the nonpoor and the poor. This is a huge simplification, but it serves our purposes in this discussion.

2. The models are ideal types. They are not intended to describe every case, or any single case; instead, the models provide pictures of welfare dynamics for large groups of people. The theoretical suggestion is that overall, the models reasonably describe the financial welfare dynamics of most individuals in the groups indicated.

3. In the interest of clarity, the models are presented in linear fashion, omitting all loops and lines of feedback. Of course, like almost everything else, financial welfare is anything but linear in reality.

4. The models give a false impression that welfare occurs in a closed world with only a few variables. This too is a simplification, not to be mistaken with reality, but it is helpful in drawing attention to key relationships.

Welfare of the Nonpoor:
Income plus Assets

Although it may seem peculiar to begin with a welfare model of the nonpoor, it is important to understand welfare dynamics of the nonpoor precisely because assets are an important part of this model. As described in chapter 4, the nonpoor benefit from large asset transfers by the government in the form of tax benefits for home ownership and retirement pensions. And the nonpoor have other sources of asset accumulation as well.

Therefore, the meaning of welfare in this discussion is quite broad, going well beyond government income transfers to the poor. Welfare refers to a more general state of economic well-being (this is consistent with broad views of welfare that have characterized the work of Robert Lampman, Alex Inkeles, and others). In order to achieve a fuller picture of welfare dynamics, all major sources of financial support are included.

As illustrated in Figure 8.2, the nonpoor have four major sources of financial support: employment, government, family, and existing assets. Each of these sources of financial support provides both income and assets for the nonpoor. It is important to note that savings are often not a residual—they are not what is "left over" after consumption is subtracted from income. Although standard economic theory tends to look at asset accumulation in this manner, the residual notion is not the best description of the process of saving in middle-class homes under welfare capitalism. *Savings often enter households as*

Figure 8.2. **Welfare Model for the Nonpoor: Income Plus Assets**

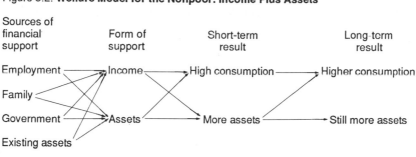

Note: In this model, consumption is increasing and the presence of assets yields welfare effects of assets (see Figure 8.1).

assets from the beginning. From this perspective, employer contributions to pension funds are not, in any meaningful sense, saved income, but, rather, direct asset accumulation. Also, tax breaks for home mortgage interest and capital gains contribute directly to asset accumulation. Secondarily, these subsidies also make housing more attractive, thus pushing up the market value, thereby contributing to owner equity.

Employment for the nonpoor, who tend to be in "good jobs," provides wages or salary as income making up 65 percent of average household income. "Good jobs" have good fringe benefits, and typically provide pension funds as assets. In a growing number of cases, employment also provides stock ownership as an additional form of asset accumulation.

Government provides massive income transfers in old age in the form of Social Security and Medicare, and huge tax breaks for accumulating assets, particularly in housing and retirement pension accounts (an estimated $107 billion in tax expenditures in these two categories for fiscal 1990; see chapter 4).

Families of the nonpoor transfer income within the family during hard times, and also transfer major assets, especially in the form of bequests.

Existing assets tend to yield both additional income and further accumulation of assets. In the case of the very rich, of course, family transfers and existing assets are the major sources of income as well as wealth accumulation.

Thus, both income and assets are received from multiple sources by the nonpoor. Even if one or two of these sources is not operative for a given household at a given time, the others are very likely to be operative. It is a diversified system of financial support.

What are the welfare results of these sources of support? In the short term, income feeds a high rate of consumption, and when income is high enough, some of it may be saved, further increasing assets. Assets tend to generate more assets, and asset earnings can be used to increase consumption. In the long term, income tends to grow, and consumption becomes still greater, while larger and larger asset earnings may further contribute to growing consumption.

For lack of space on a single illustration, welfare effects of assets are not listed in the welfare models (Figures 8.2, 8.3, and 8.4). As detailed above, the presence of assets yields welfare effects (see Figure 8.1). Presumably, the more financial assets that accumulate over time, the more asset-based welfare effects the household enjoys.

Welfare of the Poor: Income Only

Social welfare dynamics for the poor are much simpler. With few or no existing assets, the poor have three major sources of support: employment, government, and family. In each of these cases, the form of support is income alone.

Employment for the poor tends to be in low-paying, unstable jobs with few or no fringe benefits. Employment is the major source of income for the working poor, who remain impoverished even though they are working. Subsidized retirement accounts and stock ownership associated with employment are unlikely to be available to this group.

Government provides income transfers to some (but certainly not all) of the poor prior to retirement age. These are the welfare poor. The Earned Income Tax Credit provides tax relief to the working poor, but millions of the working poor, although officially impoverished, receive no government income benefits in any form. Regarding assets, the government offers the same tax rules to everyone for tax deductions for home ownership and tax deferments for retirement savings. However, for two reasons, these rules do not greatly benefit the poor. First, the poor earn so little that saving and investment is difficult. Second, ordinary tax breaks offered to poor families are nearly meaningless because income, and therefore tax liability, is so low that the tax de-

Figure 8.3. **Welfare Model for the Poor: Income Only**

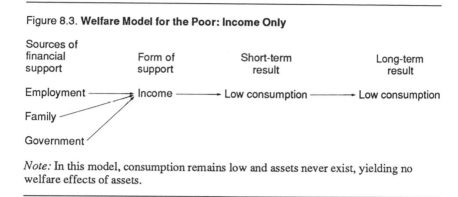

Note: In this model, consumption remains low and assets never exist, yielding no welfare effects of assets.

duction or deferment provides little incentive to save (in other words, tax policy does not reduce the relative price of asset accumulation for the poor, as it does for the nonpoor).

Family remains an important source of income in many poor households, where the intrafamily support might be in-kind rather than money transfers. For example, it is more common in poor families to provide child care for a family member and to pass along used clothing and household items. Typically, no financial assets are accumulated and passed along. In some cases, however, life insurance policies are maintained as a way to give assets to the next generation (Figure 8.3).

What are the welfare effects? In the short term, the low level of income leads to a low level of consumption. In the long term, the picture is no different—a low level of income leads to a low level of consumption. Where governmental transfers are the major income source, continual transfers are required to maintain the same level of consumption. This is the welfare trap. It is, quite literally, a trap of no assets. Assets never accumulate, yielding no asset-based welfare effects.

A Proposed Model of Welfare for the Poor: Income plus Assets

The asset-based model of social welfare proposed in this book would augment income with assets. The only difference from the current welfare model for the poor is that assets from governmental sources would become a form of support. A structure of asset accumulation

Figure 8.4. **Proposed Welfare Model for the Poor: Income Plus Assets**

Sources of financial support	Form of support	Short-term result	Long-term result
Employment ⟶	Income ⟶	Low consumption ⟶	A little higher consumption
Family			
Government ⟶	Assets ⟶	Few assets ⟶	A few more assets

Note: In this model, consumption increases in the long term, and a beginning accumulation of assets yields welfare effects of assets (see Figure 8.1).

would be established, and a portion of government transfers would be in the form of assets rather than income (Figure 8.4). In the short term, this model would yield the same low consumption, but also the accumulation of a few assets. In the long term, the model would yield a few more assets and, due to income from assets, a higher level of consumption. Most importantly, with the first accumulation of assets would come early levels of the welfare effects of assets (Figure 8.1). In short, assets would be introduced, in many cases for the first time, into the welfare dynamics of poor families. The assumption is that, over an extended period of time, income plus assets would lead to more positive welfare outcomes than the income-only model that exists at present. Families would have both financial flows and financial stocks (both springs and ponds) to manage their well-being and pursue life goals.

Conclusion

Of course, assets are very good to have. Few people would disagree. But the point of this chapter is not simply that assets have positive welfare effects. Rather, the point is that assets yield positive welfare effects that income alone does not provide. This is not to argue that assets alone explain everything about welfare, or that assets alone are the key to solving poverty. Rather, it is to suggest that *assets have important welfare effects in addition to potential consumption.*

The effects of assets are (1) to improve stability, (2) to create a cognitive and emotional orientation toward the future, (3) to stimulate development of human capital and other assets, (4) to enable focus and specialization, (5) to provide a foundation for risk taking, (6) to enhance personal efficacy, (7) to increase social influence, (8) to increase political participation, and (9) to increase the welfare of offspring.

It is quite possible that these welfare effects of assets, and perhaps others, can be arranged into a more elaborate theoretical construction. For example, some of these effects may logically or empirically precede others; certain combinations of effects may be particularly crucial to overall welfare; and so forth. These, however, are complex questions that must wait for another day. At this point, we hope simply to establish the theoretical propositions suggesting that assets, in and of themselves, have specific, and perhaps important, welfare effects.[81]

These ideas are also an effort partially to bridge the theoretical gap between the structural-level and individual-level theories of welfare discussed in chapter 3. In brief, the theory attempts to integrate the structural concept of class—as defined by asset position—with household economic and behavioral variables. Such integration is often missing in poverty and welfare analysis, an absence that pits one level of analysis against the other in an endless, and often fruitless, debate. Asset-based welfare theory may serve as a partial connection between the structural and individual perspectives. In the *life chances* tradition of Max Weber, Ralf Dahrendorf, and William Wilson, asset-based welfare theory suggests that household financial assets do more than provide a store of future consumption. Assets yield important economic, psychological, and social effects beyond consumption.

Turning to models of welfare, the perspective offered in this chapter is that the nonpoor benefit from elaborate systems of asset accumulation from all major sources of financial support (employment, family, government, and existing assets), but the poor typically receive very few assets from any source and accumulate few assets over the long term. A key element of this perspective is that, contrary to mainstream economic theory, savings are not generally a residual left over after consumption is subtracted from income. Rather, savings often enter households through various institutional arrangements. Money is guided directly into asset accumulation, and subsidized in the process. In most households, unstructured savings out of ordinary income streams is insignificant compared to institutionalized asset accumulation.

Therefore, the proposed policy solution is to introduce similar institutionalized asset accumulation processes into the welfare model for the poor by changing the nature of financial support from governmental sources. This change would require that a structure of asset accumulation be established for the poor and that governmental transfers to the poor include not only income, but assets as well.

Now, having worked out some of the theoretical issues, it is time to be more practical. How might these ideas be applied? What are the policy issues? What polices might be considered? For whom? In what form? How would the policies work? At what cost? With what implications? These challenging questions are taken up in the following chapters.

Notes

1. In this book, the word *welfare* is used in two different but related senses. In this chapter, the meaning is well-being, as in "welfare of the people" and "welfare economics." In policy-oriented chapters, the meaning is legislative, as in "welfare policy" and "welfare programs."

2. The theoretical propositions presented in this chapter are preliminary. As with all theoretical formulations, several criteria can be employed to decide if the work is likely to be useful. These criteria include the following: Is the theory logical? Is the theory simple and straightforward? Does the theory yield testable hypotheses? Is existing empirical evidence consistent with the theory? Does the theory connect with—and draw upon—other bodies of established theory? Does the theory help to make micro-macro connections—in this case, connections between individual behavior and social structure? Does the theory yield fruitful conceptual insights? Does the theory have worthwhile practical implications?

3. An earlier version of a portion of this chapter is published as "Stakeholding: Notes on a Theory of Welfare Based on Assets," *Social Service Review*, December 1990.

4. Only idealists have taken the viewpoint that accumulation of assets is actually harmful. This group includes a large number of monks, a few artists, and Karl Marx. One of the most eloquent, forceful, and sarcastic statements on the perils of asset accumulation is by Marx:

> The less you eat, drink, buy books, go to the theatre or to balls, or to the public house, and the less you think, love, theorize, sing, paint, fence, etc. the more you will be able to save and the *greater* will become your treasure which neither moth nor rust will corrupt—your *capital*. The less you *are*, the less you express your life, the more you *have*, the greater is your *alienated* life and the greater is the saving of your alienated being. Everything which the economist takes from you in the way of life and humanity, he restores to you in the form of *money* and *wealth*. And everything which you are unable to do, your money can do for you; it can eat, drink, go to the ball and to the theatre. It can acquire art, learning, historical treasures, political power; and it can travel. It *can* appropriate all these things for you, can purchase everything; it is the true *opulence*. But although it can do all this, it *desires* to create

itself, and to buy itself, for everything else is subservient to it ("Economic and Philosophical Manuscripts," in Eric Fromm, *Marx's Concept of Man*. New York: Frederick Ungar, 1966, 144, translation by Tom Bottomore).

5. For a summary of documented psychological and social effects of unemployment, see Katharine Briar and Marie Hoff. "Preventing and Alleviating the Human Costs of Unemployment," in Katharine Briar, ed., *The Unemployed: Policy and Services*, report of Working Group No. 9, 13th European Regional Symposium on Social Welfare. Helsinki: International Council on Social Welfare, 1986, 215–23.

6. Franco Modigliani and Richard Brumberg, "Utility Analysis and the Consumption Function: An Interpretation of Cross-Section Data," in Kenneth K. Kurihara, ed., *Post-Keynesian Economics*. New Brunswick, NJ: Rutgers University Press, 1954; and Milton Friedman, *A Theory of the Consumption Function*. Princeton: Princeton University Press, 1957.

7. Joseph Stiglitz and Andrew Weiss, "Credit Rationing in Markets with Imperfect Information," *American Economic Review* 71(3), 1981, 393–410; and Stephen Zeldes, "Consumption and Liquidity Constraints: An Empirical Investigation," *Journal of Political Economy* 97(2), 1989.

8. Susan Mayer and Christopher Jencks, "Poverty and the Distribution of Material Hardship," *Journal of Human Resources* 24(1), 1989, 88–114.

9. Oscar Lewis, *La Vida*. New York: Random House, 1966; and Edward Banfield, *The Unheavenly City Revisited*. Boston: Little, Brown, 1974.

10. As of December 1988, with the assistance of the "I Have a Dream" Foundation, which Eugene Lang established, 125 benefactors had pledged full college tuition to some 5,000 youngsters in twenty-four cities across the United States.

11. Max Weber, *Economy and Society*, two volumes, Guenther Roth and Claus Wittich, eds. Berkeley: University of California Press, 1968.

12. Ralf Dahrendorf, *Life Chances: Approaches to Social and Political Theory*. Chicago: University of Chicago Press, 1979.

13. Michael Sherraden, "School Dropouts in Perspective," *Educational Forum* 51(1), 1986, 15–31.

14. William Raspberry, "Key to Teen Births Is Self-Perception," *St. Louis Post-Dispatch*, December 20, 1986, 3B. This viewpoint is also expressed in publications of the Children's Defense Fund; see Marion Wright Edelman, *Families in Peril: An Agenda for Social Change*. Cambridge: Harvard University Press, 1987.

15. S.M. Segal and J. Ducette, "Locus of Control and Pre-Marital High School Pregnancy," *Psychological Reports* 33, 1973, 887–90.

16. Kate Prager, *Induced Terminations of Pregnancy: Reporting States, 1981*, National Center for Health Statistics, Monthly Vital Statistics Report, 34(4), supplement 2, July 30, 1985.

17. A. Gabriel and E.R. McAnarney, "Parenthood in Two Subcultures: White, Middle-Class Couples and Black, Low-Income Adolescents in Rochester, New York," *Adolescence* 18(7), 1983, 211–17.

18. E.S. Herold and L.M. Samson, "Difference between Women Who Begin Pill Use Before and After First Intercourse: Ontario, Canada," *Family Planning*

Perspectives 12, 1980, 304–5; and P.W. Scher, S.J. Emans, and E.M. Grace, "Factors Associated with Compliance to Oral Contraceptive Use in an Adolescent Population," *Journal of Adolescent Health Care* 3, 1982, 120–23.

19. For much of the information on teenage pregnancy, I am indebted to Audrey Mengwasser ("Teenage Pregnancy: From Virginity to Resolution," Washington University, unpublished, 1988). For the discussion of social cognitive theory, I am indebted to David Katz, relying on his manuscript-in-progress ("Information and Social Welfare") and numerous conversations.

20. R.E. Kelley and J.L. Michela, "Attribution Theory and Research," *Annual Review of Psychology* 31, 1980, 457–501; and J.H. Harvey and G. Weary, *Perspectives on Attributional Process*. Dubuque, IA: W.C. Brown, 1981.

21. Fritz Heider, *The Psychology of Interpersonal Relations*. New York: John Wiley & Sons, 1958; and R.E. Kelley, "Attribution Theory in Social Psychology," in D. Levine, ed., *Nebraska Symposium on Motivation*, vol. 15. Lincoln: University of Nebraska Press, 1967.

22. S.T. Fiske and P.W. Linville, "What Does the Schema Concept Buy Us?" *Personality and Social Psychology Bulletin* 6, 1980, 543–57; and S.E. Taylor and J. Crocker, "Schematic Bases of Social Information Processing," in E.T. Higgens et al., eds., *Social Cognition: The Ontario Symposium*, vol. 11. Hillsdale, NJ: Erlbaum, 1981.

23. L. Ross, M.R. Lepper, and M. Hubbard, "Perseverance in Self-Perception and Social Perception: Biased Attribution Processes in the Debriefing Paradigm," *Journal of Personality and Social Psychology* 32, 1975, 880–92; and C.A. Anderson, "Abstract and Concrete Data in the Perseverance of Social Theories: When Weak Data Lead to Unshakeable Beliefs," *Journal of Experimental Social Psychology* 19, 1983, 93–108.

24. D.E. Rumelhart, "Schemata in the Cognitive System," in R.S. Wyer and T.K. Srull, eds., *Handbook of Social Cognition*, vol. 1. Hillsdale, NJ: Lawrence Erlbaum Associates, 1984; and G. Mandler, *Cognitive Psychology*. Hillsdale, NJ: Lawrence Erlbaum Associates, 1985.

25. David Halle, *America's Working Man: Work, Home, and Politics among Blue-Collar Property Owners*. Chicago: University of Chicago Press, 1984, 11–14.

26. William Scott, *In Pursuit of Happiness: American Conceptions of Property from the Seventeenth to the Twentieth Centuries*. Bloomington: Indiana University Press, 1977, 6.

27. R.E. Pahl, *Divisions of Labor*. New York: Basil Blackwell, 1984.

28. Gary Becker, *The Economic Approach to Human Behavior*. Chicago: The University of Chicago Press, 1976; and Marc Nerlove, Assaf Razin, and Efraim Sadka, *Household and Economy: Welfare Economics of Endogenous Fertility*. New York: Academic Press, 1987.

29. Some unconventional "New Age" economists have suggested that informal, nonmonetized economic activity may be increasing in the post-industrial age (for example, see William Nicholls and William Dyson, *The Informal Economy*. Ottawa: Vanier Institute of the Family, 1983). I have strong doubts about this. On the contrary, it would seem that a great deal of "service" activity that was nonmonetized in the past has today become part of the formal economy (e.g., day care, food preparation, a smorgasbord of personal and business services, many

kinds of recreation, and so forth). However, it is nonetheless true that a great deal of the modern economy remains informal, and it is important to assess where this nonmonetized economic activity is taking place, and what facilitates it.

30. Adam Smith, *An Inquiry into the Nature and Causes of the Wealth of Nations.* Indianapolis: Liberty Press, 1981 (originally published in 1776), 276–77.

31. Harry Markowitz, "Portfolio Selection," *Journal of Finance* 7, 1952, 77–91; and Franco Modigliani and Gerald A. Pogue, "An Introduction to Risk and Return," *Financial Analysts Journal* 30, March-April, 1974, 68–80; and May–June, 1974, 69–88.

32. Adam Smith, *The Theory of Moral Sentiments.* Indianapolis: Liberty Press, 1976 (originally published in 1759); and Smith, *Wealth,* 1981.

33. William Graham Sumner, *What the Social Classes Owe to Each Other.* New York: Harper and Brothers, 1893, 76–78.

34. Daniel Patrick Moynihan, "Half the Nation's Children: Born without a Fair Chance," *New York Times,* September 25, 1988, E25.

35. In the corporate world, the economic value of added control is sometimes evident in market prices. Economists talk about a "control premium" as the difference between the market price of an individual share of stock and the amount it is worth as part of a block that controls the corporation. From this perspective, the premium price paid for a stock in a takeover or a leveraged buy-out situation reflects, in part, the economic value of control.

36. Lars Osberg, *Economic Inequality in Canada.* Toronto: Butterworths, 1981, 153.

37. Lester Thurow, *Generating Inequality: Mechanisms of Distribution in the U.S. Economy.* New York: Basic Books, 1975, 141.

38. James Stock and David Wise, "The Pension Inducement to Retire: An Option Value Analysis," NBER Working Paper No. 2660. Cambridge: National Bureau of Economic Research, 1988.

39. Laurence J. Kotlikoff and David A. Wise, *The Wage Carrot and the Pension Stick: Retirement Benefits and Labor Force Participation.* Kalamazoo: W.E. Upjohn Institute for Employment Research, 1989.

40. Thorstein Veblen, *The Theory of the Leisure Class.* New York: The Macmillan Company, 1899, 32–33.

41. Smith, *Wealth,* 1981.

42. Robert L. Heilbroner, *The Nature and Logic of Capitalism.* New York: W.W. Norton, 1985, 42ff.

43. Alexis de Tocqueville, *Democracy in America.* Garden City, NY: Anchor Books, 1969 (originally published in 1835), 614–15.

44. C. Wright Mills, *White Collar: The American Middle Classes.* New York: Oxford University Press, 1953; C. Wright Mills, *The Power Elite.* New York: Oxford University Press, 1956; G. Kolko, *Wealth and Power in America.* New York: Praeger, 1962; and G. William Domhoff, *The Higher Circles: The Governing Class in America.* New York: Vintage, 1971; see also Constance Perin, *Everything in Its Place: Social Order and Land Use in America.* Princeton, NJ: Princeton University Press, 1977.

45. Anthony F. Shorrocks, "UK Wealth Distribution: Current Evidence and Future Prospects," in Edward Wolff, *Growth, Accumulation, and Unproductive Activity.* Cambridge: Cambridge University Press, 1987, 29–50.

46. Denis Kessler and André Masson, "Personal Wealth Distribution in France: Cross-Sectional Evidence and Extensions," in Edward Wolff, *Growth, Accumulation, and Unproductive Activity.* Cambridge: Cambridge University Press, 1987, 141–76.

47. Smith, *Wealth,* 1981, 279.

48. Alfred Winslow Jones, *Life, Liberty, and Property.* Philadelphia: J.B. Lippincott Co., 1941.

49. J.K. Galbraith, *American Capitalism.* Boston: Houghton Mifflin, 1952, 30.

50. Tocqueville, 1969, 722–23.

51. Scott, 1977, 202.

52. Galbraith, 1952.

53. Ibid., 1952, 11.

54. Tocqueville, 1969, 636–37.

55. Sheila Rule, "Violent Reaction to New Poll Tax Is Attributed to Young Have-Nots," *New York Times,* April 6, 1990, B1.

56. Modigliani and Brumberg, 1954.

57. Shorrocks, 1987.

58. Osberg, 1981.

59. Laurence J. Kotlikoff, *What Determines Savings?* Cambridge: MIT Press, 1989.

60. Steven Venti and David Wise, "But They Don't Want to Reduce Housing Equity," NBER Working Paper No. 2859. Cambridge, MA: National Bureau of Economic Research, 1989.

61. James Duesenberry, *Income, Saving and the Theory of Consumer Behavior.* Cambridge, MA: Harvard University Press, 1967, 22.

62. Franco Modigliani, *The Debate over Stabilization Policy*, Raffaele Mattioli Lectures, Bocconi University. Cambridge: Cambridge University Press, 1986, 127.

63. For example, Edward P. Lazear and Robert T. Michael (*Allocation of Income within the Household.* Chicago: University of Chicago Press, 1988, 196–97) point out that "the connection between expenditures and welfare is not straightforward unless the preferences are specified explicitly in terms of a utility function. . . . without an explicit utility function one cannot make statements about welfare and how it might be affected by a change in expenditure. . . . expenditures do not necessarily reflect welfare in any simple straightforward way." This is a welcome elaboration of consumption-based theory, but this thinking has not yet influenced social policy-making, which relies exclusively on a definition of household welfare based on level of income (and assumed level of consumption).

64. Amitai Etzioni, *The Moral Dimension: Toward a New Economics.* New York: The Free Press, 1988.

65. Thurow, 1975, 142.

66. See, for example, W.W. Rostow, "The Take-Off into Sustained Growth," in Jason L. Finkle and Richard W. Gable, eds., *Political Development and Social Change.* New York: John Wiley & Sons, 1971.

67. For a very readable account, see James Gleick, *Chaos.* New York: Viking Penguin Books, 1987.

68. Friedman, 1957, 221.

69. The general idea of permanent income and consumption had been stated in less formal language many times before. For example, Arthur Schopenhauer, in his essay on property, wrote:

> A man never feels the loss of things which it never occurs to him to ask for; he is just as happy without them; whilst another, who may have a hundred times as much, feels miserable because he has not got the one thing he wants. In fact, here too, every man has a horizon of his own, and he will expect as much as he thinks it is possible for him to get. (Arthur Schopenhauer, *Complete Essays of Schopenhauer*. New York: Wiley Book Co., 1942, 46)

70. Modigliani and Brumberg, 1954.

71. George Gilder, *Wealth and Poverty*. New York: Basic Books, 1981.

72. Among several people who have raised the possibility of similar effects of income and assets, the thoughtful comments of Stephen Fazzari and Neil Gilbert have been very helpful.

73. A similar conclusion is reached by Hugh Heclo and Henrik Madsen, *Policy and Politics in Sweden*. Philadelphia: Temple University Press, 1987; see also Tony Horowitz, "Welfare Stagnation Besets Smug Sweden," *Wall Street Journal*, April 5, 1990, A18.

74. Melvin Kohn, Atushi Naoi, Carrie Schoenbach, Carmi Schooler, and Kazimierz Slomczynski, "Position in the Class Structure and Psychological Functioning in the United States, Japan, and Poland," *American Journal of Sociology*, 95, 1990, 964–1008.

75. Adam Smith, in *The Wealth of Nations*, assumed that interest in capital accumulation was a fundamental human characteristic. Smith did not pursue this issue, but a case might be made that human survival has depended on acquisition of certain goods, especially scarce resources, tools, and land. To the extent that complex human behavior might have biological foundations, capital accumulation, broadly defined, would be a logical candidate. In contrast, Karl Marx suggested in *Capital* that the desire to seek capital was a cultural characteristic created by capitalism. According to Marx, in a better (noncapitalist) world, a different social and moral standard would replace the drive for material acquisition. In a different way, Max Weber, in *The Rise of the Protestant Ethic and the Spirit of Capitalism*, also said that capitalism created a culture of accumulation. Under capitalism, said Weber, accumulation was an *ethos*, a spiritual calling closely interwoven with Protestant religion.

76. Lawrence Mead and Douglass North have been helpful in articulating the alternative possibility that behaviors lead to assets, rather than vice versa. A central element in this perspective is that the poor behave differently from the nonpoor—the poor have different abilities or different preferences and they do not respond in the same way to incentives. The assumption is that existing incentives are more or less the same for everyone.

77. Michael Morris and John B. Williamson, *Poverty and Public Policy: An Analysis of Federal Intervention Efforts*. New York: Greenwood Press, 1986.

78. Greg J. Duncan et al., *Years of Poverty, Years of Plenty*. Ann Arbor: Institute for Social Research, 1984.

79. Paul Andrisani, "Internal-External Attitudes, Personal Initiative, and the Labor Market Experience of Black and White Men," *Journal of Human Resources* 12, 1977, 308–38; and Paul Andrisani, "Internal-External Attitudes,

Sense of Efficacy, and Labor Market Experience: A Reply to Duncan and Morgan,'' *Journal of Human Resources* 16, 1981, 658–66.

80. Kohn et al., 1990.

81. Although this issue is not the subject of this chapter, it is also possible that assets have certain negative effects. Under some circumstances—one thinks of a profligate son of a self-made millionaire—assets might lead to too much comfort and too little effort. In other cases, assets might require so much attention that quality of life is significantly reduced, interpersonal relationships subverted, or personality distorted (see Marx's comments in note 4, above). It seems likely that these negative effects of assets, to the extent that they exist, tend to be limited to situations of substantial wealth, but these questions must wait for another time.

9 • The Design of
Asset-Based Welfare Policy

"To make chicken soup, begin with a chicken. . . ." To create wealth in poor households, begin with assets. The recipe sounds simple enough. But a good recipe does not always make good soup, and a good idea does not always make good policy. Even if asset-based welfare looks promising on paper, it faces many hurdles between the idea and the reality, between conceptualization and application. As initial steps toward application, the purposes of this chapter are to look at policy goals, precedents, and issues; to raise questions for debate; and to suggest preliminary policy guidelines.

The Goals of Asset-Based Welfare Policy

The vision that underlies this proposal is that insofar as possible, each individual should be encouraged to develop to his or her greatest potential, not only as a matter of humanistic values, but as a matter of long-term economic competitiveness of the nation, social cohesion, and vitality of our democratic political institutions.

Foremost, it is apparent that the dominant ideology of welfare policy should change. Neither the "conservative" ideology of total self-sufficiency nor the "liberal" ideology of interventionist problem solving responds to the fundamental social and economic issues that confront the United States during the last years of the twentieth century. A new and more useful ideology of welfare would emphasize participation by all citizens and the need for the nation to develop all its people to the fullest extent possible. In this regard, social policy interventions by the state, the volunteer sector, or the corporate sector should be viewed not entirely as helping, remediation, and problem solving, but rather as people-developing and nation-building. The traditional conservative focus on self-sufficiency should give way to greater understanding of mutual interdependence, and the traditional liberal focus on correcting deficiencies should give way to a focus on realizing potential. In this light, welfare expenditures would not be viewed as unproductive drains on available resources, but as essential investments in the future. To put this another way, policy would move away from support and toward growth, away from entitlement and toward empowerment. This is not to abandon the concepts of need and charity, but to recognize that full development of the poor is in the best interests of both the poor and the nation as a whole.

The idea of investment as superior to consumption is a principle long recognized in business and individual financial affairs, but strangely, it has not been recognized in welfare policy. Welfare policy for the poor has impeded rather than promoted investment. Income-based policy has sustained the economically weak, but it has not helped strengthen them. Therefore, a new welfare policy is required, a policy based on asset accumulation. This new asset-based policy would complement existing income-based policy.

The basic test of a welfare program should be: Are participants fundamentally better off after being part of the program? With income-based transfer policy, the answer, unfortunately, is very often no. With asset-based policy, the answer would be yes; participants would have more assets with which to meet life goals.

This is not entirely a humanitarian issue. There are sound practical reasons for promoting asset accumulation. In the social and political arenas, property has its duties as well as its rights. The vision of asset-based welfare policy would be of *welfare citizens* instead of welfare clients. Policy would be designed not merely to provide financial support, but also to foster participation and active citizenship.[1]

Objectives of the proposed policy are ambitious. This is not to say that asset-based welfare would solve all social problems in the United States. It would not. However, the proposal is not so much for a new "program," but rather for a new way of thinking about welfare and for implementing a new kind of policy. At the individual and household levels, objectives are (1) to make it possible for individuals to accumulate assets; (2) to promote household stability, orientation toward the future, and long-range planning; and (3) to enable individuals and families to more successfully set and achieve life goals. At the national level, objectives are (1) to reduce poverty permanently; (2) to develop a more economically astute and economically active citizenry; (3) to help improve the savings rate of the nation; and given these; (4) to help make the United States more competitive in the world economy during the twenty-first century.

Previous Applications
of Asset-Based Welfare Policy

The Jeffersonian ideal of agrarian republicanism was a major feature of mainstream political thought well into the nineteenth century. In the 1830s, political leaders such as Missouri's Senator Thomas Hart Benton and President Andrew Jackson supported land distribution to the poor: "The wealth and strength of the country are its population, and the best part of the population are cultivators of the soil. Independent farmers are everywhere the basis of society and the true friends of liberty."[2] Various land reform movements and proposals were a central feature of national politics during the pre–Civil War period.[3]

The Homestead Act of 1862, under which pioneers were given 160 acres of land, was the first major asset-based welfare policy in U.S. history. This legislation made possible the famous Oklahoma Land Rush, an indelible symbol of westward expansion. Pioneers lined up on the border of the Oklahoma Territory and raced to claim their homesteads. (A few resourceful individuals slipped into the territory ahead of the rush and claimed the best parcels of land before the honest competitors arrived. These early-arrivers were called "sooners," a nickname that Oklahomans have since adopted with some affection.) The Homestead Act and subsequent land acts gave over 200 million acres of public lands to farmers, ranchers, and timbermen. More than 200 million acres were transferred from federal and state governments to the railroads. The Morrill Land Grant Act of 1862 set aside additional millions of acres of public lands for public schools and institutions of higher education. Altogether, through various means, the federal government transferred nearly one billion acres from the public domain to private ownership during the nineteenth century, creating millions of private owners of property and facilitating the provision of public services. These programs were a major antecedent of the welfare state.[4]

With the exceptions of Civil War Pensions (another important antecedent to the welfare state) and the Freedmen's Bureau for blacks (discussed in chapter 7), land grants were the only major federal welfare programs between 1865 and 1935, and they were, of course, entirely asset-based. For pioneer families and the nation as a whole, the impact was tremendous. Land grants played a major role in the settling of the western territories and in economic development during the latter years of the nineteenth century. As one social welfare scholar has observed, the Homestead Act "was far more radical and 'welfare' oriented than much social legislation today."[5]

Traces of the Homestead Act linger in U.S. policy discussions. Proposals for landholding resurface from time to time, although with less and less political vigor as each decade passes. The Jeffersonian ideal, in its original construction as a nation of independent farmers, is not very well suited to industrial or postindustrial capitalism. However, occasionally, even today, a rural county or small town, hoping to spur economic development, offers free acreage to modern day "settlers" who make a commitment to live on the land for a specified number of years. When this occurs, the community leaders inevitably recall, with a touch of romanticism, the success of the original Homestead Act.

As described in chapter 4, with the advent of the modern welfare state, the United States has developed a number of programs for the non-poor that can be described as asset-based. For the most part, these are structured into the tax system, a form of transfer that Richard Titmuss called fiscal welfare. The two largest categories of fiscal welfare for individuals are home mortgage interest tax deductions and tax deferments for retirement pension funds. By and large, however, the poor do not participate in these welfare policies, because they tend to have jobs without retirement benefits, and often do not own their own homes. In this respect, the United States has asset-based welfare policy for the non-poor, but not for the poor. Welfare policy for the poor consists mostly of income-based transfers in cash grants, food stamps, rent subsidies, and so forth.

Some exceptions exist. The New Deal initiated home mortgage subsidies under the Federal Housing Administration (FHA) and land ownership support under the Farm Security Administration (FSA), both oriented toward ownership of property by those less able to afford it. The FHA has had a tremendous impact on housing availability. Somewhat less appreciated are the activities of the FSA. To take one example, the FSA set up ten villages, comprising some six hundred dwellings, for displaced tenant farmers in the impoverished "boot-heel" region of southeastern Missouri during the depression years. Later, a nonprofit agency, the Delmo Housing Corporation, established a home ownership plan for the occupants of this housing. The plan called for a one-hundred-dollar down payment and ten dollars per month over a period of eight years. Among the six hundred units, only three fell into default before the loans were paid in full. The ten villages and the Delmo Housing Corporation remain the basis of social organization in the bootheel region today.

During the 1980s, other asset-based welfare experiments have emerged. Among the best known are Individual Retirement Accounts (IRAs). IRAs are available to all wage earners, and to a lesser extent, to the spouses of wage earners. At this writing, each wage earner may deposit up to two thousand dollars per year in an account. In households where combined income is less than forty thousand dollars per year, taxes on the deposit and future earnings are deferred. In households with greater income, some or all of the deposit is taxed, but future earnings remain tax-deferred. IRAs are an important precedent in universal asset-based welfare policy, but unfortunately, the current system of incentives for deposits does not attract many poor depositors. In poor households, it is more difficult to spare the income and, because tax brackets are low for the poor, the tax incentive is not as great as for higher income households. However, there is great potential for expanding this basic concept into other areas of social welfare. For example, one proposal before Congress would permit use of IRA accumulations for first-time home buyers.

Another important asset-based development during the 1980s was the proliferation of state-sponsored savings plans for higher education. These savings plans take many different forms, some guaranteeing a certain rate of college tuition, and some providing tax-deferred or tax-exempt savings for college. Although universal in concept, college savings plans do not by and large serve the poor. There are as yet no special incentives or assistance for the poor to participate.

Conceptually related to college savings plans, there is in the not-for-profit sector a series of experiments—perhaps more accurately called a social movement—to guarantee college tuition to students in poor inner-city neighborhoods. The first such experiment, very well known, was initiated by businessman Eugene Lang, who promised a class of Harlem sixth graders that he would pay for their college educations if they stayed in school. Lang's experiment has grown into the "I Have a Dream" Foundation, which now functions in more than twenty-four cities serving some five thousand young people. Several other private efforts to guarantee tuition for postsecondary education also have emerged. Similarly, some corporations, such as Pizza Hut and Burger King, are beginning to grant tuition guarantees to their best employees. In the case of Pizza Hut, the guarantees can be used by the employees themselves, their children, or their grandchildren.[6] This tuition guarantee movement is of great significance for two reasons: First, it is a major application of asset-based welfare *for the poor.* Second, the corporate sector is taking the lead in developing this policy, and doing so with an enthusiasm that is unmatched in other areas of welfare participation by corporations. It seems likely that this enthusiasm has something to do with the asset character of the strategy. Corporations are clearly viewing tuition guarantees as investments toward future productivity.[7]

Within traditional federal welfare programs, other asset-based welfare experiments are beginning to take place. Many of these have been stimulated by the Corporation for Enterprise Development (CfED) in Washington, DC. Robert Friedman is the founder and former president of CfED; his basic idea is to use welfare transfers as investments in economic independence, for example, as seed capital for starting new businesses (see chapter 11).

In Western Europe, perhaps the first asset-based policy occurred in France in the 1890s, where economists proposed allocations to "popular savings," which proved successful among workers as well as the middle class.[8] In Europe to this day, employers are often required by law to deduct a portion of employees' salaries for investment in a government pension program, typically referred to as "forced savings." Also, during the 1980s, Europe has been in the vanguard in using welfare transfers as seed capital. There have been successful experiments in asset-based unemployment compensation in France, the United Kingdom, Belgium, and other European countries. Under the French and Belgian schemes, for example, recipients may elect to receive unemployment compensation in a lump sum for the purpose of starting a new business.

In general, however, experiments with asset-based welfare have not been widespread. With the major exception of the Homestead Act and other land grants in the nineteenth century, public policy in

States has not generally promoted broadly based acquisition of real or financial property. Of the policies that exist, most benefit the nonpoor. Typically, the poor have been told that they should work hard and save more, but historically, there have been few programs or incentives to encourage them to do so. The United States in particular is characterized by strong exhortations for the poor to become more thrifty, but saving by the poor has not often been facilitated by public policy. Nonetheless, the above-mentioned developments suggest that asset-based welfare (although it does not yet go by this name) may be an emerging theme in American welfare policy.

Toward a Definition of Asset Poverty

To date, there have been limited efforts in using assets as part of a definition of poverty (other than in the negative sense of asset limits to determine eligibility for income transfers). One noteworthy effort to define asset poverty is by Edward Wolff, who undertakes several alternative incorporations of household wealth into poverty calculations.[9] But calculations of this nature have not appeared very much in policy discussions. How should asset poverty be defined?

Let us begin with a traditional definition of poverty. Poverty is typically defined in an absolute sense (as opposed to a relative sense) as "inadequate resources to maintain an adequate standard of living."[10] Of course, depending on their sentiments and politics, people differ about how much money is "adequate." Others argue not for adequacy, but for equity or fairness. In either case, the notion of standard of living—level of income and consumption—is seldom questioned. Whatever the view of adequacy or equity, for policy purposes, poverty is almost always defined as too little income (and, by inference, too little consumption).

To return to the analogy at the beginning of chapter 8, if both springs and ponds are important as sources of water, that is, if both financial flows and financial stocks are important for household welfare, then it may be advisable to reconceptualize poverty, not solely as income-related, but also as asset-related. In this regard, a definition of asset poverty should be developed.

The meaning of asset adequacy would be very different from the meaning of income adequacy. In formulating income-based welfare policy, we employ almost exclusively the concept of need. We assume that people need so much money, so much food, or so much medical care. In contrast, asset-based welfare would enhance control, participation, and well-being beyond the fulfillment of immediate need; that is, beyond consumption.

But how would assets be taken into account in this revised definition of poverty? As with income poverty, there would be a choice between absolute and relative definitions. An absolute definition would specify a certain level of household assets as adequate, similar to the manner in which income poverty is currently defined in the United States. A relative definition, on the other hand, would be calculated as some percentage of median household assets.

A relative definition of asset poverty, although appealing from an egalitarian viewpoint, would be politically unrealistic. In all advanced welfare states, relative definitions of income poverty have been rejected. Instead, welfare policy is guided by absolute definitions. In other words, a given amount of income is deemed sufficient, regardless of how much income everyone else has. In Europe, relative income definitions are occasionally discussed, but such discussions take place in obscure forums and academic journals, rarely in the political process. In the United States, one seldom hears a discussion of relative poverty, even among academics. U.S. policymakers, and most of the general public, would look upon such a discussion as hopelessly idealistic and misguided.

Because asset-based policy would not be viewed differently from income-based policy in this regard, we focus here on absolute definitions. An absolute definition of asset poverty would require that some basic level of assets be deemed adequate. Again, people would differ about adequacy depending on their sentiments and politics.

Logically, deciding what level of assets is adequate would require that various welfare effects of assets be taken into account. These effects are discussed in chapter 8. They include promotion of household stability; promotion of orientation toward the future; greater focus and specialization; enhancement of personal efficacy, social power, and political participation; and passing on economic and social advantages to offspring. If assets have such effects, then theoretically, some amount of assets would yield the desired effects. This amount would be the total assets required to rise above asset poverty. At this point, in the absence of empirical research, there is little way to know what level of assets this might be. Moreover, as suggested in chapter 8, it may be that certain types of assets have certain types of welfare effects, while other types of assets have other types of welfare effects.

This is not, however, as great a stumbling block as it might seem. In the real world, the definition of asset poverty, like the definition of income poverty, would be shaped in the political process and would be, in some respects, arbitrary. After passing through a series of compromises, the definition would not be perfect, but it would be a step in the right direction.

Not for the Asset Poor and Income Rich

At this point, we encounter another potential problem in the definition of asset poverty. Some households have few or negative assets, but large incomes. Would such households be considered impoverished from an asset point of view? The answer can be divided into two parts, the logical answer and the policy answer.

The logical answer is yes, such households are asset impoverished. Assets are a different way to see poverty, and through this lens, even high consumption households can be poor. If the finances of a household consist of a rented apartment or house, loans for a new car and a boat, large consumption debts, and no savings or investments, then the household is asset impoverished. If it is possible to have poverty amid plenty under a single roof, this is what it looks like—high consumption, but no savings and accumulation. Unfortunately, this form of poverty, at the household level, is very common in the United States, although we do not often call it by its true name.

However, the policy answer is that, when incomes are above a certain level, people have *access* to asset accumulation schemes (particularly tax-advantaged home mortgages and retirement pensions). If individuals choose to ignore these opportunities, they *choose* asset poverty. Public policy should not attempt to do more for this group. A better policy strategy would be to establish stronger disincentives for consumption, such as value-added taxes and luxury taxes.

Not for the Asset Rich and Income Poor

As noted in chapter 6, a rather large proportion of Americans are officially below the income poverty line but nonetheless have significant non-income-producing assets. For the most part, these are older people who own their own homes or rural dwellers who own land. People in these circumstances are sometimes referred to as "house poor" or "land poor." This group, too, would not be eligible for asset-based welfare transfers. Increasingly, creative schemes such as reverse mortgages and equity sharing are making it possible for older people to utilize their home equity to maintain adequate consumption (although people are apparently reluctant to do so).

Another special case in this category is that of college students, who typically have neither significant assets nor large incomes. However, they do have high earnings potential—that is, human capital. For policy purposes, valuing this human capital is not a serious problem. Students would simply not be eligible for benefits oriented toward the asset poor. There is strong precedent for this position. In the past, income-based welfare policy did not give benefits to full-time students. Asset-based policy would follow this principle.[11]

Only for the Asset Poor and Income Poor

Therefore, asset poverty, for policy purposes, would be defined in conjunction with income poverty. When households are below minimum levels of both assets and income, the concept of asset poverty would become operational in public policy. In other words, only when both income and assets are low, would antipoverty asset policies be put into effect.

For some, a question may linger: Why should welfare benefits be in the form of assets rather than income? After all, income benefits can be converted into asset benefits simply by saving rather than spending. The simple answer, as pointed out in chapter 4, is that the United States has elaborate, government-sponsored, and deeply entrenched asset accumulation policies for the nonpoor. These policies operate primarily through the tax system, and most household wealth of the nonpoor is accumulated through these mechanisms. In reality, there is very little accumulation of assets through ordinary income streams in the vast majority of households (see chapter 6): it just does not happen that way. Therefore, if the nonpoor are ineffective at accumulating assets outside of special program structures, how much less likely is such accumulation for the poor? Recognizing the institutionalized nature of asset accumulation for the nonpoor, which almost everyone seems to accept as desirable, a better question is: Why not also for the poor?

Policy Framework

Asset-based welfare policy would require not merely a new way of thinking about policy *content*, but also a new way of thinking about policy *structure*. In other words, asset-based policy is not merely a matter of social programs, but of a policy framework that can, insofar as possible, integrate numerous policy efforts into a single system. This system should be designed so that a wide variety of creative asset-based welfare efforts by governments, corporations, nonprofit organizations, and households could mesh and complement one another. The system should be able to grow and adapt, facilitate experiments, discard failures, and expand successful efforts. In short, the key is to set up a policy framework within which asset-based welfare policies can develop. This system would include incentives and rules for participation within which parties can interact and experimentation can occur. In chapter 10, I suggest that a universal system of special accounts, called Individual Development Accounts, might form the basis of this policy framework.

Policy Principles

Before turning to the policy itself, it may be useful to set forth the basic principles that should guide asset-based welfare policy. Asset-based policy should: (1) complement income-based policy; (2) have universal availability; (3) provide greater incentives for the poor; (4) be based on voluntary participation; (5) not define individuals as "on welfare" or "off welfare"; (6) promote shared responsibility; (7) have specific purposes; (8) encourage gradual accumulation; (9) provide investment options; (10) promote economic information and training; and (11) foster personal development.

Complement to Income-Based Policy

In most applications, asset-based policy would not entirely replace income-based policy but would serve as a complement. The two types of policies, income-based and asset-based, often serve different purposes and could work hand in hand. For example, a welfare policy for recipients of Aid to Families with Dependent Children (AFDC) might include both an income transfer and a deposit in a long-term account for each child.

Universal Availability

The policy should be universally open to anyone who chooses to participate. Universal availability would engender a broad base of political support, as it does for current systems of Social Security, Individual Retirement Accounts, and other universal programs.

Greater Incentives for the Poor

Universal availability, however, would not mean universal incentives. Although the program would be open to everyone, incentives for participation would be greater for the poor. In most applications of asset-based welfare policy, the poor would receive a variety of supports, including direct subsidies as well as beneficial tax treatment. For at least some of the nonpoor, the program would provide beneficial tax treatment, but no direct subsidies. The rationale for this approach is that most of the nonpoor already benefit from asset-based welfare policies in home ownership and retirement pension systems. The primary purpose of the proposals in this book is to apply similar asset-based principles to welfare policies for the poor.

Voluntary Participation

All recipients of asset-based welfare policy would participate voluntarily. No one would be required to accumulate assets. In some cases, however, incentives might be so attractive that it would be foolish *not* to participate. (Still, there would be some individuals who would exercise their right to be foolish. Many nonpoor individuals make financially ill-advised decisions. For example, some of my colleagues in the university do not participate in the tax-deferred retirement system that is available, even though the university and the tax laws make it quite attractive to do so. In the American tradition, people should be allowed this freedom.)

Not "On Welfare" or "Off Welfare"

In a system of asset-based welfare, people would not be "on welfare" or "off welfare." Asset-based welfare is a long-term idea. At certain times, deposits would be made into asset accounts, and at other times, deposits would not be made. Depending on circumstances, people might be eligible to receive subsidies for deposits, and at other times they would not. The total effect would be cumulative.

Perhaps this is best illustrated by looking at the current system of Individual Retirement Accounts (IRAs), an asset-based program that, for the most part, benefits the nonpoor. People are not "on IRAs" or "off IRAs," although deposits are sometimes made into IRA accounts, and sometimes they are not. When deposits are made into IRAs, there is no judgment that the IRA-holder is on welfare, although assuredly over time the government is granting a large transfer of money. On the contrary, people who make deposits into IRAs are seen as being responsible citizens, looking after their personal welfare. Similarly, the purpose of asset-based welfare for the poor would be to establish a long-range program and non-stigmatized accumulation.

Under asset-based welfare policy for the poor, when people have achieved a certain level of asset accumulation, they would no longer be eligible for a particular direct subsidy or a particular tax treatment. In concept, this is not different from the current rules governing IRAs, wherein, at a certain level of household income, deposits are no longer tax-deferred. Under the broader asset-based welfare policy proposed in this book, programs and guidelines would cover a much greater range of policy purposes, including home ownership, college education, capital for self-employment, and so forth.

Mutual Responsibility

In no case would public subsidies support deposits without some level of mutual participation, or co-contribution, between the recipient and the government. This would serve two important purposes. First, shared responsibility would connect recipients more strongly to the program; and second, shared responsibility would make asset-based welfare more politically acceptable to the broad range of the American public.

For the very poor, in some cases, the level of shared responsibility might be quite low—as low as 10 percent matched by 90 percent. The poor would be encouraged to raise their match through earned income, income transfers, entrepreneurial ventures, fund-raising, or in other ways. Creative combinations of funding would be actively promoted.

Specific Purposes, Restricted Assets

Through the use of restricted accounts, asset accumulation would be tied to specific goals that are deemed to be in the public interest. This is appropriate because asset-based policy would be tax-benefited and subsidized. This is comparable to the current system of restricted asset-based welfare for the nonpoor in home equity and retirement pension subsidies. In other words, if an individual wants the public subsidy, she or he must hold the assets for a particular purpose or purposes.

Also, in many poor households, accumulation must be restricted to specific purposes, or it would be unlikely to occur. Carol Stack's classic study of financial interactions among the urban poor suggests that available financial assets are likely to be used by someone in the ''support network.'' These networks are characterized by strong ties and mutual obligation. For example, Carol Stack recounts:

> When Magnolia and Calvin Waters inherited a sum of money, the information spread quickly to every member of their domestic network. Within a month and a half, all of the money was absorbed by participants in their network whose demands and needs could not be refused.[12]

Similarly, it is not uncommon to hear from a welfare mother that she gave part of her rent money to a friend who was in greater difficulty than she was, hoping that the landlord would not kick either one of them out, as long as they paid something. Although systematic knowledge in this area is quite limited, it appears that, for many of the poor, the concept of individual property rights, including ownership of private assets, is slightly different from that of the middle class. Among the poor, more property is shared. Security resides, in part, in network obligations. An old saying on the street that captures this system of security is, ''If you can't make money, make friends.''

Of course, there is a great deal that is noble and appealing about the values of mutual support. The purpose of the current proposal is not to challenge these values but to develop a parallel and more financially based system of household security.

Investment Options

Regardless of the type or purpose of restricted account, individuals would have a limited set of choices for investments, such as a choice among a principal-protected, interest-bearing account; a bond fund; and a more speculative fund of common stocks.

Based on historical experience, common stocks yield a larger return than do fixed-income investments. Exact returns depend on methods of calculation. By one set of calculations, since 1926, over a period of sixty-three years, and before taxes, Standard and Poor's 500 stocks have returned 6.9 percent above the rate of price inflation; long-term U.S. bonds, 1.1 percent; and treasury bills, 0.4 percent.[13] Therefore, for long-term goals, investments in stock funds would be encouraged. For short-term goals, fixed-income investments would protect principle.

Gradual Accumulation over the Long Term

Asset-based welfare policy would not be designed to dump large assets, in a lump sum, into the lives of poor people. Rather, it would be designed for gradual accumulation. The key is to structure the system so that it would promote long-term, lifelong accumulation. This long-term orientation would promote planning and achievement of major life goals.

As pointed out in the preceding chapter, it is not only how much money people have that matters, but also where they are going financially. With income transfer programs, history has shown, people are going nowhere. But with asset accumulation, they would be going somewhere; they would be making financial progress.

Economic Information and Training

In general, the level of economic literacy in the United States is very low. In a survey of economic knowledge among high school students, scores were surprisingly low:

> More than half of all high school students in a national survey could not define basic economic terms like profit and inflation. . . . In a multiple-choice test given to more than 8,000 high school students last spring, 75 percent gave an incorrect definition for inflation, 66 percent said profits

equal something other than revenue minus cost, and 55 percent incorrectly identified the term "government budget deficit."[14]

The low scores prompted this comment from Paul Volcker, former head of the Federal Reserve: "The news is not good if you believe that a basic understanding of our economic system is important if this country is indeed to be effective in what everyone realizes is a period of global competition."[15]

Economic illiteracy appears to be a general problem for the nation, and perhaps more so for the poor. Because the poor typically do not participate in systems of asset accumulation, basic financial concepts related to savings, credit, investment, and productivity are not well known. In a world of no assets, these concepts are not salient. As one person from an impoverished background commented, "The concept of assets is meaningless to most people without resources." The person who made this comment was studying for his Ph.D., certainly very intelligent, but it was apparent in the conversation that he himself did not very clearly understand financial assets as a term. The economics of accumulation had not been a part of his life. He had never thought about it. (This incident may be difficult for some readers to believe, but it points out the very crucial cognitive effects of assets, or in this case, absence of assets. When assets are not present, the concept quite literally has no meaning.)

Asset-based welfare policy would become a structure around which economic education could occur. Asset accounts could be used as a basis for economic education and planning for the future. This might be thought of as a revitalized home economics. This revitalized home economics would focus on long-term strategies of asset accumulation, including especially a personal balance sheet, alternative choices for investments, compound earnings, and calculations of present value of long-term financial activities; and connecting these concepts to life goals, especially education and home ownership. Such a program of financial education would be designed to structure people's thoughts of their own economic life *in the long term*. Ideally, such education would take place routinely in the schools, for all students. As a by-product, long-term thinking about other personal goals would be almost inevitable.

The existence of long-term asset accumulation accounts, by themselves, would stimulate greater financial planning in many households—people would be thinking about how to use the funds to meet life goals. In addition, it would be helpful to have extensive information and education campaigns on the use of asset accounts. Wherever possible, these should be structured into the settings where people work and go to school. The best applications of financial planning are with young people in schools, where asset accounts could be used as a basis for regular financial planning and career planning exercises.

Personal Development

Asset-based welfare policy would promote and reinforce education, training, employment, and other personal development objectives by structuring subsidies and tax benefits to promote these objectives. Especially in the case of young people, the program would strongly reinforce education.

Questions

At this point, a number of questions arise. As in all matters of public policy, questions are not always easy to answer. Even after some issues are thoroughly explored, reasonable people will continue to disagree. This process of questioning and dialogue is essential to the formulation of public policy. In that spirit, this section poses some of the important questions and offers responses.

Why Special Programs for Asset Accumulation?

Some people might say that although it is a good idea to accumulate assets, such accumulation is better left to individual households without the interference of public policy. One commentator has said that assets are "the last thing people acquire and the hardest to redistribute." This view assumes, as does standard neoclassical economics, that savings are a residual—what is left over after consumption is subtracted from income.

The perspective in this book, however, is that asset accumulation typically is *not* a residual in this sense. Rather, it is an institutionalized process. For the most part, people do not accumulate assets by themselves. Asset accumulation by the majority of nonpoor households occurs through structured tax arrangements. From this perspective, it is not fully accurate to interpret savings as something left over after consumption is subtracted from income. On the contrary, for most of the nonpoor, savings enter the household *as assets* in the form of home equity and accumulations in retirement pension accounts. This money is not "saved" out of income in the traditional sense, but, rather, is accumulated through subsidized mechanisms designed for asset accumulation. Assets are not the last thing people acquire, but rather are acquired throughout the adult lifetime. In a very real sense, for the majority of nonpoor households, most existing financial and real assets were never income in the traditional sense, but rather entered the household as restricted assets. In these cases, public policy has not found it difficult to redistribute restricted assets. Why should it be difficult to do something similar for the poor?

Will the Public Support Welfare Transfers above the Safety Net Level?

In an era of large budget deficits, any proposal for more spending—perhaps especially welfare spending—will be met with strong opposition. As long as the idea of welfare policy is defined as consumption, the public, in all likelihood, will not support transfers to the poor above the safety net level.

However, if the fundamental idea of welfare policy is redefined as growth and development, there is a high probability for a shift in emphasis. In the case of asset transfers to the nonpoor through the tax system, one rarely hears objections to asset-based policy. Even though the amounts are large, asset transfers for these purposes are deemed to be desirable and enjoy widespread public support.

Don't the Poor Need Income More than Assets?

This is the most difficult question of all. In discussions of asset-based welfare, a typical first response is that poor people need income more than assets. When people do not have enough money for survival, current need takes priority over saving and accumulation. When one does not have enough to feed one's children, the issue is not saving for tomorrow, but eating today. From this perspective, it would be paternalistic to require, for example, of AFDC recipients, that a portion of their already insufficient income be diverted into a long-term, restricted account. As one former AFDC recipient, now active in social policy in the state of Missouri, puts it:

> I would like to make one point about restricted assets based on my experience. It is often difficult to separate one's professional and private lives. In this case it is impossible for me to do so. My son and I received AFDC benefits for several years. We ran out of food stamps before the end of the month more times than I care to remember. I cannot imagine how it would have felt when my child was hungry to know that I had assets which I was not allowed to touch. I sincerely doubt that this knowledge would have carried me through. I would have traded the assets in a second, to feed him. I am not sure that it is good or fair to put a person in the position of being hungry, with assets.

This a very powerful statement. Who could argue with it? Who would *want* to argue with it? How, then, is this question of inadequate consumption to be answered? The response cannot have the emotional impact of the statement above, but there are key points to be made.

First, asset-based welfare programs would be voluntary. Those who do not wish or are not able to participate in asset-based welfare programs would elect not to do so. Just as the nonpoor can choose consumption over asset accumulation, this choice would also be available to the poor. Not everyone would participate. But this does not mean that the program would be a failure. For example, making a very pessimistic estimate, if only 10 percent of poor households (more than 3 million people) chose to accumulate assets, would the program be unsuccessful? Certainly it would not.

Second, it is easy enough to say that poor households require income more than assets, and to cite many examples accordingly, but to what extent this is actually so is an open question, and the answer will vary from household to household. If the poor had equal—or stronger —incentives for asset accumulation as the nonpoor, it seems likely that some of the poor would find ways to save and accumulate assets. Even without incentives, millions of poor families make huge sacrifices, foregoing consumption, trying to pay for a child's education or accumulate a down payment for a house. It is sweepingly simplistic to say that poor people cannot save.

Consider the historical record of the United States. A major reason for industrial development during the late nineteenth and early twentieth centuries was the hard work and frugal savings habits of immigrants. Many of these immigrants were poor—dirt-poor. But they struggled and sacrificed. They put away whatever they could so their children would have greater opportunities. Savings institutions were created to serve small savers. The resulting high rate of personal savings fueled capital accumulation that helped to make industrial development possible.

Consider an analogy from development economics. In many cases, a similar no-ability-to-save thinking has been applied to poor nations. The argument is that very poor countries cannot accumulate capital until basic needs are met. However, oddly enough, there is no actual correlation between level of economic development (defined as gross national product or gross domestic product per person) and rates of net national savings. Many countries far poorer than the United States, for example, have higher rates of savings. Among so-called developing nations, Mexico has a very low rate of internal savings, while India, far poorer than Mexico, has a very high rate of internal savings, primarily because India has developed a banking system—an institutional mechanism for asset accumulation—that reaches out to the poor. In short, it is not necessarily true that poor nations cannot save.[16]

A similar faulty reasoning may be occurring among policymakers in advanced welfare states. Poor individuals, like poor nations, may find a way to save when saving is encouraged and when it is in their economic interest to do so. When the incentives are right, and the institutional mechanisms are present, at least some people will find a way to save. Perhaps they find a way through sacrifice, through harder work, or through ingenuity. But without an institutional structure to encourage the saving, this added sacrifice, harder work, and ingenuity are less likely to occur.

Ultimately, whether poor people can save, given institutional incentives to do so, is an empirical question. Imagine what might happen if we said to all AFDC mothers, whatever you can save, we will match two dollars for one dollar, in a restricted trust for your children to go to college? Who knows what would happen, but I would guess that many of the mothers would find ways to take advantage of the offer. In the final analysis, an effective institutional structure, with proper incentives, may be more important than level of income in promoting asset accumulation.

Therefore, as much as possible, asset accumulation for the poor should be *institutionalized,* as it is for the nonpoor. This would mean voluntary payroll and welfare transfer deduction programs, with matches from the federal government, accompanied by information and education programs on the availability and benefits of such programs.

Can Restricted Accounts Buffer Income Shocks?

The good thing about financial assets is their portability and flexibility; they can be used for a variety of purposes. But restricted assets would not be so portable and flexible. How would an asset-based welfare policy buffer income shocks if assets were restricted to specific purposes?

The ability to buffer income shocks depends on the form and liquidity of assets. Long-term restricted accounts would not, in themselves, serve this purpose. One possibility is to permit borrowing against restricted accounts under emergency or hardship conditions, as is now possible under 401(k) retirement plans. If such a program were put into place, the "borrower" would repay himself or herself with interest. Whether or not such a program would be practical is difficult to say. If not, then a system of restricted asset accounts would not do much to buffer short-term income shocks.

Aren't Restricted Accounts Economically Inefficient?

Standard neoclassical economic theory suggests that all public transfers are inefficient, and that transfers with restrictions are more inefficient than transfers without restrictions. Mainstream economists would prescribe, theoretically, transfers with as few restrictions as possible, thereby allowing recipients to decide freely how to use resources in the most economically efficient manner possible.

Despite this theory, as pointed out above, restricted asset transfers are the vehicle for the vast bulk of asset accumulation for the U.S. population; these occur through home mortgage tax deductions and tax-deferred retirement pension systems. Contrary to the prescription of neoclassical economists, the nation's household wealth is not accumulated so much by choice as by policy restrictions. Oddly, few economists have actively opposed these policies for the nonpoor on the grounds of inefficiency. Therefore, one assumes, what seems to be efficient enough for the nonpoor might also be efficient enough for the poor.

Would Asset-Based Policy Help the "Underclass"?

I am not very comfortable with the term "underclass." I am never certain what the term means, and it seems to me that it obscures more than it reveals. If underclass refers to the drug culture, it is helpful to bear in mind that most drug addicts do not live in poor, inner-city neighborhoods. Moreover, the nation has some 6 million drug addicts, but 18 million problem drinkers. If underclass refers to people living in hard-core poverty neighborhoods, Isabel Sawhill of the Urban Institute estimates that number at 2.5 million, only 1.1 million of whom are officially poor, and fewer still could be called behaviorally antisocial. At almost 9 million, there are far more working poor than underclass poor, and the total number of Americans in poverty is 33 million. If there is an underclass, it should not be confused, in a simplistic way, with the problems of drugs and poverty in America.

Still, there are many individuals in poverty neighborhoods who are antisocial, hard-core criminals, drug pushers, and murderers. If this is what social scientists and journalists mean by underclass, would asset-based welfare help to resolve these problems? Not likely. However, if all those on long-term public assistance are included in the underclass, would asset-based welfare help to resolve these problems? Quite possibly. Anyone who has worked with welfare mothers knows that many are careful financial managers—with so little income, they have to be. Permit me to recount an incident: A homeless, single, black mother with three children is standing in the living room of a house that she cannot move into because she has no voucher to cover the rent. She wants the house very badly, contending that she would rather remain in the shelter than go into "the projects" with her kids. She has lived on AFDC for a long time. She is distraught at not being able to move in, and she is also unhappy about having to go to budgeting classes as part of the homeless service network. She says:

> I don't need any budgeting classes. I know how to live. When you get your check you got to pay the rent first—that's the first thing. Then the gas, then the lights. I got Food Stamps for food and I got me a freezer. You got to use some money for food in the freezer so you can

get by the whole month. Then you got to put something aside for medicine when your kids get sick, and for shoes. They need shoes that fit. Then you start over the next month. That's how you get by.[17]

As a financial manager, this woman is as hard-nosed as a small town banker. If she were not, she and her children would be in very serious trouble (an AFDC transfer in Missouri is, however one wishes to measure it, not enough to live on; tremendous financial skill is required to survive from month to month). This woman is a long-term welfare recipient, but is she part of an "underclass" that is beyond help? Of course not. Would she save for her children's college education if there were some way for her to do so? Very likely she would.

Would Poor People Respond Behaviorally to Asset Accumulation the Same as Everyone Else?

In chapter 8, a number of psychological and social effects of asset accumulation are discussed, along with economic effects. Evidence in support of these effects is substantial. But several commentators have raised the possibility that poor people would not respond to asset accumulation in the same way, due to their different values. This viewpoint arises from a culture-of-poverty perspective of the conservative variety: poor people are different from the nonpoor and therein lies the problem.

In my experience, there is no reason to believe that poor people are different from the rest of us. As William J. Wilson has found among the poor in Chicago, their values are very much like everyone else's— they seek home ownership, education, a satisfactory career.[18] Very likely they would respond to asset accumulation in much the same way as everyone else. However, because there is little research on economic behavior in poor households, the question remains open. Empirical work with poor populations is necessary, ideally through asset-based demonstration projects.

Won't More People Take Advantage of the Welfare System?

If the government begins to offer asset accumulation accounts, will not more people try to take advantage of the welfare system? Charles

Murray has recognized that a major problem of income-based welfare transfers is that such transfers attract new people to welfare and, as Charles Murray says, "It is much easier to get into the welfare system than to get out of it."[19] He is correct about this. Getting off of income-based welfare is extremely problematic (indeed, it is amazing that so many families manage to do so against formidable odds).

But asset-based welfare is a very different idea. The *goal* of asset-based welfare is for poor people to accumulate assets, and public policies would encourage them to do so. Above a certain level of asset accumulation, households would not qualify for particular subsidies and incentives. In other words, the limits of government-supported accumulation would be spelled out in advance and would be applied automatically.

Still, there might be some who say that asset-based welfare recipients would not be standing on their own two feet, would not be independent, and so forth. This assertion can be met with a question: Where is the independence of the nonpoor? Each year, many nonpoor households collect asset transfers in home mortgage tax deductions and tax-deferred retirement pension funds in excess of the average annual transfers to AFDC families.[20] Do the nonpoor feel dependent in receiving these asset transfers? Hardly, although it would be much more difficult to accumulate assets otherwise. Are the nonpoor taking advantage of the system? Often as much as possible, but the system is designed for the nonpoor to do so.

The more academic version of this question is: Will not asset subsidies keep people from earning more income? This is the traditional work incentive question that has so preoccupied mainstream welfare analysts. At this point, the data are sufficient to answer that even income transfers do not reduce work behavior by very much.[21] If asset-based welfare is in the form of restricted accounts, as proposed in this book, then the resources could not be used to support immediate consumption. Without consumption support, it is difficult to see how the poor would be induced to work less.

Isn't the Proposal for Asset-Based Welfare Just Trying to Make Everyone Middle-Class?

From the political left comes the query about trying to make everyone middle class. The problem, from this perspective, is not the transferring of assets, but the idea that people who have assets think and behave differently, plan for the future, take care of their belongings, and so forth. A typical comment is as follows: "The proposal assumes that all people want the same things, that everyone wants assets. All people do not want the responsibility of a house or car, nor does everyone want a college education. To assume that everyone wants a condominium, or to play the stock market, seems absurd to me." More intellectual-sounding versions of this statement sometimes employ the phrase "bourgeois mentality," which asset-based welfare policy apparently would promote.

In response to this query, the answer would have to be yes, asset-based welfare is, in this sense, trying to make participants middle class. The policy seeks to promote accumulation of wealth, long-term thinking, active citizenship, and so forth. If this is "bourgeois mentality," then it would promote that as well.

While I appreciate the underlying concern about hollow materialistic values, it is all too easy for those who are comfortable to romanticize about poverty. One cannot find many poor people who do *not* wish to own a house and a car and send their children to school. Of course, the programs would be optional; those who reject the values inherent in asset accumulation would remain free to do so.

Would Asset-Based Welfare Policy Be Used as a Screen for the Federal Government to Withdraw from Its Commitment to the Poor?

Another query from the left, this one to be taken very seriously, is the possibility that political conservatives might use asset-based rhetoric as a way to withdraw from welfare programs altogether. A very good example of this question is currently being raised in St. Louis. With the strong support of Department of Housing and Urban Development (HUD) secretary Jack Kemp and Missouri senator Christopher Bond, the Tenant Management Association of the Carr Square public housing project is seeking to transform the project to tenant ownership. There is no doubt that Secretary Kemp and the Tenant Management group are well intentioned and highly committed to the project. Secretary Kemp is a strong proponent of home ownership. However, in this case, it is not clear that the proposal would in fact result in individual tenant ownership of the units, or when this might occur. Congressman William Clay interprets the proposal as an effort by the federal government to get out of public housing altogether.[22] At this stage, it is not possible to say which side in this debate is correct—only the experiment itself, if it goes forward, will provide the answer.

The Carr Square example illustrates that although asset-based welfare may sound appealing, the political reality of implementation may be quite complex. Different people would support the policy for different reasons, and therefore the policy might serve a variety of purposes. The possibility always exists, as with any program, that major objectives would be intentionally or unintentionally subverted. However, this is not a good reason to reject asset-based welfare. The point is that policy objectives, and particularly implementation plans, must be carefully designed and monitored.

Alternative Asset-Based Policy Directions

The major proposal suggested in this book is for restricted individual accounts in the name of each participant. However, a large number of other asset-based policy approaches are possible. Some of these are mentioned briefly below.

A wide variety of small ad hoc applications of asset-based policy occur in local communities, neighborhoods, and social service agencies, although they are not known as "asset-based policy." For example, one social service agency encourages businesses to donate used cars, for which the businesses take tax write-offs. The used cars are then given to welfare recipients who use them to get to work. The value of the cars is low enough for recipients to stay under the fifteen-hundred-dollar asset limit for AFDC. In this case, the rules of welfare policy permit the asset to be transferred, while receipt of the same amount of income would disqualify participants for AFDC.

Another example is the practice of some homeless shelters (for example, Family Haven operated by the Salvation Army in St. Louis) to do everything possible to get families to *save* while in the shelter so that when housing is located, the family has a small nest egg for a start toward stability in housing.

Also, there are numerous creative approaches to home ownership for the poor, including urban homesteading, sweat equity arrangements, and mortgage loan subsidies. Because home ownership plays so vital a role in the financial well-being of American families, all of these creative equity arrangements hold a great deal of potential. Virtually any form of home equity promotion should be encouraged.

It is also possible to consider asset accumulation strategies at the group and community levels, including community ownership of enterprises, "mutual housing," "community land trusts," and the like. Very creative asset-based solutions are possible. I have heard, for example, of a housing project that capitalizes public rent subsidy lines and uses the money to float bonds. These group asset approaches might be thought of as either local socialism or group capitalism (the difference between capitalism and socialism, at the small group level, is not always easy to determine). Such approaches seem to be particularly attractive to people on the political left, who cannot easily accept the idea of promoting individual ownership.[23]

A different asset-based strategy, also gaining in popularity, is the Employee Stock Ownership Plan (ESOP). Louis Kelso began promoting this idea in the 1950s. In 1974, the first tax code changes were enacted to subsidize ESOPs. During the next fifteen years, some ten thousand companies enrolled more than nine million workers in ESOPs.[24] There is limited evidence that companies with ESOPs have grown faster and are more productive than those without them—higher productivity seems to result when ESOPs are combined with greater participation in decision making on the part of employees.[25,26]

The employee stock ownership movement is led in Europe by the United Kingdom. Since Margaret Thatcher took office in 1979, the number of people owning stock in companies has tripled to nine million, a big step toward what Thatcher has called "my great aim of making every man and woman a capitalist." If Thatcher is serious about this goal, she is possibly more progressive than many of her critics imagine.[27]

Conclusion

In sum, asset-based welfare is a fundamental change in direction in welfare policy for the poor. It is a new path to consider when welfare proposals reach the floor for discussion. History tells us that welfare states are built piece by piece, slowly, across decades.[28]

Policymakers need not adopt an all-or-nothing perspective. Clearly, income-based policies will always play a role in welfare in the United States, probably the principal role. But this does not preclude the introduction of asset policies as complements where they are appropriate. The two basic types of policies—income-based and asset-based—can work together. As new areas of welfare policy enter the political arena, asset programs might be considered either as alternatives or as complements to traditional income-based programs.

But what would asset-based welfare policies look like? There are a wide range of possible applications. Thinking specifically of asset-based policy for the poor in the United States, at a minimum it would be desirable to expand asset limits for AFDC, Food Stamps, and other targeted welfare programs, so that poor people could begin to accumulate some wealth. More desirable still would be a system of incentives to support asset accumulation. In the next chapter, I suggest one possible policy instrument, the Individual Development Account.

Notes

1. The term "welfare citizen" is also used by Malcolm Bush (*Families in Distress: Public, Private, and Civic Responses*. Berkeley: University of California Press, 1988), although he uses it in a somewhat different sense, focusing almost exclusively on rights and very little on responsibilities.

2. Andrew Jackson, *First Annual Message to Congress*, in James D. Richardson, ed., *A Compilation of the Messages and Papers of the Presidents, 1789–1897*. Washington: U.S. Government Printing Office, 1896–1899, vol. 2, 600–601.

3. An excellent history is by William Scott, *In Pursuit of Happiness: American Conceptions of Property from the Seventeenth to the Twentieth Centuries*. Bloomington: Indiana University Press, 1977.

4. Henry Steele Commager, "Appraisal of the Welfare State," in Charles Schottland, ed., *The Welfare State*. New York: Harper Torchbooks, 1967, 84–90.

5. Charles Schottland, ed., *The Welfare State*. New York: Harper Torchbooks, 1967, 14.

6. Julie Solomon, "Managers Focus on Low-Wage Workers," *Wall Street Journal*, May 9, 1989, B1.

7. Tuition guarantee programs sponsored by the private sector, while very encouraging, have not been universally successful. In some cases, the promise of tuition, by itself, is not enough. Experience from the "I Have a Dream" Foundation suggests that good adult supervision and role models, as well as structured peer support, may be essential in keeping young people on track toward a college education. For this reason, it would be important to integrate asset-based educational programs into primary and secondary schooling (see chapter 10).

8. Douglas E. Ashford, *The Emergence of the Welfare States*. Oxford: Basil Blackwell, 1986, 88–89.

9. Edward N. Wolff, "Wealth Holding and Poverty Status in the US," a paper presented at the 20th General Conference of the International Association for

Research on Income and Wealth, Roca di Papa, Italy, August, 1987.

10. Michael Morris and John B. Williamson, *Poverty and Public Policy: An Analysis of Federal Intervention Efforts.* New York: Greenwood Press, 1986.

11. The discussion of asset-rich and income-rich households may give a false impression of all household members sharing equally in available resources. From a feminist perspective, Deborah Page-Adams has pointed out to me that women and children may in fact be asset-poor in asset-rich households, and income-poor in income-rich households. This point is well taken; however, divergent economic interests within the same household are, for the most part, beyond the scope of the proposals in this book. Individual Development Accounts, because they would be held in each person's name, would make possible asset accumulation by all household members, but they would not guarantee it.

12. Carol B. Stack, *All Our Kin: Strategies for Survival in a Black Community.* New York: Harper and Row, 1974, 36–37.

13. The source for these figures on long-term returns of investments is Ibotson Associates, Inc., Chicago. The firm says that 1926 is the earliest year for which it can obtain reliable data.

14. Deirdre Carmody, "Many Students Fail Quiz on Basic Economics," *New York Times,* December 29, 1988, 1Y and 8Y, citing results of a report by William Walstad and John Soper, *A Report Card on the Economic Literacy of U.S. High School Students.* New York: Joint Council on Economic Education, 1988.

15. Quoted in Carmody, 1988.

16. Michael Sherraden and Clemente Ruiz, "Social Welfare in the Context of Development: Toward Micro-Asset Policies—The Case of Mexico," *Journal of International and Comparative Social Welfare* 5(2), 1989, 42–61.

17. For this quotation, I am indebted to Alice Johnson, one of my doctoral students who has worked extensively on the problem of homelessness in St. Louis.

18. William J. Wilson et al., panel presentation at the Annual Meetings of the Midwest Sociological Society, St. Louis, April 1989.

19. Charles Murray, "New Welfare Bill, New Welfare Cheats," *Wall Street Journal,* October 13, 1988, A16.

20. Allow me to use my family as an example. Direct asset transfers through the tax system for housing and retirement funds to our rather average household in 1988 totaled about $6,160. Undoubtedly, most policy analysts who write about the perils of welfare dependency receive similar or greater transfers. By comparison, in 1988 a family of three on AFDC in Missouri received $282 plus $198 in Food Stamps per month, for a total of $5,760 on an annual basis.

21. Sheldon Danziger, Robert Haveman, and Robert Plotnick, "How Income Transfer Programs Affect Work, Savings, and the Income Distribution: A Critical Review," *Journal of Economic Literature* 19, 1981, 975–1028.

22. Among many news reports in St. Louis, see for example, Margaret Wolf Freivogel, "Public Housing Debate Centers on Federal Role," *St. Louis Post-Dispatch,* December 17, 1989, B1 and B6.

23. In my view, the potential for group capital is quite limited as a strategy for fighting poverty on a broad scale. Historically, as the record of communes and other utopian experiments indicates, group ownership has not been successful over the long term. Organizational and transaction costs involved in cooperative

ownership are large, often beyond the coping abilities of any group, much less the economically marginal.

24. The motivation of major companies in establishing ESOPs is not necessarily a sudden urge to share the wealth. Federal tax laws have made ESOPs very attractive. Under current law, ESOPs "offer simultaneous solutions to major problems now besetting American corporations. When a company gives stock to its employees through an ESOP, it cuts its tax bill, erects a takeover defense, clamps a lid on the cost of pensions, and perhaps even spares itself the nightmare of monumental medical benefits for future retirees. And it can do all this while moving toward the most important goal of all: boosting productivity enough to make U.S. companies more competitive in world markets" (Christopher Farrell and John Hoerr, "ESOPs: Are They Good for You?" *Business Week*, May 15, 1989, 116–23). During the first six months of 1989, U.S. corporations acquired over $19 billion of their own stock to establish ESOPs. Researchers conclude that "the main motivation for the growth of ESOPs is their antitakeover characteristics" (Myron Scholes and Mark Wolfson, "Employee Stock Ownership Plans and Corporate Restructuring: Myths and Realities," Working Paper No. 3094. Cambridge, MA: National Bureau of Economic Research, 1989).

25. Robert D. Hershey, Jr., "Including Labor in the Division of Capital," *New York Times*, April 24, 1988, E5; and Farrell and Hoerr, 1989.

26. Over a period of several decades, Kelso has developed and promoted a still broader scheme of asset distribution. His rather utopian visions of "universal capitalism" have never been taken seriously in public policy, but they are nonetheless provocative and interesting. Simply put, Kelso's idea is to make everyone a capitalist by borrowing the money and letting investment earnings repay the loans. The underlying philosophy is presented in Louis O. Kelso and Mortimer J. Adler, *The Capitalist Manifesto*. New York: Random House, 1958. A detailed plan is offered in Louis O. Kelso and Patricia Hetter, *How to Turn Eighty Million Workers into Capitalists on Borrowed Money*. New York: Random House, 1967. A chatty, somewhat revisionist version is presented by Stuart Speiser, *A Piece of the Action*. New York: Van Nostrand, 1977.

27. Thatcher has many critics (I am sometimes among them) because she has attacked and reduced welfare benefits in the United Kingdom and generated massive unemployment. On the other hand, she has made significant progress toward greater asset distribution. The spread of stock ownership, mentioned above, is one example. Perhaps more fundamental is the huge increase in home ownership and privately held pensions that Thatcher has promoted, and its pronounced effect on the distribution of household wealth. Since 1980, more than one million units of "council housing" in the United Kingdom have been sold, below market price, to residents.

> Over the last twenty-five years the value of personal wealth has approximately doubled in real terms. This substantial increase has been caused by major changes in the composition of assets and in their relative value. Of particular importance has been the rapid and continuous growth of home ownership and, from the mid-1970s, the development of occupational and other pension funds as a primary form of long-term financial savings. Together, owner-occupied houses and private pension funds account for over 60 percent of total personal sector wealth compared to less than a third twenty years ago.

The main reason for the accumulation of wealth in these forms is that access to them has been massively subsidised by the state, normally in the form of tax concessions.

The 'new wealth' is more evenly distributed than the 'old' forms which were held mainly in land and company stocks. . . . The most important feature of the new wealth is its *vertical* distribution, which cuts across the occupational class structure (Stuart Lowe, "New Patterns of Wealth: The Growth of Owner Occupation," in Robert Walker and Gillian Parker, eds., *Money Matters: Income, Wealth and Financial Welfare.* London: Sage, 1988, 149–65).

Thus, while critics might argue that Thatcher has increased human suffering, she has, in a fundamental sense, also attacked the very basis of inequality, the distribution of assets. However, as in the United States, tax-supported mechanisms for household wealth distribution in the United Kingdom do not often reach the poor. Essentially, Thatcher is stimulating asset holding by the middle class, something that, historically, the United Kingdom has not done to the same extent as has the United States. Also, at this writing, Thatcher's home ownership scheme is not going well. Interest rates are high in the United Kingdom and many of the people who purchased council housing are finding themselves unable to meet the mortgage payments. After years of stable residence, they are being put out on the street.

28. Ashford, 1986.

10 • Individual Development Accounts

How would asset-based welfare policy be put into practice? Through what mechanism would assets be accumulated? By whom? Under what circumstances? There are many possible answers to these questions, but the suggestion here is for a relatively simple and universal system of accounts similar to Individual Retirement Accounts (IRAs), which began in 1974. For the sake of discussion, let us call these new accounts Individual Development Accounts (IDAs).[1] IDAs would be optional, earnings-bearing, tax-benefited accounts in the name of each individual, initiated as early as birth, and restricted to designated purposes. Regardless of the category of welfare policy (housing, education, self-employment, retirement, or other) assets would be accumulated in these long-term restricted accounts. The federal government would match or otherwise subsidize deposits for the poor, and there would be potential for creative financing through the private sector (for example, adoption of a school by a corporation) or through the efforts of account holders themselves (for example, student fund-raising projects or student-run businesses). IDAs would be designed to promote orientation toward the future, long-range planning, savings and investment, individual initiative, individual choice, and achievement of life goals.

In many respects, IDAs would be similar to Individual Retirement Accounts (IRAs), but there would be important differences. IDAs would serve a wider range of purposes and would rely on more varied sources of deposits. In a sense, the IDA concept would *encompass* the IRA concept and add to it.[2]

In developing a single system for all types of asset-based welfare programs, the government would limit complexity and inefficiency and better integrate various asset-based welfare policies into an overall national strategy. Also, the policy would essentially operate directly to the beneficiary, with very limited intervention by a welfare bureaucracy.

Description

Within the IDA concept, it is possible to imagine many different policy designs for many different purposes. In chapter 11, specific policies are suggested. Before turning to specific policies, however, we might consider the following general guidelines:

1. In at least some form, IDAs would be available to every person in the United States. Unlike IRAs, which are available only to wage earners and their spouses, IDAs would be available to everyone.

A universal asset-based welfare policy would require greater federal resources than would a policy designed solely for the poor. For this reason, some might prefer a targeted policy.[3] However, for reasons of political stability, a universal policy is more desirable. Also, because asset-based policy would be a system of savings and investment rather than a system of consumption, the net effect of universal policy would be to encourage, with tax subsidies, more savings. Arguably, this makes sense in ways that go beyond the purposes of welfare policy (see chapter 12).

2. The system of IDAs would be connected with activities that promote individual and national development. Accordingly, deposits would be permitted only under certain circumstances and would have specified limits. For example, occasions for deposits and limits on deposits for educational IDAs might be as follows: For each completed grade of primary and secondary schooling, a deposit of up to five hundred dollars would be permitted. Successful high school graduation would enable an individual to make a deposit of twenty-five hundred dollars.

Through defining activities that merit IDA deposits and activities that would be supported by IDA withdrawals, public policy would encourage desirable citizen behaviors such as education, training, employment, national service, or other activities that are deemed to be in the long-term interests of the nation as a whole.

3. Certain IDA deposits would be subsidized for impoverished families. On a sliding scale, high-income families would bear up to 100

percent of deposited amounts, but impoverished families would receive subsidies for certain deposits.

In no case would an asset-transfer subsidy comprise 100 percent of the deposit. Some level of matching funds would always be required by the poor. These matches might come from earned income, Earned Income Tax Credits, or monthly income-based welfare transfers.

Deposit subsidies would come from a variety of sources. Most would come from the federal government through an IDA Reserve Fund. However, federal subsidies could be matched at state and local levels, and participation by the not-for-profit and for-profit sectors would be actively encouraged.

4. Individuals (or their parents or guardians) would have choices regarding how their IDA accounts are invested. There might be three basic choices for allocating IDA investments: a money market interest-bearing fund, a bond fund, and an indexed common stock fund. Individuals could allocate, and within reasonable limits, move their IDA investments from one fund to another.

This set of choices is similar to those offered by most companies under 401(k) retirement fund provisions. In place of a money market fund, many companies offer a pool of guaranteed investment contracts (GICs), and most publicly held companies also offer the employer's stock as an option. Most companies allow a shift in the investment mix two to four times a year.

5. Because asset-based welfare is a long-term concept, some of the best applications of IDAs would be for young people. Young people would be given specific information about their IDA accounts from a very early age, would be encouraged to participate in investment decisions for the accounts, and would begin planning for use of the accounts in the years ahead. Ideally, this education in the IDA system would take place in the schools as an important aspect of individual development—as important as health education, social studies, or civics. In other words, financial planning would be incorporated into the public school curriculum. As a result, education in the handling of financial assets, which now occurs "around the dinner table" in many middle- and upper-class families, and generally not in poor families, would be democratized and incorporated into each child's education. The improved economic literacy that would result from this education would benefit the nation as a whole.

Planning for use of the IDA would also serve as a mechanism for developing an orientation toward the future. Specific planning skills and planning exercises would be built around each young person's IDA. For IDA participants, these planning "exercises" would involve real funds and real plans; therefore, the learning process would be salient and meaningful in a way that no traditional economics or personal finance course ever could be.

6. IDA accounts would be set up only for long-term goals. For example, in the case of saving for postsecondary education, withdrawals without a substantial penalty would not be allowed until the individual was enrolled in a postsecondary education program.

7. Deposited funds and earnings on funds would be in whole or in part tax-benefited (sometimes tax-exempt, sometimes tax-deferred) when used for designated purposes.

8. If withdrawn for other than designated purposes, all subsidized deposits and the earnings on those deposits would revert to the IDA Reserve Fund. The remaining balance would be subject to a heavy penalty and would be fully taxable as ordinary income when withdrawn. All penalties for non-approved withdrawals would revert to the IDA Reserve Fund to help finance other IDAs. The heavy penalty for non-designated withdrawals would strongly discourage use of funds for purposes unintended by public policy.

9. A parent or legal guardian could transfer, at any time during his or her lifetime or at death, without penalty, any portion of an IDA to the IDAs of his or her children or grandchildren. Just as wealthy families pass along assets to their children, the IDA system would permit many non-wealthy parents and grandparents to pass along financial assets and opportunities to their offspring in the form of IDA account balances.

Alternatives and Variations

The above description is for a universal system of IDAs open to everyone but with deposits subsidized for the poor. As an alternative, it would be possible to design a system targeted only toward the poor. Such a system would be less expensive, but like all targeted programs, it would tend to stigmatize participants and make the program politically vulnerable. For these reasons, targeting IDAs may not be the best policy. Similar to the public approval of Social Security and IRAs, the universality of IDAs would engender widespread support.

There are many other alternatives that can be constructed by emphasizing or altering one or more of the points outlined above. For example, it might be advisable to make very large deposits early in life; to involve private foundations and private corporations more heavily; to provide a narrower or wider range of investment options; to reduce restrictions on use of accounts; or to tighten restrictions on use of accounts solely to education and job training. At this formative stage in developing the IDA concept, it is useful to consider a wide variety of possibilities. During developmental stages, experimentation with such possibilities might best be left to different states, within a general policy framework at the federal level. Certainly in the case of welfare policy in the 1980s, the states were in the forefront in creative thinking and welfare experimentation.[4]

Eligibility: Who Would Receive Assets?

The young, the old, the sick, the crazy,
Even the shiftless and the lazy,
Eat at the common human table
Spread by the Active and the Able.
The problem is, to organize
This monumental enterprise
So that—to see that all are boarded—
Both Need and Virtue are rewarded.

—Kenneth Boulding[5]

Who would be eligible for IDA accounts? How are they to be identified? And how is policy to be designed so that, as Kenneth Boulding says, both Need and Virtue are rewarded?

As a general strategy, universal policy is preferred, with asset accumulation available to all, but with different subsidies and incentives for different people. When the policy is universal, in a very important sense, all are eligible. However, for most people, there would be no public subsidy on deposits, although there would be preferential tax treatment of account balances. For the poor, deposit subsidies would be available as matching funds. Thus, everyone would be covered by the same policy, but different individuals would be covered in different ways.

Deciding who qualifies for particular subsidies would not be more difficult than it is under current income-based welfare policy. Existing income-based policy for the poor already incorporates an "asset test" to determine eligibility. In order to be eligible for the major cash and in-kind transfer programs, one must have low income and limited assets. In an IDA system, eligibility criteria based on assets would be somewhat altered—shifting to some threshold or poverty line of assets, perhaps set differently for each application, depending on goals and purposes of each program. As indicated in chapter 9, both asset and income criteria would be used. Only those who are asset poor *and* income poor would be eligible for public subsides for IDA deposits.

How Much Would They Get?

As mentioned above, some level of assets would be considered the asset poverty level, taking into account the number, ages, and relationships of people in the household. For example, the asset poverty level for each adult might be set at some portion, say 20 percent, of the median value of existing housing (similar to the manner in which the income poverty level is currently defined as three times an emergency food budget).

Asset based welfare benefits would accumulate gradually. Over the long term, policy would be designed to bring all participants up to the asset poverty level, or to some portion of it. In this regard, different applications of asset-based policy would have different purposes, and target asset levels might be set differently in each case.

Structure and Control of IDA Accounts

Each individual would have his or her own IDA account. Accordingly, money would accumulate in the name of each participant. The IDA system would function in a manner similar to that of a defined contribution retirement plan, wherein earnings accumulate in the name of each account holder, and the ultimate benefits are not defined in advance, but instead, ultimate benefits depend on the size of deposits and the success of individual investment strategies.

Where feasible, IDA savings programs would be structured into employment settings, schools, and community institutions. Access to banking facilities is a particular problem in poor neighborhoods, but a number of alternatives might be considered. In the late nineteenth and early twentieth centuries, U.S. Post Offices had savings windows. Postal savings by small investors was largely responsible for Japan's investment boom and tremendous economic growth following World War II (see chapter 12). India has extended its banking system to reach the rural poor, and the resulting increase in savings by the poor has been impressive. At certain times in the past, the United States has had savings plans available at public schools. Such policies greatly facilitate savings by ordinary people.

The entire IDA system would be directed by an independent board of trustees at the national level. Some combination of executive and legislative authority would be called for in appointing the board. Ideally, after a transition period, a portion of the board would be elected by participants in the program.

Investment of IDA funds would be overseen by the board, employing a group of private investment companies which would compete for share of investment funds on the basis of earnings performance. The board of trustees would establish basic investment guidelines, perhaps limits on types of risk or limits on investing in international securities, but the board would not participate directly in investment decisions.

Use of private sector fund managers would greatly reduce the federal bureaucracy required to manage IDA funds and would create a competitive investment situation through which investment gains are likely to be highest over the long term.

Unlike the Social Security Trust Fund (which is more of a system of promises than an existing fund), IDA accounts would be fully funded; that is, actual money would be invested in the name of each individual. Unlike money in the Social Security Trust Fund, resources in IDA accounts would not be lent at below market rates to finance other government programs, nor would accumulations in IDA accounts be used in budgetary calculations to offset deficits in other government programs.

Regarding control of withdrawals, the single IDA system would facilitate control. In the case of education and housing IDAs, arrangements with institutions of higher education and mortgage lenders would transfer funds directly to those institutions at the appropriate time. Retirement IDAs would be controlled by age, just as IRAs are today. For self-employment IDAs, if boards of local businesspeople are established to approve IDA business plans, as I think would be essential, these local boards could sign off on withdrawals.

Financing

The federal government, through appropriations to an IDA Reserve Fund, would be the principal source of money for subsidized IDA deposits. The IDA Reserve Fund would be partially replenished in later years by penalties for nondesignated use of IDA accounts. The legislative target would be to deplete the IDA Reserve Fund and reallocate resources on an annual basis. Therefore, the IDA Reserve Fund, unlike the Social Security Trust Fund, would never accumulate a large balance. Instead, asset accumulations would occur within individual accounts, as described above.

In addition, there would be a wide variety of cooperative funding mechanisms with state and local governments, corporations, foundations, and recipients. For example, local school districts might help support subsidized deposits for educational achievement. Corporations might "adopt" a school and help provide IDA deposits for its students. Young people might undertake fund-raising projects—car washes, bake sales, carnivals, and bingo games—to build IDA accounts. Student-run businesses might be developed in high schools, the profits from which would become IDA deposits. Tenant management organizations in public housing might operate businesses (as happens successfully in the Cochran Gardens housing project in St. Louis), and the profits might be used for IDA deposits. Possibilities for creative funding of IDAs are nearly endless. Many of these funding mechanisms would be exciting in and of themselves, leading to financial skills as well as enhanced awareness and enthusiasm for the IDA system and its potential.

Is More Money Required?

The biggest policy issue is cost. To what extent would asset-based welfare be paid for out of the cost of existing programs, and to what extent would "new money" be required?

In my opinion, the United States should be spending a great deal more in several key areas of social welfare, particularly those related to children in poverty. The United States has the highest child poverty rate of any industrialized country, and a major reason is the stingy welfare policy for children. Canada, for example, spends 1.6 percent of its GNP on income support for children, but the United States spends only 0.6 percent. However, not everyone is of the same opinion regarding welfare spending, and the arguments in this book do not rest on the supposition that welfare spending will be greatly increased.

Nonetheless, some welfare spending would have to be redirected. There is no such thing as a free lunch, and each IDA program would have a price tag (suggestions for specific asset-based welfare programs and estimated costs are taken up in the next chapter). Resources would come from (1) rechanneling of expenditures from current welfare programs, particularly transfers to the nonpoor, and (2) creative nonfederal government financial support from corporations, foundations, interested individuals, state and local governments, and welfare recipients themselves.

In many respects, at the outset, the key issue is not the initial amount of funding, but its structure. As a system of asset accumulation for the poor becomes structured and proves its worth, additional funding and creative approaches to funding can be developed.

From Where Would the Money Come?

If federal money is to be rechanneled from current programs, from where would this additional funding come? At this point, an astute policy advocate might say that this question is best left to legislators. If the program is worthwhile and a good investment for the nation, legislators should find the money for it.

On the other hand, in an age of large budget deficits and an overwhelming belief that new programs cannot be funded, legislators are extremely reluctant to allocate "new money." Therefore, the more politically possible, although more difficult, approach is to consider reallocation of existing expenditures. But which existing expenditures?

Of course, it is easy to answer, as many welfare advocates do, that billions should be cut from defense and rechanneled to social services. With the dramatic developments in Eastern Europe, everyone is talking about a "peace dividend" and how it might be used. Scrapping the B2 bomber and foregoing a few aircraft carriers would free tens of billions of dollars for more constructive endeavors. I am strongly in favor of making these cuts, and it now appears that some of them will in fact be made. However, I will not rely on the "peace dividend" to support the proposals for asset-based welfare policy.

Instead, I will stick to the territory I know best—welfare policy.

Here, too, there is enough misguided spending to make possible a wide range of more constructive programs. In health care, housing, and retirement security, benefits to the nonpoor soak up tens of billions of dollars that could be used for other purposes. Focusing on tax expenditures alone, below is a selected list of possible savings (estimated tax savings are for the year 1990, based on data from the United States Joint Committee on Taxation):[6]

1. Fully tax Social Security benefits, raising an additional $21.0 billion per year; and tax railroad retirement benefits, raising an additional $0.4 billion. These changes would make public retirement systems less regressive.

2. Remove 50 percent of the tax deferment for pension contributions and earnings, raising $24.2 billion; and remove 50 percent of the tax deferment for IRAs and Keogh plans, raising an additional $5.6 billion. Under current policy, massive tax expenditures for personal retirement funds benefit the nonpoor almost exclusively.

3. Remove the tax exclusion for employer-contributed medical insurance premiums and medical care, raising $32.6 billion; and also tax miscellaneous fringe benefits (other than medical and retirement benefits) raising an additional $5.8 billion per year. Employee fringe benefits constitute a parallel welfare system, primarily for the nonpoor. It is one thing to receive such benefits, but quite another for those benefits to be additionally supported by preferential tax treatment.

4. Eliminate 50 percent of home mortgage interest tax deductions, raising $12.7 billion, but not across the board. All the revenues would be raised by eliminating mortgage tax deductions on loan amounts exceeding the median price of existing housing, and for mortgage loans on second homes. The rationale for this suggestion is that anyone who wishes to own an above-average house, or two houses, is free to do so, but he or she should not be subsidized out of the public purse for this luxury. Subsidizing luxury housing is also, from a macroeconomic perspective, a poor use of the nation's investment dollars. At the macroeconomic level, housing is a very unproductive investment—it is actually more a form of consumption.[7]

5. Eliminate 100 percent of tax deferments for capital gains on sales of principle residences, raising $10.3 billion; and eliminate 100 percent of the exclusion of capital gains on sales of personal residences for persons who are age fifty-five and over, raising an additional $3.4

billion. Supporting home ownership is one thing, but supporting the *gains* from home ownership is quite another. These measures subsidize asset accumulation by the nonpoor. Also, all these tax benefits for home ownership, whatever the form, push up the price of housing, making it less affordable for those at the bottom.

6. Eliminate 100 percent of the exclusion of capital gains at death, raising $5.4 billion. Why should capital gains be excluded at death? (Death is not a standard social welfare category in the United States, but in the current discussion, it would be difficult to omit this substantial asset transfer to the nonpoor.)

These are a few of the possibilities for reallocation of current tax expenditures. Other savings could be identified from direct budgetary expenditures, but for the moment, we will let these go. The overall logic of the above proposals is that they reduce some of the huge transfers through the tax system to the nonpoor. Some of these transfers are asset-based; that is, they contribute directly to asset accumulation. A portion of these public resources could be, and should be, rechanneled toward asset accumulation by the poor.

The total annual savings on tax expenditures for the above recommendations is $121.4 billion. In my opinion, all of the suggestions are reasonable. But if these measures seem too drastic to some, even one-fourth of these savings would provide enough resources to operate a wide variety of asset-based welfare programs for the poor. If choices are to be made, I would recommend the first, fourth, and sixth, above —fully taxing Social Security and railroad retirement benefits, eliminating home mortgage interest tax deductions on loans above the median price of existing housing, and removing the capital gains exclusion at death. Together, these three measures would save $38.5 billion annually.

Perhaps these suggestions are not far removed from current public opinion. For example, there seems to be a growing consensus that the nonpoor receive too much from the Social Security system. A *New York Times* editorial entitled "Target Social Security on the Needy"[8] suggests that benefits to those who are already well-off should be cut back. The editorial attacks the "liberal" view that the best way to protect the poor is to give excessive benefits to the nonpoor. The suggestion from the *New York Times* is to tax all Social Security benefits. The Ford Foundation has also proposed taxing all Social Security benefits to finance welfare policy reform.[9] When one of the nation's leading newspapers and one of the nation's leading private foundations take this position, it is possible that greater taxing of Social Security benefits might soon be on the political agenda.[10]

Conclusion

Unlike traditional welfare programs, IDA accounts would introduce real assets into the lives of many poor people who would otherwise be without them. IDAs would be a different approach to welfare policy, an approach that emphasizes individual development and combines social provision with individual responsibility and individual control. IDAs would enable the poor to bring their own cards to the table and make their own deal.[11]

Through defining activities that merit IDA deposits and activities that would be supported by IDA withdrawals, the federal government could reinforce education, training, employment, national service, and other activities that are in the long term interests of the nation as a whole.

Assets are the key to economic development. Individual and family development is not built on receiving and spending a certain amount of monthly income. Rather, development is built on planning for the future, accumulating savings, investing, using financial assets to support life goals, and passing along assets to offspring. IDAs would provide a mechanism for even the very poorest people in the nation to accumulate and handle assets to meet individual and family goals. As a result, the current trend toward widening economic inequality would be attenuated and possibly reversed.

In the process, the IDA system would provide an education in the functioning of the economic system. Instead of the current situation wherein large numbers of people are without assets, many more people would have a "stake" in the financial system. Through considering investment decisions, many would become knowledgeable and would learn lessons that would carry over into other aspects of their financial affairs—into other forms of saving, investment, and entrepreneurial activity. This increase in the number of people who are financially aware and financially active would greatly benefit the economy as a whole.

IDAs would also generate a new pool of savings for investment (see

(see chapter 12). In a nation where the low savings rate and low rate of capital formation are serious and continuing problems, this additional mechanism for savings and investment would be very desirable.

Notes

1. An alternative to the term "Individual Development Accounts" might be "Individual Development and Enrichment Accounts." The latter would have the acronym IDEAS, perhaps an appropriate description of the purposes of these accounts.

2. In December 1989, Treasury secretary Nicholas Brady outlined a "family savings plan" that would create special multipurpose accounts, with tax-free interest and dividends, and deposit limits of five thousand dollars per year. President Bush proposed the creation of Family Savings Accounts (FSAs) in early 1990. In spirit, the administration's plan is consistent with my proposal for IDAs. The major differences are that FSAs could be used for *any* purposes and would provide no deposit subsidies for the poor. In my view, if the federal government is to provide tax benefits (a subsidy), then their purposes should be restricted to major social and economic goals of the nation, such as housing, education, self-employment, and retirement security. Also, in my view, because the poor do not generally benefit from such plans due to their low tax liabilities, subsidies for the poor should be primarily in the form of deposit subsidies.

In September 1989, Senator Lloyd Bentsen proposed wider use of IRA accounts for first-time home buyers and college expenses (see Susan Rasky, "Revival Is Urged for Wider IRAs," *New York Times*, September 13, 1989, 1). This proposal is very consistent with my proposal for IDAs, although Bentsen's plan does not include deposit subsidies for the poor.

In August 1989, Senator William Roth proposed a system of flexible IRAs, which could be used for housing and education, and he included a deposit subsidy for the poor in the form of a tax credit of $500 to $2000 for those with incomes under $25,000. This idea comes closest to my proposal for IDAs; however, I think it would be preferable to make the deposit subsidy directly. With direct deposit subsidies, even those with too little income to be taxed could participate.

3. For sound reasoning in support of targeted policy, see Neil Gilbert, *Capitalism and the Welfare State*. New Haven: Yale University Press, 1983.

4. David Osborne, *Laboratories of Democracy*. Cambridge: Harvard Business School Press, 1988.

5. Kenneth Boulding, *Principles of Economic Policy*. Englewood Cliffs, NJ: Prentice-Hall, 1958, 233.

6. U.S. Congress, Joint Committee on Taxation, *Estimates of Federal Tax Expenditures for Fiscal Years 1990–1994*. Washington: U.S. Government Printing Office, 1989.

7. Housing and banking industry lobbyists strongly oppose limiting home mortgage interest tax deductions in any way. Initiatives in this direction, although very sensible, would be met by heated opposition.

8. "Target Social Security on the Needy," *New York Times*, December 29, 1988, 18Y.

9. Ford Foundation, *The Common Good: Social Welfare and the American Future.* New York: Ford Foundation, 1989. Views on the political feasibility of greater taxation of Social Security benefits differ; see National Academy of Social Insurance, *Social Policy: Looking Backward, Looking Forward.* Washington: National Academy of Social Insurance, 1989.

10. It is well established that recipients of most non-means-tested entitlements, such as Social Security retirement benefits, receive much more than the actuarial value of their contributions to the insurance trust funds. In other words, they are receiving large income transfers they have not earned. Martha Ozawa ("Social Insurance and Redistribution," in Alvin Schorr, ed., *Jubilee for Our Times: A Practical Program for Equality of Income.* New York: Columbia University Press, 1977, 123–77) and others have cogently argued this point for years. Curiously, this giveaway program to the nonpoor has only recently reached the table for serious policy discussion. Most economists and policy-makers have long preferred the fiction that large Social Security retirement benefits are somehow due to affluent Americans. Indeed, most economists have argued that Social Security is a progressive system because in proportion to contributions, poor people receive more benefits. But in actual dollars of unearned transfer, affluent people receive more, and since the transfer portion of Social Security is entirely unearned, the dollar size of the transfer should be the important point. On top of this, life expectancy for poor people, on the average, is less than for nonpoor people, and therefore, the poor collect retirement benefits for fewer years (the life expectancy difference between blacks and whites is even greater). In these fundamental ways, Social Security is a regressive system.

11. For this phrase, I am indebted to Doug Ross, President of the Corporation for Enterprise Development.

11 • Examples, Proposals, Costs

There are many possible applications for Individual Development Accounts, but some are much better than others. Americans are more interested in specific welfare needs, such as housing, food, medical care, child care, and education, than in poverty as an abstract economic concept.[1] For example, the general public is more sympathetic to the need for basic shelter than to the idea that everyone should have a certain level of income. Poverty as a general concept does not capture the nation's imagination, but concrete human problems and aspirations *do* capture the nation's attention and concern. Therefore, a primary consideration in policy-making is to construct asset-based welfare targeted toward basic needs and specific goals.

Asset-based welfare is not a solution for all social problems. For some welfare issues, such as food and health care, income-based policies are preferable. However, asset-based policies would be preferable in situations where accumulation is desirable and feasible. Some of the most promising applications for IDAs appear to be in the financing of postsecondary education, home ownership, capital for self-employment, and funds for retirement security. In this chapter, we look at these possibilities.

IDAs for Postsecondary Education

Young people are, in many ways, the best target for asset-based welfare policy because asset accumulation is a long-term process. Patterns of saving and investment should begin as early in life as possible. Also, connecting welfare policy to educational achievement is a sensible national strategy. There is a growing realization that the United States must educate all its children more effectively or we will suffer economically in the decades ahead. In short, welfare for education is not a purely humanitarian issue—it is an essential national investment.

The Growing Importance of Postsecondary Education

The cost of going to college is rising fast, but the cost of not going to college is rising even faster. Economic returns on a college education exploded during the 1980s. In 1986, according to data from the Census Bureau, male college graduates in the labor force earned 39.2 percent more than did male high school graduates, but the difference was only 23.8 percent in 1979. Nearly comparable changes occurred for female college graduates, who earned 40.5 percent more than did female high school graduates in 1986, up from 27.9 percent in 1979.

Higher education is increasingly important for success in the labor market. In 1988, 26 percent of adult workers were college graduates, up from 21 percent in 1978. Another 20 percent had one to three years of college education, up from 16 percent in 1978. The proportion with only a high school diploma remained stable, at about 40 percent. And the proportion without a high school diploma stood at 15 percent in 1988, down from 24 percent in 1978. Labor force participation is highly related to educational achievement. In 1988, the participation rate was 88 percent for college graduates, 83 percent for those with one to three years of college, 77 percent for high school graduates, and only 61 percent for those who had not completed high school.

Also, people with the highest levels of education have the lowest levels of unemployment. In March 1988, the unemployment rate for college graduates was 1.7 percent; for those with one to three years of college, it was 3.7 percent; for those with a high school diploma it was 5.4 percent; and for those who had not completed high school the unemployment rate was 9.4 percent. The relationship of education to employment is likely to be even stronger in the years ahead. As more and more jobs become highly skilled, those without education will be increasingly likely to be among the unemployed.

How Families Cope

In the United States, financing a college education has become a serious problem. Tuition, room and board, and other college costs are rising faster than the rate of inflation. Between 1978 and 1988, the cost of living increased 87 percent, but the cost of attending a public college increased 114 percent, and the cost of attending a private college increased 141 percent. For the 1987–88 academic year, the American College Testing Program estimates that average family income required to finance college education ranged from $49,866 for a two-year public college to $94,804 for a private university. (By these calculations, only 18 percent of children, aged eighteen or younger, live in households that can afford, out of ordinary income, even the least expensive college education. Existing assets or loans are required by the vast majority of households.) In the face of these high and sharply rising costs, cuts in federal college aid during the 1980s seriously damaged the educational opportunities of many young people.

Blacks have been affected more than whites. According to statistics from the American Council of Education, in 1978 the percentage of 18- to 24-year-olds attending college was 31.1 percent for whites and 29.7 percent for blacks—not a great difference. By 1988, however, the rate for whites had increased to 38.1 percent, while the rate for blacks had fallen to 28.1 percent. At the beginning of the 1980s, total black enrollment at the undergraduate level stood at about 11 percent of all college students. By the 1984–85 school year, black enrollment was down to 8.8 percent of the undergraduate population. Incredibly, this sharp decline occurred during a period when the proportion of black high school graduates was rising. Also, fewer black students than white students graduate from college. Of all black freshmen in 1980, only 31 percent had graduated by 1986, compared with 55 percent of whites.

The reason for this growing racial discrepancy in higher education is not difficult to understand. Black families are more than twice as likely as white families to live below the income poverty line. But more important, as noted in chapter 6, the average black family has only one-twelfth the net assets of the average white family. Therefore, college costs, for the vast majority of black families, cannot be financed either out of income flows or by using the family's very limited assets. Consequently, cutbacks in public support for higher education during the 1980s have made it impossible for many black families to send their children to college. They simply cannot afford it.

Those who do attend college, white and nonwhite, are assuming large debt burdens. In 1976, loans made up 17 percent of all college aid; but by 1986, loans accounted for 50 percent. In 1986, students graduating from private colleges owed an average of almost nine thousand dollars in student loans. Those graduating from public colleges owed an average of seven thousand dollars. Many graduate students complete their master's and doctoral degrees owing between twenty thousand dollars and thirty thousand dollars in student loans. These debts restrict career choices and financial independence. In the face of such debts, low-paying but important professions, such as social work and teaching, are much less attractive. Large purchases, particularly purchases of homes, are delayed.

In addition, the loan default rate is very high. Defaults on college loans cost the federal treasury $1.8 billion in 1989. In the Guaranteed Student Loan (GSL) Program, loans through 1987 totaled over $70 billion, with outstanding debt almost doubling between 1982 and 1987. During this period, defaults increased by 276 percent. Of the 1.18 million borrowers who obtained their last loan in 1983, a remarkable 18 percent (228,000) had defaulted by September of 1987. Default rates were highest at vocational schools, where 35 percent had defaulted. Default rates at traditional two-year and four-year colleges were 12 percent. There was a 33 percent default rate for those who attended school for one year or less, and an 11 percent default rate for those who attended longer.[2] These dismal results of college loan programs are not good for individuals and they are not good for the nation. The United States needs a better way to finance higher education.

Policy Development for IDAs in Education Has Already Begun

The best known asset-based program in postsecondary education was the GI Bill. Initiated in June 1944, the GI Bill provided World War II veterans with five hundred dollars per year for education plus fifty dollars per month for living expenses. President Robert Hutchins of the University of Chicago warned that "colleges and universities will find themselves converted into educational hobo jungles," but his prediction proved to be incorrect. Veterans did indeed flock to college campuses, but according to almost all observers, they were a mature and successful group of students. By 1947, in its peak year, the GI Bill supported 49 percent of all students enrolled in higher education. This tuition-guarantee policy played a key role in the postwar economic expansion, and was one of the most successful U.S. social programs ever undertaken. Other versions were initiated after the Korean and Vietnam wars.

At local and state levels, there are today a number of recently introduced and very creative asset-based educational policies (although they do not yet go by this name). For example, in the Cleveland public schools, students in grades seven through twelve can earn scholarship money in basic courses. An A is worth forty dollars, a B twenty dollars, and a C ten dollars. By graduation, a straight-A student can earn as much as forty-eight hundred dollars. The money is available only to graduates and is held in escrow for college or training up to eight years following graduation. The program is financed by foundations, corporations, and individuals. Rhode Island plans a Rhode Island Children's Crusade to guarantee college tuition and provide tutoring to low-income students. Milwaukee also plans a college guarantee for high school graduates.

Perhaps the best-known example of asset-based educational policy, mentioned in chapter 8, is Eugene Lang's promise to Harlem sixth graders that he would pay for their college tuition if they would stay in school. Lang's "I Have a Dream" Foundation is expanding these opportunities and is being replicated around the country. At this writing, Lang's "I Have a Dream" Foundation in St. Louis has promised students at three different primary schools six thousand dollars each (in current dollars) for college tuition. The donors are anonymous.

Avron Fogelman, a Memphis real estate developer and co-owner of the Kansas City Royals, announced in 1987 that he would subsidize tuition perpetually for disadvantaged Memphis-area public school students who go to Memphis State University. "Fogelman has put up an initial $2.5 million, and will add some $2 million annually over ten years. The first beneficiaries will be current seventh graders. To receive the assistance, needy students must, among other things, maintain passing grades and take part in some kind of public service activity."[3]

In 1988, Gerald Greenwald, then an auto executive, offered fifty scholarships to fifth graders at his alma mater in University City, Missouri. He started a program for businessmen to invest in community schools, dubbing it the "Believers Program." Only fifth graders who have a financial need and are enrolled in the federal food lunch program are eligible for selection in the Believers Program, which is to pay tuition and fees for up to four years at a Missouri state college or technical school.

These programs are not without their problems. For example, the "I Have a Dream" Foundation in St. Louis has had a somewhat bumpy beginning. The program has unclear plans and guidelines. School officials are sometimes resistant. For most children and their families, say social workers who have worked in the program, money for tuition, by itself, is not enough. They agree, however, that one important effect of the money is changing parents' attitudes about the future educational possibilities for their children. Parents are becoming more interested and involved in their children's schooling.

At the state level, some forty states now have, or are considering, savings and credit plans to help pay for college education. At least ten states have already offered prepaid savings plans, and a dozen more have passed laws authorizing such plans. For example, Michigan, as of 1989, had signed up more than forty thousand students and has a trust fund of $265 million invested to underwrite the bills when parents start cashing in tuition guarantees. State tuition plans take several forms. The two main approaches are prepayment of tuition, or "tuition guarantees," (as in Michigan), and tax-exempt, zero-coupon college savings bonds (as in Illinois). Altogether, about $1 billion in prepaid tuition plans of one kind or another were purchased in 1988.[4]

Results so far have been mixed. The major drawback of state-defined systems is their geographic rigidity. In the United States, where the average family moves every five years, the inflexibility in state-defined systems eventually will cause problems and limit participation.[5]

As a partial response, the Congress has recently created tax-exempt savings accounts for college expenses. Beginning in 1990, parents with joint incomes under ninety thousand dollars can receive tax breaks on income from Series EE U.S. Savings Bonds if receipts are applied toward tuition and fees at any college, university, or vocational school. These accounts have restrictive conditions, and in their present form, they may not be an attractive vehicle for college savings. Nonetheless, they represent an important step toward a national asset-based policy for financing postsecondary education.

The recent wave of interest in tax-exempt tuition plans embodies the principle of long-term asset accumulation, and these plans are quite possibly a turning point in the way many people think about financing higher education. However, such plans, like their predecessors in private universities, benefit primarily middle- and upper-class families. The plans provide no government contributions or matching funds for the poor.

A Proposal for Educational IDAs

Following the lead of state college tuition plans, IDAs would be a departure from the current basic approach to educational financing. The present system functions—and dysfunctions—primarily by loans. Another way to describe current college financing is as a system of negative assets or liabilities. In contrast, IDAs for education, would be accumulated *prior* to college; they would be a system of positive assets. Features of an IDA system for postsecondary education might be as follows:

1. For the most part, IDA deposits would be related to benchmark achievements. For example, occasions for deposits and deposit limits might be as follows: A one-thousand-dollar deposit would be allowed at birth. For each completed year of primary and secondary schooling, a deposit of up to five hundred dollars would be permitted. Also, student fund-raising projects and student businesses would be encouraged to add to IDA balances. Successful high school graduation would enable an individual to make a deposit of up to twenty-five hundred dollars.

A variation might be to include deposits for participation in Head Start or other approved preschool programs. Increasingly, research data suggest that the preschool years are crucial to future educational achievement.

Completing a year of recognized military or civilian national service might earn a deposit of, say, five thousand dollars. Deposits for national service would be fully earned by each individual. The GI Bill was tremendously successful in promoting higher education among World War II veterans, and this concept should be reinstituted in the form of IDA deposits for military personnel. In addition, the United States may eventually adopt a voluntary civilian national service, wherein young people would have an opportunity to work for a year or two in natural resource conservation, social services, literacy education, disaster relief, or other constructive activities. In exchange for a period of approved national service, a young person would receive a stipend from the federal agency, state agency, local agency, private organization, or some combination of organizations that sponsored the service project. This stipend would be deposited directly into the individual's IDA.[6]

Some might argue that it is inappropriate to offer financial incentives for people to go to school—that educational achievement should provide its own incentives. However, for many young people, especially in inner-city schools, incentives for educational achievement are not readily apparent. Many young people are not convinced that completing a high school education will get them a job.[7] An IDA would not only provide incentives for current education, but would also build a financial base for future education.

2. Certain IDA deposits would be subsidized for poor people. On a sliding scale, nonpoor families would bear 100 percent of the deposited amounts for educational achievement, while impoverished families would receive subsidies of up to 90 percent for these deposits.

The proposed IDA system would partially offset inequities in quality of education that exist in the United States. Poor families are much more likely to live in poor neighborhoods with below average schools. But if these families were eligible for subsidized IDA deposits, then in spite of inferior schools, impoverished young people would have greater motivation to succeed in primary and secondary schooling and to proceed to college or other advanced training.

3. Young people would be given specific information about their IDA accounts from a very early age. They would be encouraged to participate in investment decisions for the accounts, and would begin planning for uses of the accounts in the years ahead. Ideally, this "education" in the IDA system would take place in the schools as an important aspect of individual development. Where possible, school savings banks would be established. Financial planning would be incorporated into the curriculum. In other words, education in the handling of financial assets would be democratized and incorporated into each child's education. IDAs would provide a real and important example for each child on the necessity for planning for the future. Specific planning skills and planning exercises would be built around each young person's IDA. The improved economic literacy that would follow from this financial education would benefit the nation as a whole.[8]

4. All deposited funds and earnings on the funds would be tax-

exempt if used for education or training, or expenses concurrent with education and training, such as child care. Because the primary purpose of IDAs would be individual development through education and training, there would be a strong incentive to use IDAs for this purpose. Unlike IRAs, which are tax-deferred, IDAs would be completely tax-exempt if used for education and training.

5. No withdrawals would be permitted until the holder reached the age of eighteen (or graduation from secondary school if it comes first). The primary purpose of IDAs would be to provide resources for individual development following high school graduation. The years prior to age eighteen would be viewed as a learning and planning period, a time in which young people prepared themselves to use their IDA accounts as effectively as possible.

6. For individuals between the ages of eighteen and thirty-five, educational IDA funds would be available only for education and training, and for no other purpose.

7. After age thirty-five, individuals could transfer educational IDA funds, without penalty, to educational IDAs of their children or grandchildren.

8. After age thirty-five individuals could disband educational IDA funds, in which case participants would receive only the amount of their original deposits plus associated earnings, minus a 10 percent penalty. The income would be fully taxed upon withdrawal. The penalty amount, all deposit amounts from other sources, plus all earnings on those deposits, would revert to the IDA Reserve Fund. The rationale for these restrictions is that the money would have been set aside, at public expense, for particular purposes. If those purposes were not fulfilled, then the money should be available to others who might make better use of it.

Issues and Observations

If access to postsecondary education is to be broadened, one major concern is how to improve small proprietary schools, some of which offer inferior education. A large number of poor people use these schools and unfortunately, often receive shoddy education or job training. To some extent, this was a problem with the original GI Bill, and it is a problem today in the Guaranteed Student Loan (GSL) program. At this writing, there is a scandal in St. Louis caused by training schools "recruiting" homeless and destitute "students," making out-landish promises, signing admission papers and GSL papers, and then leaving the "students" with large debts and a bad credit rating. Very often, the nation's taxpayers are left with the bill for defaulted loans in these situations. In response to this problem, there is a need to improve considerably the quality of small institutions for postsecondary educa-tion and training. This is not a new problem—not one that would be created by educational IDAs—but it is a problem that requires serious attention.[9]

The above proposal for educational IDAs assumes that the federal government has an important role to play in establishing a nationwide system that encourages savings and investment for future education, and particularly, helps make higher education more accessible to mi-norities and the poor.

America is moving into an information, service, and high technology future in a more competitive international economy. The nation's success in this transition will require the brain power, commitment, and productiv-ity of all members of society. Educational financing policy should be developed that facilitates education of the population to the fullest extent possible, and in addition, inspires future orientation and long-term thinking. Individual Development Accounts would be a step in this direction.

In the years ahead, debates about educational financing are likely to be intense. Asset accumulation for education, initiated at a very early age, should be considered as an option in these discussions.

In a rather bold departure from the current discussion, a proposal by Robert Haveman would create capital accounts of as much as twenty thousand dollars for each person in the nation at the age of eighteen, to be used for education, training, and health care.[10] Thus, the primary oritentation would be to develop and maintain human capital. Have-man's proposal merits careful consideration as an asset-based policy that reaches the entire population. However, I believe it would be preferable for young people to accumulate assets *over their lifetimes*, so that they learn to invest and plan, rather than have a large sum given to them all at once at the age of eighteen.

IDAs for Housing Policy

For reasons of both financial security and social status, housing is a critical asset for American families. Home ownership is part of the

American Dream. According to data from the American Housing Survey, the 64 percent of U.S. households that own homes have, on the average, more rooms, more floor space, and more yard space.[11] Owning is also generally cheaper than renting. At all annual income levels below forty thousand dollars, home owners, on average, pay a smaller proportion of their income on housing than do renters.[12] Moreover, experience shows that once people own their homes, they go to extraordinary efforts to make the monthly mortgage payments.

After forty years of expansion, the percentage of owners has dropped for the first time since the 1930s. Home ownership stood at 44 percent in 1940, rose to a peak of over 65 percent in 1980, and was down to under 64 percent in 1988. The decline was only slight, but its impact was not uniform. The greatest decline was among the young. For people ages twenty-five to twenty-nine, the percentage owning their own homes dropped sharply, from 44 percent in 1979 to 36 percent in 1987. Some have suggested that home ownership among the young has dropped because single people are choosing a different lifestyle and prefer to rent, but this theory is not supported by the data. A recent Harvard study shows that much of the ownership decline is among young married couples with children, who are likely to want their own homes, but cannot afford to buy.[13]

The primary reasons for growing housing problems are threefold. There have been (1) a decline in the number of low-cost units available, (2) an increase in the number of families in poverty, and (3) a decrease in real wages earned by the young and the poor. These factors have made the housing market very difficult for first-time home buyers.

Housing is expensive for the poor. Low-income families pay a large and growing share of their incomes for housing. In 1985, of the poor who rented housing, 63 percent paid more than half of their incomes for rent and utilities, compared to only 8 percent of the nonpoor. Incredibly, 45 percent of poor renters paid at least 70 percent of their incomes for rent and utilities. Of the poor who owned their own homes, 46 percent paid more than half of their incomes for housing costs, compared to only 4 percent of the nonpoor.

As one might expect under these circumstances, housing is becoming less adequate for the poor. One in five poor households, about 2.7 million people, live in housing classified as substandard by HUD. The poor are more likely to live in units with rat infestation, holes in the floor, and exposed wiring.[14] Eviction rates for renters are up nationwide, primarily for non-payment of rent. Waiting lists for public housing have reached one million names nationwide.

Homelessness is the most dramatic manifestation of the growing inaffordability of housing. Estimates of the number of homeless people in the United States range from three hundred thousand to 3 million. According to the U.S. Conference of Mayors, nearly one in four homeless adults has a job, yet cannot afford shelter. Families, often single mothers with young children, are the fastest growing segment of the homeless population (now comprising about half of all the homeless), primarily because there is a growing shortage of housing that is affordable on an AFDC income.[15]

Homelessness is only the most visible sign of housing inaffordability. Researchers have also found a substantial decrease in "housing independence" among the poor, that is, more poor people are living with parents or in multifamily households.[16] Although this problem tends to be overlooked by the general public and policymakers, it is very serious. In St. Louis, I have been shocked to find eight or ten impoverished people, often representing three generations of the same family, crammed into squalid little apartments in desperate neighborhoods. They peer out distrustfully, their faces and their living conditions terribly reminiscent of Jacob Riis's photographs of urban tenements at the turn of the century.[17] This is the *other half*, the *other America* that few middle-class Americans see. Our urban areas are divided. Traveling from one part to the other feels like crossing a national border from a developed to an undeveloped country. In rural areas, the quality of housing for impoverished people is no better.[18]

In response to growing housing needs, most would agree that federal housing policy has not been successful. There is not enough "low-income housing" (note the income concept again), and housing policy is oriented primarily toward rent subsidies. The nation's 1.4 million public housing units are in disrepair. The cost of renovating public housing is estimated at $21 billion.[19] In 1987, only 29 percent of poor renter households received any type of federal, state, or local housing subsidy.

During the 1980s, federal aid to housing was severely cut back. Between 1981 and 1988, the largest reductions in welfare appropriations came in the area of subsidized housing, which plunged from more than $30 billion in 1981 to $8 billion in 1988, more than an 80 percent reduction with inflation taken into account.[20] As a percentage of the federal budget, the HUD budget fell from 7 percent in 1980 to 1 percent in 1988. In addition, privately held low-cost housing stock is being lost to "gentrification" in many urban areas.

Moreover, the nation's low- and moderate-income housing supply could be further reduced in the 1990s because of the expiration of more than 1 million federal rental subsidy contracts. Today, there are some 2 million privately owned, federally subsidized housing units in the United States, and almost 1 million additional units whose occupants receive federal rent subsidies. Rents are set at no more than 30 percent of the tenant's income. But subsidies will run out on more than 0.7 million units by 1995 and on more than 1.4 million units by the year 2000. Where property values have appreciated, this will be an opportunity for the owners to exit from subsidized housing, and poor tenants will be forced to leave.

On top of this, new low-cost housing is not being built very rapidly. Under the Reagan administration, federal subsidies for construction of low-income housing were virtually abolished. The number of subsidized units under construction shrank to twenty-five thousand in 1989, down from an average of 1 million units per year between 1976 and 1982. It is also anticipated that the Tax Reform Act of 1986, in the long-term, will reduce investment in housing, contributing further to the shortage.[21] Therefore, the shortage of low-cost rental housing is expected to grow.

To put this in perspective, in fiscal year 1988, direct federal spending on low-income housing assistance programs of all kinds totaled $13.9 billion. But during the same year, federal tax expenditures to home owners totaled $53.9 billion. In 1988, the number of households with incomes below ten thousand dollars per year was nearly the same as the number of households with incomes above fifty thousand dollars per year, but the higher-income group received, on the average, *three times more* housing assistance than did the lower-income group.[22] Considering how many people are homeless and ill-housed, this pattern of public expenditures is not merely unfair, but inhumane and senseless.

Examples of Asset Ideas for Housing

Housing is where asset-based welfare policy is most familiar, and possibly where it has the most potential. Because home ownership is a widely shared American value, asset-based policy may be more readily acceptable and workable in this area than in many others.

Under an asset-based housing policy, subsidies would go for equity accumulation rather than for rent. Perhaps eventually, public housing projects would become privately owned condominiums. It is likely that, under these circumstances, housing projects would start to look better than they do today. The government would no longer be responsible for maintenance, and it can be predicted that owners would put more personal effort into improving the properties. With subsidies for principle and interest provided by the government, private sector contractors would recognize a market and build more low-cost housing. Perhaps it would be called "low-asset housing" rather than "low-income housing."

Housing is a very troubled area of social policy, but it is also a very creative area. At local and state levels, there are a wide range of asset-based examples, including arrangements for sweat equity, "granny" housing, urban homesteading programs, and shared equity.[23] Various forms of collective ownership have also been proposed and tested, under such labels as social sector housing, mutual housing, community land trusts, and the like.

One popular approach is housing trust funds. Revenue for these funds comes from real estate activities, development projects, or program-generated funds. Dozens of such funds now exist; the majority are at the municipal level, but some are at county and state levels as well. Most housing trust funds support rent subsidies, but a few support individual mortgages, frequently targeting low- and moderate-income families.[24]

Another well-known example of asset-based housing is Habitat for Humanity, made famous by Jimmy Carter's involvement as a volunteer. Habitat has built or renovated more the three thousand low-cost homes using voluntary labor. The organization also provides interest-free home loans, which are paid back into a revolving loan fund.

Numerous asset-based housing initiatives exist in major cities. St. Louis has several examples. Larry Rice, a religiously oriented service provider and advocate for the homeless, has developed a program in which homes are rehabilitated by the homeless, who are trained in carpentry and other building and maintenance skills. In the process, they earn title to the house.

Bertha Gilkey, director of the Tenant Affairs Board at Cochran

Gardens public housing project in St. Louis, is one of a handful of dynamic public housing leaders who, with the enthusiastic support of HUD Secretary Jack Kemp, are attempting to transform a number of public housing projects. Gilkey grew up in public housing in St. Louis when it was a desirable place to live, and over the years she watched it sink into disrepair, crime, and drugs. Since the mid-1970s, she has been trying to pull it back up by organizing tenants, clearing out drug pushers, enforcing maintenance standards, and involving residents in management. The tenant management group receives HUD maintenance money and creates jobs for residents. In addition, the group has started a development company—they now build federally subsidized housing units. They have also started several businesses and given tenants shares of ownership, and they are moving toward tenant ownership of the public housing complex itself. As Gilkey says, being poor does not take away your ability to hope, to dream, to be creative. Cochran Gardens has become an international model for tenant management; Gilkey has been featured on ''60 Minutes,'' and she is now a successful housing consultant.

Secretary Kemp has cited Gilkey's success, as well as that of Kimi Gray of the Kenilworth-Parkside public housing project in Washington, DC. Kemp is promoting tenant ownership. Unfortunately, the HUD plans for tenant ownership do not necessarily call for full property rights of individual tenants. Tom Bethell offers an incisive conservative critique.[25] From the liberal side, Congressman William Clay (Democrat, Missouri) is opposed to a plan to transform the Carr Square project in St. Louis to private ownership. Clay cites the expenses of maintenance and upkeep, which he believes are beyond the reach of the poor.

Another St. Louis example is a program called ''A Dwelling Place,'' which was set up with $100,000 in 1988 by the Roman Catholic Archdiocese. The program offers loans at 2 percent interest to cover a 5 percent down payment and closing costs. An additional $150,000 was pledged for 1989 and was slated to provide loans to thirty or more families by the end of that year. Minimum income of $17,000 is required for participation.

State-sponsored home ownership plans of all kinds have blossomed in recent years. Michigan again appears to be in the lead in asset-based policy. Early in 1989, Governor James Blanchard proposed that first-time home buyers in Michigan earn tax-free interest on savings invested three to ten years in state-issued bonds. The earnings on savings were guaranteed to keep up with inflation in housing costs. This program marks the first time that a state has directly assisted first-time buyers with a down payment. The program is modeled after Michigan's college savings plan. Other states are said to be formulating similar programs, and the National Association of Realtors is seeking a similar program nationwide.

Many private companies are also beginning to help employees with housing, and even trade unions are exploring trust fund arrangements to provide grants and loans for housing. Some observers predict that housing assistance is likely to be a major new employee benefit in the years ahead. However, most of these workplace programs will not benefit the poor.

Capturing some of these trends, some analysts have proposed comprehensive plans to meet America's housing needs, including asset-based approaches. One comprehensive plan calls for a down payment assistance loan program, a lease-purchase home buying program, an employer-assisted home ownership plan, a mortgage interest rate buy-down fund, and shared equity mortgages.[26]

A Proposal for Housing IDAs

As indicated above, many state and local programs have led the way in asset-based housing policy. George Bush's "thousand points of light" are surely out there, and the efforts are encouraging, but unfortunately, these relatively small efforts cannot begin to replace the tremendous housing void created by the retreat of federal housing policy in the 1980s. If Americans are to be reasonably housed, the gap must be filled, but not solely by rent subsidies. The federal government should move away from rent subsidies and toward home ownership by the poor.

In order to do so, the government should employ creative and successful elements of the experiments described above. Specifically, the focus should be on accumulation of assets for down payments. Down payments are the most critical barrier to home ownership.[27] Remarkably, research indicates that mortgage default rates do not vary with income. Once the down payment is made, people have a commitment to their homes. The general experience with low-income home ownership programs is that home owners go to great lengths to meet their monthly mortgage payments.

Steps have already been taken in the right direction. In 1989, legislation appeared in Congress, introduced by Senator Alfonse D'Amato (Republican, New York) and Senator Alan Cranston (Democrat, California), which would allow first-time home buyers and others who have not owned a home for three years to use money from an Individual Retirement Account or a 401(k) savings plan as a down payment on a house. (The legislation also called for easing of restrictions on mortgages insured by the Federal Housing Administration.) Both Senator Lloyd Bentsen and President George Bush, proposed, in the fall of 1989, that IRAs could be used for down payments by first-time home buyers. Also in the fall of 1989, an unlikely partnership of the advocacy-oriented National People's Action of Chicago and the solidly establishment Mortgage Insurance Companies of America have proposed a Home Ownership Made Easier (HOME) plan which would provide federal matches in special accounts for housing down payments by the poor. This basic idea of special accounts for down payments should be expanded, as follows:

1. IDAs for housing would be open to those eighteen years of age and over who are first-time home buyers or who have not owned a home for three years or longer. In other words, the program would not be restricted to people who qualify for IRAs (Individual Retirement Accounts) or other pension systems but instead, would be open to everyone based only on housing status.

2. There would be an annual deposit limit of two thousand dollars per individual account, and an overall limit of fifteen thousand dollars, after which no further deposits would be permitted.

3. Impoverished individuals below specified income and asset criteria would be eligible for deposit subsidies from the federal government of up to 90 percent of deposited amounts.

4. Housing IDA funds would be available only for down payments, capital improvements, repairs, or use as a mortgage payment reserve fund.

5. IDA funds could be applied only toward the purchase of dwellings that did not exceed the median price of existing housing in that locality. The rationale for this restriction is that, although home ownership is desirable, public funds should not be used to support above-average accommodations. If people want to live in an above-average style, they are free to do so, but tax dollars should not be used to support personal luxury.

6. Housing IDAs could be pooled for joint ownership in any way

that holders of the funds and lending agencies deemed sensible and appropriate. The rationale for this provision is that, with the growing diversity in types of families, and the rising cost of housing, the one-family-in-one-house concept is not necessarily the best solution for everyone.

7. Following a period of ten years from the initiation of the IDA, account balances could be transferred, without penalty, to housing IDA accounts of children or grandchildren. A variation might be to permit transfers to educational IDAs of children and grandchildren as well.

8. After a period of ten years from the initiation of the IDA, if not used for housing, IDA housing funds could be disbanded, in which case the holder of the fund would receive only his or her original deposits and associated earnings, less a 10 percent penalty. Income tax would be paid on the full amount withdrawn. The penalty amount and all other deposited amounts and associated earnings would revert to the IDA Reserve Fund.

It is very difficult to predict how many individuals, both poor and nonpoor, might participate in a program of housing IDAs as outlined above. But if, say, 10 million individuals deposited an average of fifteen hundred dollars per year in IDAs exclusively for housing, for a total of $15 billion per year, this pool of capital would have a large impact on low-cost housing construction.

Many variations on the above model are possible. For example, asset-based housing policy for the poor might also apply to accumulations for major fix-up, remodeling, or additions to existing housing below a certain market value.

Another interesting possibility would be long-term housing IDAs set up when children are very young, with small deposits, say $250, permitted every year. Such deposits would be subsidized for children in poverty. Because this model would help create long-term planning and future orientation for children in poverty, it might be preferable to the model described above, or it might be implemented simultaneously with the model above.

IDAs for Self-Employment

Although patterns of economic production have drastically changed during the last one hundred years, the United States is still, to a significant extent, an entrepreneurial nation. During 1988, 8.6 percent of all measured employment was self-employment—7.6 percent of nonagricultural employment and 44.1 percent of agricultural employment.[28] Of all business ventures, self-employment, both full- and part-time, is the most common type of business in the country; businesses with employees actually represent a minority of total businesses. Self-employment grew during the 1980s and grew much more rapidly among women than among men.[29] One study found that one-half of all proprietors stated they started or acquired their businesses with less than five thousand dollars in capital.[30] Small business is also the most flexible and dynamic sector of the U.S. economy. Between 1980 and 1986, America generated 10.5 million new jobs. More than one-third of these came from small businesses with less than twenty employees; this represented twice their share of total employment growth in the economy.[31] While it is possible to overly romanticize self-employment, there is no doubt that small, entrepreneurial ventures are an important wellspring not only of employment, but also of business ideas and future economic productivity.

Surprisingly, triggers for entrepreneurship are more often negative than positive. Self-employment often begins with loss of job, loss of spouse, or being trapped in unemployment or a dead-end job. A Department of Labor study found that, without any support, 7.7 percent of workers displaced in 1979 and reemployed in 1984 had created jobs for themselves. In industries such as finance and services, construction, and utilities, the rate exceeded 11 percent.[32] Overall, the biggest difference between growing and declining regions of the country is not in job-loss rates, which are remarkably similar, but in job-creation rates and firm-formation rates.[33]

Self-employment is often something other than a vehicle to wealth for the dashing entrepreneur. The self-employed, on average, do not earn large incomes, and self-employment plays a key role in economic security for many of the poor. Among single-parent households, self-employed women often see their efforts more in terms of balancing work and family life than in achieving entrepreneurial success. In other words, the emphasis is more on self-sufficiency and personal control than on growth and riches.

To finance their small businesses, the self-employed often rely on an informal pattern of personal savings plus help from friends, family members, and associates. This system of finance works remarkably well, and altogether may be larger than the venture capital industry in size. However, informal financing tends not to work very well in poor communities where social networks include few significant assets. Consequently, the poor have a difficult time accumulating seed capital for a business.

To make matters worse, the current income-based welfare system for the poor is institutionally opposed to capital accumulation. The welfare system is oriented toward catching cheaters rather than promoting self-development. This catch-the-cheaters orientation is especially detrimental to efforts to be self-employed and to start a new business.

The AFDC system poses significant obstacles to self-employment. The restrictive treatment of self-employment income and assets makes it almost impossible to achieve self-sufficiency while still on welfare. Those who determine eligibility often make no distinction between personal and business assets. A typewriter or cash from an unsecured business loan may be counted as an asset in determining AFDC eligibility. Deductions for capital equipment or depreciation, usually recognized as legitimate expenses in businesses, are not allowed to AFDC recipients. Certain supplies may or may not be allowed as deductions. For example, one welfare mother was denied deductions for cleaning supplies for starting a janitorial service—on the grounds that they could be used for household consumption. In addition, business income can vary greatly, especially during start-up, and one month of high income can make a person ineligible for AFDC, even though this may represent a return on investment and effort from prior months and may be needed for reinvestment in the business. Although states have the authority to set up accounting periods of up to one year for self-employed AFDC recipients, few states do so.

Unemployment Insurance also discourages self-employment. In most jurisdictions, the only safe strategy for an unemployed person, without jeopardizing receipt of unemployment compensation, is to search for a comparable job, however unlikely the success. The dislocated worker who tries to start a business becomes ineligible for benefits since he or she is no longer "ready, available, and searching for work."

As a possible alternative, a welfare system that encourages self-employment would not only help some of the poor, but could stimulate entrepreneurial ventures across the board. In the years ahead, this would seem to be a very sensible national strategy.

Fortunately, there are some precedents and models from which we might learn. During the 1980s, eight European countries—Belgium, Denmark, France, Ireland, the Netherlands, Spain, Sweden, and the United Kingdom—began to remove disincentives and encourage self-employment among unemployed welfare recipients. These initiatives in Europe have helped to create more than 250,000 small businesses. France and the United Kingdom have the most extensive programs. The program in France is known as *Chomeurs Createurs* and the program in the United Kingdom is called the Enterprise Allowance Scheme. The latter allows the unemployed to continue receiving unemployment benefits for one year while they start a new business. Experience with European programs suggests that self-employment is a viable option for 2 percent to 3 percent of transfer payment recipients. Although the percentage is small, a similar figure for the AFDC program in the United States would translate into sixty thousand to ninety thousand self-employed people, not an insignificant number.

In the United States, several states have used Job Training Partnership Act (JTPA) money to fund entrepreneurial training. Ohio, for example, has used $550,000 in JTPA Title III funds to train 217 dislocated workers to start businesses. Some states and localities have established seed capital for revolving loan funds. Beginning in 1990, Missouri will have an "incubator program," with a 50 percent tax credit to encourage savings for small entrepreneurial efforts. But the experience to date in the United States has been piecemeal and inconsistent. The Corporation for Enterprise Development (CfED) in Washington, DC, has taken the lead in experimenting with self-employment welfare models for possible broader application.

Self-Employment Options under AFDC

It may be surprising to some, but most single mothers are not on welfare, and a very large number hold full-time jobs. Some 55 percent to 60 percent of single mothers work outside the home. But in 1986, almost half of these 6.3 million single mothers earned less than ten thousand dollars per year. Although there has been extensive interest in welfare-to-work programs in the United States, it is clear that there are not enough well-paying jobs. People can work full time and still be in poverty. Indeed, the most likely impact of the Family Support Act of 1988 is that some single mothers will leave the welfare roles, but will still be poor.[34] The need for job creation and employment alternatives is evident. Therefore, a self-employment option should be added to welfare-to-work programs.

Taking the lead in this area, CfED is mounting a multiyear, multistate Self-Employment Investment Demonstration (SEID). Iowa, Michigan, Minnesota, Mississippi, and New Jersey are committed to participating. Federal waivers of regulations that hamper self-employment efforts have been sought in each of these states—all seek a package of waivers that allow acquisition of limited amounts of cash, equipment, and inventory without threatening welfare benefits, applying to the first year or the first two years of the demonstration. Other waivers will be sought, as necessary, to maintain Medicaid and Food Stamps during this period. These experiments are being independently evaluated by the Manpower Demonstration Research Corporation.

Unemployment Insurance as Seed Capital for Self-Employment

Unemployment Insurance is a mainstay of the modern welfare state, but it is a system whose effectiveness is highly questionable. From the conservative side, Martin Feldstein has argued that unemployment compensation creates incentives in an economic downturn to reduce employment rather than wage rates.[35] Liberal observers have also questioned Unemployment Insurance as currently structured. For example, Robert Kuttner has urged a stronger focus on reemployment by using some Unemployment Insurance funds to provide job training and subsidize wages.[36]

In addition, the Unemployment Insurance system teeters on insolvency. It has inadequate reserves at the state level, and was severely strained during the steep recession of 1981–82. To improve solvency, federal and state policies have tightened eligibility. The proportion of the unemployed who actually received benefits fell from as high as 70 percent during the late 1970s, to 34 percent in 1984. Despite this tightening of eligibility, it is projected that in a future recession, many states will be unable to pay benefits without borrowing billions of dollars from the federal government.[37]

Evidence indicates that unemployed workers are about twice as likely to start businesses as employed workers, but with less success.[38] Perhaps public policy can begin to improve on this situation.

As a hopeful response, Congress enacted a tiny provision at the end of 1987 which would allow three states to handle unemployment compensation a little differently, using unemployment payments to start small businesses. The new program is based on the *Chomeurs Createurs* in France and the Enterprise Allowance Scheme in the United Kingdom. The U.S. pilot program will help one thousand to two thousand jobless workers in Massachusetts, Minnesota, and Oregon by enabling them to use unemployment benefits as seed capital. Applicants must have an idea and a thoughtful business plan. Abt Associates of Cambridge, Massachusetts, is designing and evaluating the experiments.

A Proposal for Self-Employment IDAs

As the above experiments suggest, it may be possible to restructure AFDC payments and Unemployment Insurance for self-employment at little additional cost. Even on this basis, there is reason to believe that creative results are possible.

Under a more expansive asset-based view, self-employment IDAs might be universally available, and deposits into IDAs for the poor might be matched, say at one dollar of matching funds for every one-dollar deposit by the holder of the IDA, if the money is used as seed capital to start a new business.

1. IDAs for self-employment would be open to anyone eighteen years of age and over, with the restriction that the money be used as seed capital to start a business venture.

2. There would be an annual deposit limit of five thousand dollars per individual account, and an overall limit of fifteen thousand dollars, after which no further deposits would be permitted.

3. There would be tax exemptions for all participants as long as accounts were used exclusively for starting a new business or for expenses concurrent with running the business, such as child care in the case of single parents.

4. Impoverished individuals below specified income and asset criteria would be eligible for deposit subsidies from the federal government of up to 50 percent of deposited amounts.

5. Self-employment IDA funds would be available for use without penalty only after a business plan is developed and approved by a

voluntary local review board made up of businesspeople. (This local review process could occur through the existing Private Industry Councils, which implement the Job Training Partnership Act, thus avoiding creation of an additional organizational structure.)

6. Self-employment IDAs could be pooled for joint ownership in any way that holders of the funds and local boards deemed sensible and appropriate.

7. After a period of ten years from the initiation of the IDA, if not used for self-employment, IDA funds could be disbanded, in which case the holder of the fund would receive only his or her original deposits and earnings on those deposits, less a 10 percent penalty. Income tax would be paid on the full amount received. All other amounts and earnings would revert to the IDA Reserve Fund.

As with other IDA possibilities, several interesting variations of employment-related IDAs are possible. For example, IDAs might be used to support job training and/or labor market mobility in the geographic sense. The Ford Foundation has issued a recommendation for lump sum payments of Unemployment Insurance and AFDC grants to persons in declining labor markets to enable them to "move to areas of more promising economic opportunity."[39] This is a step toward asset-based policy. But why assets only for moving? Some people might prefer to stay and create their own employment, and public policy should encourage them to do so.

IDAs for Retirement Pensions

People are living longer and staying healthier longer. For a very large number of people, retirement is no longer a time for "being put out to pasture" but rather another active stage of life. As the population ages, the nation will need its retirees as productive citizens, if not in the formal labor market, then in useful community service. But in order to be contributing members of the community, rather than a drain on the community, retirees must have a degree of financial security. At this point, it is clear that Social Security retirement benefits, even when augmented by Supplemental Security Income (SSI), provide only a bare minimum of financial security. A system of individually held retirement funds would not replace Social Security or SSI, but would supplement these old-age income transfers.

Moreover, most of the American work force does not have occupational pension coverage—either because of low-benefit jobs, or because employees have changed jobs before becoming vested in a defined benefit retirement plan (typical defined-benefit pension plans do not allow employees to take money with them when they change jobs). Occupational pension plan coverage grew after World War II, reaching a peak of 45.7 percent of the labor force in 1979, and then began a decline and reached 41.8 percent by 1985.[40] According to the Social Security Administration, among full-time workers, the percentage with employer-sponsored pension plans fell from 50 percent in 1979 to 46 percent in 1988. The absence of pensions is especially acute in small businesses. Fewer than one in five workers in companies with twenty-five or fewer employees is offered a company pension plan, compared to five of every six workers in companies with more than five hundred employees.

As U.S. employers seek ways to cut costs, declining trends in private pension coverage will very likely continue. Moreover, because corporations increasingly use the capital in pension funds for other purposes, there is, in some cases, a question about the security of these funds for future retirees.

Even where pensions are available, workers are not always able to take advantage of them. About 90 percent of all private pensions are defined-benefit plans as opposed to defined-contribution plans. A participant in a defined-benefit plan typically is required to work for a number of years prior to being vested. Effective January 1989, based on provisions of the Tax Reform Act of 1986, employees can be vested after five years of employment instead of ten. But even the new five-year rule is not a remedy for the problem. Median job tenure for American workers is only 4.4 years. According to the Bureau of Labor Statistics, an estimated 59 percent of all current workers will lose some or all of their retirement benefits during their working lives because they change jobs.

The problem is getting worse. As many as one-half of all new jobs pay wages below the poverty level, and almost none of these jobs have retirement benefits. According to a 1988 report of the Democratic staff of the Senate Budget Committee, "half of the new jobs generated in the last eight years were at wages below the poverty level for a family of four" (which was $11,611 in 1987 dollars). Different observers count differently, but it is clear that jobs paying below the poverty level, and without retirement benefits, are growing faster than any other kind.

A Proposal for Retirement IDAs

Recognizing that millions of Americans are working but remain in poverty, the government might take steps to promote asset accumulation by the working poor in the form of retirement pensions, matching contributions from the poor themselves. In essence, the federal government would, for those with "bad jobs" and no benefits, make available the same sort of institutionalized retirement schemes that are currently enjoyed by those with "good jobs" and good benefits. Unlike current income-transfer programs, which discourage work, this asset-based support for the working poor would incorporate strong work incentives.

IDAs for retirement pensions could be developed through an expansion of Simplified Employee Pensions (SEPs), a little-known plan designed by Congress in 1978 as an alternative for small businesses that cannot afford to pay high start-up and operating costs of conventional employee pension plans. An SEP allows workers to take retirement money with them from job to job—in other words, the pension is portable. Under current law, an employer can contribute up to 15 percent of each worker's salary or thirty thousand dollars annually, whichever is less. All workers, even part-time workers, are eligible. SEPs are defined-contribution plans; that is, the money belongs to each employee immediately. It is like an IRA that the employer sets up for the workers. If employees change jobs, they can transfer the SEP balance to a new SEP account or to an IRA. In very small businesses (fewer than twenty-five employees), in lieu of employer contributions, employees may contribute themselves. As with an IRA, earnings are not taxed until retirement. Income tax and a 10 percent penalty are imposed on withdrawals prior to the age of 59 years and 6 months. SEPs can also be set up by the self-employed.

Some points that build on this concept follow (it does not really matter if this asset accumulation fund is called an expanded SEP, an expanded IRA, or a retirement IDA, but for discussion purposes, and to relate it to the proposals above, let us call it a retirement IDA):

1. IDAs for retirement would be open to those eighteen years of age and over who are employed.

2. For accounts with subsidized deposits, there would be an annual deposit limit of two thousand dollars per account.

3. Impoverished individuals below specified income and asset criteria would be eligible for deposit subsidies from the federal government of up to 50 percent of deposited amounts.

4. After a period of ten years from the initiation of the IDA, the fund could be disbanded, in which case the holder of the fund would receive only his or her original deposits and earnings on those deposits, less a 10 percent penalty. Income tax would be paid on the full amount received. All other amounts and earnings would revert to the IDA Reserve Fund. A variation might be to permit retirement IDA funds to be transferred, without penalty, to educational or housing IDAs of children and grandchildren.

The rationale for IDAs in education, housing, and self-employment is obviously *investment.* Retirement is a somewhat different case in that the rationale supposedly is *security* in the later years. Ironically, however, even retirement-oriented IDAs are not likely to stimulate consumption in retirement but rather intergenerational transfer of wealth, because in fact, the elderly do not decrease very much of their wealth by spending during retirement.[41]

Multipurpose IDAs

Above are four suggestions for IDAs for specific purposes—educational financing, home ownership, capital for self-employment, and retirement pension funds. They are presented as separate proposals, but it may be desirable to combine elements of different proposals to create more flexible, multipurpose IDAs, to be used for education, housing, self-employment, retirement, and/or other approved purposes as the holder of the IDA thinks best. Whether or not this is desirable is open to discussion. Certainly, this possibility should be considered. Two questions are of central concern in this discussion: (1) What does the federal government wish to subsidize and for whom? and (2) What are the trade-offs between freedom of choice and control of program quality?

Children in Poverty and IDAs

Turning to the most difficult welfare issue in America, the growing number of women and children in poverty, it might be helpful to consider how the above proposals for IDAs can help solve this problem. Under an asset-based welfare policy, using IDAs, AFDC families would have the option of putting a portion of such payments, matched with as much as nine dollars for every one dollar deposited, into IDAs for housing, future education of children, self-employment, or possibly other development activities. As a further incentive to make such deposits, state and local governments, foundations, or corporations might offer to match IDA deposits as well. The asset-based program would not replace AFDC, Food Stamps, or other income-based programs; rather, the two types of welfare policies would complement one another.

There is very little precedent in the United States for encouraging savings and investment of funds in poverty households. But if the long-term goal of AFDC is the abolition of poverty, then savings and investment may be more important than consumption, and those families that can find a way to save for their children's future, with attractive subsidies and incentives, might find a way to do so.

An Individual Example: Amanda Smith

It might be helpful to illustrate how an IDA might work for an individual. Because some of the best applications of IDAs are with children for educational purposes, let us focus on these. We take the case of Amanda Smith, born in 1990 in Junction City. Amanda is one of two children in a family headed by a single mother. The mother works as a waitress. Family income is typically below ten thousand dollars per year, and there are no significant financial assets in the household. The family is among the working poor and does not receive AFDC. In the absence of an IDA system, Amanda Smith's prospects for financing a college education are slim. Indeed, she would very likely abandon this possibility early in life. On the other hand, imagine the existence of an IDA program. With an IDA for Amanda Smith, the following might occur (see Table 11.1):

Deposits into Amanda's account (in 1990 dollars) are as follows: $1,000 at birth; $500 for completing each year of schooling grades kindergarten through eleven; an extra $60 in grade eight and an extra $280 in grade eleven earned in class projects; $2,500 for completing grade twelve (high school graduation); and a $5,000 stipend for completing one year of national service following high school.[42] For her

Table 11.1

Example: Amanda Smith's IDA Account
(assumes a 3 percent real return on investments)

Year	Age	Events	Deposit	With-drawal	Earnings*	Balance
1990	0	birth	$1,000	$ 0	$ 0	$1,000
1991	1	—	0	0	30	1,030
1992	2	—	0	0	31	1,061
1993	3	—	0	0	32	1,093
1994	4	—	0	0	33	1,126
1995	5	grade K	500	0	34	1,660
1996	6	grade 1	500	0	50	2,210
1997	7	grade 2	500	0	66	2,776
1998	8	grade 3	500	0	83	3,359
1999	9	grade 4	500	0	101	3,960
2000	10	grade 5	500	0	119	4,579
2001	11	grade 6	500	0	137	5,216
2002	12	grade 7	500	0	156	5,872
2003	13	grade 8 and class project	560	0	176	6,608
2004	14	grade 9	500	0	198	7,306
2005	15	grade 10	500	0	219	8,025
2006	16	grade 11 and class project	780	0	241	9,046
2007	17	grade 12	2,500	0	271	11,817
2008	18	national service	5,000	0	355	17,171
2009	19	college	0	2,500	515	15,186
2010	20	college	0	2,500	456	13,142
2011	21	college	0	2,500	394	11,036
2012	22	college	0	2,500	331	8,867
2013	23	—	0	0	266	9,133
2014	24	—	0	0	274	9,407
2015	25	—	0	0	282	9,689
2016	26	—	0	0	290	9,979
2017	27	—	0	0	299	10,278
2018	28	—	0	0	308	10,586
2019	29	—	0	0	317	10,903
2020	30	—	0	0	327	11,230
2021	31	—	0	0	337	11,567
2022	32	—	0	0	347	11,914
2023	33	—	0	0	357	12,271
2024	34	—	0	0	368	12,639
2025	35	—	0	0	379	13,018
2026	36	graduate school	0	3,500	390	9,908
2027	37	graduate school	0	3,500	297	6,705
2028	38	—	0	0	201	6,906
2029	39	—	0	0	207	7,113
2030	40	—	0	0	213	7,326
2031	41	—	0	0	220	7,546
2032	42	—	0	0	226	7,772
2033	43	transfer to children's IDAs	0	5,000	233	3,005

Table 11.1 *(continued)*

Year	Age	Events	Deposit	With-drawal	Earnings*	Balance
2034	44	—	0	0	90	3,095
2035	45	—	0	0	93	3,188
2036	46	—	0	0	96	3,284
2037	47	—	0	0	99	3,383
2038	48	—	0	0	102	3,485
2039	49	—	0	0	105	3,590
2040	50	—	0	0	108	3,698
2041	51	—	0	0	111	3,809
2042	52	—	0	0	114	3,923
2043	53	—	0	0	117	4,040
2044	54	—	0	0	121	4,161
2045	55	—	0	0	125	4,286
2046	56	—	0	0	129	4,415
2047	57	—	0	0	133	4,548
2048	58	—	0	0	137	4,685
2049	59	—	0	0	141	4,826
2050	60	—	0	0	145	4,971
2051	61	—	0	0	149	5,120
2052	62	—	0	0	154	5,274
2053	63	—	0	0	158	5,432
2054	64	—	0	0	163	5,595
2055	65	transfer to grandchildren's IDAs and close account	0	5,763	168	0

Notes: Figures in this table reflect an estimated average 3 percent real return on investment. This estimate is based on historical experience. Since 1926, over a period of sixty-three years, and before taxes, Standard and Poors's 500 stocks have returned 6.9 percent above the rate of price inflation; long-term U.S. bonds have returned 1.1 percent; and treasury bills have returned 0.4 percent. (*Source:* Ibotson Associates, Inc., Chicago.) Assuming a mixed portfolio of 50 percent stocks and 50 percent bonds and cash, a estimated 3 percent return is reasonable, perhaps slightly conservative.

In interpreting data in the table, note that the real return basis of calculations essentially changes all figures into 1990 dollars. For example, the $3,500 spent for graduate school in the year 2026 or the $5,763 transferred to grandchildren's IDAs in the year 2055 are comparable to the same amounts of money in 1990. In reality, with inflation, actual dollar amounts in future years would be much higher.

*As a simplification, the 3 percent earnings are calculated on the balance from the preceding year, and not on additions or subtractions during the current year.

national service, Amanda works for the Junction City recycling program, developing and implementing strategies for community education to increase the number of city residents who recycle cans, glass bottles, plastic containers, and newspapers. As a result of this experience, she develops an interest in solid waste disposal and other ecological issues.

The sources of the deposits into Amanda Smith's IDA account are as follows: Deposits at birth and for educational progress, totaling $9,500, result from a matching contribution whereby the federal government contributes 80 percent and the state government contributes 10 percent for every 10 percent deposited by the Smith family. The 10 percent match from the Smith family is made at considerable sacrifice, but given the strong financial incentives and the prospect of college education for her children, Amanda's mother decides to make this sacrifice.

The added $60 in eighth grade and $280 in Amanda's junior year of high school result from class projects organized for the purpose of raising funds for deposits into the IDAs of everyone in the class. In eighth grade, the class project is a schoolwide flea market, which earns $30 for each student in the class. A local corporation contributes $1 for each dollar that the children have earned, bringing the deposit to $60 for each student. As juniors, Amanda's class organizes an ethnic food fair, theater presentation, and raffle, with most of the supplies donated by local restaurants and other businesses. This project is a huge success and nets $140 per student. Again, a local corporation contributes $1 for each dollar that the children have earned, bringing the deposit to $280 for each student.

The national service stipend of $5,000 is provided through joint funding between Junction City and a major soft drink company that has a bottling facility in the city. For her national service, Amanda works for one year helping to survey residents and design a recycling center for metals, glass, and newspaper in Junction City.

Total deposits into Amanda Smith's IDA over a period of eighteen years are $14,840. No other deposits are made into the account for the remainder of her life (see Table 11.1).

While in school, Amanda, along with all her classmates, has learned about the existence of her IDA account and how it works. She has learned to make investment decisions for her account, and she has undertaken many planning exercises for use of her account in the future.

How does Amanda use her IDA account? If we assume that she earns an average 3 percent real return on her IDA investments, she has $17,171 (in 1990 dollars) in her account by her nineteenth birthday. After some careful thought and advice from her high school counselor and city officials with whom she worked during her national service year, Amanda has decided to pursue her interest in solid waste disposal. She enrolls in Central State College to study mechanical engineering and urban planning. For each of the next four years she withdraws $2,500 per year to help with the costs of a college education. (This amount is comparable to current limits on undergraduate borrowing under the Guaranteed Student Loan Program. In many cases, $2,500 is not enough to finance a full year of college education. The reality of college financing, for most students, is a "package" of personal resources, grants, loans, and earned income. The IDA would be one source of financing among others. In many cases, at public institutions, $2,500 per year would completely replace the need for borrowing.) At the end of college, Amanda Smith's IDA balance is down to $8,867. She is not required to spend all of her assets for her undergraduate education.

She receives her bachelor's degree in engineering and takes a job with a firm that designs and constructs solid waste recovery facilities. She marries and has two children, and continues to work full-time. However, her advancement at her company is hindered by child care responsibilities and lack of an advanced degree. While the children are young, she does not think it possible to go back to school for her master's degree.

At age thirty-six, when the children are older and more independent, Amanda decides that she can return to school. She elects to apply to a Master's in Business Administration (MBA) program, and she is admitted. In the intervening years, the balance in her IDA account has grown again to $13,018 (in 1990 dollars). During each of the next two years, she withdraws $3,500 to help pay for her schooling. Following graduation, by prior agreement, she returns to her company and is soon given a promotion.

A few years later, at the age of forty-three, thinking that she will probably not be financing any more of her own education, Amanda Smith decides to transfer, without penalty, $5,000 into the IDA accounts of her children to help them with their college educations. At this point, her children are seventeen and twenty years old and, even though they have IDAs of their own, they can use the additional assets to help finance college and graduate school.

At age sixty-five, Amanda Smith has an IDA balance that has again grown to $5,763, and certain that she will not be needing it, she transfers, without penalty, the entire balance to the IDA accounts of her grandchildren, closing her own account.

Total withdrawals and transfers from Amanda's account, until her sixty-fifth birthday, have been $27,763 in real (inflation-adjusted) dollars, almost twice the amount of the original deposits.

Discussion of Amanda Smith Example

Amanda Smith's case is, of course, an idealized example, but it illustrates important features of an educational IDA system. Most notably, modest IDA deposits early in life have the potential to generate substantial returns over time, helping to finance a great deal of education.

The best strategy for use of the IDA is illustrated in Amanda Smith's case. She uses the account to meet her current educational objectives, but she is careful to leave a large enough balance so that earnings accumulate for her next major withdrawal. This fundamental strategy would be taught to young people as they planned and prepared for use of their IDAs.

The proposed IDA system is ideally suited to ongoing educational achievement and personal development. Mid-career supplemental education and retooling, as illustrated in Amanda Smith's case, will likely become more common as the economy changes rapidly in the decades ahead. IDAs would facilitate this educational pattern because they would provide a financial base from which earnings could be withdrawn periodically over a lifetime.

After Amanda's personal educational goals are achieved, she uses her IDA account to help with her children's education, but again she is careful to leave a balance that accumulates earnings. Later she is able to help her grandchildren. This ability to pass along significant assets to offspring is a major difference between the rich and the poor. Children in wealthy families know from birth that they will be able to go to college, and take it for granted that they will do so. Children in poor families make no such assumption, and indeed often assume otherwise. An IDA system, over the long term, would change these assumptions in many poor families. IDAs for education would make it possible for more families to provide a "start in life" for their children and grandchildren.

While not everyone would use the IDA account as wisely as does Amanda Smith, the existence of such accounts would greatly encourage long-range planning, development of educational objectives and investment strategies, and prudent use of resources to meet personal and family goals.

How Much Would Asset-Based Welfare Cost?

At this point in the discussion, the reader may be saying something like, "All of this talk about asset-based welfare is fine, but how much would asset-based welfare cost?" In this section, cost estimates are made for the asset-based policies described above. It is impossible to make precise estimates without knowing specific guidelines and the scope with which IDA programs might be implemented. The best way to proceed is to make certain assumptions about program characteristics and size, and then estimate on the basis of those assumptions. Even then, the figures are sometimes based on rather imprecise information. However, the reader will at least know the basis of the estimates, which are "in the neighborhood," given assumptions about guidelines and numbers of participants.

Before we turn to these estimates, two brief points about costs for asset-based welfare policy should be made. First, as mentioned previously, a *structure* for asset-based welfare is the most critical element in policy design, even more important than the dollar expenditures of the policy at the outset. Once a structure is in place that facilitates asset accumulation by the poor—even if it is funded modestly at the outset—through creative approaches the programs might expand. Second, asset-based welfare, in a very important sense, is not a cost, but rather a system of *investment*. By and large, the policy would not subsidize consumption but rather would subsidize savings. To the extent that public funds would subsidize asset-based welfare, the public treasury would be depleted, but simultaneously, in many individual accounts, wealth would accumulate. The stimulus of public incentives would draw household resources into new savings, and to this extent, the national savings rate would increase. (The possibility that IDA savings would only be transferred from other household savings must be considered. To some extent, this would occur. However, experience with IRAs suggests that new savings would be generated. Of course, in poor households, with no savings at the outset, the possibility of transfer would not exist.)

Having made these two points, let us turn to cost estimates. Ultimately, costs will depend on what programs are adopted and on the scale of these programs. The effort here is to estimate on the high side by giving figures for substantial and widespread applications of the asset-based welfare proposals outlined above. In each case, more lim-

Table 11.2

Estimated Costs to the Federal Government for Individual Development Account Proposals, First Year
(billions of dollars)

Type of IDA	Deposit subsidy to the poor	Tax expenditure to the poor	Tax expenditure to the nonpoor	Total
Education	2.8	0.6	1.6	5.0
Housing	5.6	1.2	4.9	11.7
Self-emploment	1.2	0.3	3.3	4.8
Retirement	5.4	1.7	0*	7.1
Total	15.0	3.8	9.8	28.6

Notes: Estimated costs for the first year assuming universal programs, with deposit subsidies to the poor and tax benefits to all. In calculating tax expenditures, the marginal tax rate for the poor is taken as 15 percent, and for the nonpoor, 30 percent. See text for details of estimates. Tax expenditures would increase after the first year as earnings on deposits are untaxed.

*There would be no additional tax expenditures for the nonpoor for retirement IDAs, because these benefits already exist in the form of IRAs and other tax-deferred private pension plans.

ited and less costly applications would be possible, and during an experimental phase, desirable.

There are two major types of public costs associated with the proposals described in the preceding chapter—direct subsidies for deposits into IDAs of the poor, and tax benefits for all those, poor and nonpoor, who hold IDAs (for a summary, see Table 11.2). Let us first address the cost of annual subsidies for deposits into IDAs of the poor.

Federal Deposit Subsidies

IDAs for Education

It is possible to envision a program in which no deposit subsidies are made at all; only tax incentives for educational savings (this is similar to the plan for tax-exempt earnings on U.S. Savings Bonds that took effect in 1990). Or taking the educational IDA proposal described above, *maximum* costs of the federal government for deposit subsidies would be as follows: 80 percent of a $1,000 deposit at birth for some 750,000 children born into poverty households each year, at an annual cost of $0.6 billion; plus 80 percent of annual deposits of $500 for each year of education completed for some ten million children (between the ages of five and eighteen) living in poverty, at an annual cost of $4.0 billion; and 80 percent of $2,500 deposits for an estimated 600,000 high school graduates living in poverty, for an annual cost of $1.2 billion. (For these deposits, state governments would contribute 10 percent, and recipient households would contribute the remaining 10 percent.) Total annual federal cost, based on these maximum esti- mates, would be $5.8 billion (on total deposits of $7.25 billion).

These figures assume, however, that *all* children would continue in school, and *all* families would choose to participate (because a 10 percent match would be required, some families would choose not to participate). If, for one reason or another, impoverished families partic- ipated at only 60 percent of the maximum rate in a given year, the cost to the federal government would be reduced to $3.5 billion. The above figures also assume that all impoverished households would be subsi- dized for deposits into educational IDAs at a rate of 80 percent. If the federal subsidy rate were set on a sliding scale (which would be essen- tial for avoiding a "notch" effect), and averaged only 65 percent, the federal contribution would be reduced to $2.8 billion (on total deposits of $4.4 billion). Given the policy parameters outlined above, expendi- tures in this range seem most likely

IDAs for Housing

The first recommendation in housing would be to rechannel a portion of current income-based federal expenditures and create asset-based housing programs at no additional cost to the federal treasury. In par- ticular, tax expenditures for rental housing developers should be phased out in favor of direct equity subsidies for poor households. As much as possible, the money should go directly to the poor in the form of ownership, rather than to developers.

Because the nation's housing is so woefully inadequate, however, and because federal expenditures for housing have been so dramati- cally cut back in recent years, a significant expansion of federal effort toward home ownership by the poor is desirable. Based on the propos- als outlined above, if average deposits are $1,500 annually, and the federal government picks up an average of 75 percent of this amount for, say, 5 million participating poverty households, the annual cost to the federal government would be $5.6 billion (on total deposits of $7.5 billion).

IDAs for Self-Employment

Self-employment is not for everyone, nor is it a panacea for poverty in America, but it can play a significant role in helping some families overcome poverty. Because of the self-control it offers, it is a particularly attractive option for some single-parent households with young children.

As indicated by experiments developed by CfED, self-employment options may be funded by current Unemployment Insurance and AFDC resources. These programs can be restructured at little or no additional cost. Or, to give greater attention to impoverished households, asset-based policy might match self-employment IDA deposits on a basis of one dollar matched for each dollar deposited, *if and only if* the money is used as seed capital to start a new business. Let us assume: (1) that only 5 percent of 16 million impoverished individuals between the ages of eighteen and sixty-four participate (based on experience in Europe, this estimate is probably high); (2) that the average participant achieves total deposits at only 60 percent of the five-thousand-dollar annual limit, or three thousand dollars; and (3) that the average match by the federal government is 50 percent (that is, a match of one dollar for one dollar). Given these assumptions, the total federal cost would be $1.2 billion annually (on total deposits of $2.4 billion).

IDAs for Retirement Pensions of the Working Poor and Others Not Covered by Private Pension Systems

Under existing SEP and IRA retirement plans alone, all working people currently have access to private retirement funds. However, the current programs are not of great benefit to the working poor, who often cannot afford to make the deposits themselves, and for whom the tax incentives are small or non-existent.

A program of retirement IDAs would subsidize deposits for the working poor, who number almost 9 million people (both full time and part time). If the federal government provides a one-for-one match for all deposits at an average participation rate of 60 percent on maximum deposits of two thousand dollars, then annual deposit subsidies would total $5.4 billion (on total deposits of $10.8 billion). Expenditures in this range seem most likely.

Additional Tax Expenditures for the Poor

We turn now to tax expenditures that would be required to support the programs outlined above. For analytical purposes, we divide these tax expenditures into two categories: tax expenditures to the poor and tax expenditures to the nonpoor.

If deposit subsidies are made in accordance with the estimates above, then participation by the poor would be widespread. Including matches from state governments and participants, total annual deposits into accounts for education would be $4.4 billion; for housing, $7.5 billion; for self-employment, $2.4 billion; and for retirement pensions, $10.8 billion; totaling $25.1 billion in annual IDA deposits for the poor. If the average marginal tax rate for IDA participants in this group is 15 percent,[43] then tax expenditures for the first year would be as follows: $0.6 billion for educational IDAs; $1.2 billion for housing IDAs; $0.3 billion for self-employment IDAs; and $1.7 billion for retirement IDAs. Together, these tax expenditures for the poor would total $3.8 billion in the first year. This level of tax expenditure would gradually increase because earnings on deposits are also tax-exempt or tax-deferred.

Additional Tax Expenditures for the Nonpoor

Even though no IDA deposit subsidies would be available to the non-poor, the programs described above would be open and tax-benefited to nonpoor participants. The proposal is that all deposits, as well as earnings, are tax-benefited for all participants. This would be the most extravagant model from the standpoint of the federal treasury, but it would also stimulate the most savings and capital accumulation, and would generate the broadest base of political support. (An alternative would be to make deposits tax-deductible only up to a certain income level, as is the current arrangement for IRAs.)

To estimate the extent of tax expenditures to the nonpoor for the IDA programs outlined above, it is necessary first to estimate levels of participation. These estimates are uncertain—guesstimates would be a better description. How many would participate? Perhaps the best data to determine the answer to this question is the IRA participation rate in 1986, the last year in which all IRA deposits were tax-deferred for all participants. Total employment during 1986 averaged about 110 million. Of this number, about 101 million were nonpoor. Therefore, the *potential* total IRA contributions for all nonpoor workers (at $2,000 each) was about $202 billion. However, during that year, only $38.3 billion was deposited into IRAs.[44] Assuming that IRA deposits by the poor were negligible, then *actual* IRA deposits by the nonpoor were roughly 20 percent of potential deposits. Although 20 percent is probably an outside estimate, let us assume that this participation rate by the nonpoor would hold for all the IDA programs described above (incentives would be very similar).

In the case of educational IDAs, there are three major types of potential deposits from households to consider: $1,000 at birth, $500 for each year of schooling, and $2,500 for high school graduation. Applying the 20 percent participation rate to nonpoor age cohorts of about 2.7 million, we can estimate annual deposits of $0.5 billion at birth, $3.5 billion for years of schooling completed, and $1.4 billion at high school graduation, for a total of $5.4 billion in educational deposits annually. If the nonpoor have an effective marginal tax rate of 30 percent, then the tax expenditure for educational IDAs to the nonpoor would be $1.6 billion in the first year.[45]

Turning to housing IDAs, if we take the nonpoor 18- to 64-year-old population of about 135 million individuals, and estimate that 30 percent do not already own a home, and a participation rate of 20 percent for IDA deposits on $2,000, then total deposits would be $16.2 billion. At an average marginal tax rate of 30 percent, the tax expenditure would be $4.1 billion.

Use of IDAs for self-employment by the nonpoor is even more difficult to estimate. In 1989, the total civilian labor force was about 123 million. Roughly 110 million of these were nonpoor. If 10 percent of the nonpoor labor force are potentially interested in IDAs for self-employment, but the average participation rate on maximum annual deposits of $5,000 is only 20 percent, then total deposits would be $11.0 billion. Assuming an effective marginal tax rate of 30 percent, the total tax expenditure to the nonpoor during one year for self-employment IDAs would be $3.3 billion.

The equivalent of retirement IDA's for the nonpoor is already implemented in the form of 401(k), 403(b), SEP, Keogh, IRA, and other tax-deferred retirement programs. These tax expenditures are already in place and the proposal here would add nothing to them.

Total Costs to the Federal Government

As indicated in Table 11.2, the total costs (direct costs plus tax expenditures) for all four proposed IDA programs would be $28.6 billion. Tax expenditures would increase gradually because earnings in IDA accounts would also be tax-benefited.

In the long run, IDA programs would reduce income-based welfare expenditures in education, housing, and retirement security. Quite probably, these effects would be substantial, but they would not occur immediately. For example, an IDA housing policy, if implemented on the scale indicated above, would greatly expand home ownership within a period of ten to fifteen years, easily bringing the ownership percentage up from its current 64 percent to 80 percent or 85 percent. At that point, neither public rent subsidies nor asset-based housing subsidies would be required on nearly so large a scale.[46]

Also, it would be well to bear in mind that the recommended programs here are asset-based, that is, the policies would support accumulation rather than consumption. In effect, if we look at the nation's economy as a whole, these are not expenditures but rather savings and investment. The total estimated annual deposits for the above programs is $57.7 billion (see Table 11.3). If much of this is new savings—evidence from IRAs indicates that much of it would be new savings[47]—then a broad system of IDAs would generate a substantial boost in the nation's household savings rate.

Experimentation, Demonstration, Evaluation

In some respects, asset-based welfare is a new way to think about antipoverty policy. As a welfare policy reform, it is uncomplicated but rather sweeping in its implications. If the idea is judged to have merit, it surely cannot be implemented all at once, but rather will require many experimental efforts, starts and stops, and renewed initiatives, and much evaluation, discussion, and so forth. (A reasonable analogy might be the negative income tax, a very striking idea when it was introduced in the 1960s, but one that met with opposition as specific proposals were presented. Gradually, however, it seems that the nega-

Table 11.3

Estimated Annual Deposits under IDA Proposals
(billions of dollars)

Type of IDA	Deposits by the poor	Deposits by the nonpoor	Total
Education	4.4	5.4	9.8
Housing	7.5	16.2	23.7
Self-employment	2.4	11.0	13.4
Retirement	10.8	0*	10.8
Total	25.1	32.6	57.7

Note: See text for details of estimates.

　*There would be no additional saving by the nonpoor for retirement IDAs, because incentives and mechanisms already exist in the form of IRAs and other tax-deferred private pension plans.

tive income tax idea is finding expression through the Earned Income Tax Credit and tax credits for child care.)

As indicated in the numerous examples mentioned in this chapter, many asset-based welfare policies are already being tested, in one form or another, at local, state, and federal levels. These experiments should be carefully monitored, and where successful, expanded. Most importantly, policymakers and the general public might begin to see these isolated experiments as part of a larger movement toward asset-based welfare policy, and give asset-based demonstration projects special scrutiny as welfare reform proposals are considered.

At the federal level, asset-based policies, because they would be new and untested in most applications, should be developed first in small demonstration programs, or in particular geographical locations. Problems of implementation will inevitably arise. For example, one problem will be how to assure that resources in restricted accounts are used for the purposes specified. The tremendous need for public information and education will present other problems. Institutionally, it may be possible to use the schools, traditional welfare organizations, housing authorities, banks, savings and loans, credit unions, investment companies, and other institutions to develop asset-based programs. As particular approaches prove successful, as problems are worked out, and as regulations are developed, programs should be expanded.

Another approach would be to target IDAs to particular populations on an experimental basis. One possibility is to target single-parent families. Another possibility is to target a particular geographical area, such as an impoverished region, a particular state, a city, or a neighborhood. Another possibility is to target a particular age-group. Asset-based welfare, because of its long-term nature, is ideally suited to application with the young. Another possibility is to target a particular social problem, for example, teen parents. Another possibility is to target by race. Blacks, more than any other minority group, have been excluded from asset accumulation. The "forty acres and a mule" promised by the Freedmen's Bureau was never delivered; this missed opportunity is one of the greatest social policy errors in American history. Perhaps we should initiate a modern equivalent, something like forty shares of IBM and a college savings account.

Demonstration projects, especially those in educational financing, would ideally be conducted over a period of twenty-five or thirty years; however, this is not very practical. As an alternative, a truncated version of the educational IDA program could be established, perhaps designed as a five-year experiment. It might begin with sophomores in high school and follow them until two years after high school graduation. An entire sophomore class in a school would comprise the experimental group, and a control group would be established in a similar high school elsewhere. The experimental group would have IDA accounts sufficient to provide a realistic opportunity for a college education or other post-high school training, and they would intensively plan for future use of IDAs while in high school. While a demonstration project of this nature would not be a perfect test of the educational IDA concept, it would yield a strong indication of the likely effects.

Although this book suggests a specific IDA policy, a number of different asset-based policy approaches are possible, many of them complementary. Asset limits for current recipients of means-tested income transfers might be eased or eliminated altogether. The Earned Income Tax Credit might be used to build asset accumulation accounts for the working poor. Postal savings and/or school savings programs might be re-established. There are numerous possibilities, but before we can proceed, the nation, and particularly the welfare policy establishment, must come to see that income-based antipoverty policy is insufficient. Tinkering with the income flows will not do the job. It is necessary to shift to asset-based policy.

Notes

1. Susan Mayer and Christopher Jencks, "Poverty and the Distribution of Material Hardship," *Journal of Human Resources* 24(1), 1989, 88–114.

2. U.S. General Accounting Office, "Defaulted Student Loans: Preliminary Analysis of Student Loan Borrowers and Defaulters." Washington: U.S. Government Printing Office, 1988.

3. Ezra Bowen, "Needy Kids, Perpetual Aid," *Time*, November 30, 1987, 70.

4. Joseph Michalak, "For Quick Sale: College Nest Eggs," *Education Life, New York Times*, August 7, 1988, 47–49; Joseph Michalak, "That College Bill," *Education Life, New York Times*, January 8, 1989, 12 and 14; and Gary Putka, "Anxious Parents Flock to Tuition Schemes," *Wall Street Journal*, March 8, 1989, C1.

5. Robert Plotnick has reminded me that households with school age children probably move less, on the average, than other households, and that statistics on moving include in-state moving. Therefore, state-defined college savings plans may work well for many people. However, mobility would still be a problem for many, as well as the fact that a large number of young people choose to attend colleges outside of their home state.

6. Similar educational benefits for national service have been proposed by Michael Sherraden and Donald Eberly, eds., *National Service: Social, Economic, and Military Impacts*. New York: Pergamon Press, 1982; Donald Eberly, "National Service Education Fund" (unpublished paper). Washington: National Service Secretariat, 1985; and Charles Moskos, *A Call to Civic Service*. New York: The Free Press, 1988.

7. Michael Sherraden, "School Dropouts in Perspective," *Educational Forum*, 1986, 15–31.

8. A growing number of business schools are teaching investment to their students by letting them invest real money, usually a portion of the school endowment. These experiments are widely viewed as a financial and educational success. In a similar way, Individual Development Accounts could be used in the educational process in primary and secondary schools. The amounts of money would be less, and the investment lessons not as complex as those learned by business students, but the results in economic education are likely to be no less dramatic.

9. The problem of quality of proprietary school is an example of an old issue in welfare policy—the maximization of choice versus quality control. This issue shows up in many circumstances, often taking the form of cash versus in-kind transfers.

10. Robert Haveman, *Starting Even: An Equal-Opportunity Program to Combat the Nation's New Poverty*. New York: Simon and Schuster, 1988.

11. U.S. Bureau of the Census, *American Housing Survey, 1985*. Washington: U.S. Government Printing Office, 1989.

12. Paul Leonard, Cushing Dolbeare, and Edward Lazere, *A Place to Call Home: The Crisis in Housing for the Poor*. Washington: Center on Budget and Policy Priorities and Low Income Housing Information Service, 1989.

13. William Apgar, Jr. and Denise DiPasquale, *The State of the Nation's Housing*. Cambridge, MA: Harvard University Joint Center for Housing Studies, 1989.

14. Leonard et al., 1989.

15. Alice Johnson, "Female-Headed Homeless Families and the Housing Market," *Affilia, Journal of Women and Social Work* 4(4), 1989, 23–39.

16. Rebecca Blank and Harvey Rosen, "Recent Trends in Housing Conditions among the Urban Poor," NBER Working Paper No. 2886. Cambridge, MA: National Bureau of Economic Research, 1989.

17. Jacob Riis, *How the Other Half Lives: Studies among the Tenements of New York*. New York: Charles Scribner's Sons, 1903.

18. Edward Lazere, Paul Leonard, and Linda Kravitz, *The Other Housing Crisis: Sheltering the Poor in Rural America*. Washington: Center on Budget and Policy Priorities, 1989.

19. Carol Steinbach, "Shelter-Skelter," *National Journal*, April 8, 1989, 851–55.

20. Center on Budget and Policy Priorities, "New Reductions in Low Income Programs in FY 1988." Washington: Center on Budget and Policy Priorities, 1988.

21. Lawrence Gouldner, "Tax Policy, Housing Prices, and Housing Investment," Working Paper No. 2814. Cambridge, MA: National Bureau of Economic Research, 1989.

22. Leonard et al., 1989.

23. Mary Nenno, *New Money and New Methods: A Catalog of State and Local Initiatives in Housing and Community Development*. Washington: National Association of Housing and Redevelopment Officials, 1986.

24. Mary E. Brooks, *A Survey of Housing Trust Funds*. Washington: Center for Community Change, 1988.

25. Tom Bethell, "Tenant Ownership: Will Anyone Bother to Buy?" *Wall Street Journal*, January 10, 1990, A10.

26. David Schwartz, Richard Ferlauto, and Daniel Hoffman, *A New Housing Policy for America*. Philadelphia: Temple University Press, 1988.

27. Apgar and DiPasquale, 1989.

28. U.S. Bureau of Labor Statistics, *Employment and Earnings, January 1989*. Washington: U.S. Government Printing Office, 1989, Table 23. Officially measured self-employment understates the extent of self-employment in the economy. Unmeasured business activity in a wide variety of legal and illegal activities is common, especially for U.S. blacks (see Ivan Light, "Immigrant and Ethnic Enterprise in North America," *Ethnic and Racial Studies* 7(2), 1984, 195–216).

29. Jules H. Lichtenstein, "Measuring Self-Employment as a Micro-Business Phenomenon," a paper presented at a conference, "The Self-Employment Strategy: Building the New Economy," Toronto, October 1989.

30. Faith Ando & Associates, Inc., *Minorities, Women, Veterans, and the 1982 Characteristics of Business Owners Survey: A Preliminary Analysis*, Report no. PB89–115091/AS. Springfield, VA: National Technical Information Service, 1989.

31. Lichtenstein, 1989.

32. U.S. Department of Labor, *Alternative Uses of Unemployment Compensa-*

tion, Washington, DC: U.S. Government Printing Office, 1986.

33. In this section, I am borrowing from publications from the Corporation for Enterprise Development (CfED), particularly those by Robert Friedman, president, and Rona Feit, senior policy analyst.

34. Phoebe Cottingham and David Ellwood, eds., *Welfare Policy for the 1990s*. Cambridge: Harvard University Press, 1989.

35. Martin Feldstein, "Temporary Layoffs in the Theory of Unemployment," *Journal of Political Economy*, October 1970, 937–58.

36. Robert Kuttner, "Getting Off the Dole: A Proposal to Reform the Unemployment Compensation System," *The Atlantic Monthly*, September 1985, 74–79.

37. U.S. General Accounting Office, *Unemployment Insurance: Trust Fund Reserves Inadequate*. Washington: U.S. Government Printing Office, 1988.

38. Lichtenstein, 1989.

39. Ford Foundation, *The Common Good: Social Welfare and the American Future*. New York: Ford Foundation, 1989.

40. Richard Lee Deaton, *The Political Economy of Pensions: Power, Politics, and Social Change in Canada, Great Britain, and the United States*. Vancouver: University of British Columbia Press, 1989.

41. Laurence J. Kotlikoff, *What Determines Savings?* Cambridge: MIT Press, 1989.

42. This assumes a national service plan similar to that proposed in Sherraden and Eberly, 1982; and Moskos, 1988.

43. Precise data on marginal tax rates (MTR) are not available. The statutory MTR for all individual income below $23,900 in 1988 was 15 percent. According to estimates by the staff of the Joint Committee on Taxation, the average effective tax rate (ETR) for 1988 was only 0.5 percent on incomes below $10,000, and 4.4 percent on incomes between $10,000 and $20,000 (U.S. Congress, Joint Committee on Taxation, "Data on Distribution by Income Class of Effects of the Tax Reform Act of 1986," an unpublished paper prepared by the staff, October 1, 1986). The latest data relating MTR and ETR are from 1985 (U.S. Internal Revenue Service, Statistics of Income, *Individual Income Tax Returns, 1985*. Washington: U.S. Government Printing Office, 1988). These data are particularly out of date because of changes in the 1986 Tax Act. However, during 1985, when the MTR was 15 percent, the ETR was 7.9 percent. In terms of these figures, it is certain that the average MTR for individuals in poverty is less than 15 percent, but 15 percent is used here as an outside estimate.

44. IRA deposit figures are from the Revenue Analysis Division of the Joint Committee on Taxation.

45. Again, precise data on effective marginal tax rates (MTR) are not available. In 1988, the statutory MTR for all individual income above $23,900 and below $61,650 was 28 percent, and for all income above $61,650 and below $123,790, the rate was 33 percent. According to estimates by the staff of the Joint Committee on Taxation, the average effective tax rates (ETR) for 1988 ranged from 7.5 percent on incomes between $20,000 and $30,000 to 22.3 percent on incomes over $200,000 (U.S. Congress, Joint Committee on Taxation, 1986). The latest data relating MTR and ETR are from 1985 (U.S. Internal Revenue Service, 1988). As mentioned previously, these data are particularly out of date because of changes in the 1986 Tax Act. However, during 1985, when the MTR was 30

percent, the ETR was 16.1 percent. In terms of these figures, it is certain that the average MTR for nonpoor individuals is less than 30 percent, but 30 percent is used here as an outside estimate.

46. If IDAs were implemented on a large scale, a number of other indirect cost effects, both positive and negative, would occur. Regarding educational IDAs, for example, the demand for higher education would eventually increase; the quality of the labor supply would later improve; increased labor productivity would follow; and so forth. Estimating these effects would be extremely challenging, and is beyond the scope of the current discussion.

47. Daniel Feenberg and Jonathan Skinner, "Sources of IRA Saving," NBER Working Paper No. 2845. Cambridge, MA: National Bureau of Economic Research, 1989.

12 • The Integration of Welfare Policy with Economic Goals of the Nation

In the preceding chapters, I have attempted to lay the theoretical groundwork and provide a concrete proposal for asset-based welfare policy. Throughout the book, and especially in the theoretical section, the primary focus has been on individuals and households. It has been an analysis at the microeconomic level. In this chapter, we turn briefly to a more macroeconomic perspective—a discussion of asset issues at the national level. I draw the conclusion that asset-based welfare policy does not necessarily conflict with economic goals of the nation. Unlike income-based policy, asset-based policy would help to build financial capital, contributing in some measure to the nation's long-term economic prosperity.

Keynes, Consumption, and the Welfare State

Savings and investment, throughout the course of history, have almost always been viewed as desirable. However, prior to and immediately following World War II, there was widespread concern about the possibility of too much savings. This thinking was influenced by John Maynard Keynes, whose consumption-oriented theories warned of the possibility of too much savings. In Keynesian theory, oversavings can result in reduced demand, leading to depressed economic activity.

Prior to Keynes, economists generally did not worry about oversavings. Say's Law (after Jean Baptiste Say, a French economist) suggested that there could never be an excess of savings because savings or their equivalent must be spent either as consumption or as investment. In other words, aggregate demand for all goods must always equal aggregate supply. This thinking was an article of faith among economists for over one hundred years. As Franco Modigliani observes:

> The fact that capital is a necessary condition for economic development, and that it is in very limited supply, has been widely recognized. . . . this attitude toward capital can be traced back to the origins of economics and it is for this reason that saving has typically been regarded as a virtuous social act.
>
> Nonetheless, it must be borne in mind that there has been a brief but influential interval during which, under the impact of the Great Depression and Keynes' *General Theory*, saving came to be regarded with suspicion, as potentially economically disruptive and harmful to social welfare. The period in question was between the mid-1930s to the late 1940s or early 1950s. Thrift was a potential enemy because it might result in an "inadequate" demand—that is, in an aggregate demand lower than the capacity of the economy. Indeed, the act of saving was seen as reducing one component of demand, consumption, without systematically and automatically giving rise to an expansion of the other component, investment. . . . In particular, oversaving was seen as having played a major role in the Great Depression, and there was widespread fear that it might occur again in the post-war period. . . . It is interesting that the impetus for the systematic study of saving behaviour was largely the result of this concern with the role of saving and the danger of oversaving. . . . Furthermore, in view of the concern at that time, it is not surprising that the emphasis was placed on the determinants of consumption as a component of aggregate demand. Thus, the subject came to be known as the study of the 'consumption function' rather than of the disaving function.[1,2]

Although the majority of economists have revised their thinking on the possibility of oversavings and its supposed negative effects, Keynes's influence has had a far more lasting impact, and is very much with us today, but it is sometimes unrecognized because *it is structured into the policies of the welfare state*. The Keynes-Beveridge welfare state that emerged before and after the Second World War, with its emphasis on employment and transfer income, was, and is, based decidedly on consumption, and very little on savings and investment.[3]

As shown in chapter 4, federal welfare expenditures, including both direct expenditures and tax expenditures, totaled $776 billion in fiscal year 1990. This large sum represents 53 percent of all federal expenditures. Of the $776 billion, the largest share (84 percent) is non-targeted and goes mostly to the nonpoor as income support. A significant portion of this income support for the nonpoor is in the form of direct welfare transfers masquerading as "social insurance." Relatively little (16 percent) of all federal welfare spending goes to targeted "safety net" programs for the poor. For both the nonpoor and the poor, the bulk of welfare expenditures is intended to support a higher level of immediate consumption.[4]

In this sense, the current design of U.S. social policy is flawed at its base. This is not to speak against materialism (although this might also be in order), but against consumptionism. In the United States, as Budget Director Richard Darman has said, we not only want things, we want them *now*, regardless of our ability to pay for them, and regardless of how our current indulgence might affect future generations.[5] Today, in the presence of large U.S. budget deficits and low economic growth, the wisdom of consumption-oriented social policies should be explicitly questioned. A different idea of the welfare state is required, a welfare state based less on spending and consumption, and more on savings and investment.

Low Savings

Compared with other industrialized nations, the United States is not saving very much. Although savings is difficult to define, and measurements vary, virtually all indicators record a slowdown in savings during the 1980s.[6] The net U.S. national savings rate—personal, corporate, and government combined—averaged only 3 percent to 4 percent during the 1980s, compared to about 7 percent to 8 percent during the 1950s, 1960s, and 1970s.

It may be helpful to compare the U.S. savings rate with those of other nations. According to data from the Office of Management and Budget, between 1980 and 1987, net savings as a percent of national income was 20.3 percent in Japan, 10.8 percent in West Germany, 9.9 percent in Canada, 8.6 percent in France, 6.3 percent in the United Kingdom, and 4.2 percent in the United States.[7]

The national savings rate has three primary components: personal savings, corporate savings, and government savings. The personal savings rate in the United States rose to a postwar high of over 9 percent in the early 1970s, but then declined sharply through 1987. In 1980,

Ronald Reagan made the low U.S. savings rate a theme of his presidential campaign, and one of the primary justifications for the huge tax cuts to corporations and wealthy individuals embodied in the 1981 tax law. Contrary to Reagan's predictions, however, personal savings as a percentage of disposable personal income fell from 7.5 percent in 1981 to 3.2 percent in 1987, the lowest level since 1947. Corporate savings declined dramatically during the 1980–82 recession and did not recover throughout the decade. In the public sector, federal government deficits (dissavings) expanded remarkably during the 1980s. Budget deficits averaged only 0.1 percent of GNP between 1950 and 1969; but during the 1980s, deficits averaged 4 percent of GNP.

No one can say whether the U.S. savings rate will recover. At this writing, it appears that the overall federal deficit may be eliminated gradually by rising surpluses in the Social Security Trust Fund.[8] But a larger question hangs over the future of private savings, both corporate and household. Possibly, American businesses will become more profitable and be able to retain some of the profits as savings, although the massive debt positions of many corporations will cut into future profits.

On the personal side, the maturing of the baby boomers means that this age-group is moving into a stage of life typically characterized by more savings. These are the "couch potato" years, when major purchases are already made, salaries are higher, and people begin to think about retirement. In 1989, the personal savings rate rose to over 5 percent, an encouraging trend. However, other observers point out that baby boomers have married later, and unlike their parents, they will be struggling with mortgage payments and college tuition for their children well into their fifties and sixties. Consistent with this view, one study finds that Americans born after 1940 save less in their peak saving years than do Americans born before 1940. People born before 1940 are saving at around 10 percent; people born after 1940 are saving at around 4 percent.[9] These findings should give pause to those who predict that demographic changes alone will greatly alter personal savings rates.

Rising Debt

Internally, debt increased in all sectors of the U.S. economy during the 1980s, a pattern uncharacteristic of economic expansions. During an expansion, debt is usually reduced. Instead, by the end of 1989, there was

$9.7 trillion in government and private debt outstanding in the United States, having risen 50 percent faster than GNP during the 1980s.[10]

A large portion of the debt is federal government debt. The total federal debt, at this writing, is about $3 trillion. To put this almost unfathomable number in perspective, one trillion dollars in hundred-dollar bills, placed end to end, across land and sea, would reach around the earth at the equator thirty-four times. The federal debt is three times this amount, meaning that the line of hundred-dollar bills would go around the earth more than one hundred times.[11]

Corporations have fared no better than government. Between the end of 1979 and the end of 1988, the private debt of nonfinancial institutions rose from $2.9 trillion to $6.7 trillion.[12] Interest payments of U.S. corporations as a percentage of pretax earnings rose from 18 percent in 1985 to a debilitating 34 percent in 1989. Moreover, corporate debt is unevenly distributed; many companies are highly leveraged; and the stage is set for business bankruptcies in these companies during the next recession.

Like government and businesses, consumers have relied on borrowing to expand their spending. During the 1980s, U.S. household liabilities rose faster than household assets.[13] About 40 percent of the growth in household spending between 1983 and 1988 was financed by installment debt and home equity loans, up from 20 percent in previous cyclical expansions. Consumer installment credit, adjusted for inflation, surged 60 percent between 1980 and 1988.

In sum, the nation has gone dramatically into hock. I believe it was Senator Moynihan who commented that, during the 1980s, the United States "borrowed a trillion dollars and threw a party." However, he was speaking only about the federal government when he made this statement. The nation as a whole borrowed and spent several trillions, with precious little to show for it.

Of course, debt is not necessarily bad—as long as it is used to develop productive capacity for future economic growth. But in the United States during the 1980s, little of the massive debt-ridden spending was toward capital investment.

Low Growth in Capital and Sluggish Investment

The accumulation of capital is essential for economic development. A high pool of savings provides a stable source of funding for corporations, supports government borrowing, lowers and stabilizes interest rates, reduces dependence on foreign capital, and enables more people to afford major purchases like houses and automobiles, which in turn keep the economy growing. Indeed, the process of capital accumulation is seen by some economists as the driving force in economic history.[14]

Unfortunately, since the mid-1960s, net private capital has grown more slowly in each successive business upswing.[15] Despite the lengthy economic expansion of the 1980s, domestic net worth, adjusted for inflation, increased only 18.4 percent between 1978 and 1988. The net worth of U.S. corporations—other than banks and financial businesses—actually *declined* in real terms during the 1980s.[16]

With declining net worth has come declining investment. Net annual investment declined from 7.2 percent of GNP during the 1960s, to 6.9 percent during the 1970s, to 4.8 percent during the 1980s. The United States now has the lowest rate of investment among the major industrial economies. In 1989, total capital investment in Japan, as a percentage of GNP, was well over double that of the United States.

The nature of U.S. investment has also changed during the 1980s. Much more has been spent in leveraged purchasing of other companies rather than in building new productive capacity. This "paper entrepreneurship" has generated quick profits for some investors, but in many respects, has not been of benefit to the economy as a whole.[17]

With the shortage of U.S.-generated investment capital, the value of foreign assets in this country has been rising more rapidly than the value of U.S. assets abroad. At the end of 1988, foreigners owned nearly $1.3 trillion worth of assets in the United States compared with $0.7 trillion worth of assets owned by the United States abroad.[18] Although there is some debate about how U.S. foreign assets are valued, and about whether the United States is in fact "behind" in assets held abroad, the trend has decidedly not been in the United States's favor.

Investment in public sector infrastructure—ports, airports, highways, bridges, water systems, sewage systems, mass transit—has declined as well. Investment in physical capital slid from 24.3 percent of federal spending in 1960 to 11.0 percent in 1990. As a proportion of private capital stock, public capital stock declined from more than 30 percent in 1970 to less than 24 percent in 1988.[19] This too has affected productivity. Private sector production and delivery of goods and services depend fundamentally on public sector capital stock. When a shipment is late due to bad roads or workers cannot get to work on time, productivity suffers. Productivity growth during the 1970s and 1980s was approximately half that of the 1950s and 1960s.

Explanations of Savings Patterns:
The Role of Institutions

There are many possible reasons for variations in savings rates. Some of these explanations are consistent with Modigliani's life cycle hypothesis (LCH), which suggests that people save while they work and then spend during retirement. Other explanations are not consistent with the LCH. As pointed out in chapters 6 and 7, individuals save for a variety of reasons other than retirement. Also, a wide range of institutional incentives and disincentives affect savings behavior, above and beyond the motives of individuals. These institutional factors include, especially, taxation policies and the accessibility of savings mechanisms.[20]

For example, one study examines the divergent savings patterns between the United States and Canada: "Private saving rates in the United States and Canada diverged dramatically over the last decade. . . . This difference in saving rates is largely the result of different tax structures and of the interaction between taxation and inflation." Measures to promote savings in Canada were instituted between 1972 and 1976. Canadians can now contribute up to thirty-five hundred dollars per year, tax free, to Registered Retirement Savings Plans, which are similar to IRAs in the United States. In addition, Canadians are not taxed on their first one thousand dollars of investment income each year. The effects of these institutional incentives have been very great indeed. Canadian personal savings rose from 3.3 percent of GNP between 1957 and 1971 to 7.6 percent between 1972 and 1985.[21]

Looking at another example, before World War II, Japan had one of the lowest savings rates among major nations. Following Japan's defeat, this rate plunged into dissavings. With most of the nation in rubble, the country needed massive capital investment. There was little possibility of borrowing abroad and no Marshall Plan was instituted for Japan. In this environment, the American Occupation brought in Joseph Dodge as the economic adviser. Dodge proposed very large income tax rates and tax exemptions for the interest earned on postal savings bank deposits. Against strong opposition from Keynesian economists, who urged demand stimulation, Dodge succeeded in pushing through his savings-oriented reforms. Six months later, the Japanese savings rate turned up and kept climbing. Practically every Japanese, including low-income individuals, had a savings account, and many had multiple accounts. The savings from these accounts, in large measure, created the pool of low-cost capital that financed the remarkable postwar recovery of the Japanese economy.[22,23]

It is important to note in the two examples above that *changes in institutional incentives for savings* were responsible for increased savings rates. It is all too easily—and incorrectly—assumed that other countries save more than the United States because of vaguely defined cultural differences. The popular press seems to view Americans as foolishly consumption-oriented, while the Japanese are seen as having a national characteristic of thriftiness. But at earlier times, Americans saved a great deal; and prior to World War II, the Japanese did not save much at all. There is simply no long-term historical evidence to support the notion that thriftiness is any more a cultural characteristic in Japan than in the United States. The Japanese savings rate rose after World War II only after strong institutionalized savings programs were established. In short, millions of individual Japanese have responded to incentives created by public policy.

In contrast, during the postwar period, the political economies of the United Kingdom and the United States did not create strong incentives for savings and investment, but rather created strong incentives for consumption. Tax codes encouraged debt over equity. During this period, there was little debate in Western Europe and the United States about the wisdom of this strategy—the consumption-driven economy was widely viewed as desirable. However, in retrospect, more skepticism would have been desirable. The major economic results of the postwar period are now clear: An investment-driven economy, over the long term, is superior to a consumption-driven economy. It is also clear that public policy has a leading role to play in determining one type of economy or the other.

The Role of Social Policy

America needs an investment boom, preferably from internal rather than external sources. This is not simply a matter of national pride, but of practical necessity. If the United States wants its standard of living to rise in the long run, it will have to consume less and save more. How best to improve overall savings is beyond the scope of this book, except for one element in the equation: social policy.

The ideal role of the federal government in social policy-making is long-term. Policy-making at the national level is not suited to short-term adjustments. It does not respond very well to business cycles, social upheavals, or unforeseen crises of any kind. The federal policy-making apparatus is too cumbersome and too slow; the timing is often bad. Therefore, the primary role of the federal government should be to establish a coherent set of long-term rules and incentives—taxes, expenditures, regulations, and general goals—that will be in the best interests of society as a whole, through all of its ups and downs. As suggested in this book, promotion of asset accumulation should be a major part of this long-term social policy strategy. It happens that capital accumulation is also consistent with the economic goals of the nation. Thus, although it is not usually thought of in these terms, *welfare policy should be, in part, a vehicle to develop capital*.

Welfare policy is typically viewed as a set of expenditures in long-term conflict with capital accumulation. There is a pervasive assumption among intellectuals in Western political economies that this conflict is inevitable. The suggestion in this book is that welfare policy, if asset-based, would not compete with—but rather would contribute to—capital accumulation and economic growth.

The heavily consumption-focused welfare state is no longer serving the best interests of the nation. Income-based policy has eased suffering under advanced capitalism, and will continue to do so, but this policy has not promoted economic development of poor households. Welfare policy should be based on a different conception of well-being, one that is more oriented toward the long term. Through the institutions and polices of the welfare state, the United States should encourage individual savings and investment.[24]

Would Individual Development Accounts Increase Savings?

Would Individual Development Accounts (see chapters 9 through 11) really increase the national savings rate? We cannot, in the absence of empirical evidence, be certain of the extent to which this would occur.

However, two points should be mentioned.

First, the nonpoor, although they would not receive deposit subsidies, would receive tax benefits. In this regard, IDAs would be very similar to the original IRAs, and we can look at the experience of IRAs to make predictions. A common critique of IRAs is that people shift money from other savings, thus not increasing the overall savings rate. However, the majority of studies suggest that shifting of funds for IRAs has been minimal. One study finds little substitution: "The vast majority of Individual Retirement Account contributions represent new saving."[25] IRA savings totaled about $45 billion in 1986, one-fourth of all U.S. personal savings during that year. Another study concurs that most money saved in IRA accounts is new savings: "We can decisively rule out reshuffling."[26] Moreover, IRA contributors are more likely to save in other forms as well.[27] To the extent that a program of Individual Development Accounts would provide tax benefits to the nonpoor, we can anticipate that the savings behavior would be similar to that of IRA participants: With attractive tax incentives, people would find new money to save.[28]

Second, as described in chapter 11, direct subsidies for IDAs, in the form of matching deposits, would go only to the poor. Of course, these subsidies would only be a transfer from government savings to personal savings. There is an open question about the extent to which the poor would participate with their own money. Total new savings of the poor would certainly be more modest than savings of the nonpoor. However, almost by definition, the asset poor would not be reshuffling assets in order to take advantage of an IDA program. They have no assets to reshuffle. Almost all their contributions to IDA accounts would be new savings. However small these amounts, they would contribute at least a little to the national savings rate.

Conclusion

Before savings by the poor are dismissed as inevitably inconsequential, we might recall Japan's postwar experience with millions of small savers, who played a decisive role in the process of capital formation. The United States, at this juncture in history, has lost virtually all institutional savings mechanisms for the poor. Indeed, current welfare policy *prevents* the poor from saving. As a nation, the United States would do well to re-create savings mechanisms for the poor in the form of IDAs, poor people's banks, postal savings, school-based savings, or other institutional arrangements that offer both convenient access and strong incentives to save.

In the postwar decades, the United States has been very clever in extending consumption and debt to virtually the entire population. This has occurred through all sorts of creative mechanisms, ranging from time payment plans, to credit card purchases, to home equity loans. Surely, if we make up our minds to do so, we can be similarly creative in extending savings and investment. In order to extend asset accumulation to the poor, a structured program and system of incentives would be required. A key point of this book is that welfare policy is a major vehicle that might be used for this purpose.

Notes

1. Franco Modigliani, *The Debate over Stabilization Policy*, Raffaele Mattioli Lectures, Bocconi University. Cambridge: Cambridge University Press, 1986, 121–23.

2. In fairness, Keynes is often wrongly interpreted regarding his warning on excess savings. He warned just as firmly against excess consumption. It seems very likely that Keynes, if he were alive today, would join in the questioning of very large budget deficits. He believed in using fiscal policy to dampen swings in the economy in *either* direction, and he was always ready to change his course accordingly. As one story goes, in the late 1930s, Keynes was chided by a friend for changing an economic analysis. Reportedly, Keynes responded to his friend: "When the facts change, I change my mind. What do you do, Sir?"

3. The modern Western welfare state is sometimes referred to as the Keynes-Beveridge welfare state. William Beveridge, like John Maynard Keynes, was highly influential in shaping welfare policies in the postwar United Kingdom, and indirectly in much of Western Europe and the United States.

4. The major exceptions to consumption-oriented welfare policy are the approximately $107 billion (fiscal year 1990) in transfers through the tax system that contribute directly to asset accumulation, mostly for the nonpoor, in the form of home equity and retirement pension funds. However, in macroeconomic terms, the portion of this capital that goes to housing, although desirable for individuals and families, is not the most productive investment for the nation as a whole. On the other hand, the large accumulations in retirement pension accounts *do* provide capital for investment—indeed, pension funds are now the single largest pool of investment capital in the United States.

5. Budget director Richard Darman's well-publicized phrase is cultural "now-now-ism" to describe America's consumption habits. This, says Darman, is a "short hand label for our collective short-sightedness, our obsession with the here and now, our reluctance to address the future." The entire nation, he says, is like the spoiled child in the television commercial who screams, "I want my Maypo! I

want it NOW!'" (see Alan Murray, "Dick Darman Wants His Maypo!" *Wall Street Journal*, July 31, 1989, A1).

6. Michael Boskin, "Issues in the Measurement and Interpretation of Saving and Wealth," Working Paper No. 2633. Cambridge, MA: National Bureau of Economic Research, 1988.

7. National savings rates for a single year, according to figures from the Organization for Economic Cooperation and Development (OECD), were as follows in 1987: Japan, 16.6 percent; France, 13.0 percent; West Germany, 12.2 percent; Canada, 9.4 percent; the United Kingdom, 5.6 percent; and the United States, 3.9 percent.

8. The Social Security Trust Fund will accumulate large surpluses well into the next century—unless Senator Moynihan's provocative proposal to cut Social Security taxes eventually alters this plan.

9. Michael Boskin and Lawrence Lau, "An Analysis of Post-War U.S. Consumption and Savings, Part II: Empirical Results," Working Paper No. 2606. Cambridge, MA: National Bureau of Economic Research, 1988.

10. In 1948, only three years after the close of an expensive war, total debt was less than that year's GNP. By 1980, the debt to GNP ratio had risen to 1.4; and by 1989 it was over 1.8.

11. In addition, as few people are aware, the federal government lends almost as much money as it borrows, and many of these loans are of questionable quality. From 1980 to 1988, while federal budget deficits totaled $1.4 trillion, the government issued $0.4 trillion of new direct loans, and $0.8 trillion in new primary loan guarantees. These figures omit secondary guarantees, deposit insurance, and activities of government-sponsored enterprises. Although accounting practices are often shoddy, and therefore the actual size of U.S. government obligations is not clear, the General Accounting Office warns that the U.S. government now lends, guarantees, or insures, about $5 trillion. Growing exposure to losses from these programs—from Guaranteed Student Loan defaults to savings and loan bailouts—suggests that federal credit may be out of control (William G. Gale, "The Big Debt Overhang," *Wall Street Journal*, October 25, 1989, A22).

12. In 1979, corporate debt in the United States equaled about 30 percent of the nation's annual output; by 1989, it was nearly 40 percent. Between 1984 and 1988, there was a net increase of $0.4 trillion in outstanding corporate bonds, much of it in the form of low-quality "junk bonds."

13. Household debt rose from 25 percent of disposable income in 1983 to 31 percent in 1987. In terms of GNP, household debt rose from 52 percent of GNP in 1983 to 62 percent in 1987.

14. Richard B. Du Boff, *Accumulation and Power: An Economic History of the United States*. Armonk, NY: M.E. Sharpe, 1989.

15. Like savings, investment—particularly net investment—is very difficult to measure. More confidence can be placed in the trends than in the exact numbers. Some analysts have argued that with increased international mobility of capital, the savings rate within a given country does not matter vis-à-vis investment. However, Martin Feldstein and Phillippe Bacchetta ("National Saving and International Investment," Working Paper No. 3164. Cambridge, MA: National Bureau of Economic Research, 1990), in a study of twenty-three industrial countries, conclude that a one-dollar increase in net domestic savings was associated with a

seventy-nine-cent increase in net domestic investment during the years 1980 through 1986, down somewhat from a ninety-one-cent increase during the 1960s and an eighty-six-cent increase during the 1970s. Thus, whereas mobility of international capital is playing a larger role, domestic saving is still the dominant factor in determining rates of investment. Moreover, the effect occurs very quickly. When savings change, according to Feldstein and Bacchetta, one-quarter of the effect on investment occurs within one year; one-half, within three years; and four-fifths, within six years.

16. U.S. Federal Reserve Board, *Balance Sheets for the U.S. Economy, 1949–1988*. Washington: U.S. Government Printing Office, 1989.

17. Taking a broader perspective, the role of accumulated wealth at the national level serves more than economic purposes. Many years ago, in the heyday of U.S. postwar prominence, John Kenneth Galbraith recognized the political and social importance of accumulated capital:

> One of the profound sources of American strength has been the margin of error provided by our endowment. . . . Wealth does more than provide a margin of error. . . . The cost of free education, social security, assistance to farmers and like measures of domestic welfare have been deeply disguised by the general increase in income. . . . Had the assessment of these costs been directly against the static incomes of those who paid but did not benefit, the debate concerning them would have been a good deal more bitter than it was. Wealth, and especially growing wealth, has not only been a solvent for mistakes. It has also been a solvent for what, in its absence, might have been grave social strains (John K. Galbraith, *American Capitalism*. Boston: Houghton Mifflin, 1952, 112–13).

18. U.S. Federal Reserve Board, 1989.

19. David Alan Aschauer, "Public Spending for Private Profit," *Wall Street Journal*, March 14, 1990, A14.

20. Many other factors might also affect savings rates. In one rather interesting study, it was found that countries tend to save less when a large fraction of their population thinks that a war is likely to occur during the next ten years. At the time of the study, the country that most expected another world war, and had the lowest savings rate, was the United States (Joel Slemrod, "Fear of Nuclear War and Intercountry Differences is the Rate of Saving," Working Paper No. 2801. Cambridge, MA: National Bureau of Economic Research, 1989). If this relationship between war expectations and savings is not entirely spurious, then the historic changes in the Soviet Union, by lowering expectations of world war, might contribute to a higher savings rate in the United States as well as throughout the world. This is a happy prospect, but it should be viewed with a measure of caution.

21. Lawrence Summers and Chris Carroll, "Why Have Private Saving Rates in the United States and Canada Diverged?" Working Paper No. 2319. Cambridge, MA: National Bureau of Economic Research, 1987.

22. Peter Drucker, "Japan's Not-So-Secret Weapon," *Wall Street Journal*, January 9, 1990, A14; and Fumio Hayashi, "Japan's Saving Rate: New Data and Reflections," Working Paper No. 3205. Cambridge: National Bureau of Economic Research, 1989.

23. The tax-benefited Japanese savings accounts were so successful that they were abandoned in 1988 under international pressure to boost consumption rather than savings.

24. Regarding benefits to the poor, the thinking in this book differs somewhat from that of Peter Peterson and Neil Howe (*On Borrowed Time: How the Growth in Entitlement Spending Threatens America's Future.* San Francisco: ICS Press, 1988), who argue very persuasively that entitlement-stimulated consumption is ruining the American economy and that more investment is needed. Peterson and Howe's vision is to better invest money in order to create a healthy economy, which, in turn, would provide a surplus to help the poor. My proposal, somewhat in contrast, is to make it possible for the poor, along with everyone else, to do the investing themselves. This might be thought of as an investment strategy *from the bottom*, merging the idea of social policy with the idea of economic development.

25. Steven Venti and David Wise, "Have IRAs Increased U.S. Saving? Evidence from Consumer Expenditure Surveys," Working Paper No. 2217. Cambridge, MA: National Bureau of Economic Research, 1987.

26. Daniel Feenberg and Jonathan Skinner, "Sources of IRA Saving," Working Paper No. 2845. Cambridge, MA: National Bureau of Economic Research, 1989.

27. Venti and Wise, 1987.

28. Also, if Social Security benefits were fully taxed to help pay for an IDA program (as suggested in chapter 11), we might expect that personal savings would rise as a result. Martin Feldstein ("Social Security, Induced Retirement and Aggregate Capital Accumulation," *Journal of Political Economy*, 82, 1974, 905–26) finds that Social Security depresses personal savings by 30 percent to 50 percent. Therefore, if Social Security benefits to the nonpoor are reduced through taxation, it is likely that personal savings would rise.

13 • Summary and Conclusion

The theme of this book can be summarized very simply: Asset accumulation and investment, rather than income and consumption, are the keys to leaving poverty. Therefore, welfare policy should promote asset accumulation—stakeholding—by the poor. An asset-based welfare policy would seek to combine welfare assistance with economic development.

The Current Vision:
Income-Based Policy for the Poor

Up to the present time, welfare theory and debate, from both conservative and liberal viewpoints, has taken for granted that income is an adequate definition of well-being, at least for the poor. This assumption is the foundation of the modern welfare state, and it has shaped almost all antipoverty policy (see chapters 2 through 5). This policy is characterized by means-tested cash transfers in programs like Aid to Families with Dependent Children, and transfers of goods and services in programs like Food Stamps, Medicaid, and rental subsidies for housing. The basic idea of these programs is to support a minimum level of consumption. In 1990, these means-tested programs totalled $125 billion in federal expenditures (see chapter 4).

This income-based support has greatly eased human suffering, and is absolutely essential, but it has not reduced poverty in any fundamental sense. Income-transfer policy for the poor is called *income maintenance*. After more than a half century of income-maintenance policy, we have confirmed that it is correctly named. The policy leads not to development but only to maintenance.

Asset-Based Policy for the Nonpoor

Over the years, the United States has developed a number of programs that can be described as asset-based, and they have been quite successful, but they have benefited the nonpoor almost exclusively. Most of these programs are structured into the tax system. The largest are tax subsidies for corporate and individual retirement pensions and home ownership. Through these two categories of tax transfers, totalling $107 billion in 1990 (see chapter 4), most American households have accumulated most of their wealth. In the vast majority of households, ordinary saving and investment outside the structure of these tax benefits is very limited.

The poor, by and large, do not benefit from these major tax benefits because they usually have jobs without retirement benefits, and they are less likely to be home owners. For those impoverished individuals who do have retirement funds or own their homes, tax benefits are small or nonexistent due to low marginal tax rates. Thus, the United States has asset-based policy for the nonpoor, but not for the poor.

A Different Vision:
Asset-Based Policy for the Poor

A more equitable and more productive policy would be to create a universal asset accumulation system open to all Americans, but with special incentives for the poor. In short, welfare policy would be designed, in part, to encourage and facilitate savings and investment among the poor.

Why are assets important? What do assets do for individuals and families that income alone does not do? Assets have important welfare effects *beyond consumption.* Simply put, when people are accumulating assets, they think and behave differently and the world responds to them differently as well. Assets (1) improve household stability; (2) psychologically connect people with a viable, hopeful future; (3) stimulate development of other assets, including human capital; (4) enable people to focus and specialize; (5) provide a foundation for risk taking; (6) increase personal efficacy, (7) increase social influence, (8) increase political participation, and (9) enhance the welfare of offspring (see chapter 8). Taken together, this cluster of effects far surpasses consumption as a long-term antipoverty strategy. In general, assets *connect* people to the economy and the society. If, as William Julius Wilson concludes, persistent poverty results from social and economic isolation,[1] then asset-based welfare policy would be a step toward breaking that pattern of isolation.

To a great extent, this policy could be funded by reallocating excessive welfare expenditures that currently go to the nonpoor, especially those that support luxury housing and excessive retirement benefits to people who do not need the money. Also, creative funding from the private sector and from participants would be encouraged. Early evidence suggests that asset-based welfare policy, because it is built on savings and investment, would be viewed very positively by the private sector.

An Emerging Trend

In recent years, a number of asset-based welfare experiments have emerged. The most well known are retirement accounts such as 401(k), 403(b), Keogh, Simplified Employee Pensions, and Individual Retirement Accounts. These tax-deferred retirement funds are an important precedent in universal asset-based welfare policy, although the current system of tax subsidies does not attract many poor depositors.

Another important asset-based development during the 1980s has been the proliferation of state-sponsored savings plans for higher education. These savings plans take many different forms, some guaranteeing a certain rate of college tuition, and some providing tax-deferred or tax-exempt savings for college. Although these programs are universal in concept, there are, as yet, no special incentives or assistance to encourage the poor to participate in them.

Conceptually related to college savings plans, there is in the private sector a series of experiments to guarantee college tuition to students in poor inner-city neighborhoods. The first such experiment was by businessman Eugene Lang, who promised a class of Harlem sixth graders that he would pay for their college educations if they stayed in school. Lang's experiment has grown into the "I Have a Dream" Foundation, which now functions in more than twenty-four cities serving some five thousand young people. Other business leaders and corporations have followed Lang's example, as have some local and state governments. This tuition guarantee movement is of great significance for two reasons. First, it is a major application of asset-based welfare *for the poor*. And second, the corporate sector is playing a major role in developing this policy, which suggests that other creative asset-based initiatives, with cooperation between the public and private sectors, might be feasible.

Within traditional federal welfare programs, other asset-based welfare experiments are beginning to appear. Many of these have been stimulated by the Corporation for Enterprise Development in Washington, DC, which has promoted the idea of Transfer Payment Investment—giving welfare recipients the option of accumulating income transfers as capital for self-employment.[2]

These experiments suggest that asset-based welfare policy may be an emerging theme in the United States. As such programs develop, policymakers and the general public might begin to see these apparently isolated experiments as part of a larger movement toward asset-based policy. The concept should be further expanded to include more asset-based programs for the poor. At this writing, the Congress is considering capital gains tax cuts for the rich and Family Savings Plans for the middle class. Why not an asset accumulation policy for the poor as well?

Policy Proposal:
Individual Development Accounts

The proposal in this book is for a relatively simple and universal system of accounts. For the sake of discussion, I have called these Individual Development Accounts (IDAs). IDAs would be optional, earnings-bearing, tax-benefited accounts in the name of each individual, initiated as early as birth, and restricted to designated purposes. Regardless of the category of welfare policy (housing, education, self-employment, retirement, or other), assets would be accumulated in these long-term restricted accounts. The federal government would match or otherwise subsidize deposits for the poor, and there would be potential for creative financing from the private sector and account holders themselves. IDAs would be designed to promote long-range planning, savings and investment, and achievement of life goals.

The following principles would guide an IDA policy:
1. IDAs would complement rather than replace income-based policy;
2. IDAs would be universally available;
3. There would be greater subsidies for the poor;
4. Participation would be voluntary;
5. Responsibility would be shared—even the poorest people would be required to match government subsidies for deposits;
6. Accounts would be restricted for specific purposes, with heavy penalties for non-designated use;

7. Accumulation would be gradual;

8. There would be a limited number of investment options; and

9. The system would be used to increase economic information and training (see chapters 10 and 11).

In many respects, IDAs would be similar to IRAs, but there would be important differences: IDAs would be available to everyone; they would begin much earlier in the life cycle; they would serve a wider range of purposes; and they would rely on more varied sources of deposits, including government matching funds for the poor. In a sense, the IDA concept would encompass the IRA concept and expand it.

There are many possible applications for Individual Development Accounts. In general, asset-based policies would be preferable in those situations where accumulation is highly desirable and has important consequences. The most promising applications appear to be in financing of postsecondary education, home ownership, capital for self-employment, and funds for retirement security (see chapter 11).

Structure and Control of IDA Accounts

Asset-based welfare policy requires not only a new way of thinking about policy content, but also a new way of thinking about policy structure. In other words, asset-based policy is not merely a matter of social programs, but of a policy framework that can, insofar as possible, integrate numerous policy efforts into a single system. This system should be designed so that a wide variety of creative asset-based welfare initiatives by governments, corporations, nonprofit organizations, and households can mesh and complement one another. The system should be able to grow and adapt, facilitate experiments, and expand successful efforts.

Therefore, the structure for asset-based welfare is the most critical element in policy design. Once a structure is in place that facilitates asset accumulation by the poor, even if modestly funded at the outset, then through creative approaches and where success is proven, the programs might expand.

The IDA system would function in a manner similar to a defined contribution retirement plan, with perhaps three investment options—a stock fund, a bond fund, and a money market fund. Deposits and earnings would accumulate in the name of each account holder, who would make decisions on investments among the three options. Ultimate benefits would not be defined in advance, but instead would depend on the success of individual investment strategies.

The entire IDA system would be directed by an independent board of trustees at the national level, overseeing a group of private investment companies which would compete for share of investment funds on the basis of earnings performance. The board of trustees would establish basic investment guidelines, but the board would not participate directly in investment decisions (see chapter 10).

Use of private sector fund managers would greatly reduce the federal bureaucracy required to manage IDA funds, and would create a competitive investment situation through which investment gains are likely to be highest over the long term.

Unlike the Social Security Trust Fund, IDA accounts would be fully funded in the name of each participant, that is, actual money would be set aside and invested in individual accounts. Unlike the Social Security Trust Fund, resources in IDA accounts would not be lent at below market rates to finance other government programs, nor would accumulations in IDA accounts be used in budgetary calculations to offset federal government deficits.

In developing a single system for all types of asset-based welfare programs, the government would limit inefficiency and better integrate various asset-based welfare policies into an overall strategy. Also, the policy would essentially operate directly to the beneficiary, with very limited intervention by a welfare bureaucracy.

Alternatives

The proposal for Individual Development Accounts is only one possible application of asset-based welfare policy. This proposal is presented to give substance to the idea, and hopefully, to initiate wider discussion and debate. Other ownership and equity-oriented polices are possible as well, as complements or as alternatives to IDAs. These include poor people's banks, school-based savings, postal savings, urban homesteading programs, and investment clubs for the poor. Although some of these suggestions may sound peculiar at first, these are the types of programs that must be developed if poverty is to be reduced in the United States. In general, the key is to establish institutionalized, trustworthy, opportunities and incentives for ordinary people, including the poor, to save and invest for the long term. These institutional mechanisms—far more than vague "cultural characteristics"—are responsible for high savings rates in some countries, such as Japan, and low savings rates in other countries, such as the United States (see chapter 12).

Demonstration, Experimentation, Research

In this book, I have attempted to cover a lot of ground, both theoretically and practically. While I hope this effort will stimulate a new way of thinking about well-being and welfare policy, I am under no illusion that all of the questions have been answered. Indeed, ten additional questions arise for each one that is addressed. A great deal of work remains to be done. In my view, there are two major agendas for future inquiry.

The first agenda is practical. If the program of Individual Development Accounts—or some other asset-based welfare proposal—is deemed to be a promising idea, how can this strategy be effectively tested and implemented? Experiments and demonstration projects should focus on what structures of IDA incentives are most successful and for whom they succeed. Problems of implementation will inevitably arise. For example, one problem will be how to assure that resources in restricted accounts are used for the purposes specified. The tremendous need for public information and education will present other problems. Institutionally, it may be possible to use the schools, traditional welfare organizations, housing authorities, private banks, investment companies, and other institutions to develop asset-based programs. As particular approaches prove successful, as problems are worked out, and as regulations are developed, programs should then be expanded.

As indicated by the several examples mentioned in the book, asset-based welfare policy is already evolving in one form or another at local, state, and federal levels. Also, savings plans and asset accumulation schemes have been widely applied in "developing" countries. All of these experiments should be carefully monitored. New U.S. experiments should be introduced in small demonstration projects. Most importantly, policy makers should give asset-based proposals special scrutiny as welfare reform proposals are considered. In the short term, this practical research agenda will be in the forefront.

The second agenda is theoretical. It involves the confirmation and elaboration of welfare effects of asset accumulation. These are summarized in the nine propositions presented in chapter 8, including improved household stability, greater orientation toward the future, and development of other assets, including human capital. The nine propositions stand on substantial empirical support and connect with established theories. Moreover, I have found that these propositions have strong intuitive appeal to most people. However, the propositions must be more carefully specified and confirmed. To what extent, for whom, and under what circumstances, are psychological, social, and economic effects of assets accumulation realized? Can the propositions be elaborated and refined? Is it possible to move toward more precise explication of some of the propositions? Can the propositions be combined into a more complex theory? Ultimately, the development and testing of this theoretical knowledge about the effects of asset-holding could be far-reaching in its impact on theories of welfare and social policy. If the propositions turn out to be fruitful, the theoretical research agenda will require a series of carefully designed studies over a period of years.

Welfare as Investment

In closing, the following thought comes to mind: It is probably a strategic error to think about welfare policy for the poor as a separate, residual function. Such policy should be integrated with the major social, economic, and political purposes of the nation. In essence, assistance to the poor should not be viewed entirely in humanitarian terms, but also as an investment in the future. This is not to abandon the ideas of need and caring, but simply, in addition, to recognize and articulate that well-being and productivity of the poor are in the economic and social interests of society as a whole.

In an age of advanced industrial capitalism, where brains are more important than brawn, it is in everyone's interests to have more people function as effectively as possible. The ideas in this book suggest that the way to achieve this goal is to make more people stakeholders. This might be thought of as a more democratic capitalism. The underlying assumption is that the national economic pie is not finite. It can grow with the spirit and ability of the people. Paradoxically, the more people who have a piece of the pie, the faster it will grow.[3]

Therefore, it would seem to be in the nation's interest to promote, through welfare policy, broader participation in asset accumulation. Robert Morris reminds us that ideas about welfare policy do not remain the same over time, and that periodically there are transformations in U.S. history under which new concepts of welfare are forged.[4,5] It is not unreasonable to guess that the United States is poised for such a period of reconceptualization. The concepts of asset accumulation and investment, rather than income and spending, may provide a theoretical and practical foundation for this new direction.

Notes

1. William J. Wilson, *The Truly Disadvantaged: The Inner City, the Underclass, and Public Policy.* Chicago: University of Chicago Press, 1987.

2. Robert E. Friedman, *The Safety Net as Ladder: Transfer Payments and Economic Development.* Washington: The Council of State Policy and Planning Agencies, 1988.

3. Regarding the invigorating effects of widespread asset accumulation, one of the more enduring statements is by Sir Francis Bacon: "Wealth is like muck. It is not good but if it be spread."

4. Robert Morris, *Rethinking Social Welfare: Why Care for the Stranger?* New York: Longman, 1986; also William McLoughlin, *Revivals, Awakenings and Reform.* Chicago: University of Chicago Press, 1978.

5. Edward Weaver, former executive director of the American Public Welfare Association, in personal communication, suggests that

> The 'great awakening' rationale might better be characterized as a 'crisis' which cannot be avoided. To call the policy actions in the mid-1930s or the late 1960s the result of great awakenings (which sounds like we act out of positive enlightenment), is a real stretch. Those policy advances were possible because of an overarching crisis which threatened to destroy all of us—rich and poor alike.

If Weaver is correct about this interpretation, perhaps the growing crises of the failure of income-transfer policy in reducing poverty and the shortage of domestically generated capital in the United States might spur the nation toward asset-based welfare policy.

Selected References

Abramovitz, Mimi. 1983. "Everyone Is on Welfare: The Role of Redistribution in Social Policy Revisited." *Social Work*, 28(6):440–45.

———. 1988. *Regulating the Lives of Women*. Boston: South End Press.

Adler, Mortimer. 1984. *A Vision of the Future*. New York: Macmillan.

Ahluwalia, M.S. 1976. "Income Inequality—Some Dimensions of the Problem." In *Redistribution with Growth*, ed. H. Chenery et al. London: Oxford University Press, 3–37.

Aldrich, Nelson W., Jr. 1988. *Old Money: The Making of America's Upper Class*. New York: Alfred A. Knopf.

Ando, Faith, and Associates, Inc. 1989. *Minorities, Women, Veterans, and the 1982 Characteristics of Business Owners Survey: A Preliminary Analysis*, Report No. PB89–115091/AS. Springfield, VA: National Technical Information Service.

Andrisani, Paul. 1977. "Internal-External Attitudes, Personal Initiative, and the Labor Market Experience of Black and White Men." *Journal of Human Resources*, 12:308–38.

———. 1981. "Internal-External Attitudes, Sense of Efficacy, and Labor Market Experience: A Reply to Duncan and Morgan." *Journal of Human Resources*, 16:658–66.

Angle, John. 1986. "The Surplus Theory of Social Stratification and the Size Distribution of Personal Wealth." *Social Forces* 65:293–326.

Apgar, William, Jr., and DiPasquale, Denise. 1989. *The State of the Nation's Housing*. Cambridge, MA: Harvard University Joint Center for Housing Studies.

Arrow, Kenneth J. 1985. "Distributive Justice and Desirable Ends of Economic Activity." In *Issues in Contemporary Macroeconomics and Distribution*, ed. George R. Freiwel. Albany: State University of New York Press, 134–56.

Ashford, Douglas E. 1986. *The Emergence of the Welfare States*. Oxford: Basil Blackwell.

Auerbach, Alan J., and Kotlikoff, Laurence J. 1989. "Demographics, Fiscal Policy, and U.S. Saving in the 1980s and Beyond." Working Paper No. 3150. Cambridge, MA: National Bureau of Economic Research.

Bane, Mary J., and Ellwood, David. 1983. "Slipping into and out of Poverty: The Dynamics of Spells." Working Paper No. 1199. Cambridge, MA: National Bureau of Economic Research.

Banfield, Edward. 1974. *The Unheavenly City Revisited*. Boston: Little, Brown.

Barlow, Robin; Brazer, Harvey; and Morgan, James. 1985. *Economic Behavior of the Affluent*. Washington, DC: The Brookings Institution.

Beach, Charles M. 1989. "Dollars and Dreams: A Reduced Middle Class? Alternative

Explanations." *Journal of Human Resources* 24 (1): 162–93.

Becker, Gary S. 1976. *The Economic Approach to Human Behavior*. Chicago: University of Chicago Press.

Birdsall, William C. 1986. "The Value of the Official Poverty Statistics." Working Paper No. 86–01. Ann Arbor: School of Social Work, University of Michigan.

Blank, Rebecca M. 1986. "How Important is Welfare Dependence?" Working Paper No. 2026. Cambridge, MA: National Bureau of Economic Research.

Blank, Rebecca, and Rosen, Harvey. 1989. "Recent Trends in Housing Conditions among the Urban Poor." NBER Working Paper No. 2886. Cambridge, MA: National Bureau of Economic Research.

Blau, Francine D., and Graham, John W. 1989. "Black/White Differences in Wealth and Asset Accumulation." Working Paper No. 2898. Cambridge, MA: National Bureau of Economic Research.

Blau, Peter M., and Duncan, Otis Dudley. 1967. *The American Occupational Structure*. New York: John Wiley & Sons.

Blinder, Alan S. 1976. "Inequality and Mobility in the Distribution of Wealth." *Kyklos* 29:607–38.

Block, Fred; Cloward, Richard A.; Ehrenreich, Barbara; and Piven, Frances Fox. 1987. *The Mean Season: The Attack on the Welfare State*. New York: Pantheon Books.

Boskin, Michael. 1988. "Issues in the Measurement and Interpretation of Saving and Wealth." Working Paper No. 2633. Cambridge, MA: National Bureau of Economic Research.

Boskin, Michael, and Lau, Lawrence. 1988. "An Analysis of Post-War U.S. Consumption and Savings, Part II: Empirical Results." Working Paper No. 2606. Cambridge, MA: National Bureau of Economic Research.

Boulding, Kenneth. 1958. *Principles of Economic Policy*. Englewood Cliffs, NJ: Prentice-Hall.

Bourdieu, Pierre. 1973. "Cultural Reproduction and Social Reproduction." In *Knowledge, Education and Cultural Change*, ed. Richard Brown. London: Tavistock.

———. 1984. *Distinction: A Social Critique of the Judgement of Taste*. Cambridge, MA: Harvard University Press.

Bowles, Samuel. 1972. "Schooling and Inequality from Generation to Generation." *Journal of Political Economy* 80:S219–51.

Briar, Katharine, ed. 1986. *The Unemployed: Policies and Services*, Report from Working Group 9. Thirteenth European Regional Symposium on Social Welfare. Helsinki: International Council on Social Welfare.

Brittain, John A. 1977. *The Inheritance of Economic Status*. Washington, DC: Brookings Institution.

Browne, R.S. 1974. "Wealth Distribution and Its Impact on Minorities." *The Review of Black Political Economy* 4 (4): 27–37.

Buchanan, James M., and Wagner, Richard E. 1977. *Democracy in Deficit: The Political Legacy of Lord Keynes*. New York: Academic Press.

Burtless, Gary. 1986. "The Work Response to a Guaranteed Income: A Survey of Experimental Evidence." In *Lessons from the Income Maintenance Experiments*, ed. Alicia Munnell. Boston: Federal Reserve Bank of Boston.

———. 1987. "Inequality in America: Where Do We Stand?" *The Brookings Review* (Summer): 9–16.

Bush, Malcolm. 1988. *Families in Distress: Public, Private, and Civic Responses*. Berkeley and Los Angeles: University of California Press.

Butler, Stuart, and Kondratas, Anna. 1987. *Out of the Poverty Trap: A Conservative Strategy for Welfare Reform.* New York: Free Press.

Carter, Charles 1968. *Wealth.* New York: Basic Books.

Charles, Murray. 1984. *Losing Ground: American Social Policy 1950–1980.* New York: Basic Books.

Coleman, James S. 1988. "Social Capital in the Creation of Human Capital." *American Journal of Sociology* 94:S95-S120.

Commager, Henry Steele. 1967. "Appraisal of the Welfare State." In *The Welfare State,* ed. Charles Schottland. New York: Harper Torchbooks, 84–90.

Cottingham, Phoebe H., and Ellwood, David T., eds. 1989. *Welfare Policy for the 1990s.* Cambridge, MA: Harvard University Press.

Cowell, F.A. 1977. *Measuring Inequaltiy.* Oxford: Philip Allan.

Dahrendorf, Ralf. 1979. *Life Chances: Approaches to Social and Political Theory.* Chicago: University of Chicago Press.

Danziger, Sheldon, and Gottschalk, Peter. 1986. "Work, Poverty, and the Working Poor: A Multifaceted Problem." *Monthly Labor Review* 109:17–21.

———. 1988–89. "Increasing Inequality in the United States: What We Know and What We Don't." *Journal of Post Keynesian Economics* 11 (2): 174–95.

Danziger, Sheldon; Gottschalk, Peter; and Smolensky, Eugene. 1989. "How the Rich Have Fared." *American Economic Review* 79 (2): 310–14. Papers and Proceedings of the Annual Meeting of the American Economic Association, New York, December 1988.

Danziger, Sheldon; Haveman, Robert; and Plotnick, Robert. 1981. "How Income Transfer Programs Affect Work, Savings, and the Income Distribution: A Critical Review." *Journal of Economic Literature* 19:975–1028.

Danziger, Sheldon, and Plotnick, Robert. 1986. "Poverty and Policy: Lessons of the Last Two Decades." *Social Service Review* 60 (1): 34–51.

Davis, Kingsley, and Moore, Wilbert. 1945. "Some Principles of Stratification." *American Sociological Review* 10 (2): 242–49.

Deaton, Richard Lee. 1989. *The Political Economy of Pensions: Power, Politics, and Social Change in Canada, Great Britain, and the United States.* Vancouver: University of British Columbia Press.

de Tocqueville, Alexis. [1835] 1969. *Democracy in America.* Garden City: Anchor Books.

Dobelstein, Andrew W. 1986. *Politics, Economics, and Public Welfare,* 2nd ed. Englewood Cliffs, NJ: Prentice-Hall.

Domhoff, G. William. 1971. *The Higher Circles: The Governing Class in America.* New York: Vintage.

Du Boff, Richard B. 1989. *Accumulation and Power: An Economic History of the United States.* Armonk, NY: M.E. Sharpe, Inc.

Du Bois, W.E.B. 1968. *Black Reconstruction.* Cleveland: Meridian Books.

———. [1903] 1970. *The Souls of Black Folk.* Greenwich, CT: Fawcett Publications.

Duesenberry, James. 1967. *Income, Saving and the Theory of Consumer Behavior.* Cambridge, MA: Harvard University Press.

Dugdale, Richard L. 1910. *The Jukes.* 4th ed. New York: G.P. Putnam's Sons.

Duncan, Greg, et al. 1984. *Years of Poverty, Years of Plenty.* Ann Arbor: Survey Research Center, Institute for Social Research, University of Michigan.

Duncan, Greg; Hill, Martha; and Hoffman, Saul. 1988. "Welfare Dependence within and across Generations." *Science* 239:467–70.

Edelman, Marian Wright. 1987. *Families in Peril: An Agenda for Social Change.* Cambridge, MA: Harvard University Press.

Ellwood, David T. 1987. "Understanding Dependency: Choices, Confidence, or Culture?" Paper prepared for the U.S. Department of Health and Human Resources, Center for Human Resources, Brandeis University.

————. 1988. *Poor Support: Poverty in the American Family.* New York: Basic Books.

Ellwood, David T., and Summers, Lawrence H. 1985. "Poverty in America: Is Welfare the Answer to the Problem?" Working Paper No. 1711. Cambridge, MA: National Bureau of Economic Research.

Etzioni, Amitai. 1988. *The Moral Dimension: Toward a New Economics.* New York: Free Press.

Farkas, George; Grobe, Robert; and Sheehan, Daniel. 1990. *Human Capital or Cultural Capital.* Hawthorne, NY: Aldine de Gruyter.

Feenberg, Daniel, and Skinner, Jonathan. 1989. "Sources of IRA Saving." NBER Working Paper No. 2845. Cambridge, MA: National Bureau of Economic Research.

Feldstein, Martin. 1970. "Temporary Layoffs in the Theory of Unemployment." *Journal of Political Economy* 78:937–58.

————. 1974. "Social Security, Induced Retirement and Aggregate Capital Accumulation." *Journal of Political Economy* 82:905–26.

Feldstein, Martin, and Bacchetta, Phillippe. 1990. "National Saving and International Investment." Working Paper No. 3164. Cambridge, MA: National Bureau of Economic Research.

Finn, Charles. 1989. *Mortgage Lending in Boston Neighborhoods, 1981–1987.* Boston: Boston Redevelopment Authority.

Fiske, S.T., and Linville, P.W. 1980. "What Does the Schema Concept Buy Us?" *Personality and Social Psychology Bulletin* 6:543–57.

Foner, Philip S. 1955. *The Life and Writings of Frederick Douglass.* 4 vols. New York: International Publishers.

Ford Foundation. 1989. *The Common Good: Social Welfare and the American Future.* New York: Ford Foundation.

Franklin, John Hope. 1969. *From Slavery to Freedom.* New York: Vintage Books.

Frazier, E. Franklin. 1962. *Black Bourgeoisie.* New York: Collier.

Friedman, Milton. 1957. *A Theory of the Consumption Function.* Princeton, NJ: Princeton University Press.

Friedman, Robert E. 1988. *The Safety Net as Ladder: Transfer Payments and Economic Development.* Washington, DC: The Council of State Policy and Planning Agencies.

Fromm, Eric. 1966. *Marx's Concept of Man.* Trans. Tom Bottomore. New York: Frederick Ungar.

Galbraith, John K. 1952. *American Capitalism.* Boston: Houghton Mifflin.

————. 1958. *The Affluent Society.* Boston: Houghton Mifflin.

Gans, Herbert. 1972. "Positive Functions of Poverty." *American Journal of Sociology* 78:275–89.

Gilbert, Neil. 1983. *Capitalism and the Welfare State.* New Haven: Yale University Press.

————. 1986. "The Welfare State Adrift." *Social Work* 31 (4): 251–55.

Gilbert, Neil, and Gilbert, Barbara. 1989. *The Enabling State: Modern Welfare Capitalism in America.* New York: Oxford University Press.

Gilder, George. 1981. *Wealth and Poverty.* New York: Basic Books.

Glazer, Nathan. 1988. *The Limits of Social Policy.* Cambridge, MA: Harvard University Press.

Goddard, Henry H. 1912. *The Kallikak Family*. New York: Macmillan.

Gough, Ian. 1979. *The Political Economy of the Welfare State*. London: Macmillan.

Gouldner, Lawrence. 1989. "Tax Policy, Housing Prices, and Housing Investment." Working Paper No. 2814. Cambridge, MA: National Bureau of Economic Research.

Granovetter, M. 1985. "Economic Action and Social Structure: The Problem of Embeddedness." *American Journal of Sociology* 91:481–510.

Halle, David. 1984. *America's Working Man: Work, Home, and Politics among Blue-Collar Property Owners*. Chicago: University of Chicago Press.

Harmon, J. H., Jr.; Lindsey, Arnett; and Woodson, Carter G. 1929. *The Negro as a Business Man*. College Park, MD: McGrath.

Harrington, Michael. 1962. *The Other America*. New York: Macmillan.

———. 1984. *The New American Poverty*. New York: Holt, Reinhart, and Winston.

Haveman, Robert. 1988a. "Conclusion." In *Modelling the Accumulation and Distribution of Wealth*, ed. Denis Kessler and André Masson. Oxford: Clarendon Press, 323–28.

———. 1988b. *Starting Even: An Equal-Opportunity Program to Combat the Nation's New Poverty*. New York: Simon and Schuster.

Hayashi, Fumio. 1989. "Japan's Saving Rate: New Data and Reflections." Working Paper No. 3205. Cambridge, MA: National Bureau of Economic Research.

Heclo, Hugh, and Madsen, Henrik. 1987. *Policy and Politics in Sweden*. Philadelphia: Temple University Press.

Heider, Fritz. 1958. *The Psychology of Interpersonal Relations*. New York: John Wiley & Sons.

Heilbroner, Robert L. 1985. *The Nature and Logic of Capitalism*. New York: Norton.

Henretta, John C. 1979. "Race Differences in Middle Class Lifestyle: The Role of Home Ownership." *Social Science Research* 8: 63–78.

Higgs, Robert. 1982. "Accumulation of Property by Southern Blacks before World War I." *American Economic Review* 72 (4): 725–37.

Hoff, Marie D. 1986. "Response to the Catholic Bishops' Letter on Economic Justice: Implications for Social Welfare." Ph.D. diss. University of Washington.

Hunter, Robert. 1904. *Poverty*. New York: Macmillan.

Hurd, Michael, and Mundaca, Gabriela. 1988. "The Importance of Gifts and Inheritances among the Affluent." NBER Working Paper No. 2415. Cambridge, MA: National Bureau for Economic Research.

Hurst, Charles E. 1979. *The Anatomy of Social Inequality*. St. Louis: C.V. Mosby.

Huxley, Thomas H. [1894] 1902. *Evolution and Ethics and Other Essays*. New York: D. Appleton.

Janowitz, Morris. 1976. *Social Control of the Welfare State*. Chicago: University of Chicago Press.

———. 1978. *The Last Half-Century*. Chicago: University of Chicago Press.

Jencks, Christopher et al. 1972. *Inequality: A Reassessment of the Effect of Family and Schooling in America*. New York: Basic Books.

Johnson, Alice. 1989. "Female-Headed Homeless Families and the Housing Market." *Affilia, Journal of Women and Social Work* 4 (4): 23–39.

Jones, Alfred Winslow. 1941. *Life, Liberty, and Property*. Philadelphia: J.B. Lippincott.

Kearl, James; Pope, Clayne; and Wimmer, Larry. 1980. "The Distribution of Wealth in a Settlement Economy: Utah, 1850–1870." *Journal of Economic History*, 40:477–96.

Kelley, R.E., and Michela, J.L. 1980. "Attribution Theory and Research." *Annual Review of Psychology* 31:457–501.

Kellogg, Paul, ed. 1909–14. *The Pittsburgh Survey*, 6 vols. New York: Russell Sage Foundation.

Kelso, Louis O., and Adler, Mortimer J. 1958. *The Capitalist Manifesto*. New York: Random House.

Kelso, Louis O., and Hetter, Patricia. 1967. *How to Turn Eighty Million Workers into Capitalists on Borrowed Money*. New York: Random House.

Kessler, Denis, and Masson, André. 1987. "Personal Wealth Distribution in France: Cross-Sectional Evidence and Extensions." In *Growth, Accumulation, and Unproductive Activity*, ed. Edward Wolff. Cambridge: Cambridge University Press, 141–76.

——— eds. 1988. *Modelling the Accumulation and Distribution of Wealth*. Oxford: Clarendon Press.

Kluegel, James, and Smith, Eliot. 1986. *Beliefs about Inequality*. New York: Aldine de Gruyter.

Kohn, Melvin; Naoi, Atushi; Schoenbach, Carrie; Schooler, Carmi; and Słomczyński, Kazimierz. 1990. "Position in the Class Structure and Psychological Functioning in the United States, Japan, and Poland." *American Journal of Sociology* 90:964–1008.

Kolko, Gabriel. 1962. *Wealth and Power in America*. New York: Praeger.

Kotlikoff, Laurence J. 1989. *What Determines Savings?* Cambridge: MIT Press.

Kotlikoff, Laurence J., and Summers, Lawrence. 1981. "The Role of Intergenerational Transfers in Aggregate Capital Accumulation." *Journal of Political Economy* 89:706–32.

Kotlikoff, Laurence J., and Wise, David A. 1989. *The Wage Carrot and the Pension Stick: Retirement Benefits and Labor Force Participation*. Kalamazoo: W.E. Upjohn Institute for Employment Research.

Kuznets, Simon. 1955. "Economic Growth and Income Inequality." *American Economic Review* 45:1–28.

Lampman, Robert. 1962. *The Share of Top Wealth-Holders in National Wealth, 1922–1956*. Princeton, NJ: Princeton University Press.

———. 1971. *Ends and Means of Reducing Income Poverty*. Chicago: Markham Publishing Co.

———. 1984. *Social Welfare Spending: Accounting for Changes from 1950 to 1978*. Orlando: Academic Press.

Lazear, Edward P., and Michael, Robert T. 1988. *Allocation of Income within the Household*. Chicago: University of Chicago Press.

Lazere, Edward; Leonard, Paul; and Kravitz, Linda. 1989. *The Other Housing Crisis: Sheltering the Poor in Rural America*. Washington, DC: Center on Budget and Policy Priorities.

Leiby, James. 1985. "Moral Foundations of Social Welfare and Social Work: A Historical View." *Social Work* 30:323–30.

Lenski, Gerhard. 1966. *Power and Privilege: A Theory of Social Stratification*. New York: McGraw-Hill.

Leonard, Paul; Dolbeare, Cushing; and Lazere, Edward. 1989. *A Place to Call Home: The Crisis in Housing for the Poor*. Washington, DC: Center on Budget and Policy Priorities and Low Income Housing Information Service.

Levitan, Sar, and Shapiro, Isaac. 1987. *Working but Poor: America's Contradiction*. Baltimore: Johns Hopkins University Press.

Levitan, Sar; Mangum, Garth; and Pines, Marion. 1989. *A Proper Inheritance: Investing in the Self-Sufficiency of Poor Families*. Washington, DC: Center for Social Policy Studies, George Washington University.

Levy, Frank. 1987. *Dollars and Dreams: The Changing American Income Distribution.* New York: Russell Sage Foundation.

Lewis, Oscar. 1966. *La Vida.* New York: Random House.

Lichtenstein, Jules H. 1989. "Measuring Self-Employment as a Micro-Business Phenomenon." Paper presented at conference, The Self-Employment Strategy: Building the New Economy, Toronto.

Lieberson, Stanley. 1980. *A Piece of the Pie: Black and White Immigrants Since 1880.* Berkeley and Los Angeles: University of California Press.

Light, Ivan. 1984. "Immigrant and Ethnic Enterprise in North America." *Ethnic and Racial Studies* 7 (2): 195–216.

Lowe, Stuart. 1988. "New Patterns of Wealth: The Growth of Owner Occupation." In *Money Matters: Income, Wealth and Financial Welfare,* ed. Robert Walker and Gillian Parker, London: Sage, 149–65.

Lowi, Theodore. 1969. *The End of Liberalism.* New York: Norton.

McLoughlin, William. 1978. *Revivals, Awakenings and Reform.* Chicago: University of Chicago Press.

McNulty, Paul. 1980. *The Origins and Development of Labor Economics.* Cambridge: MIT Press.

MacPherson, C. B., ed. 1978. *Property: Mainstream and Critical Positions.* Toronto: University of Toronto Press.

Malthus, Thomas Robert. [1798] 1970. *An Essay on the Principle of Population.* London: Penguin Books.

Mandler, G. 1985. *Cognitive Psychology.* Hillsdale, NJ: Lawrence Erlbaum Associates.

Marable, Manning. 1983. *How Capitalism Underdeveloped Black America.* Boston: South End Press.

Margo, Robert. 1984. "Accumulation of Property by Southern Blacks before World War I: Comment and Further Evidence." *American Economic Review* 74 (4): 768–76.

Markowitz, Harry. 1952. "Portfolio Selection." *Journal of Finance* 7:77–91.

Marshall, Alfred. 1920. *Principles of Economics.* 8th ed. London: Macmillan.

Marx, Karl. [1849] 1950. *Wage Labour and Capital.* In *Selected Works. In Two Volumes.* Moscow: Foreign Languages Publishing House.

———. [1867] 1967. *Capital,* 3 vols.

Massey, Douglas, and Eggers, Mitchell. 1990. "The Ecology of Inequality: Minorities and the Concentration of Poverty, 1970–1980." *American Journal of Sociology* 95 (5): 1153–88.

Mayer, Susan, and Jencks, Christopher. 1989. "Poverty and the Distribution of Material Hardship." *Journal of Human Resources* 24 (1): 88–114.

Mead, Lawrence. 1986. *Beyond Entitlement: The Social Obligations of Citizenship.* New York: Free Press.

———. 1989. "The Logic of Workfare: The Underclass and Work Policy." *Annals of the American Academy of Political and Social Science* 501:156–69.

Meier, August, and Rudwick, Elliott. 1976. *From Plantation to Ghetto.* 3d ed. New York: Hill and Wang.

Miller, S.M., and Roby, P. 1970. *The Future of Inequality.* New York: Basic Books.

Mills, C. Wright. 1953. *White Collar: The American Middle Classes.* New York: Oxford University Press.

———. 1956. *The Power Elite.* New York: Oxford University Press.

————. 1959. *The Sociological Imagination*. New York: Oxford University Press.

Minsky, Hyman. 1986. *Stabilizing an Unstable Economy*. New Haven: Yale University Press.

Mishra, Ramesh. 1984. *The Welfare State in Crisis*. New York: St. Martin's Press, 176–78.

Modigliani, Franco. 1986. *The Debate over Stabilization Policy*. Raffaele Mattioli Lectures, Bocconi University. Cambridge: Cambridge University Press.

Modigliani, Franco, and Brumberg, Richard. 1954. "Utility Analysis and the Consumption Function: An Interpretation of Cross-Section Data." In *Post-Keynesian Economics*, ed. Kenneth K. Kurihara. New Brunswick, NJ: Rutgers University Press.

Modigliani, Franco, and Pogue, Gerald A. 1974. "An Introduction to Risk and Return." *Financial Analysts Journal* 30 (March–April): 68–80; and (May–June): 69–88.

Morris, Michael, and Williamson, John B. 1986. *Poverty and Public Policy: An Analysis of Federal Intervention Efforts*. New York: Greenwood Press.

Morris, Robert. 1986. *Rethinking Social Welfare: Why Care for the Stranger?* New York: Longman.

Murray, Charles. 1984. *Losing Ground: American Social Policy 1950–1980*. New York: Basic Books.

————. 1988. *In Pursuit of Happiness and Good Government*. New York: Simon and Schuster.

Nenno, Mary. 1986. *New Money and New Methods: A Catalog of State and Local Initiatives in Housing and Community Development*. Washington, DC: National Association of Housing and Redevelopment Officials.

Nerlove, Marc; Razin, Assaf; and Sadka, Efraim. 1987. *Household and Economy: Welfare Economics of Endogenous Fertility*. New York: Academic Press.

Niebuhr, Reinhold. 1932. *The Contribution of Religion to Social Work*. New York: Columbia University Press.

North, Douglass. 1981. *Structure and Change in Economic History*. New York: Norton.

Novak, Michael, et al., eds. 1988. *The New Consensus on Family and Welfare*. Washington, DC: American Enterprise Institute.

O'Connor, James. 1973. *The Fiscal Crisis of the State*. New York: St. Martin's Press.

Offe, Claus. 1984. *Contradictions in the Welfare State*. Cambridge: MIT Press.

O'Hare, William P. 1983. *Wealth and Economic Status: A Perspective on Racial Inequality*. Washington, DC: Joint Center for Political Studies.

————. 1985. *Poverty in America: Trends and New Patterns*. Population Bulletin 40, no. 3. Washington, DC: Population Reference Bureau.

Okun, Arthur. 1975. *Equality and Efficiency: The Big Tradeoff*. Washington, DC: The Brookings Institution.

Oliver, Melvin, and Shapiro, Thomas. 1990. "Wealth of a Nation: A Reassessment of Asset Inequality in America Shows at Least One Third of Households Are Asset-Poor." *American Journal of Economics and Sociology* 49:129–51.

Olson, Mancur. 1965. *The Logic of Collective Action: Public Good and the Theory of Groups*. Cambridge: Harvard University Press.

Osberg, Lars. 1981. *Economic Inequality in Canada*. Toronto: Butterworths.

Osborne, David. 1988. *Laboratories of Democracy*. Cambridge, MA: Harvard Business School Press.

Osthaus, Carl R. 1976. *Freedmen, Philanthropy, and Fraud: A History of the Freedman's Savings Bank*. Urbana: University of Illinois Press.

Oubre, Claude F. 1978. *Forty Acres and a Mule: The Freedmen's Bureau and Black Land Ownership*. Baton Rouge: Louisiana State University Press.

Ozawa, Martha N. 1977. "Social Insurance and Redistribution." In *Jubilee for Our Times*, ed. Alvin Schorr. New York: Columbia University Press, 123–77.

———. 1986. "The Nation's Children: Key to a Secure Retirement." *New England Journal of Human Services* 6 (3): 12–19.

Pahl, Raymond E. 1984. *Divisions of Labor*. New York: Basil Blackwell.

Parsons, Talcott. 1951. *The Social System*. Glencoe, IL: Free Press.

Peterson, Peter G., and Howe, Neil. 1988. *On Borrowed Time: How the Growth of Entitlement Spending Threatens America's Future*. San Francisco: Institute for Contemporary Studies.

Pinker, Robert. 1982. *Theory, Ideology, and Social Policy*, SWRC Reports and Proceedings No. 26. Kensington, New South Wales: Social Welfare Research Center.

Piven, Frances Fox, and Cloward, Richard A. 1971. *Regulating the Poor: The Functions of Social Welfare*. New York: Vintage.

———. 1982. *The New Class War: Reagan's Attack on the Welfare State and Its Consequences*. New York: Pantheon.

———. 1987. "The Contemporary Relief Debate." In *The Mean Season: The Attack on the Welfare State*, ed. Fred Block, et al. New York: Pantheon, 45–108.

Plotnick, Robert. 1989. "Directions for Reducing Child Poverty." *Social Work* 34:523–530.

Pratt, John W., and Richard J. Zeckhauser. 1985. *Principals and Agents: The Structure of Business*. Boston: Harvard Business School Press.

Radner, Daniel. 1990. "Assessing the Economic Status of the Aged and Nonaged Using Alternative Income-Wealth Measures." *Social Security Bulletin* 53 (3): 2–14.

Rainwater, Lee. 1987. "Class, Culture, Poverty, and Welfare." report prepared for the U.S. Department of Health and Human Resources, Harvard University.

Rainwater, Lee; Martin Rein; and Joseph Schwartz. 1986. *Income Packaging and the Welfare State: A Comparative Study of Family Income*. Oxford: Clarendon Press.

Rank, Mark. 1986. "Family Structure and the Process of Exiting from Welfare." *Journal of Marriage and the Family* 48:607–618.

Riis, Jacob. 1903. *How the Other Half Lives: Studies among the Tenements of New York*. New York: Charles Scribner's Sons.

Rodgers, Harrell R., Jr. 1990. *Poor Women, Poor Families*. Rev. ed. Armonk, NY: M.E. Sharpe, Inc.

Rostow, W.W. 1971. "The Take-Off into Sustained Growth." In *Political Development and Social Change*, ed. Jason L. Finkle and Richard W. Gable. New York: John Wiley & Sons.

Ruggles, Patricia, and Williams, Robertson. 1989. "Longitudinal Measures of Poverty: Accounting for Income and Assets Over Time." *Review of Income and Wealth* 35 (3): 225–43.

Rumelhart, D. E. 1984. "Schemata in the Cognitive System." In *Handbook of Social Cognition*. Vol. 1, ed. R.S. Wyer and T.K. Srull. Hillsdale, NJ: Lawrence Erlbaum Associates.

Sawhill, Isabel V., ed. 1988. *Challenge to Leadership: Economic and Social Issues for the Next Decade*. Washington, DC: Urban Institute Press.

Scholes, Myron, and Wolfson, Mark. 1989. "Employee Stock Ownership Plans and Corporate Restructuring: Myths and Realities." Working Paper No. 3094.

Cambridge, MA: National Bureau of Economic Research.

Schopenhauer, Arthur. 1942. *Complete Essays of Schopenhauer*. New York: John Wiley & Sons.

Schottland, Charles, ed. 1967. *The Welfare State*. New York: Harper and Row.

Schumpeter, Joseph. 1939. *Business Cycles: A Theoretical, Historical, and Statistical Analysis of the Capitalist Process*. New York: McGraw-Hill.

Schwartz, David; Ferlauto, Richard; and Hoffman, Daniel. 1988. *A New Housing Policy for America*. Philadelphia: Temple University Press.

Scott, William. 1977. *In Pursuit of Happiness: American Conceptions of Property from the Seventeenth to the Twentieth Centuries*. Bloomington: Indiana University Press.

Seidman, Edward. 1986. "Justice, Values and Social Science: Unexamined Premises." In *Redefining Social Problems*, ed. Edward Seidman and Julian Rappaport. New York: Plenum Press.

Shammas, Carole; Salmon, Marylynn; and Dahlin, Michael. 1987. *Inheritance in America: From Colonial Times to the Present*. New Brunswick, NJ: Rutgers University Press.

Shapiro, Isaac, and Greenstein, Robert. 1988. *Holes in the Safety Net*. Washington, DC: Center on Budget and Policy Priorities.

———. 1989. *Making Work Pay: A New Agenda for Poverty Policies*. Washington, DC: Center on Budget and Policy Priorities.

Sherraden, Michael. 1986. "School Dropouts in Perspective." *Educational Forum* 51 (1): 15–31.

———. 1988. "Rethinking Social Welfare: Toward Assets." *Social Policy* 18 (3): 37–43.

Sherraden, Michael, and Ruiz, Clemente. 1989. "Social Welfare in the Context of Development: Toward Micro-Asset Policies—The Case of Mexico." *Journal of International and Comparative Social Welfare* 5 (2): 42–61.

Shorrocks, Anthony F. 1987. "UK Wealth Distribution: Current Evidence and Future Prospects." In *Growth, Accumulation, and Unproductive Activity*, ed. Edward Wolff. Cambridge: Cambridge University Press, 29–50.

Skocpol, Theda. 1985. "Bringing the State Back In: Strategies of Analysis in Current Research." In *Bringing the State Back In*, ed. Peter B. Evans, Dietrich Rueschmeyer, and Theda Skocpol. Cambridge: Cambridge University Press, 3–37.

Slemrod, Joel. 1989. "Fear of Nuclear War and Intercountry Differences is the Rate of Saving" Working Paper No. 2801. Cambridge, MA: National Bureau of Economic Research.

Smith, Adam. [1759] 1976. *The Theory of Moral Sentiments*. Indianapolis: Liberty Press.

———. [1776] 1981. *An Inquiry into the Nature and Causes of the Wealth of Nations*. Indianapolis: Liberty Press.

Smith, J. Owens. 1987. *The Politics of Racial Inequality: A Systematic Comparative Macro-Analysis from the Colonial Period to 1970*. Westport, CT: Greenwood Press.

Smith, James D., and Franklin, Stephen D. 1974. "The Concentration of Personal Wealth, 1922–1969." *American Economic Review* 64:162–67.

Smith, James P. 1988. "Poverty and the Family." In *Divided Opportunities: Minorities, Poverty, and Social Policy*, ed. Gary Sandefur and Marta Tienda. New York: Plenum Press.

Smolensky, Eugene; Danziger, Sheldon; and Gottschalk, Peter. 1988. "The Declining

Significance of Age in the United States: Trends in the Well-Being of Children and the Elderly since 1939.'' In *The Vulnerable: America's Young and Old in the Industrial World*, ed. John Palmer, Timothy Smeeding, and Barbara Torrey. Washington, DC: Urban Institute Press.

Sosin, Michael. 1986. *Private Benefits: Material Assistance in the Private Sector.* Orlando: Academic Press.

Sowell, Thomas. 1975. *Race and Economics.* New York: Longman.

———. 1981. *Ethnic America.* New York: Basic Books.

———, ed. 1988. *Mainstreet Capitalism: Essays on Broadening Share Ownership in America and Britain.* New York: New Horizons Press.

Spencer, Herbert. [1850] 1880. *Social Statics.* New York: D. Appleton.

Stack, Carol B. 1974. *All Our Kin: Strategies for Survival in a Black Community.* New York: Harper and Row.

Stack, Carol B., and Semmel, Herbert. 1975. ''Social Insecurity: Welfare Policy and the Structure of Poor Families.'' In *Welfare in America: Controlling the "Dangerous Classes,"* ed. Betty Reid Mandell. Englewood Cliffs, NJ: Prentice-Hall, 89–103.

Steinberg, Stephen. 1985. ''Human Capital: A Critique.'' *Review of Black Political Economy* 14 (1): 67–74.

Stephens, John D. 1979. *The Transition from Capitalism to Socialism.* London: Macmillan.

Stevens, Beth. 1985. ''Blurring the Boundaries: How the Federal Government Has Shaped Private Sector Welfare Benefits.'' Working Paper No. 3, Taxation, Project on the Federal Social Role. Washington, DC: National Conference on Social Welfare.

Stiglitz, Joseph, and Weiss, Andrew. 1981. ''Credit Rationing in Markets with Imperfect Information.'' *American Economic Review* 71 (3): 393–410.

Stock, James, and Wise, David. 1988. ''The Pension Inducement to Retire: An Option Value Analysis.'' NBER Working Paper No. 2660. Cambridge, MA: National Bureau of Economic Research.

Summers, Lawrence, and Carroll, Chris. 1987. ''Why Have Private Saving Rates in the United States and Canada Diverged?'' Working Paper No. 2319. Cambridge, MA: National Bureau of Economic Research.

Sumner, William Graham. 1893. *What the Social Classes Owe to Each Other.* New York: Harper and Brothers.

Tawney, R.H.[1920] 1978. ''Property and Creative Work.'' In *Property: Mainstream and Critical Positions*, ed. C.B. MacPherson. Toronto: University of Toronto Press, 135–51.

Taylor, S.E., and Crocker, J. 1981. ''Schematic Bases of Social Information Processing.'' In *Social Cognition: The Ontario Symposium.* Vol. 11, ed. E.T. Higgens, et al. Hillsdale, NJ: Erlbaum.

Thurow, Lester. 1975. *Generating Inequality: Mechanisms of Distribution in the U.S. Economy.* New York: Basic Books.

———. 1980. *The Zero-Sum Society.* New York: Penguin Books.

Tidwell, Billy J. 1988. ''Black Wealth: Facts and Fiction.'' In *The State of Black America 1988*, ed. National Urban League. Washington, DC: National Urban League, 193–238.

Titmuss, Richard. 1965. *Commitment to Welfare.* London: Allen and Unwin.

Tomer, John F. 1987. *Organizational Capital.* New York: Praeger.

U.S. Bureau of the Census. 1986. *Household Wealth and Asset Ownership, 1984,*

Current Population Reports, Household Economic Studies, Series P–70, No. 7. Washington, DC: U.S. Government Printing Office.

————. 1989. *American Housing Survey, 1985.* Washington, DC: U.S. Government Printing Office.

U.S. Department of Labor. 1986. *Alternative Uses of Unemployment Compensation.* Washington, DC: U.S. Government Printing Office.

U.S. Small Business Administration. 1987. *The State of Small Business.* Washington, DC: U.S. Government Printing Office.

Veblen, Thorstein. 1899. *The Theory of the Leisure Class.* New York: Macmillan.

Venti, Steven, and Wise, David. 1987. "Have IRAs Increased U.S. Saving? Evidence from Consumer Expenditure Surveys." Working Paper No. 2217. Cambridge, MA: National Bureau of Economic Research.

————. 1989. "But They Don't Want to Reduce Housing Equity." NBER Working Paper No. 2859. Cambridge, MA: National Bureau of Economic Research.

Washington, Booker T. 1909. *The Story of the Negro.* Vol. 2. New York: Doubleday, Page & Co.

Weber, Max. [1904–05] 1958. *The Rise of the Protestant Ethic and the Spirit of Capitalism.* New York: Charles Scribner's Sons.

————. [4th German ed., 1956] 1968. *Economy and Society.* 2 vols., ed. Guenther Roth and Claus Wittich. Berkeley and Los Angeles: University of California Press.

Weisbrod, Burton A., and Hanson, W. Lee. 1968. "An Income-Net Worth Approach to Measuring Economic Welfare." *American Economic Review* 8:1315–19.

Wells-Barnett, Ida B. [1892, 1894, and 1900] 1969. *On Lynchings.* New York: Arno Press.

Wilensky, Harold. 1975. *The Welfare State and Equality: Structural and Ideological Roots of Public Expenditures.* Berkeley and Los Angeles: University of California Press.

Williamson, Oliver. 1985. *The Economic Institutions of Capitalism.* New York: Free Press.

Wilson, William J. 1987. *The Truly Disadvantaged: The Inner City, the Underclass, and Public Policy.* Chicago: University of Chicago Press.

Wise, David T. 1988. "Saving for Retirement: The U.S. Case." Paper presented at a conference. Cambridge, MA: National Bureau of Economic Research.

Wojtkiewicz, Roger; McLanahan, Sara; and Garfinkle, Irwin. 1987. "The Growth of Families Headed by Women: 1950 to 1980." IRP Discussion Paper no. 822–87. Madison: Institute for Research on Poverty.

Wolff, Edward N. 1990. "Wealth Holding and Poverty Status in the U.S." *Review of Income and Wealth.* Based on a paper presented at the 20th General Conference of the International Association for Research on Income and Wealth, Roca di Papa, Italy, August 1987.

————. 1987. "Estimates of Household Wealth Inequality in the U.S., 1962–1983." *Review of Income and Wealth* 33 (3): 231–42.

————, ed. 1987. *International Comparisons of the Distribution of Household Wealth.* Oxford: Clarendon Press.

————. 1989. "Trends in Aggregate Household Wealth in the U.S., 1900–1983." *Review of Income and Wealth* 35 (1): 1–29.

Wrong, Dennis. 1961. "The Oversocialized Conception of Man in Modern Sociology." *American Sociological Review* 26:183–93.

Zeldes, Stephen. 1989. "Consumption and Liquidity Constraints: An Empirical Investigation." *Journal of Political Economy* 97 (2): 305–46.

Index

Abramovitz, Mimi, 53
Abt Associates, 256
Abundance, 19–20
Achievements, 240
Accumulated capital, 292n.17
Accumulation behavior, 124
Addams, Jane, 85
Adler, Mortimer, 104
Adolescence, 154
AFDC. *See* Aid to Families with Dependent Children
AFDC-UP. *See* Aid to Families with Dependent Children-Unemployed Parent
African-Americans, 131–139. *See also* Blacks
Age, 25–26
Agricultural subsidies, 76n.30
Aid to Families with Dependent Children (AFDC), 3, 54, 63–64, 78, 92n.29
    Individual Development Accounts and, 261
    self-employment and, 253, 254–55
Aid to Families with Dependent Children-Unemployed Parent (AFDC-UP), 75–76n.21
Aldrich, Nelson, Jr., 80–81, 126
All Our Kin (Stack), 104
Andrisani, Paul, 175
Appearances, 103
Aristocracy, 163
Ashford, Douglas, 41
Asset-based policy, 189–219
    alternative directions for, 214–15
    asset poverty and, 195
    defined, 6

Asset-based policy *(continued)*
    framework of, 199
    goals of, 189–91
    history of, 191–95
    nonpoor and, 294–95
    poverty and, 295–96
    principles of, 199–205
    questions about, 205–14
Asset maintenance, 76n.30
Asset poverty, 195–99, 225
Asset rich, 197–98
Assets, 95–120. *See also* Capital; Wealth
    conservatives and, 82, 165
    consumption and, 188n.27
    defined, 5, 96–97, 106–7, 117n.9
    distribution of, 107–15
    foreign, 285
    income and, 97–100
        nonpoor welfare and, 68, 176–78
        poor welfare and, 179–80
    inequality of, 121–44
        African-Americans and, 131–39
        inheritance in, 123–24, 140–41n.16
        institutions in, 124–25
        patterns of, 125–31
    negative effects of, 182–83n.4, 188n.81
    Social Security and, 77n.32
    tests for, 6, 64
    theory of, 145–88
        behavior in, 174–75
        future orientation in, 151–56
        household stability in, 149–50
        human capital in, 156–57
        income in, 171–74

Assets *(continued)*
  offspring in, 166–67
  permanent assets in, 170–71
  personal efficacy in, 160–62
  political participation in, 165–66
  risk-taking in, 159–60
  social influence in, 162–64
  specialization in, 157–59
  sufficiency in, 168–70
  utility in, 167–68, 186*n.63*
  welfare models in, 175–80
  types of, 100–106
  welfare and, 43–45
Attitudes, 174–75
Automobiles, 214

Baby boomers, 283
Bacchetta, Phillippe, 291–92*n.15*
Bacon, Francis, 302
Banfield, Edward, 38
Basic needs, 62
Becker, Gary, 103
Behavior, 174–75, 187*n.76*, 211
Believers Program, 238–39
Benito Juarez, Mexico, 105–6
Benton, Thomas Hart, 191
Bentsen, Lloyd, 232*n.2*, 250
Bethell, Tom, 248
Black Code, 135
Blacks, 8–9, 26, 29, 40
  assets of, 131–39, 142*n.46*, 143*n.56*
  higher education of, 236
  social networks of, 188*n.20*
Blanchard, James, 248
Blau, Peter, 122
Blinder, Alan, 141*n.22*
Blue-collar workers, 156
Bond, Christopher, 213
Bordieu, Pierre, 103
Borges, Jorge Luis, 151
Borrowing, 150. *See also* Debt
Boulding, Kenneth, 224
Bourgeois mentality, 213
Bowles, Samuel, 122
Brady, Nicholas, 232*n.2*
Brittain, John, 121
Brumberg, Richard, 44, 123, 167, 170
Budget, 75*n.17*
Bureaucracy, 82
Burtless, Gary, 42

Bush, George, 130, 232*n.2*, 249, 250
Butler, Stuart, 38, 81, 82

Callinicos, Alex, 39
Canada, 286
Capital, 111–12, 117*n.9*, 118*n.25*,
    284–85. *See also* Assets; Wealth
  accumulated, 292*n.17*
  cultural, 103
  financial, 72, 106–7, 112
  human, 72, 102, 156–57, 117*n.13*. *See
    also* Human capital
  organizational, 104
  political, 104
  redistribution of, 71, 72, 75*n.16*, 88
  social, 103–4, 118*n.20*
Capital (Marx), 187*n.75*
Capital gains, 229–30
Capital markets, 150
Capitalism, 13, 41, 100, 187*n.75*
  interest groups and, 90*n.5*
  radical left on, 87–88, 89
Capitello, Grace, 129
Cars, 214
Carter, Jimmy, 247
Case management, 85
CfED. *See* Corporation for Enterprise
    Development
Chances, life, 39–40, 152
Children, 54, 166–67
  housing accounts for, 251
  poor, 25–26, 71–72, 260–61
Citizens, welfare, 190
Civil rights movement, 137
Civil service retirement, 66
Class theory, 36
Clay, William, 214, 248
Cloward, Richard, 86, 105
Cochran Gardens, 247–48
Cognitive theory, 154–55
Coleman, James, 104
College, 132, 152. *See also* Higher
    education
College students, 198
Commitment, 213–14
Community ownership, 215, 217*n.23*
Conflict theories, 36
Conservatism
  assets and, 82, 165
  welfare reform and, 79–83

Consumer debt, 291n.13
Consumption, 11, 280–82, 287,
    290nn.2,4
  assets for, 118n.27
  income and, 6, 42–43, 90n.6, 91n.16
Control, 145–47, 153, 172–73,
    185n.35, 298–99
Copyrights, 102
Corporate debt, 284, 291n.12
Corporation for Enterprise Development
    (CfED), 194, 254, 255
Cranston, Alan, 250
Credit, 102, 128, 149–50
Criminals, 210
Crisis, 302
Cultural capital, 103
Culture, 173–74
Culture of poverty, 38, 81–82, 85, 138

Dahrendorf, Ralf, 39, 40, 122, 152, 181
D'Amato, Alfonse, 250
Danziger, Sheldon, 18, 19, 78
Darman, Richard, 282, 290n.5
de Crèvecoeur, St. John, 12
Dean, Dizzy, 20
Death, 230
Debt, 10, 150, 283–84, 291nn.10,12,13
Defined-benefit plans, 161, 258
Defined-contribution plans, 161–62
Delmo Housing Corporation, 193
Democracy, 41, 81, 163, 166
Demonstration programs, 274, 275,
    300–301
Deposit subsidies, 241, 268–73
Direct expenditures, 61–62, 66–67
Distribution of assets, 107–15
Distribution of income, 16–20
Diversification, 159
Dodge, Joseph, 286–87
Douglass, Frederick, 134
Down payments, 249
Drucker, Peter, 120
Du Bois, W.E.B., 133, 134
Duncan, Greg, 38, 85, 122
Duncan, Otis Dudley, 122
Durable household goods, 102, 169
"Dwelling Place, A," 248

Earned Income Tax Credit, 178
Economic growth, 11
Economic Justice for All, 51

Economic literacy, 203–4, 241, 276n.8
Economic power, 126, 161, 162–63,
    168
Economy, 10
Edelman, Marian Wright, 38, 83
Education, 59, 62
  economic, 203–5, 241, 276n.8
  higher. See Higher education
  proprietary schools, 242–43, 276n.9
Efficiency of investment, 52, 72–73,
    209–10
Ellwood, David, 38, 85, 121
Emancipation Proclamation, 132
Employee Stock Ownership Plan
    (ESOP), 215, 218n.24
Employment, 60, 177
  housing assistance and, 249
  poverty and, 4–5, 29–30, 62, 178
Entitlements, 98–99
Entrepreneurs, 96, 285
Equal opportunity, 84
Equity, 51, 71–72
  home. See Home equity
  sweat, 157
ESOP. See Employee Stock
    Ownership Plan
Etzioni, Amitai, 168
Eugenics movement, 37, 46n.7
Europe, 254
Existing assets, 177
Experimentation, 273–75, 300–301

Family
  nonpoor, 177
  poor, 27–28, 33n.29, 33–34n.34, 179
Family Savings Account (FSA),
    232n.2
Family Support Act of 1988, 86
Farm Security Administration (FSA),
    192
Farm subsidies, 76n.30
Federal government, 177, 178, 243,
    288
  debt of, 284, 291n.11
  welfare policy of, 50–77. See also
    Welfare state
Federal Housing Administration
    (FHA), 192
Feldstein, Martin, 141n.22, 255,
    291–92n.15, 293n.28

Females, 26, 27
FHA. *See* Federal Housing
     Administration
Financial assets, 106–7, 112
Financial planning, 7, 223
Financial securities, 101
Finn, Charles, 143*n.50*
Fiscal welfare, 53, 67–68, 192
Fluidity of assets, 105–6
Focus, 157–59
Fogelman, Avron, 238
Food Stamps, 64
Forbes, 95
Ford Foundation, 257
Foreign assets, 285
Freedman's Bank, 133–34
Freedmen's Bureau, 133
Freedom of decision, 164
Friedman, Milton, 71, 170
Friedman, Robert, 194
FSA. *See* Family Savings Account;
     Farm Security Administration
Fully restricted assets, 99
Functionalist theory, 35–36
Fungible wealth, 113
Future orientation, 151–56

Galbraith, John Kenneth, 52, 165,
     292*n.17*
GI Bill, 140*n.2*, 237–38
GIC. *See* Guaranteed investment contract
Giddens, Anthony, 39
Gilbert, Barbara, 38, 76*n.30*
Gilbert, Neil, 38, 48*n.38*, 73, 76*n.30*
Gilder, George, 95, 171
Gilkey, Bertha, 247–48
Gini coefficient, 111, 120
Glazer, Nathan, 82
Gottschalk, Peter, 18, 19
Gradual accumulation, 203
Grand welfare state, 54–60
Granovetter, Mark, 104
Gray, Kimi, 248
Great awakening, 302
Great Depression, 37
Greenwald, Gerald, 238
Growth, 11
GSL. *See* Guaranteed Student Loan
Guaranteed investment contract
     (GIC), 222

Guaranteed Student Loan (GSL), 237,
     242–43

Habitat for Humanity, 247
Halle, David, 156
Hanson, W. Lee, 107
Hard assets, 101
Harrington, Michael, 21, 37, 84
Haveman, Robert, 38, 42, 43–44, 84,
     107, 243
Head Start, 240
Health care, 55–59
     nonpoor welfare and, 66, 67–68
     poor welfare and, 61
High school, 152–53
Higher education, 132, 152
     Individual Development Accounts
          for, 222, 234–43
     cost of, 268–69
     taxes and, 272
     savings plans for, 193
Hispanics, 26
Holiday, Billie, 14, 122
HOME. *See* Home Ownership Made
     Easier
Home equity, 73, 114–15, 150
     blacks and, 136–37
     subsidies for, 247
Home ownership, 127, 156, 214–15,
     230
     black, 136, 137, 143*n.53*
     Individual Development Accounts
          for, 243–51
     cost of, 269–70
     taxes and, 272
     United Kingdom, 218–19*n.27*
Home Ownership Made Easier
     (HOME), 250
Homelessness, 245
Homestead Act of 1862, 191
Horizontal equity, 51
Household durable goods, 102, 169
Household income, 42–43
Household net worth, 110
Household stability, 149–50
Household time use, 157
Household wealth, 43–45
Housing, 59, 67. *See also* Home
     ownership

Housing and Urban Development
(HUD), 213
Howe, Neil, 66, 67, 70, 72, 293n.24
HUD. See Housing and Urban
Development
Human capital, 72, 102, 156–57,
117n.13
conservatives and, 81
poor welfare state and, 62
Hunter, Robert, 21
Hurd, Michael, 141n.16
Hutchins, Robert, 237
Huxley, Thomas, 80

"I Have a Dream" Foundation, 183n.10,
194, 216n.7, 238, 239, 296
IDA. See Individual Development
Account
Immigrants, 208
Incentives, 200, 207, 208, 259, 286–87
Income, 5, 29, 42–43, 53–54
asset-based policy and, 206–9
assets and, 97–100
nonpoor welfare and, 68, 176–78
poor welfare and, 178–80
consumption and, 6, 42–43, 90n.6,
91n.16
middle class, 126
permanent, 149, 170, 187n.69
welfare effects of, 171–74
Income abundance, 19–20
Income-based policy, 3–5, 199–200,
294
Income distribution, 16–20
Income inequality, 122
Income maintenance, 294
Income poverty, 20–30
assets and, 197–99, 112–15
defined, 120
Income rich, 197
Income security, 55, 62, 64, 66, 67
Income shock, 149, 209
Individual Development Account
(IDA), 220–79
control of, 226
costs of, 267–73
description of, 221–23
for education, 222, 234–43
eligibility for, 224–25
example of, 261–66

Individual Development Account
(IDA) (continued)
experimentation with, 273–75,
300–301
financing, 227–31
for housing, 243–51
multipurpose, 260
national savings and, 288–89
poor children and, 260–61
for retirement, 257–60
for self-employment, 251–57
structure of, 225–26
summary of, 297–301
target asset levels for, 225
taxes and, 223, 241–42, 271–73
variations of, 223–24
Individual Retirement Account (IRA),
99, 193, 201, 232n.2, 250, 289
Individual theories, 35–36, 37, 39, 79,
181
Industrialization, 108
Inequality, 35–40
asset, 121–44
African-Americans and, 131–39
inheritance in, 123–24, 140–41n.16
institutions in, 124–25
patterns of, 125–31
income, 122
Informal social capital, 103–4, 118n.20
Inheritance, 123–24, 140–41n.16, 223
Inkeles, Alex, 176
Institutions, 124–25, 127, 128, 209
radical left and, 88
savings and, 286–87
Insurance, 51, 70–71
Intangible assets, 102–5
Interest groups, 90n.5
Interest income, 18
Intergenerational transfers, 123–24,
141n.20
Investment, 13, 190, 203, 267, 301–2
efficiency of, 52, 72–73, 209–10
national, 285–86
IRA. See Individual Retirement
Account

Jackson, Andrew, 191
Janowitz, Morris, 36, 64, 73
Japan, 286–87, 292n.23
Jefferson, Thomas, 12, 165

Jencks, Christopher, 107, 122, 150
Job Training Partnership Act (JTPA), 254
Johnson, Alice, 217*n.17*
Joint ownership, 250–51
Jones, Alfred Winslow, 163
JTPA. *See* Job Training Partnership Act
Jukes family, 37

K-wealth, 44, 163
Kallikaks family, 37
Kelso, Louis, 215, 218*n.26*
Kemp, Jack, 213, 248
Kessler, Denis, 44, 141*n.22*, 163
Kettering, Charles F., 8
Keynes, John Maynard, 280, 281, 290*n.2*
Keynes-Beveridge welfare state, 281, 290*n.3*
King, Martin Luther, 133
Kondratas, Anna, 38, 81, 82
Kotlikoff, Laurence, 44, 123, 140*n.16*, 167
Kuttner, Robert, 255
Kuznets, Simon, 108

Labor income, 17
Lampman, Robert, 51, 52, 70, 75*n.16*, 108, 176
Land ownership, 12, 191–92. *See also* Ownership; Property
  black, 133, 134, 135, 136, 142*n.46*
  political participation and, 165–66
Lang, Eugene, 151–52, 156, 183*n.10*, 193–94, 238, 296
Law of the Haves, 121–22
LCH. *See* Life cycle hypothesis
Leaky bucket syndrome, 7
Left, 86–89
Lenin, Vladimir, 87
Letters from an American Farmer (de Crèvecoeur), 12
Levitan, Sar, 38, 48*n.39*
Lewis, Oscar, 38, 84–85
Liberal middle, 83–86
Life chances, 39–40, 152
Life cycle hypothesis (LCH), 123, 170, 286
Liquidity constraints, 149–50

Literacy, economic, 203–4, 241, 276*n.8*
Loans, 236–37
Locus of control, 153
Logic-of-capitalism, 41
Long-term goals, 223
Lorenz curve, 120
Losing Ground (Murray), 21, 25
Loss replacement, 51, 70–71
Lynchings, 135

Machines, 101
Malthus, Thomas, 36
Manufacturing jobs, 30
Marginal tax rates (MTR), 278*n.43*, 278–79*n.45*
Markowitz, Harry, 159
Marx, Karl, 87, 88, 104, 108, 117*nn.9*, *13*, 162, 182*n.4*, 187*n.75*
Marxism, 86–89
Masson, André, 44, 141*n.22*, 163
Matching funds, 222
Mayer, Susan, 107, 150
Mead, Lawrence, 38, 81, 187*n.76*
Means-tested transfers, 53
Measurement, 20, 21–22
Medical insurance premiums, 229
Mental labor, 89
Mental retardation, 13
Michigan, 248
Middle class, 68, 126–27, 151, 212–13
Military service, 66–67, 76*n.28*, 240
Mills, C. Wright, 84
Minimum provision, 51, 70
Minority children, 54
Mishra, Ramesh, 38
Modernization approaches, 41
Modigliani, Franco, 44, 123, 167, 170, 281, 286
Money, 95, 143*n.53*
Money savings, 101
Moon, Marilyn, 107
Moralistic view, 81
Morrill Land Grant Act of 1862, 191
Morris, Robert, 38, 302
Mortgage interest, 229, 232*n.7*
Motivation, 4
Moynihan, Daniel, 27, 54, 160, 284
MTR. *See* Marginal tax rates
Mundaca, Gabriela, 141*n.16*

Murray, Charles, 4, 21, 25, 38, 42, 45, 82, 211–12
Mutual responsibility, 201–2

National development, 221
National goals, 280–93
  capital growth and, 284–85
  consumption and, 280–82, 290n.4
  debt and, 283–84, 291n.10
  institutional incentives and, 286–87
  investment and, 285–86
  savings and, 282–83, 288–89
  social policy and, 287–88
National Longitudinal Survey (NLS), 175
National service, 240–41, 261, 263–64
Natural resources, 102
Negotiations, 164
Neoclassical economic theory, 35
Net financial assets, 112
Net worth, 110, 114
Network, 104, 118n.20
New Deal, 192
New York Times, 230
NLS. See National Longitudinal Survey
Noncash benefits, 21, 32n.14
Nonmonetized economy, 184n.29
Nonpoor welfare state, 64–70, 76n.26
  asset-based policy for, 289, 294–95
  model of, 176–78
Nonwhites, 26. See also Blacks
North, Douglass, 187n.76
Novak, Michael, 38
Now-now-ism, 290n.5
Nutrition assistance, 60, 62

Occupational welfare, 53
Offspring, 54, 166–67. See also Children
Old Money (Aldrich), 80
Oliver, Melvin, 112
Ordered segmentation, 36
Organizational capital, 104
Orshansky, Molly, 21
Osberg, Lars, 167
Other America, The (Harrington), 21, 37

Ownership, 83, 215, 217n.23. See also Home ownership; Joint ownership; Land ownership; Property
Oxford English Dictionary, 96
Ozawa, Martha, 233n.10

Page-Adams, Deborah, 217n.11
Panel Study of Income Dynamics (PSID), 24, 174
Paper entrepreneurship, 285
Parents, 27, 239. See also Single parents
Partially restricted assets, 99
Participation, 49n.47, 165–66
Patents, 102
Path dependence, 150
Peace dividend, 228
Pension funds, 73, 115, 120n.53, 141n.25. See also Retirement plans
Permanent assets, 170–71
Permanent income, 149, 170, 187n.69
Personal development, 160–62, 205
Personality of poverty, 84
Peterson, Peter, 66, 67, 70, 72, 293n.24
Piven, Frances Fox, 86, 105
Planning, 7, 223
Plotnick, Robert, 70, 78, 276n.5
Policy, welfare, 40, 41, 50, 77. See also Welfare state
Political capital, 104
Politics, 41, 165–66
Poor welfare state, 60–64, 70, 75n.19
Portfolio theory, 159
Positional effects, 128
Poverty, 6, 13, 50, 84, 85, 169
  asset, 195–99, 225
  asset-based policy and, 295–96
  children in, 25–26, 71–72, 260–61
  culture of, 38, 81–82, 85, 138
  housing and, 244–46
  income. See Income poverty
  income-based policy and, 294
  savings and, 129–31, 207–9, 214, 289–90
  subsidized deposits for, 241, 268–73
  theories of, 35–40
  welfare models of, 178–80
Poverty (Hunter), 21
Poverty gap, 23
Poverty level, 21, 22–24, 63, 81

Power, 126, 161, 162–63, 168
Pregnancy, 153
Principal-and-agent theory, 39
Private Industry Councils, 257
Productivity, 52, 72, 157
Property, 18, 100, 101. *See also*
    Home ownership; Land
    ownership; Ownership
  blacks and, 131
  political participation and, 165–66
Proprietary schools, 242–43, 276*n.9*
Protestant Ethic, 95
PSID. *See* Panel Study of Income
    Dynamics
Public goods, 117*n.10*
Public investment, 285–86
Public support, 206

Race, 26, 28–29, 110
Radical left, 86–89
Radner, Daniel, 107
Rainwater, Lee, 121
RAM. *See* Reverse annuity mortgage
Raspberry, William, 153
Reagan, Ronald, 283
Real property, 101
Reconstruction, 134
Redistribution of capital, 71, 72,
    75*n.16,* 88
Reese, Pee Wee, 20
Replacement of loss, 51, 70–71
Reserve Fund, 242
Restricted accounts, 202, 209–10
Retirement plans, 66–67, 68, 70,
    161–62. *See also* Pension funds
  Individual Development Accounts
    for, 257–60
  cost of, 270–71
  taxes and, 272–73
  middle class and, 127
  taxation of, 229
  working poor and, 128
Reverse annuity mortgage (RAM), 167
Rice, Larry, 247
Right, 79–83
Riis, Jacob, 245
*Rise of the Protestant Ethic and the
    Spirit of Capitalism, The*
    (Weber), 187*n.75*
Risk-taking, 159–60

Ross, Doug, 233*n.11*
Roth, William, 232*n.2*

S-wealth, 44, 163
Savings, 10, 101, 123–24, 133, 170
  excess, 280–81
  institutions and, 286–87
  national, 280–81, 282–83, 288–89
  nonpoor and, 176–77
  poor and, 129–31, 207–9, 214,
    289–90
  Social Security and, 293*n.28*
Sawhill, Isabel, 38, 210
Say, Jean Baptiste, 280
SCF. *See* Survey of Consumer
    Finances
Schemata, 154–55
Schopenhauer, Arthur, 187*n.69*
Schudson, Charles B., 130
Schumpeter, Joseph, 102
Securities, 101
Security, 260
Segmentation, 36
SEID. *See* Self-Employment
    Investment Demonstration
Self-employment
  Individual Development Accounts
    for, 251–57
  cost of, 270
  taxes and, 272
  measurement of, 277*n.28*
Self-Employment Investment
    Demonstration (SEID), 255
SEP. *See* Simplified Employee Pension
Service jobs, 30
Settlement houses, 85
Shapiro, Isaac, 38
Shapiro, Thomas, 112
Shared responsibility, 201–2
Shorrocks, Anthony, 44, 163, 167
SI. *See* Survivors Insurance
Simplified Employee Pension (SEP),
    259
Single parents, 27–28, 63, 85, 86, 254
SIPP. *See* Survey of Income and
    Program Participation
Situation of poverty, 85
Slavery, 131, 132
Smith, Adam, 8, 160, 162, 163,
    187*n.75*

Smith, James D., 108
Social capital, 103–4, 118*n.20*
Social class, 35–40
Social Darwinism, 37, 79, 80
Social influence, 162–64
Social insurance, 51, 70–71
Social mobility, 122
Social network, 104, 118*n.20*
Social problems, 81
Social Security, 51, 53–54, 71, 72,
    77*n.32*
  benefit taxation and, 229, 230–31,
    233*n.10*
  savings and, 293*n.28*
  supplement to, 257
  surpluses in, 283, 291*n.8*
Social services, 60, 62
Social welfare, 53, 287–88
Socialism, 87
"Sooners," 191
Sowell, Thomas, 131, 132
Specialization, 157–59
SSI. *See* Supplemental Security
    Income
Stability, 98, 149–50
Stack, Carol, 104, 202
Stakeholding, 5–7
States, 41, 276*n.5*
Statistics, 20, 21–22
Structural theories, 36, 37, 39, 181
Structure, 267, 298–99
Student loans, 236–37
Subsidized deposits, 241, 268–73
Sufficiency, 168–70
Summers, Lawrence, 123
Sumner, William Graham, 160
Supplemental Security Income (SSI),
    257
Supply-side economics, 82–83
Survey of Consumer Finances (SCF),
    110
Survey of Income and Program
    Participation (SIPP), 109
Survivors Insurance (SI), 54
Sweat equity, 157
Sweden, 173

Tangible assets, 101–2, 106, 117*n.10*
Targeted benefits, 60–64, 70, 75*n.19*,
    223, 274–75
Tawney, R.H., 100

Taxes, 67–68, 75*n.16*, 125, 229–30
  Individual Development Accounts
    and, 223, 241–42, 271–73
  negative, 273–74
Tenure system, 160
Thatcher, Margaret, 215, 218–19*n.27*
Theories
  asset-based, 145–48. *See also*
    Assets, theory of
  welfare, 35–41
Theory of the Leisure Class, The
    (Veblen), 162
Thurow, Lester, 123, 124, 141*n.20*,
    161, 168
Tidwell, Billy, 8–9
Titmuss, Richard, 53, 67, 68, 192
Tocqueville, Alexis de, 13, 95, 163,
    165
Tomer, John, 104
Trade, 10
Training schools, 242–43
Trust funds, 247
Truth, Sojourner, 132
Tuition plans, 194, 216*n.7*, 239–40
Two-parent families, 27

Unbounded assets, 170
Underclass, 210–11
Underdeveloping nation, 9–11
Unemployment, 149, 235
Unemployment Insurance, 253,
    255–56
United Kingdom, 215, 218–19*n.27*
United States, 9–11, 12–14
Universal policy, 200, 221, 224
Unrestricted assets, 100
Utility, 167–68, 186*n.63*

Veblen, Thorstein, 162, 172
Vertical equity, 51
Veterans, 66–67, 76*n.28*
Vision, 7–9
Volcker, Paul, 204
Voluntary participation, 200, 207

War, 292*n.20*
War on Poverty, 83
Washington, Booker T., 134
Wealth, 7, 8–9, 111–12. *See also*
    Assets; Capital

Wealth *(continued)*
  fungible, 113
  household, 43–45
Wealth of Nations, The (Smith), 8,
    162, 187*n.75*
Wealth and Poverty (Gilder), 96
Wealthy, 125–26
Weaver, Edward, 302
Weber, Max, 13, 39, 95, 152, 181,
    187*n.75*
Weisbrod, Burton, 107
Welfare, 41–45, 49*n.47*, 176, 182*n.1*
  fiscal, 53, 67–68, 192
  investment as, 301–2
  occupational, 53
  on or off, 201
  social, 53, 287–88
  theories of, 35–41
  vision of, 7–9
Welfare citizens, 190
Welfare policy, 40–41, 50–77. *See
    also* Welfare state
Welfare poor, 115, 129–31
Welfare reform, 78–92
  conservative right on, 79–83
  liberal middle on, 83–86
  radical left on, 86–89
Welfare state, 50–77
  characteristics of, 52–54

Welfare state *(continued)*
  conflicting goals of, 50–52
  consumption and, 280–82, 290*n.4*
  grand, 54–60
  interpretation of, 70–73
  Keynes-Beveridge, 281, 290*n.3*
  nonpoor. *See* Nonpoor welfare
    state
  policy and, 41, 54
  poor, 60–64, 70, 75*n.19*
  theories of, 40–41
Well-being, 16, 42–45, 176
Wells, Ida B., 135
*What the Social Classes Owe to Each
    Other* (Sumner), 160
Whites, 29
Wilkins, Roger, 85
Williamson, Oliver, 118
Wilson, William J., 36, 38, 39, 40, 84,
    181, 211
Wisconsin, 85
Wise, David, 123
Withdrawals, 223, 242
Wolff, Edward, 107, 108, 109, 111,
    195
Women, 26, 27
Work disincentive, 42, 86
Work incentive, 259
Working poor, 29–30, 128–29

Michael Sherraden is Associate Professor at the George Warren Brown School of Social Work, Washington University. He received his bachelor's degree at Harvard and his master's and doctoral degrees at the University of Michigan. Sherraden has studied and written in the areas of social administration, social welfare history, employment policy, and youth policy. He recently coauthored with Donald Eberly *The Moral Equivalent of War? A Study of Non-Military Service in Nine Nations.*